MASTERS & JOHNSON INSTITUTE
ETHICS CONGRESS

ETHICAL ISSUES IN SEX THERAPY AND RESEARCH

VOLUME 2

MASTERS & JOHNSON INSTITUTE
ETHICS CONGRESS

Ethical Issues in Sex Therapy and Research

VOLUME 2

EDITED BY

WILLIAM H. MASTERS, M.D.

Co-Director, Masters & Johnson Institute

VIRGINIA E. JOHNSON, D.Sc.(Hon.)

Co-Director, Masters & Johnson Institute

ROBERT C. KOLODNY, M.D.

Associate Director, Master & Johnson Institute

SARAH M. WEEMS, M.A.

Editorial Assistant, Masters & Johnson Institute

Little, Brown and Company

BOSTON

PRINTED IN THE UNITED STATES OF AMERICA
MV

PARTICIPANTS

E. JAMES ANTHONY, M.D.

Blanche F. Ittleson Professor of Child Psychiatry and Director,
Eliot Division of Child Psychiatry, Washington University School
of Medicine, St. Louis, Missouri

DAVID H. BARLOW, Ph.D.

Professor of Psychology, State University of New York, Albany

ROBERT J. BAUM, Ph.D.

Professor of Philosophy and Director, Center for the Study of the
Human Dimensions of Science and Technology, Rensselaer
Polytechnic Institute, Troy, New York

MAE A. BIGGS, R.N., B.S.N., M.S.

Senior Clinician and Director of Training Supervision,
Masters & Johnson Institute, St. Louis, Missouri

THERESA L. CRENSHAW, M.D.

Director, The Crenshaw Clinic; Co-Director, Division of Human Sexuality,
University of California, San Diego, School of Medicine;
Assistant Clinical Professor, Department of Reproductive Medicine,
University of California, San Diego

H. TRISTRAM ENGELHARDT, JR., Ph.D., M.D.

Rosemary Kennedy Professor of the Philosophy of Medicine,
The Joseph and Rose Kennedy Institute of Ethics, Georgetown University,
Washington, D.C.; Member of Board of Directors,
Masters & Johnson Institute, St. Louis, Missouri

CHARLES FRIED, LL.B.

Professor of Law, Harvard Law School, Cambridge, Massachusetts

PAUL H. GEBHARD, Ph.D.

Director, Institute for Sex Research, Indiana University, Bloomington

JOSHUA S. GOLDEN, M.D.

Professor of Psychiatry, Assistant Dean for Student Affairs, and
Director, Human Sexuality Program, School of Medicine,
University of California, Los Angeles

SAMUEL GOROVITZ, Ph.D.

Professor and Chairman, Department of Philosophy,
University of Maryland, College Park

RICHARD GREEN, M.D.

Professor, Department of Psychiatry and Behavioral Science, and
Department of Psychology, State University of New York, Stony Brook

SAMUEL B. GUZE, M.D.

Spencer T. Olin Professor, Head of Department of Psychiatry,
and Vice-Chancellor for Medical Affairs, Washington University
School of Medicine; Member of Board of Directors,
Masters & Johnson Institute, St. Louis, Missouri

SEWARD HILTNER, Ph.D., D.D.

Professor of Theology and Personality. Princeton Theological Seminary,
Princeton, New Jersey

FREDERICK G. HUMPHREY, Ed.D.

Associate Professor of Family Relations, University of Connecticut, Storrs;
President, American Association for Marriage and Family Therapy

R. CHRISTIAN JOHNSON, Ph.D.

Research Associate, School of Education, Stanford University,
Stanford, California

VIRGINIA E. JOHNSON, D.Sc. (Hon.)

Co-Director, Masters & Johnson Institute, St. Louis, Missouri

ALBERT R. JONSEN, Ph.D.

Professor of Ethics in Medicine, School of Medicine, University
of California, San Francisco

ALEX H. KAPLAN, M.D.

Professor of Clinical Psychiatry, Washington University School of Medicine,
St. Louis, Missouri; Associate Medical Director, St. Louis Psychoanalytic
Institute; President, American Psychoanalytic Association

MIRIAM F. KELTY, Ph.D.
Human Development Study Section, National Institutes of Health,
Bethesda, Maryland

ROBERT C. KOLODNY, M.D.
Associate Director and Director of Training,
Masters & Johnson Institute, St. Louis, Missouri

JUDITH B. KURIANSKY
Doctoral Psychology Clinic, New York University, New York

JUDITH LONG LAWS, Ph.D.
Assistant Professor of Sociology and Psychology,
Cornell University, Ithaca, New York

NAT LEHRMAN
Senior Vice-President and Associate Publisher,
Playboy Enterprises, Chicago

STEPHEN B. LEVINE, M.D.
Associate Professor of Psychiatry and Director, Sexual Dysfunction Clinic,
Case Western Reserve University, Cleveland, Ohio

HAROLD I. LIEF, M.D.
Professor of Psychiatry and Director of the Division of Family Study,
The University of Pennsylvania School of Medicine, Philadelphia;
Director, Marriage Council of Philadelphia, Philadelphia

JOSEPH LoPICCOLO, Ph.D.
Professor of Psychiatry and Director, Sex Therapy Center,
State University of New York, Stony Brook

RUTH MACKLIN, Ph.D.
Associate for Behavioral Studies, The Hastings Center, Institute of Society,
Ethics and the Life Sciences, Hastings-on-Hudson, New York;
Associate Clinical Professor of Community Health,
Albert Einstein College of Medicine, Bronx, New York

JAY MANN, Ph.D.
Associate Clinical Professor of Medical Psychology, School of Medicine, University of
California, San Francisco; Clinical Assistant Professor of Psychiatry and Behavioral
Science, Stanford University School of Medicine, Stanford; Chief of Family Study
Unit, Veterans Administration Medical Center, Palo Alto, California

WILLIAM H. MASTERS, M.D.
Co-Director, Masters & Johnson Institute, St. Louis, Missouri

WALTER L. METCALFE, JR., J.D.
Attorney, Armstrong, Teasdale, Kramer & Vaughan; Member of Board of
Directors, Masters & Johnson Institute, St. Louis, Missouri

JOHN MONEY, Ph.D.
Professor of Medical Psychology and Associate Professor of Pediatrics,
The Johns Hopkins University School of Medicine, Baltimore, Maryland

FRITZ REDLICH, M.D.
Professor of Psychiatry, University of California at Los Angeles; Associate Chief of
Staff for Education, Brentwood Veterans Administration Hospital, Los Angeles

ARVIL C. REEB, JR., M.S.S.W.
Associate Professor in Psychiatry (College of Medicine) and Chief Clinical
Social Worker (Student Health), University of Kentucky, Lexington

IRA L. REISS, Ph.D.
Professor of Sociology, University of Minnesota, Minneapolis

LORNA J. SARREL, M.S.S.W.
Assistant Clinical Professor of Social Work in Psychiatry and in Obstetrics and
Gynecology, Yale University School of Medicine, New Haven, Connecticut

PHILIP M. SARREL, M.D.
Associate Professor of Obstetrics and Gynecology and Associate Professor of
Psychiatry, Yale University School of Medicine, New Haven, Connecticut

PATRICIA SCHILLER, M.A., J.D.
Executive Director and Founder, American Association of Sex Educators, Counselors,
and Therapists; Secretary-General and Treasurer, World Association for Sexology;
Director, National Institute of Sex Education, Counseling and Therapy; Assistant
Professor of Obstetrics and Gynecology and Director of Human Sexuality
Program, Howard University College of Medicine, Washington, D.C.

SALLIE SCHUMACHER, Ph.D.
Associate Professor of Psychiatry (Psychology), Head of Section on Marital Health,
and Director of Marital Health Clinic, The Bowman Gray School of Medicine
of Wake Forest University, Winston-Salem, North Carolina

RALPH SLOVENKO, LL.B., Ph.D.
Professor of Law and Psychiatry, Wayne State University
Law School, Detroit, Michigan

MARTHA STUART
Independent Video Producer (Martha Stuart Communications, Inc.), New York;
Lecturer, Yale University School of Public Health, New Haven, Connecticut

ROBERT L. STUBBLEFIELD, M.D.
Medical and Executive Director, Silver Hill Foundation, New Canaan, Connecticut;
Clinical Professor of Psychiatry, Yale University School of Medicine,
New Haven, Connecticut

**RAYMOND W. WAGGONER,
M.D., Sc.D.**

Professor and Chairman Emeritus, Department of Psychiatry, University
of Michigan, Ann Arbor; Member of Board of Directors,
Masters & Johnson Institute, St. Louis, Missouri

**RICHARD WASSERSTROM,
LL.B., Ph.D.**

Professor of Law and Philosophy, School of Law,
University of California, Los Angeles

**JEROME F. WILKERSON,
M.Div., Ph.D.**

Director, Newman Center, Washington University Medical Campus,
St. Louis, Missouri

TASK FORCE

ROBERT C. KOLODNY, M.D.
(Chairperson)

H. TRISTRAM ENGELHARDT, JR.,
Ph.D., M.D.

CHARLES FRIED, LL.B.

JOSHUA S. GOLDEN, M.D.

RICHARD GREEN, M.D.

ALBERT R. JONSEN, Ph.D.

HAROLD I. LIEF, M.D.

RUTH MACKLIN, Ph.D.

JAY MANN, Ph.D.

LORNA J. SARREL, M.S.S.W.

PHILIP M. SARREL, M.D.

RAYMOND W. WAGGONER,
M.D., Sc.D.

RICHARD WASSERSTROM,
LL.B., Ph.D.

JEROME F. WILKERSON,
M.Div., Ph.D.

PREFACE

The decade of the 1970s was marked by increasing public and professional attention to principles of ethical conduct in all branches of science and health care. Simultaneously, the seventies saw the birth of sex therapy as a full-fledged discipline and a concomitant proliferation of research related to human sexuality. It should be no surprise that the ethical propriety of both sex therapy and sex research was questioned by some critics; indeed, such scrutiny is warranted to guard against the tendency for technological considerations in any newly developing field to overshadow fundamental considerations of ethics and values.

In 1974, the Masters & Johnson Institute (then known as the Reproductive Biology Research Foundation) decided to organize and sponsor a series of professional meetings to provide a forum for nationally recognized experts from diverse disciplines—including the health-care sciences, philosophy, law, and theology—to discuss ethical problems associated with sex therapy and research, with a long-range goal of formulating a coherent set of ethics guidelines for the field of sexology. The first step in this direction was a conference held January 22–23, 1976, the proceedings of which were transcribed and published in W. H. Masters, V. E. Johnson, and R. C. Kolodny, Eds., *Ethical Issues in Sex Therapy and Research* (Boston: Little, Brown and Co., 1977). The purpose of the initial meeting was to identify and discuss pertinent ethical issues in therapeutic and investigative approaches to human sexuality.

Following the 1976 conference, with the assistance of Ruth Macklin, Fritz Redlich, H. Tristram Engelhardt, Jr., and Jerome F. Wilkerson, a fourteen-member task force was recruited to prepare background papers on five general topics supplementing those presented and discussed at the first conference and to draft a set of ethics guidelines for consideration at a subsequent conference. The task force met twice as a group during 1977 to examine and discuss the background papers and to plan the larger meeting. Their deliberations were sometimes tranquil, sometimes heated, but always intellectually stimulating and semantically rigorous. Many telephone calls, letters, and smaller meetings supplemented and facilitated this process, as each assigned paper and the draft of guidelines underwent two revisions before being distributed—in December, 1977—to those persons who had accepted invitations to the upcoming Ethics Congress.

Approximately two dozen experts were invited to attend the conference held January 25–27, 1978, in addition to the thirty-two persons who had been present at the 1976 meeting. Despite a blizzard that forced closing of the St. Louis airport and temporarily immobilized most of the eastern United States, forty-four of those invited gathered in St. Louis to participate in this program.

The first day of the Ethics Congress included an evening session and consisted of a series of panel discussions of the background papers, followed by open dialogue with members of the audience. On the second day, after an initial panel discussion of the prepared draft of guidelines, the format shifted from the plenary session to concurrent small group discussions, which lasted for approximately five hours. For these discussions, each group focused its attention primarily on a single specified section of the draft of guidelines. Each group was asked to prepare a summary of their deliberations and recommendations for presentation in plenary session the next day. (Transcribed tape recordings of the small group discussions have not been reproduced in the present volume, since inclusion of this material would have tripled the number of pages without a commensurate gain in content. The summary report of each group discussion provides a recapitualtion of the points of consensus and matters of dispute that characterized these sessions.)

The third and final day of the Ethics Congress was reserved for presentation of reports from the discussion groups, followed by a lively three-and-one-half-hour open discussion of the proposed draft of the ethics guidelines. Immediately upon adjournment of the larger gathering, the task force met to synthesize comments, criticism, and suggestions from participants into a revised version of the guidelines, which subsequently underwent additional minor changes before the final revision was completed in March 1978.

Although the Masters & Johnson Institute organized and sponsored this program and provided its sole financial support, the resulting guidelines are truly a testimonial to the collaborative efforts, energies, and expertise of the many individuals who participated in various stages of planning, discussion, and meeting together. A particular measure of gratitude is due to the members of the Board of Directors of the Masters & Johnson Institute, whose enthusiasm and regard for this work allowed us to spend both money and time freely in its pursuit. In addition, we are indebted to our publisher, Fred Belliveau, for his unstinting encouragement and assistance.

We can find no better closing for our prefatory remarks than the concluding lines of the preamble to the guidelines: "Recognizing that the development of new knowledge and changes in mores may necessitate reappraisal of what is beneficial or detrimental in the context of sex therapy and sex research, it is expected that this document will undergo revision and interpretation. It is hoped that these guidelines will serve as a flexible instrument, since unanimity of opinion rarely exists in the interpretation of what is ethical or unethical." Only time will tell what impact this work may have. We hope that it provides a stimulus for critical thinking and responsible professionalism.

W. H. M.
V. E. J.
R. C. K.
S. M. W.

St. Louis

CONTENTS

xvii

I
BACKGROUND
PAPERS

INFORMED CONSENT: METHODOLOGICAL, RESEARCH, AND TREATMENT ISSUES

RICHARD GREEN

Consent and consideration of when and to what degree it is "informed" and freely given engages individuals and institutions at several levels. In this paper a variety of research strategies typically employed by sex researchers and therapists are examined as they relate to issues of informed consent. The strategies are so varied that no common denominator of informed consent can address every strategy. Thus, this manuscript is divided into several areas. They include questionnaire research, laboratory research, field survey research, observational studies, research that takes place in the context of therapy and research that does not, manipulative and nonmanipulative counseling, "useless" research, research and treatment of children, and institutional consent.

QUESTIONNAIRE RESEARCH

The design employed in questionnaire research typically includes a controlled cognitive stimulus comprising standardized questions. The respondent is in control of his or her responses to questionnaire items. When an individual consents to answer a questionnaire following the pattern, "When did you first do such-and-such," "How often have you done such-and-such," the researcher's expectation is that the respondent will complete each item. However, prior to beginning the questionnaire, the respondent does not know every item to be asked. Neither the investigator nor the respondent can know a priori the extent to which a question might be upsetting. Usually, the respondent has not given consent to being asked a given question, let alone consenting to answer it.

An introductory statement should outline the areas that will be covered in the questionnaire. Questionnaires should also contain a statement to the effect that if a question is asked that the respondent does not wish to answer or finds upsetting, the respondent may skip it. However, removal of all such "risk" would eliminate all questionnaire research.

LABORATORY RESEARCH

Next, consider laboratory physical contact measures. Such measures employ invasive or noninvasive strategies and instruments. *Invasive* generally connotes that the body is penetrated by a testing instrument, whether it be a needle or catheter inserted in an artery or vein, a photoelectric cell placed in the vagina, or a pressure transducer placed in the rectum [1–3]. To varying degrees these measures have become standardized procedures, used in a wide range of physiological explorations. An instrument representing different degrees of "conventional" data collection would be an indwelling venous catheter for monitoring levels of sex steroids in contrast to the vaginal photoplethysmograph.

Individuals are likely to give a fuller degree of informed consent to use of the more invasive instruments if they are first shown the instrument, told where the instrument is to be placed, apprised of any discomfort and physical risks, and given an explanation of the kinds of data that will be recorded and why the information is of value (at least to the researcher). The psychodynamics of those who volunteer for such research comes into question here. How does their motivation, perhaps not of a fully conscious nature, contribute to the degree to which they are informed? Is an individual with a strong need for sexual exhibitionism consenting to the same study as an individual with a strong need to promote the collection of scientific data? Is the symbolic meaning of their consent comparable? I suggest not. There should be some type of psychiatric screening of applicants to minimize the possibility of detrimental effects to a subject as a result of research participation.

FIELD SURVEY RESEARCH

Next, consider field survey research, particularly collection of data from unique groups. The possibility of both invasion of privacy and stigmatization exists when a particular feature is identified in members of a group. For example, less than systematic research has conveyed to the scientific community and to the general public the view that various behavioral problems—for example, criminal behavior—are associated with atypical chromosomal karyotypes such as XXY and XYY [4]. The extent, if any, to which the atypical sex chromosome contributes to these behaviors has not been systematically assessed because of unrepresentative samples. Since the XXY and the XYY karyotypes are found in approximately 1 in 500 consecutive male births, there are many more persons with these configurations outside of prisons than inside. The degree, if any, to which the presence of either of these karyotypes is linked with susceptibility to certain kinds of undesirable behaviors can be assessed only with representative sampling. One research strategy was to karyotype all neonatal males born in hospitals in Boston and longitudinally follow those male infants exhibiting the abnormal karyotype with systematic behavioral assessments at regular intervals.

Several problems arise here regarding informed consent. What does one tell the families of study subjects? Does one tell them that their children have an abnormal sex chromosome configuration? If so, what does one tell them about its possible significance? Is it ethical to withhold either the discovery of the abnormal karyotype or the potential implications of the karyotype? Will alerting parents to this information so modify the parent-child relationship as to distort the behavioral outcome? Will disclosure induce damaging rather than helpful effects to the child along with contamination of the research design? If the public (and its microcosm, the family) perceives the abnormal karyotype as being associated with unacceptable behavior, to what extent is the family (and the affected child) stigmatized?

An alternative strategy would be to karyotype all newborn children without looking at the karyotype until a number of years later, meanwhile following the children behaviorally. This presents the problem of withholding information: Children with an abnormal karyotype might need some special considerations if, in fact, they are more vulnerable to certain kinds of maladjustment. Another strategy would be to follow a large number of children developmentally and then karyotype them at age 12. In this situation, information has not been withheld. Any child exhibiting inadequate impulse control or any other behavioral difficulty could be effectively counseled in such a study, with knowledge of the karyotype unknown to either the investigator or the family. This issue has been more fully discussed elsewhere [5–10].

In a study done in the Dominican Republic, a genetically transmitted deficiency of the 5-alpha-reductase enzyme, which converts testosterone to dihydrotestosterone, has become a focus of inquiry. Research interest is due to the effects on the development of the external male genitalia and the questions posed with respect to psychosexual development. The syndrome with its extended family history has so far been found only in the Dominican Republic [11]. Persons with this rare syndrome are born in an intersexed state: Although they have testes and the 46,XY karyotype of a normal genetic male, they look more like females than males at birth. Generations ago such persons were raised in the feminine role. However, at puberty their "clitoris" grows, approaching male penile proportions, and they appear to switch their sexual identity from female to male. Their erotic attractions are reported to be toward females. Study of this unusual disorder has generated interest in the role of testosterone and dihydrotestosterone at different periods, pre- and postnatally, on differentiation of the genitalia and on the development of sexual identity. Of especial psychological interest is the reported capacity for these persons to "switch" sexual identity after what has traditionally been viewed as the critical period for the immutable establishment of such identity (that is, the first two and one-half to three years of life) [12–14].[1]

[1] A long-term study of 33 male pseudohermaphrodites in the Dominican Republic was conducted to determine the contribution of androgens to the formation of male-

Efforts are being made by investigators to trace the family trees of persons with this genetic trait. Observations might be made on the intrafamily patterns of socialization existing for these children from birth onward. What kind of informed consent can and should be obtained from parents and children who are to be studied in these villages? Aside from the capacity of children to give informed consent, discussed later in this essay, what does one tell the potential research subjects, their relatives, and the other townspeople? To what extent does a study of these individuals stigmatize the children and their families? To what extent does the study process contaminate the natural course of psychosexual development?

Who is to give the informed consent? Should it be the Dominican Republic, the head of the village, the parents, the children? What types of group pressures are brought to bear on any families unwilling to be studied? To begin with, this is not a large population. The investigators need every subject they can get. While the subjects may be informed of what is transpiring, are they in fact consenting? Their rights of privacy, their immunity to group pressure, and the advancement of scientific knowledge should be preserved, but how? Perhaps the only topics for study should be those deemed not offensive or sensitive to the potential research subjects, reinforced by the assurance of confidentiality. Remuneration for inconvenience may be given, but not in such measure that it would constitute bribery or coercion. Consent should be given by the persons being studied, at the very least.

RESEARCH INVOLVING OBSERVATION

Observational studies may be conducted in private, in laboratory settings, or in the field. They may be conducted with or without the awareness of those who are being observed. The observa-

---

gender identity. The results of this study are reported by J. Imperato-McGinley, R. E. Peterson, T. Gautier, and E. Sturla, Androgens and the evolution of male-gender identity among male pseudohermaphrodites with 5α-reductase deficiency, *New England Journal of Medicine* 300:1233–1237, 1979.

tion may be made from a distant point at which the observer is not engaging in the social matrix with those under observation, or it may be more proximal (as with participant observation, in which the observer interacts with the observee, with or without the observee's awareness that a study is being conducted).

In a laboratory setting one may be measuring psychophysiological levels of sexual arousal in response to a variety of potentially erotic stimuli. These stimuli may be of either a socially acceptable or an unacceptable nature; they may be either "normal" or "abnormal." They may include conventional sexual stimuli or stimuli of an illegal or atypical nature (for example, pedophilia or homosexuality). The individual who consents to participate in research in which responses to these patterns of stimuli are measured runs the risk of revealing both to self and to others the potential for erotic arousal to unacceptable, abnormal, atypical, or illegal stimuli. Does the individual run the further risk of developing new erotic associations in response to such stimuli? Can the individual be psychologically harmed by self-awareness of the erotically arousing potential of such stimuli? Can the individual consenting to participate in such a study be fully and truly informed of all the possible responses and consequences? Probably not. Is it potentially more harmful to spell out the possible consequences in the informed consent form that must be signed prior to participation? Possibly.

Consider a naturalistic setting, as examplified by the doctoral dissertation that led to the book *Tearoom Trade* [15]. In this study the investigator, posing as a lookout for police in a public men's room frequented by persons looking for brief, anonymous homosexual encounters, was in fact recording the behaviors staged in such a setting, unbeknownst to the "actors." This study clearly raises an issue of invasion of privacy in itself. However, the study did not stop here. Surreptitiously, the investigator also noted the license plates of the automobiles belonging to persons stopping by the men's room, traced the automobiles' owners, and at some later interval, under the guise of a public survey, interviewed these individuals about their marital lives and sexual practices. The interviewer did not relate to the interviewees the circumstances under which the initial observation had been made.

No one was publicly identified in the dissertation or in the book However, these individuals did not consent to being studied in the first place, nor were they truly informed when they consented to the subsequent interview. The names and addresses of all subjects can be destroyed, of course, and in this case no one appeared to have been harmed. But were these persons' rights violated? Yes. Were the study subjects not harmed primarily because of genuine concern for their protection on the part of the investigator? Yes. Might they have been harmed significantly in the hands of a less concerned investigator? Yes. Can such research be carried out in any other way in order to ensure adequate controls on the conduct of the investigator? I do not know. If not, should such research methods be eliminated from social and behavioral science? Probably.

Let us consider participant observation of a different sort: Suppose a person or team studying group sex or "swinging" parties joins a club of "swingers" to investigate the phenomenon. Their research consideration is that paper-and-pencil instruments do not tap the vital dimensions of the experience and that a volunteer sample would not be representative of the population to be studied. Thus, they argue for participant observation—perhaps without the subjects being aware that they are engaged in a study. While this would at first appear similar to the *Tearoom* study cited above, consider next the possibility of the investigator actively participating in the swinging activities of the club, in contrast to merely watching others so engaged. (In the latter strategy investigators might announce to the membership that they are present as scientific observers, will protect anonymity, and will not be actively participating. Would this announcement contaminate the research?) A reasonable argument can be made that direct participant observation, without the subjects' awareness, is the only way to explore the genuine texture of the phenomenon under study. However, to what extent is objective evaluation contaminated by the researcher's subjective experience of being both spectator and actor? Dimensions are added and subtracted by either strategy. To what degree is the noninvestigator actor victimized by the absence of either component of the double-barreled term *informed consent?* Here again, the actor's privacy is infringed upon and he or she is at the mercy of the investigator. However, the actor is also at the mercy of the other members of the club—an issue of group confidentiality, which will be addressed below.

RESEARCH INVOLVING STAGED EVENTS

Next, consider staged events or manipulations of the environment. The goal is to collect data on behavioral change in a standardized situation. The use of confederates and false feedback is common in such research. In one paradigm an investigator looks at the possibilities of experimental modification of attitudes in a direction that the subject might previously have considered unacceptable. An individual with exclusively heterosexual arousal patterns and a given attitude toward homosexuality may be a subject in a penile plethysmographic experiment in which both heterosexual and homosexual stimuli are presented. The subject is given false feedback to indicate that he is showing genital responsivity to homosexual stimuli. To what extent does such false feedback modify the individual's attitudes toward homosexuality? (For a model, see Valins [16].) Experimenters typically "debrief" subjects upon completion of such a study. During this phase of the experiment, subjects are told of the nature of the false feedback. This is done to allay any anxieties on the subjects' part that they do, in fact, have homosexual arousal patterns, which could be psychologically traumatic for some persons. However, is it possible to assess prior to the study the extent to which such trauma can be eliminated by debriefing? Should subjects be told at the outset of the experiment that some form of deception will take place? Would such communication render the study meaningless? For some research subjects the experience may be traumatic, at least temporarily, and it is impossible to foresee whether there will be any long-term detrimental effects.

Consider staged events in which heterosocial skills are taught. Here an individual (for example, a rapist or a pedophile) is seen as lacking necessary heterosocial skills vis-à-vis an adult of the other sex. This "defect" renders him unable to negotiate a socially appropriate heterosexual interaction. The individual is introduced to a training program of heterosocial skills, in which he is taught a graduated set of comfortable responses including preliminary verbal and physical gestures, eye contact, and a gradient of socially appropriate seductive remarks designed to lead two strangers into a sexual situation [17–20]. One strategy for assessing the efficacy of such intervention is to place the subject in a waiting room while the therapist is allegedly delayed by a telephone call. A female confederate enters the waiting room, ostensibly as a patient, and proceeds to enact a social script suggesting the possibility of heterosocial overtures. When this contrived situation includes a pre- and post-intervention comparison, it is possible to assess the degree to which the patient's heterosocial skills have been modified. But the individual has not been informed of this manipulation or consented to it. On the other hand, it can be argued that if a patient were informed of the possibility of such intervention ensuing during the course of treatment, it would nullify the potential validity of such a manipulation. However, there appears to be no risk of harm to the subject, and the potential benefit is clear.

The risk-benefit ratio with respect to society and to the individual must always be considered. In a nontreatment situation with a normal person, the risk may be minimal and the benefit minimal or null. The benefit to the larger society may be greater than the benefit to the individual. With a patient desirous of behavioral change, the risk may be minimal and the benefit considerable. The benefit to society at large may also be considerable.

RESEARCH IN THE CONTEXT OF THERAPY

Next, consider research taking place in the context of therapy. This type of research engages issues of randomization between treatment modes. In clinical outcome studies involving sexual behavior, several interventions may be pitted against one another in an effort to delineate the most efficacious method of treatment. Sometimes the investigator has a hypothesis that a given mode of intervention will be the most effective. Sometimes patients have an idea that one mode or another will be more effective. To what extent does the therapist have an obligation to inform patients that they are in a treatment mode considered a priori less likely to induce the desired behavioral change? To what degree should the therapist be responsive to allocating patients to their preferred mode of treatment? Can there be true randomization of groups if the patient has the option to select the mode of intervention? Should the informed consent statement reveal to the subject the possible second-best nature of his or her treatment?

What of placebo intervention? Consider a study in which varieties of sexual dysfunction are being investigated by several treatments. It is unclear which treatment mode is most effective, and the investigator is not convinced, on the basis of the available literature, that any treatment is effective in itself. One hypothesis is that it is merely the couple's solicitation of help that is the catalyst for desired change. Should patients be told that some of them are entering into a treatment that is not anticipated by the investigator to yield much benefit? Consider the possibility that a married couple has consulted the therapist as a court of last resort: The relationship is on the brink of dissolution, the only possible salvation being a rapid improvement in the sexual relationship. The marriage may be irretrievably broken while placebo intervention is taking place if no improvement occurs.

If subjects are told that some of them will enter into a placebo treatment, what safeguards should be introduced? It should be mandatory to monitor the progressive status of the marital relationship and to transfer individuals from nonintervention to a direct intervention treatment cell when there is rapid deterioration and immediate risk of dissolution of a marriage. It might also be wise to inform all patients that there will be a placebo interval in which patients are not necessarily expected to show change, followed by a crossover to treatment modalities expected to induce change.

Let us move on to nonrandomized studies. Consider psychosurgery. In West Germany, a series of nearly 90 male sex offenders were treated with stereotaxic brain surgery of the ventromedial nucleus of the hypothalamus [21]. There is considerable controversy about the ethics of such intervention. To what extent can incarcerated persons or persons under threat of incarceration give noncoercive consent? Is coercive consent equivalent to nonconsent and therefore unethical, even if the alternative (nonintervention) is potentially more destructive to the individual? Denial of treatment because of inability to give noncoercive consent could be construed as a greater violation of the individual's rights; the result may be indefinite incarceration. (For a fuller discussion, see the federal government's recommendations on research involving prisoners [22].)

The issue of psychosurgery for sex offenders is even more complex in that basic science researchers note little evidence from nonhuman investigations to suggest that the procedures invoked will produce the desired effects in human subjects. Thus, the ethical question must involve theoretical and scientific considerations. To rule out the possibility of a placebo effect of this dramatic intervention, it might be required that sham surgery be performed. It would then be possible to compare those individuals in whom part of the hypothalamus had been destroyed with those in whom it had not. However, it would be necessary to inform the patients prior to surgery that some would undergo a sham procedure. Is it possible that telling someone who has undergone the real procedure that he may have had a sham procedure would diminish the benefits of the surgery (which might, in fact, be somewhat effective)? (Here we postulate an interaction between the physiological effects of the surgery and the psychological power of suggestion.) Is it ethical to subject someone to a procedure in which there is a risk of permanent injury (from the sham procedure) without genuine expectation of benefit? What if the observable benefit can only be attributed to the placebo effect? Could the risk of the sham procedure be minimized by elimination of some components (for example, modified anesthesia, no penetration of brain tissue by electrodes) without loss of the desired placebo effect? If the placebo works, should all patients be told they are having the real procedure? If so, are they truly informed? No. Are they helped? Yes.

Sex-reassignment surgery poses another dilemma. While it has not yet been seriously challenged, it has been suggested that a court might consider the procedure to be mayhem [23, 24]. If such surgery were adjudged mayhem, the individual could not legally give informed consent, since one cannot consent to an illegal act [23, 24]. The definition of mayhem generally stipulates that the injury must have been willfully imposed by the perpetrator, in this case the physician. Until recently, it was believed that surgery was the only effective treatment for transsexualism. In recent years, however, a few individuals described as transsexuals appear to have been "cured" by nonsurgical means [25, 26]. In the event that a transsexual demands surgery and refuses behaviorist intervention, has the individual given informed consent to the surgery? Has the willfully harmful aspect of the surgeon's actions been removed if the option of nonsurgical treatment was presented? If the surgeon and psychiatrist sincerely believe, based on a review of all data, that they are helping the patient, is the risk of mayhem eliminated? They would appear at least to have acted ethically.

MANIPULATIVE AND NONMANIPULATIVE COUNSELING

Individuals consult a clinic for a variety of sexual disorders. To what extent do they give informed consent to the wide variety of procedures that may ensue from the moment they arrive for their first appointment? Specific interventions may include masturbation or the use of visual and narrative erotic stimuli. Patients may consider such procedures offensive. How many therapists spend the first hour describing their philosophy of treatment and preparing their clients for the various stages of therapy that their program entails? How many practitioners instruct prospective patients, at the end of the introductory session, to go home and discuss whether they wish to engage in such a therapeutic undertaking? It can be argued that the nature of the therapist-patient relationship is such that a coercive element exists from the very beginning. It can be argued that the patient is under duress, and thus no informed consent can be given. Can the elements of coercion be mitigated if the first hour is spent exclusively describing the treatment philosophy, postponing history-taking until the second appointment? The revelation of one's personal sexual history may establish a relationship that makes it impossible for the patient to enter into subsequent treatment procedures without the presence of coercion.

Consider group counseling. When a contract is drawn between therapist and patient regarding the privileged communication that will ensue during the course of counseling, to what extent does this privileged communication extend to other patients in the group? Are clients or patients in the group bound to medical confidentiality? Are clients apprised of the potential risk of breach of confidentiality?

"USELESS" RESEARCH

In some studies, even though the parties consent, it is difficult to know whether any useful information might emanate from the study. There may be some minimal hazard for research subjects, even though they have consented to participate. Consider the possibility that it might be very difficult to formulate a theory for which the data collected would provide definite value. Consider that the research findings may have no practical application. In such a case, any risk outweighs the potential benefit. If it can be shown that neither risk nor benefit exists and the investigator(s) and subject(s) still wish to engage in the research, that can be considered their business. However, if the project requires public funding, the proposal may not be enthusiastically embraced by Congress.

RESEARCH AND TREATMENT OF CHILDREN

Consider the question of informed consent by minors. This will be dealt with only briefly here, since there is a more extensive discussion of the topic elsewhere in this conference. When a child is involved in a research study, he or she has generally been brought by the parents. The parents may be reimbursed for their time. The child is typically not reimbursed. To what extent do children have full comprehension of what is going to happen when they agree to accompany their parents to the laboratory or to the doctor's office? What if some of the procedures introduced (such as venipuncture) are frightening to the child? What if the parents are promised more money for their participation if they permit blood samples to be collected from the child? Is this not coercion, particularly in a family in need of additional income? Payment should be the same, irrespective of the child's participation in all phases of a project.

What of treatment of children? What if parents want their child to embark upon a course of therapy to eliminate a behavior that the parents consider objectionable? Can the child give an informed consent, either legally or morally, to enter therapy? Some children may be willing to enter therapy because of distress that they hope to alleviate. However, they cannot give legal consent, even though volitionally they are on the side of intervention. What if the child is neither legally capable of giving consent nor volitionally in favor of intervention? What responsibility does the therapist have to refrain from treating or studying the child if the child is reluctant to participate? Should the therapist proceed on the basis that the intervention is likely to benefit the child in the long run? Courts have upheld the rights of minors, upon achieving majority status, to bring action against physicians for acts alleged as injurious, although perpetrated with parental consent, during the time of the person's minority status.

What is the responsibility of the investigator or clinician when a child refuses to undergo a specific type of treatment invoked by the parents, even after the child has received a full explanation of the procedures? Is the clinician's responsibility to the person who has legal guardianship and control over the child, or is it to the child? Are the rights of the child to be appreciated at the same level of complexity as those of the adult? Does the therapist's responsibility rest with what he or she considers most useful for the child, with what the child thinks would be most useful, or with what the parents think would be most useful?

I suggest that there be informed consent forms for children, written in language fully understandable by the child, presented to the child by an individual in the absence of the investigator or parents, with a full explanation of the procedures that the proposed research or treatment entails.

OTHER PROBLEMS

Consider observation and monitoring of behaviors during therapy. This may include audio-recording and videotaping, the keeping of notes by therapists, and the keeping of diaries by patients. Who is the audience for these scenarios? Typically it is research assistants and secretaries. Yet, when a patient signs the usual informed consent papers, the material is described as medically confidential. How much does the subject know about the various channels through which personal data will flow? Can proper safeguards be instituted to ensure that information is adequately disguised by the principal investigator prior to its being passed on to peripheral personnel? While there exists a general mandate for confidentiality on the part of all professional personnel, research associates, secretaries, and others engaged in the project, to what degree can the patient or subject count on this confidentiality remaining inviolate?

Data pass through many hands before being reduced to multiple correlation coefficients. Prior to entering a study or treatment program, patients should be made aware of all persons who may review data in which they can be identified. They should be aware that leaks of information and breaches of confidentiality may occur. We have an ethical responsibility to educate project personnel and clinic staff members regarding the umbrella mandate of confidentiality.

To what extent is the remuneration of research subjects coercive? To what extent is it unequally coercive across socioeconomic classes? While it can be argued that research subjects should be reimbursed for their time and inconvenience, are individuals more in need of economic gain more likely to participate in activities they would otherwise find objectionable? To what extent is it coercive to require deposit of funds prior to the rendering of therapeutic services, with the sum forfeited unless the individual completes an extended treatment program? This is an "incentive" technique employed by some behavior-oriented therapy programs to minimize attrition. While most human subject research committees provide the subject with the option to withdraw from a study at any time, there is an element of coercion present when an individual has a financial investment in continuing participation.

INSTITUTIONAL CONSENT

Finally, institutions should also be able to give or refuse informed consent to be studied. Investigators must not enter institutions under false pretexts (for example, masquerading as patients in order to obtain research information). While quality control of institutions must be maintained and monitored, deceptive monitoring policies are a basic infringement on rights, whether the victim is an institution or an individual. Some type of equilibrium must be found between public accountability and the right to be left alone.

Informed consent is a deceptively simple term. When applied to the strategies of sex research and the practices of sex therapy, it engages issues of a psychologically symbolic nature far more subtle than in other specialties involving *Homo sapiens.* Sex research and sex therapy have evolved increasingly sophisticated methodological principles. With evolution goes responsibility. Let us hope the profession meets the challenge more successfully than has the species.

REFERENCES

1. Geer, J., Morokoff, P., and Greenwood, P. Sexual arousal in women: The development of a measurement device for vaginal blood volume. *Archives of Sexual Behavior* 3:559–564, 1974.
2. Heiman, J. Use of the vaginal photo-plethysmograph as a diagnostic and treatment aid in female sexual dysfunction. Paper presented at Annual Meeting of the American Psychological Association, 1975, in Chicago, Illinois.
3. Bohlen, J., and Held, J. Personal communication, 1977.
4. Money, J., Wiedeking, C., Walker, P., Migeon, C., Meyer, W., and Borgaonkar, D. 47,XYY and 46,XY males with antisocial and/or sex-offending behavior. *Psychoneuroendocrinology* 1:165–178, 1975.
5. Beckwith, J., Elseviers, D., Gorini, L., Mandansky, C., and Csonka, L. Harvard XYY study. *Science* 187:298, 1975.
6. Culliton, B. J. Patients' rights: Harvard is site of battle over X and Y chromosomes. *Science* 186:715–717, 1974.
7. Culliton, B. J. XYY: Harvard researcher under fire stops newborn screening. *Science* 188:1284–1285, 1975.
8. Franzke, A. Telling parents about XYY sons. *New England Journal of Medicine* 293:100–101, 1975.
9. Green, R. Ethical Issues and Requirements for Sex Research with Humans: Confidentiality (designated discussion). In W. H. Mas-

ters, V. E. Johnson, and R. C. Kolodny (Eds.), *Ethical Issues in Sex Therapy and Research.* Boston: Little, Brown, 1977. Vol. I, pp. 106–114.

10. Money, J.   Issues and Attitudes in Research and Treatment of Variant Forms of Human Sexual Behavior. In W. H. Masters, V. E. Johnson, and R. C. Kolodny (Eds.), *Ethical Issues in Sex Therapy and Research.* Boston: Little, Brown, 1977. Vol. 1, pp. 119–132.
11. Peterson, R., Imperato-McGinley, J., Gautier, T., and Sturla, E. Male pseudohermaphroditism due to steroid 5α-reductase deficiency. *American Journal of Medicine* 62:170–191, 1977.
12. Money, J., Hampson, J., and Hampson, J.   An examination of some basic sexual concepts: The evidence of human hermaphroditism. *Bulletin of the Johns Hopkins Hospital* 97:301–319, 1955.
13. Money, J., Hampson, J., and Hampson, J.   Imprinting and the establishment of gender role. *Archives of Neurology and Psychiatry* 77:333–336, 1957.
14. Stoller, R.   *Sex and Gender: On the Development of Masculinity and Femininity.* New York: Science House, 1968.
15. Humphreys, L.   *Tearoom Trade: Impersonal Sex in Public Places.* Chicago: Aldine, 1970.
16. Valins, S.   Emotionality and information concerning internal reactions. *Journal of Personality and Social Psychology* 6:458–463, 1967.
17. Barlow, D.   The Treatment of Sexual Deviation: Towards a Comprehensive Approach. In K. Calhoun, H. Adams, and K. Mitchell (Eds.), *Innovative Methods in Psychopathology.* New York: Wiley, 1974.
18. Abel, G., Blanchard, E., Barlow, D., and Mavissakalian, M.   Identifying specific erotic cues in sexual deviations by audiotaped descriptions. *Applied Behavioral Analysis* 8:247–260, 1975.
19. Laws, D., and Serber, M.   Measurement and Evaluation of Assertive Training with Sexual Offenders. In R. Hosford and S. Moss (Eds.), *The Crumbling Walls: Treatment and Counseling of the Youthful Offender.* Champaign, Ill.: University of Illinois Press, 1974.
20. Serber, M.   Teaching the nonverbal components of assertive training. *Journal of Behavior Therapy and Experimental Psychiatry* 3: 179–183, 1972.
21. Rieber, I., and Sigusch, V.   Psychosurgery on sex offenders and sexual "deviants" in West Germany. *Archives of Sexual Behavior* 8: 523–527, 1979.
22. National Commission for the Protection of Human Subjects of Biomedical and Behavioral Research. *Report and Recommendations: Research Involving Prisoners.* DHEW Publication No. (OS) 76–131 (Washington, D.C.: U.S. Government Printing Office, 1976).

23. Holloway, J.   Transsexuals and Their "Legal Sex." In R. Green and J. Money (Eds.), *Transsexualism and Sex Reassignment*. Baltimore: Johns Hopkins University Press, 1969.

24. Holloway, J.   Transsexuals: Legal considerations. *Archives of Sexual Behavior* 3:33–50, 1974.

25. Barlow, D., Reynolds, E., and Agras, W.   Gender identity change in a transsexual. *Archives of General Psychiatry* 28:569–576, 1973.

26. Davenport, C., and Harrison, S.   Gender identity change in a female adolescent transsexual. *Archives of Sexual Behavior* 6:327–340, 1977.

PROBLEMS OF CONSENT IN SEX RESEARCH: LEGAL AND ETHICAL CONSIDERATIONS

CHARLES FRIED

LEGAL LIABILITY

I shall not address the potential liability under statutes forbidding consensual conduct, such as prostitution, fornication, lewd and lascivious carriage, or adultery, which might arise from therapeutic and nontherapeutic sex research activities. These issues have been adequately considered in a review article by Leroy [1]. Moreover, they are somewhat irrelevant to our particular focus, which is the importance of consent. In a sense, of course, they bear on the question of consent to the extent that the consensual crimes are crimes in which consent is no defense. But our concern is rather with ways in which defective consent or failure to obtain consent may raise legal or ethical problems. For that reason it seems justifiable to put aside the kinds of problems that would be raised even if the consent were as good as you please.

CRIMINAL AND CIVIL ASSAULT

The first and most basic form of criminal liability that must be considered is liability for assault and battery. These notions, which are the same in civil law for all intents and purposes, are ancient and persistent expressions of the basic value of personal integrity. It is not physical harm that is the gravamen of the wrong here, but the offense to personal dignity, the offense to the right to control access to one's person. It is not harm or the threat of harm that is involved, but any actual or threatened offensive contact.

Consent is crucial to this notion: With consent, what may have been offensive becomes inoffensive.[1] But it is quite clear that for consent to do its work, it must be free consent and informed consent.[2] Thus, consent at the point of a gun, for instance, is no consent at all. On the other hand, if someone consents because of a hardship that the person obtaining the consent has not imposed (or has not imposed improperly), then consent to that person's impositions should not be ineffective in principle. A simple example: If I consent to experimental surgery in response to a threat, the consent is obviously invalid and the threat and the surgery itself are an assault and a battery. On the other hand, if I consent to surgery under the "threat" of serious illness—for instance, a ruptured appendix—then the consent is quite effective. After all, it is not the surgeon who is imposing the threat of the ruptured appendix upon me. That the party giving the consent must know what he or she is consenting to is equally obvious, though in practice what this means is a matter of considerable controversy.[3]

These general principles are applicable in the criminal as in the civil law. There are, however, these differences: First, the person (in a criminal case, the state) complaining of the unwarranted intrusion must bear different burdens of proof. In a criminal prosecution he must prove his case beyond a reasonable doubt, while in a civil case he must only prove that the facts are more likely to have occurred than not. Second, in a criminal case it should be possible in principle for a person charged with battery to claim that though there may not have been consent, he believed that there was. In a

[1] For example, Burrows v. Hawaiian Trust Co. (1966); Goldnamer v. O'Brien (1896); Wright v. Starr (1919).

[2] For example, Thibault v. Lalumiere (1945); People v. Steinberg (1947).

[3] For example, a student who consents to a hazing does not consent to a severe beating in the course of that hazing when the possibility of a physical injury was not revealed to him (People v. Lenti [1964]). Similarly, a patient's consent to exploratory surgery does not include consent to a mastectomy in the course of such surgery where the patient did not know that a mastectomy might be performed (Corn v. French [1955]). But consent to any medical treatment or procedure deemed necessary to a physician has been held to be effective consent for a biopsy, since the patient knew he was consenting to any treatment (Bradford v. Winter [1963]).

civil action this claim might hold only where the person who believed in the fact of the consent believed this reasonably. A classic case is that of the doctor who was sued by a non-English-speaking immigrant who joined a line with large numbers of other immigrants awaiting vaccination. Though the immigrant claimed she did not consent to the vaccination, the court held that the jury could absolve the defendant if it found that he reasonably believed that she had so consented.[4] (A further complication, which the cases do not permit us to resolve, relates to whether the aggrieved party must somehow have done something to create this reasonable but mistaken impression.)

In a criminal case, however, there are good grounds for arguing that a person should not be held liable for battery even though he was negligent in believing there was consent. The idea is that battery is not a crime that is committed merely negligently. There are a number of examples of this principle in respect to the crime of rape: A recent decision in the House of Lords held that a person cannot commit rape negligently; if he believes that the woman consents, that "good faith" belief insulates him from the charge no matter how unreasonable the belief was.[5] Although many advocates of women's rights have been outraged by this decision, it is in perfect accord with principles maintaining that the most serious criminal offenses—battery and rape among them—cannot be committed except intentionally or at least recklessly.[6]

Application to Sex Research

When these principles are applied to our area of concern, there are numerous situations in which therapeutic and nontherapeutic sex research might involve the researcher or others in responsibility for assault, battery, or rape charges. (The rape charge is simply the assault and battery charge translated to sexual contacts.)

Any research or therapeutic technique involving touching obviously raises these dangers if there is no consent or no effective consent to the touching. Even a routine pelvic examination without effective consent—performed, for example, on an unconscious

---

[4] O'Brien v. Cunard S.S. Co. (1891).
[5] Directors of Public Prosecution v. Morgan (1975).
[6] For example, Talmadge v. Smith (1894); Garratt v. Dailey (1955).

patient in a nonemergency or administered by a person who pretends to be a qualified physician—may constitute battery. The charge could also be brought in respect to those purported "therapeutic" maneuvers involving actual sexual contact between therapist and patient if the therapist has abused his or her authority so as to make the consent ineffective by virtue of fear or ignorance.[7] Certainly those cases where mentally deficient, mentally ill, or minor persons are led to believe that the sexual contact is in fact part of the therapy would constitute cases of assault, battery, and rape.[8] A more interesting problem relates to possible charges of assault, battery, and rape in respect to sexual contacts between the patient-subject and others besides the therapist. For instance, if the therapist provides a partner surrogate or is otherwise implicated in a situation that leads to sexual contact, not only the surrogate or other person in the contact but the therapist himself or herself might be liable, by the doctrine of vicarious liability. Once again, of course, consent would vitiate the charge.

In this respect the situation of minors is particularly important, for there is a question as to when the consent of a minor is effective. In the medical area, the old law held that a minor could give no effective consent, and that therefore only those things could be done that were either required by some emergency necessity or were consented to on the minor's behalf by a person having legal custody of the minor.[9] As to the latter category, it has been held until quite recently that such consent could only be given in the best interest of the child—that is, that no risk or actual harm to the child could be consented to on behalf of the child for the good of others.[10]

[7] Cf. *Commonwealth* v. *Goldenberg* (1959), *cert. denied* (1959) (patient's failure to protest upon initiation of sexual intercourse by physician does not constitute consent where patient was possibly drugged and where physician represented the intercourse as part of the patient's medical treatment); *Belcher* v. *Carter* (1967) (a patient's consent to touching by a physician is not consent at all if the patient lacks sufficient knowledge and understanding as to what is contemplated by the physician); *Natanson* v. *Kline* (1963) (consent given under duress and out of fear arising from the intentional overstatements of the physician that the patient needed a particular treatment is not valid consent).

[8] For example, *Bishop* v. *Liston* (1924) (a minor cannot consent to rape); *People* v. *Gibson* (1922) (a minor cannot effectively consent to indecent familiarities).

[9] *Zoski* v. *Gaines* (1939); *Moss* v. *Rishworth* (1920).

[10] For a discussion of the old view, see Freund [2]. Examples of the modern approach are found in *Bonner* v. *Moran* (1941) and in *Hart* v. *Brown* (1972).

This common law principle has recently come under considerable attack. The argument is made that children can make significant contributions as research subjects to the well-being of mankind generally, and that indeed only children can provide certain research benefits that would ultimately redound to other children. This has led to a very widespread view that children may be used as research subjects in therapeutic and nontherapeutic research, even where they are exposed to hazards not solely for their own personal well-being, provided that the hazards are minimal; that the use of children is unavoidable; that an important benefit would otherwise be forgone; and, finally, that the child's consent is obtained when and wherever possible [3]. It is sometimes added that the benefits of such research should redound either to children generally or, in the case of therapeutic research, to children sharing the same disease from which the research subject is suffering [4]. Thus, a 12-year-old might be used as a research subject in a protocol involving some hazards and discomfort and often no immediate benefits, if that 12-year-old agreed to participate (and, of course, if the 12-year-old's parent[s] or guardian also consented).

These general principles have application to sex research. I shall refer to them in considering the possible forms of civil and criminal liability for various forms of research. I have so far spoken of possible liability for assault, battery, and rape in connection with research involving contacts that are specifically sexual in nature. The notorious case of *People* v. *Martin* (1955) [5], in which a psychiatrist engaged in homosexual relations with an alleged therapeutic intent toward the disturbed boys in his charge, serves as an adequate example for the proposition that even the expanded notions of consent on behalf of children are not likely to be applied to this kind of conduct. One might argue that our unwillingness to allow a minor to consent to such contact or to take seriously a guardian's consent on his behalf represents simply a prudish prejudice. Such a dispute would not be fruitful, as no practical applications of the resolution of the deliberation can be imagined. The obvious problems of abuse of fiduciary relationship—which are prominent enough when the subject is an adult—are exacerbated in the case of children.

A more realistic problem relates to possible vicarious liability in cases where minors are encouraged or perhaps only given easy occasions for sexual contact either among their peers or with adults other than the researcher-therapist. The possibility of prosecution for this kind of vicarious liability seems to me much more plausible than in the case of adult patient-subjects. It should be noted that even if there is not vicarious liability for assault, battery, or rape in such cases, liability for negligence on charges of either creating, encouraging, or failing to prevent the occasions for such contact are an entirely familiar aspect of the legal landscape.

Research Involving Drugs and Behavior Modification Techniques

A less esoteric form of criminal liability for assault or battery relates to drugs and behavior modification techniques. This may come as a surprise to nonlawyers, but administering a drug to a person against his wishes or by deception is as much a case of battery as injecting such a drug into the person by force against his will.[11] Indeed, the point can be carried even farther: To give a person a drug where there is deception as to the nature of the drug will also constitute battery,[12] for there is contact with the person—even though the person may take the pill himself—and the consent is vitiated by fraud and deception. This point is firmly established in the law, and the only matter of controversy relates to the degree of deception necessary to constitute the offense. Thus, if a person thinks he is drinking tea but in fact is drinking tea with drugs in it, there is firm precedent for the proposition that this constitutes a battery.[13] If, however, a drug is given whose properties and effects have not been fully described, it is not clear that there is a battery. At this point it is plainly a matter of degree. A practical implication of these principles would be that the administration of a placebo might well constitute a battery—particularly where the administration was guided not by concern for the welfare of the patient but by extrinsic motives, such as the furtherance of research.

In the area of behavior modification, the possibility of civil and criminal liability is very much in the picture. Behavior modification techniques of the type known as aversion therapy have sometimes

---

[11] For example, *Commonwealth* v. *Stratton* (1873); *State* v. *Monroe* (1897).

[12] *People* v. *Steinberg* (1947) (nurse who injects a patient with water instead of vaccine serum has committed a battery).

[13] Cf. *Smith* v. *Smith* (1940) (slander action involving factual situation in which wife allegedly poisoned husband's milk).

included administration of electric shocks, drugs producing unpleasant results such as nausea or loss of capacity to breathe, and—
in some instances—even physical beatings. All of these "negative
reinforcers" constitute unequivocal acts of battery unless some
excuse can be found to justify their use. Consent, of course, is the
obvious form of justification that might be invoked. However, caution must be exercised. If the consent is obtained from children or
persons with diminished capacity, it may not be possible to get
fully valid consent, and therefore the conduct can only be validated
on grounds of therapeutic necessity. This is a high hurdle indeed,
particularly if the behavior modification technique is not in the
category of accepted practice. Where the behavior modification
takes place in the context of a research protocol, the theoretical
possibilities of criminal and civil liability become particularly lively.
In a research protocol there is a greater dilution of therapeutic purpose, at best; moreover, some research contexts require the use of
deception as to the purposes or features of the research protocol.
Such deception may itself vitiate the consent, thus failing to insu-
late the researcher from criminal and civil liability for battery upon
the person of the subject.

The law is clear that consent to what would be battery may be
withdrawn at any time, even if one has contracted not to withdraw
the consent and has perhaps received a benefit.[14] The behavior
modification subject who shouts "Stop" in response to receiving
painful stimuli must be obeyed at the risk of a charge of battery.

Finally, it is becoming more difficult to obtain the valid consent
of persons confined in prisons or mental institutions.[15] The recommendations of the National Commission for the Protection of Human Subjects would severely limit the use of prisoners in biomedical research on just this skeptical premise. It seems at least plausible
that the strictures of the National Commission would be generalized beyond research using drugs and other such interventions to
include behavioral research and behavior modification techniques.
There is, after all, little difference between the harm suffered from
receiving a series of electric shocks and a transient mild rash caused
by a drug administered experimentally. I shall have occasion to

[14] *Shetter* v. *Rochelle* (1966), *modified on other grounds* (1966); *State* v. *Auld*
(1949).

[15] For an excellent discussion of the issues involved in this area, see Annas,
Glantz, and Katz [4], pp. 103–138, 139–193.

return to the recommendations of the National Commission in discussing government regulations. Their relevance here is simply to illustrate a climate of opinion that might serve to undermine the consent of confined persons and thus leave the researcher exposed to criminal and civil liability for conduct that would constitute a battery without that consent.

There are serious problems regarding the consent even of nonconfined persons who seek behavior modification therapy or drug therapy for sexual disorders. The disorder or dysfunction itself may be viewed as a form of mental infirmity, such that a judge or jury may extrapolate from it, treating the local symptom as a sign of a larger volitional or cognitive disability. To the extent that the therapy is unconventional, either the therapeutic validity or necessity of the procedure or both may well be questioned. This doubt, combined with vitiated capacity to consent, may place tortious imposition on the person. The danger is exacerbated when the behavior modification technique or the drug is administered in part or wholly for research purposes.

MAYHEM

Mayhem is an ancient common law felony ranking equal to rape and behind murder in seriousness. It is defined as any intentional mutilation or serious and permanent injury inflicted upon a person involving loss of function or loss of a member; the paradigm cases often cited are amputation of a limb or blinding. (Since the mutilation or deprivation of function must be intentional, surgical procedures that have such drastic but undesired sequelae do not constitute mayhem.) This serious felony has great relevance to sex research and sex therapy. Both psychosurgery and sex-reassignment surgery would seem clearly to fall within the definition of mayhem. Moreover, mayhem is akin more to murder than to battery or rape inasmuch as consent is no defense at all.[16] Just because consent is not sufficient to excuse mayhem,[17] the researcher or therapist runs a greater risk in this area, since his conduct is more explicitly sub-

[16] *Kaimowitz* v. *Department of Mental Health* (1973).

[17] Consent would, however, be necessary to excuse most cases of therapeutic mayhem—an amputation against the wishes of a competent subject would still be criminal.

ject to ex post facto scrutiny by a possibly hostile judge. I should not wish to be too alarming in this regard; I know of no mayhem prosecutions growing out of either psychosurgery or sex-reassignment surgery. This must be because the overall beneficent purpose is exculpatory. Obviously, amputations and mutilations have been going on for centuries in the context of proper surgery, and justification is found in the therapeutic purpose of the procedure: It is better that the eye should perish than that the whole body die. It is interesting to note, however, that in traditional Roman Catholic theology, sterilization is viewed as a case of mutilation (that is, the equivalent of mayhem) in spite of an admittedly beneficent ultimate purpose. The means are condemned.

INFLICTION OF EMOTIONAL DISTRESS

In many jurisdictions it is a civil wrong to inflict grave emotional distress on another person. In almost all jurisdictions, however, the tort is only committed if there is a purpose to inflict the distress. The paradigm cases involve vicious practical jokes, as where pranksters provided a woman with a bathing suit that dissolved on contact with water,[18] or told a woman that her husband had been killed in an accident;[19] or in cases involving the harassing techniques of collection agencies.[20] The tort has, however, recently been extended in a number of jurisdictions (including California). Thus, extreme emotional distress is actionable even if the conduct was negligent—if it was foreseeable that the distress or some other harm would occur. The classical cases are the distress suffered by a parent who witnesses the accidental death of a child, though the parent was in no physical danger,[21] or the distress experienced by the family of the bereaved when the ashes of the deceased are mislaid at the crematory.[22]

There is here a fertile field for legal liability in social science research generally and in sex research in particular. Researchers who frighten, embarrass, or alarm subjects as part of the research proto-

[18] *Restatement (Second) of Torts* §46, Comment d, Illustration 3 (1965).
[19] *Wilkinson* v. *Downton* (1897).
[20] *Bowden* v. *Spiegel, Inc.* (1950); *Duty* v. *General Finance Co.* (1954).
[21] *Dillon* v. *Legg* (1968).
[22] *Kneass* v. *Cremation Society* (1918).

col are plainly inflicting such distress intentionally. They may have a further purpose other than simply the infliction of distress, but then so does the credit collection agency (which is, after all, only seeking to collect a just debt). We might reflect, for instance, on experiments in which the subject is falsely told that he has reacted positively to homosexual stimuli, in order to gauge his reaction to this revelation. Similarly, staged "accidents" may also create distress in the passersby, and such distress is in a sense intentionally inflicted. Let us suppose one consents to the infliction of emotional distress; I do not see why a truly informed consent would not justify the infliction, in such a case. But in many social science experiments that risk emotional distress, deception is a crucial part of the experiment: This facet of its nature precludes fully informed consent. The problem of deception vitiating consent might be circumvented if consent were obtained to participate in an experiment avowed to have among its features the infliction of emotional distress and the use of deception. There is no precedent that I can cite to ascertain whether this would succeed in insulating the researcher from liability, though I suspect that the greater the distress the less the likelihood that such second-order consent would be considered sufficient.

It is also possible that certain therapeutic or therapeutic-research techniques used in treating sexual dysfunctions might involve the infliction of emotional distress by confronting the patient-subject with painful truths and insights. This raises interesting and wholly unexplored issues. Truth is a defense of defamation,[23] but is it a defense against infliction of emotional distress? If in my paradigm case (*Wilkinson* v. *Downton* [1897], cited above) the victim's husband had indeed been killed in an accident, would a person who revealed this fact in a brutal manner intending to cause pain be absolved because what he stated was in fact true? The issue, though interesting, is not an important one in itself; but it leads quite naturally into questions of malpractice and negligence, considered below. As to these, it seems clear that purely verbal manipulations by therapists acting in an unprofessional manner and with harmful intent would be grounds for civil liability in negligence. However,

[23] *Wertz* v. *Sprecher* (1908); *Fort Worth Press Co.* v. *Davis* (1936).

the conduct leading to the alleged distress must be outrageous and the distress must be great before there is a finding of liability.[24] These are elastic concepts, but the therapist-researcher had best beware.

INVASION OF PRIVACY

Invasion of privacy is a tort, and the injured party may recover compensatory and punitive damages for the violation. There are two forms of violation of privacy that are relevant to this area: (1) There may be an offensive intrusion, as in the case of spying or otherwise collecting information against a person's wishes; (2) there may be an offensive divulging of information that has been given in confidence. Consent justifies conduct that would be tortious under either of these headings, but even where there is no consent there is a crucial question whether the conduct or the information was truly private, that is, whether the person viewing the conduct or divulging the information was entitled to do so. Public figures have no right to privacy, at least in respect to their public doings,[25] and it is a matter of considerable controversy how much privacy even ordinary persons enjoy when they expose themselves to public view in public places.[26] These questions are of great interest and importance to behavioral research and to sex research in particular. Consider the Humphreys research into the so-called tearoom trade [6]. There is considerable ambiguity as to whether the subjects of the research were or were not in a public setting (and thus exposed to whatever observations the researcher wished to make). There is ample authority for the proposition that whether a place is a public (as opposed to a private) place is a question not of property law so much as of the reasonable expectations of the parties involved;[27] the grievance of Humphreys's research subjects is better grounded on that basis. On the other hand, there

[24] *Savage* v. *Boies* (1954); *Wilson* v. *Wilkins* (1930).

[25] *New York Times Co.* v. *Sullivan* (1964), *motion den.* (1964).

[26] *Berg* v. *Minneapolis Star & Tribune Co.* (1948) (photograph taken in courtroom does not violate any right of privacy the subject of the photo might possess); *Gill* v. *Hearst Publishing Co.* (1953) (photograph taken at Farmers' Market in Los Angeles).

[27] *Katz* v. *United States* (1967).

is a series of cases dealing with informants and police spies, which hold that there is no vitiating invasion of privacy when someone pretends to be someone other than he is or to be acting with motives other than he has in order to collect information from persons and in settings to which he would not have access were he to declare himself.[28] The concept is ambiguous but important here. In participant-observer research, as in the work of spies, informants, and undercover agents, subjects give consent to the act of observation by the person doing the observing, but the consent is not fully informed: The subject does not know the observer's true purposes (or perhaps even his true identity). It is like consenting to administration of a drug whose risks and benefits have not been fully revealed, or which is given for purposes that have not been fully explained.

The divulging of confidential information is also a persistent concern in this area. The information observed as well as the information divulged is peculiarly sensitive, and plainly of the sort that the right to privacy is intended to protect. When the information is divulged to others in breach of either a tacit or explicit agreement, there seems to be a clear violation of privacy.[29] However, such disclosure may take place against the wishes of the researcher. Private information may be subpoenaed from the researcher. It would seem that if he acts under process of law, he should be immune from civil liability. But might it not be argued that by failing to destroy the data prior to a subpoena—to do so after a subpoena would be contempt of court—he negligently created the situation that the authorities were able to exploit? Even so, it is questionable whether the law would simultaneously require the information and give redress to a person who is aggrieved by the handing over of the information in response to that requirement. Yet, to the extent that violations of privacy are a matter of concern in the design of the experiment, this hazard must be considered and means should be devised for minimizing it.

A further problem relates to revelation of private information by persons who are not subject to the researcher-therapist's control but

---

[28] *United States* v. *White* (1971); *Hoffa* v. *United States* (1966); *Osborn* v. *United States* (1966).
[29] *Chaplin* v. *National Broadcasting Co., Inc.* (1953).

who obtain the information within the context of the research-therapy situation. Thus, group therapy poses great dangers of unwarranted revelations by other participants in the group. What is the responsibility of the group leader? At the very least, he or she should make each participant aware of the risks involved and of the limited power of the group leader to control group members. On the other hand, excessive emphasis on this point is unlikely to be conducive to the desired context of mutual free disclosure. A variation on this problem is raised in therapy in which a person reveals intimate facts about a spouse—information that the spouse has not consented to have revealed. The problem is compounded because the therapist does not have a therapeutic responsibility to the spouse who is not his patient.

INTERFERENCE WITH ADVANTAGEOUS RELATIONS

There is a form of civil liability that has been used by marriage partners and business partners to obtain redress against a third person who has interfered with some "advantageous relation" such as a family relation or contractual relation. Alienation of affections, loss of consortium, criminal conversation, and enticement are some of the common causes of action founded on interference with an advantageous family relation.[30] It is a theoretical possibility that a therapist counseling choices or conduct incompatible with an existing family relation might find himself or herself the defendant in such an action. Since the plaintiff will not have been the patient in the case, informed consent will not operate against that plaintiff. This form of action has also been threatened, though never consummated, by the wife of a husband who underwent sex-reassignment surgery.[31] I am told that such surgery is now not usually practiced unless the physician is assured that there are no currently existing marital ties.

[30] In the business sphere, the cause of action typically grows out of the use of a business name or a very similar name by a competitor. Thus, a charitable organization is protected from the use of a similar name by a commercial corporation where such use is likely to result in financial loss (*Golden Slipper Square Club* v. *Golden Slipper Restaurant & Catering, Inc.* [1952]).
[31] *Burnell* v. *Catazone* (1971).

MALPRACTICE

Finally, there is the catchall category of malpractice, which has increasing power and range of application and surely applies in the area of sex research and sex therapy. It covers any conduct that a judge and jury find substandard—whatever the intent and whatever the subjective degree of care—that results in mental or physical harm.[32] Quite plainly, both patients and research subjects in all forms of sex research and therapy are potential malpractice plaintiffs. What is the bearing of consent on this tort? Since malpractice is in general a form of negligence, the general maxim applies that one cannot by contract waive the right to sue in negligence: The closest one may come is that the consent may be a consent to encounter the very risks that might otherwise be held to be negligent. The line of separation is a fine one. In effect, the distinction is this: The patient or subject may not state beforehand that as a condition of participating in a given research project or undergoing a given course of therapy he or she agrees not to bring an action if the therapist or researcher is negligent. But one *may* agree beforehand to undergo a particular risk, which risk might otherwise be deemed to have been excessive and negligently imposed. To put the matter differently, one cannot consent to negligent treatment in general, but one may consent to a particular form of treatment, if the consent is free and knowledgeable, even when that treatment would otherwise be held to have been negligent. The point is primarily of theoretical interest since, if the treatment would have been held negligent absent the consent, it should not be a difficult matter for counsel to propose and a jury to accept some particular in respect to which the informed consent was deficient and therefore ineffective.

The question becomes, therefore, What constitutes malpractice or negligence in, say, experimentation? It involves taking unreasonable risks, risks that a prudent practitioner would not have taken in the defendant's circumstance. Since the defendant's circumstances are those of a researcher, the question arises as to what standard is to be applied. In respect to therapy, the usual legal standard is the standard of the profession. It is not at all clear that

[32] For example, *Boyce v. Brown* (1938); *Ault v. Hall* (1928); *Incollingo v. Ewing* (1971).

this standard would or even should be applied to researchers. There is a strong case to be made that in respect to researchers, the standard should be a community and not a professional standard: After all, the question of the standard of reasonable care is remitted to the medical profession only because the medical profession is presumed to be acting in the best interests of the patients. The researcher by hypothesis is pursuing research purposes, rather than the welfare of the patient—at least to the extent that the research is not wholly aimed at the situation of the particular patient. To allow the standards of the researcher to govern in that instance seems inappropriate inasmuch as those standards are in possible conflict with the welfare of the patient. The standards of the researcher should no more govern than should the standards of automobile manufacturers govern due care in the design or manufacture of automobiles. I might illustrate the potential application of the doctrine of malpractice to this area by citing the English case of *Werner* v. *Landau* (1961), in which a psychoanalyst was found guilty of negligence and required to pay damages of 6,000 pounds on account of emotional distress suffered by a patient, because the analyst maintained wholly innocent social contacts after cessation of therapy, having reason to believe that such contacts might be harmful to the former patient.

GOVERNMENT REGULATIONS

The principal regulations bearing on this field of endeavor are the directives of the Department of Health, Education, and Welfare pertaining to research involving human subjects,[33] with which every institution receiving DHEW funds must comply when engaging in such research. Compliance is required even if the particular research project is not federally funded. Moreover, a number of states have recently adopted or are considering similar laws governing the use of human subjects.

The DHEW guidelines require approval by an institutional review board of any research involving human subjects.[34] The institutional review board (IRB) must include persons from outside the

[33] 42 U.S.C. §289 1.
[34] 42 U.S.C. §289 1–3(a).

particular institution as well as persons not engaged in research.[35] In addition to determining whether the risk-benefit ratio of a research proposal is appropriate, the IRB must ascertain whether the research subjects have given informed consent.[36] The guidelines require informed consent wherever a subject is exposed to "risks"; *risk* is defined as including "expos[ure] to the possibility of injury, including physical, psychological, or social."[37] A subject is considered to be at risk in any procedure that is employed for purposes other than to meet the needs of the subject.[38] Arbitrary or random assignment of subjects to different treatment or study groups in the interests of a research project, rather than in the strict interest of the individual subject, introduces the possibility of exposing subjects to additional risks. Even comparison of two or more established and accepted methods of treatment may potentially involve exposure of at least some of the subjects to added risk.[39] Thus, it would seem that almost all sex research places the subject at some type of risk—if only psychological or sociological risk. Only the use of well-established procedures with no research purposes or manipulation would be excluded.

It is clear that a literal application of these regulations would ban research involving deception or even nondisclosure. How does such research go forward? First, there is a caveat in the guidelines permitting disclosures in the context of informed consent to be tailored to therapeutic needs as established within the context of a professional-patient relationship. Moreover, institutional review boards may at their discretion determine that a variety of experiments using deception, such as the Milgrim experiments [7] or the *Tearoom Trade* research, do not put subjects at risk. Such judgments are open to criticism. The guidelines of the American Psychological Association addressed specifically to this kind of research and to the supposed necessity for deception in the conduct of it, tacitly recognize the existence of risk (as defined in the NIH guidelines) by stating that where deception is used, the researcher assumes a correspondingly heavier burden of responsibility for ascer-

[35] 42 U.S.C. §289 1–3(b).
[36] 45 C.F.R. §46 102(b)(3) (1976).
[37] 45 C.F.R. §46 103(b) (1976).
[38] 45 C.F.R. §46 103(b) (1976).
[39] 41 Fed. Reg. 26572 (1976).

taining that the risks to the subject are minimal; are justified; or are easily dispelled by postexperimental debriefing. However, even if a risk is minimal, justified, or likely to be dispelled, it is still plain that it exists or did exist at some point. Thus, there is a real question as to whether a large amount of behavioral research, much of which includes research into sexual behavior, is not in fact in violation of the NIH guidelines. Perhaps it is in response to this problem that the National Commission for the Protection of Human Subjects, established by legislation in 1975,[40] has been assigned as one of its specific tasks the formulation of guidelines for behavioral research, including the kinds of research in which the problem of deception is most crucial. The Commission has not yet formulated a report on these matters, but it has commissioned a number of papers on this very problem by prominent social scientists. Its staff includes behavioral scientists.

Finally, to the extent that sex research involves the use of drugs, the legislation under which the Food and Drug Administration operates requires randomized double-blind testing of new drugs, but at the same time requires informed consent of all research subjects.[41] This consent, including the information that one may be participating in a double-blind placebo study, may be dispensed with only in "exceptional" cases. The exceptional cases that the regulations seem to envisage are cases of therapeutic research in which the revelation of certain risks or aspects of the research might endanger the situation of the patient.

A NOTE ON DECEPTION

There is currently raging battle on the use of deception in behavioral research (for a brief synopsis of the issues, see Warwick [7]). Many nontherapeutic social-psychological protocols in the area of sexual behavior and attitudes involve the use of deception.

[40] National Research Act, Pub. L. No. 93–348, 88 Stat. 348 (codified at 42 U.S.C. §289 1 [1974]). The Commission was completing its work as this manuscript was being prepared for publication. Accordingly, the author does not include a discussion of the final report of the Commission.
[41] See 21 C.F.R. §§310, 312, 314; 21 U.S.C. §355(b)(1).

I shall not argue this well-worn subject in detail here. Rather, I will simply suggest the main lines of my own approach.

First, we may grant that if deception is forbidden, certain research projects will not be able to go forward; if the use of deception is constrained, some projects will be aborted while others will go forward only at great expense or with less efficacy. The advocates of deception bring out this obvious fact as if it were a knockdown argument. The reverse is true. If it were *not* the case that forbidding deception would indeed hamper or prevent certain research projects, then one would indeed wonder why deception is used at all. Thus, the fact that adherence to a principle has the effect of preventing one from doing exactly what he would have done anyway can hardly serve as an objection to requiring truly informed consent.

What then of the claim of freedom of inquiry and the pursuit of pure knowledge? I am a rigid Kantian believer in the right to pursue knowledge freely and without restraint. But that is the researcher's right, and obviously one cannot exercise this right by deliberately and intentionally violating the rights of others. For instance, one cannot pursue this right by kidnapping research subjects or by embezzling funds in order to finance one's research. And if research subjects have as much right to be informed and as much right not to be deceived as researchers have to pursue research, then the answer is that researchers by all means should exercise their rights, but by no means should they violate the rights of others in the process.

If it is suggested that the right not to be deceived is not a right that people value strongly, let us put the question to those who will be deceived *in the particular case*, rather than abide by the self-serving assertions of researchers. Surveys prove nothing by showing that most pools of potential research subjects could not care less about deception in the usually benign case: We are dealing with rights, and rights belong to individuals rather than to pools of people. It may well be that the population as a whole also does not lay much store by the right of doctoral candidates in psychology to pursue research, but it would hardly be thought that the right of a researcher should depend on the results of such a survey. Rights are personal and can only be waived by the person.

The legal implications of this position are at present indeterminate. It is clear that consent to what would otherwise constitute battery is inoperative consent, if obtained by deception. Consequently, deceptive experiments involving infliction of pain, bodily contact, or administration of medication expose the experimenter to a serious hazard of substantial legal liability. I suspect that a few large damage awards against experimenters would have a wonderfully purifying effect on the experimental climate. However, the bases of liability are more tenuous in cases where no physical impingements are involved. Consent is a defense to the intentional infliction of extreme emotional distress; deception there too would remove a defense that might otherwise be available. But since the distress must be extreme, the issue is seldom likely to arise. Consent is a defense to an actionable invasion of privacy; if an experimenter obtains private information by deception, his defense would once again be nullified. But before suit could be brought, there would have to be a demonstration of substantive invasion: for example, intrusion into an intimate area of concern or publication of confidential information. Behavior in a public place is not subject to such protection, so that even covert observation in a public setting is not actionable. The definition of a private place is itself a controversial matter, and ordinary property notions are not dispositive. (Thus, a public toilet has been held to be a private place, while a private restaurant or movie lobby is a public place.)

In general, then, the question of deception is and perhaps should be the reverse side of the coin of substantive rights. If a person has a substantive right to privacy, to property, to physical integrity, or to dignity, consent to a waiver of those rights cannot be effective if obtained by deception. Deceptive practices are thus subject to whatever legal liability would obtain in the absence of consent.

REFERENCES

1. Leroy, D. H. The potential criminal liability of human sex clinics and their patients. *St. Louis University Law Journal* 16:586–603, 1972.
2. Freund, P. A. Ethical problems in human experimentation. *New England Journal of Medicine* 273:687–692, 1965.

3. McCormick, R. A. Experimentation in children: Sharing in sociality. *Hastings Center Report* 6:41–46, December 1976.
4. Annas, G., Glantz, L., and Katz, B. *Informed Consent to Human Experimentation.* Cambridge, Mass.: Ballinger, 1977. P. 94.
5. Donnelly, R., Goldstein, J., and Schwartz, R. *Criminal Law.* New York: Free Press of Glencoe, 1962. Pp. 11–28.
6. Humphreys, L. *Tearoom Trade: Impersonal Sex in Public Places.* Chicago: Aldine, 1970.
7. Warwick, D. P. Social scientists ought to stop lying. *Psychology Today* 8:38–40, 105–106, February 1975.

CASES

Ault v. *Hall,* 119 Ohio State 422, 164 N.E. 518 (1928).
Belcher v. *Carter,* 13 Ohio App. 2d 113, 234 N.E. 2d 311, 312 (1967).
Berg v. *Minneapolis Star & Tribune Co.,* 79 F. Supp. 957 (D. Minn. 1948).
Bishop v. *Liston,* 112 Neb. 559, 199 N.W. 825 (1924).
Bonner v. *Moran,* 126 F.2d 121 (D.C. Cir. 1941).
Bowden v. *Spiegel, Inc.,* 96 Cal. App. 2d 793, 216 P. 2d 571 (1950).
Boyce v. *Brown,* 51 Ariz. 416, 77 P.2d 455 (1938).
Bradford v. *Winter,* 215 Cal. App. 2d 448, 30 Cal. Reptr. 243 (1963).
Burnell v. *Catazone* (Sup. Ct. of County of Orange, Cal., Civil Action No. 184985, filed July 21, 1971).
Burrows v. *Hawaiian Trust Co.,* 417 P.2d 816 (Hawaii, 1966).
Chaplin v. *National Broadcasting Co., Inc.,* 15 F.R.D. 134 (S.D.N.Y. 1953).
Commonwealth v. *Goldenberg,* 338 Mass. 377, 155 N.E. 2d 187 (1959), *cert. denied,* 359 U.S. 1001 (1959).
Commonwealth v. *Stratton,* 114 Mass. 303 (1873).
Corn v. *French,* 71 Nev. 280, 289 P. 2d 173 (1955).
Dillon v. *Legg,* 69 Cal. Reptr. 72, 411 P. 2d 912 (1968).
Directors of Public Prosecution v. *Morgan,* [1975] 2 All E.R. 347 (House of Lords).
Duty v. *General Finance Co.,* 154 Tex. 16, 273 S.W. 2d 64 (1954).
Fort Worth Press Co. v. *Davis,* 96 S.W.2d 416 (Tex. Civ. App. 1936).
Garratt v. *Dailey,* 46 Wash. 2d 197, 279 P. 2d 1091 (1955).
Gill v. *Hearst Publishing Co.,* 40 Cal. 2d 224, 253 P.2d 441 (1953).
Golden Slipper Square Club v. *Golden Slipper Restaurant & Catering, Inc.,* 371 Pa. 92, 88 A. 2d 735 (1952).
Goldnamer v. *O'Brien,* 98 Ky. 569, 33 S.W. 831 (1896).
Hart v. *Brown,* 29 Conn. Sup. 368, 289 A. 2d 386 (1972).
Hoffa v. *United States,* 385 U.S. 293 (1966).

Incollingo v. *Ewing*, 444 Pa. 263, 299, 282 A.2d 206 (1971).

Kaimowitz v. *Department of Mental Health* (Cir. Ct. of Wayne Co., Mich., July 10, 1973).

Katz v. *United States*, 389 U.S. 347 (1967).

Kneass v. *Cremation Society*, 103 Wash. 521, 178 P. 450 (1918).

Moss v. *Rishworth*, 222 S.W. 225 (Tex. Comm. App. 1920).

Natanson v. *Kline*, 186 Kan. 393, 350 P. 2d 1093 (1963).

New York Times Co. v. *Sullivan*, 376 U.S. 254, *motion den.*, 376 U.S. 967 (1964).

O'Brien v. *Cunard S.S. Co.*, 154 Mass. 272, 28 N.E. 266 (1891).

Osborn v. *United States*, 385 U.S. 323 (1966).

People v. *Gibson*, 232 N.Y. 458, 134 N.E. 531 (1922).

People v. *Lenti*, 44 Misc. 2d 118, 253 N.Y.S. 2d 9 (1964).

People v. *Martin* (Superior Ct. of Littletown County, Conn., Oct. 4, 1955) (discussed in [5]).

People v. *Steinberg*, 190 Misc. 413, 73 N.Y.S. 2d 475 (1947).

Savage v. *Boies*, 77 Ariz. 355, 272 P. 2d 349 (1954).

Shetter v. *Rochelle*, 2 Ariz. App. 358, *modified on other grounds*, 2 Ariz. App. 607, 411 P. 2d 45 (1966).

Smith v. *Smith*, 194 S.C. 247, S.E. 2d 584 (1940).

State v. *Auld*, 2 N.J. 426, 67 A. 2d 175 (1949).

State v. *Monroe*, 121 N.C. 677, 28 S.E. 547 (1897).

Talmadge v. *Smith*, 101 Mich. 370, 59 N.W. 656 (1894).

Thibault v. *Lalumiere*, 318 Mass. 72, 60 N.E. 2d 349 (1945).

United States v. *White*, 401 U.S. 745 (1971).

Werner v. *Landau*, 105 Sol. J. 257, on appeal, 105 Sol. J. 1008 (C.A. 1961).

Wertz v. *Sprecher*, 82 Neb. 834, 118 N.W. 1071 (1908).

Wilkinson v. *Downton*, [1897] 2 Q.B. 57.

Wilson v. *Wilkins*, 181 Ark. 137, 25 S.W. 2d 428 (1930).

Wright v. *Starr*, 42 Nev. 441, 179 P. 877 (1919).

Zoski v. *Gaines*, 271 Mich. 1, 260 N.W. 99 (1939).

ISSUES OF PRIVACY AND CONFIDENTIALITY IN SEX THERAPY AND SEX RESEARCH[1]

RICHARD WASSERSTROM

Many if not all of the ethical problems of confidentiality that are peculiar to the provision of sex therapy or to the conduct of sex research arise because of the special connection felt by many persons to hold between sex and privacy. That is, problems arise because there are connections in our culture between sexual activity and privacy and between information about a person's sex life and a person's individual right to privacy. For this reason, the identification and analysis of the problems of confidentiality in sex research and sex therapy can be undertaken most productively in the context of a theory that takes into account the nature and value of privacy, the significance of privacy in respect to sexual matters, and the relationship between privacy and confidentiality. Such a theory should indicate why privacy and confidentiality may be thought to have such a special role in the sexual area and should suggest ways in which thinking about more specific topics and problems might proceed.

The present inquiry proceeds on this assumption. The first portion of this paper presents a theory of privacy and examines its relationship to sexuality: The theory provides an account of various

[1] This paper was written with the assistance of Joshua S. Golden, whose substantial contributions were of great help to the author. Some of the ideas in the paper are contained in R. Wasserstrom, Privacy and the Law, in R. Bronaugh (Ed.), *Philosophical Law* (Westport, Conn.: Greenwood, 1978), pp. 148–166.

kinds of privacy; of reasons why some types of privacy might be of particular importance and value; of reasons why privacy might require or justify confidentiality; and of reasons why privacy and confidentiality in respect to sexual matters might often be of unusual importance and significance to some individuals. The second portion of the paper examines various situations in which the maintenance of confidentiality in respect to sexual information and sexual behavior can be an issue for therapy or research, as well as some implications of the underlying theory of privacy for these situations. The final part of this essay raises tentative questions about the previously developed theory of privacy, confidentiality, and sexuality and about the assumptions on which it is based, and presents a possible alternative theory of social attitudes and values concerning sexual matters.

A THEORY OF PRIVACY AND ITS IMPORTANCE TO SEXUAL MATTERS

PRIVACY AND CONFIDENTIALITY

A number of different claims are made in the name of privacy. One thing that many but by no means all of them have in common is that they involve the question of the kind and degree of control that a person ought to be able to exercise in respect to access by others to knowledge or to the disclosure of information about himself or herself. Even when the focus is on information, it is evident that information about oneself is not all of the same type; control over some kinds of information may appropriately be more important to a person than control over other kinds of information. For this reason, it is necessary to identify some of the different types of personal information over which persons might desire to retain substantial control, and to describe the situations in which this information comes into being. One way of doing this is to consider three situations and look at the ways in which they resemble one another and differ from one another.

First, one can, if one wishes, look "inward" and become aware of the ideas that are running through one's mind, the various emotions one is experiencing, and the variety of bodily sensations one is having—for example, an itch on one's scalp or a pain in one's side. The most direct, the best, and often the only evidence of one's mental states—one's dreams, conscious thoughts, hopes, fears, and desires—consists in the individual's deliberately revealing them. The only reasonably certain way for a person to obtain very detailed and accurate information about what another person is thinking, fearing, imagining, desiring, or hating and how he or she is experiencing it, is for one person to tell or show the other. If one does not, the ideas and feelings remain within the person and are—in some sense, at least—known only to him or her. Because a person cannot read another person's mind, these things about a person are known only to him or her in a way in which other things are not, unless there is a deliberate decision to disclose them. They occupy a unique place, for the most part, in respect to the possibility of access by others.

The situation in respect to what is going on within one's body is similar in some ways to that of mental events and in some respects different. There are things going on in one's body that are like one's thoughts, fears, and fantasies. For example, if a person has a slight twinge of pain in his penis, there is no way for anyone else to know about it unless the person having the pain chooses to disclose it. However, there are other things about one's body to which this privileged position does not pertain. One cannot tell very well what one's own ribs look like; one cannot tell by the presence of one's own semen whether it contains sperm. These facts about a person's body can be known at least as well by another individual.

So there are some facts about one's body that can be known in a way others cannot know them—that can be known to others only if they are deliberately disclosed. And there are other facts about one's body that the person himself or herself does not know in this special way and that can be learned quite as well by someone or something outside of the individual.

Second, there is some information that is private only by virtue of the setting in which the information is disclosed or communicated. For example, suppose that a person has broken an arm and is in a private room with the door closed, alone except for the doctor who sets the break. Here it is the setting that makes the behavior distinctive and relevant. If no one can see the patient and the doctor, then no one is in a position at that time to know about the broken arm. This kind of case can be described as a case of things being done in private, meaning only that they are done in a setting in which there did not appear to be anyone present—other than the person with whom one was talking or interacting—who was in a position to hear what was being said or to see what was being done. Of course, this is privacy in an extremely weak sense, and for at least two reasons: The information is less within the individual's control than is information about his or her mental states (as yet unrevealed) because the other person present can, if he or she chooses, reveal what he or she has learned. In addition, there is nothing about the *character* of the information that seems to make revelation a source of concern.

This last point leads to the third kind of case. Suppose that, instead of having a broken arm set by a doctor, a person visits a therapist in the therapist's office, with the door closed, in order to discuss what the patient regards as a very loathsome sexual fantasy. Such a conversation takes place in private in the same sense in which the broken arm was treated in private: No one else could see or hear what was going on. But this situation has an additional quality that the other example did not possess. When a person consults a therapist, he or she typically expects that what is said will not be overheard by anyone else and will also be kept in confidence by the recipient of the information. It involves what might be called a private *kind* of communication. Such is not the case with much information about oneself; absent special or unusual circumstances, individuals have no particular interest in retaining control over the disclosure of many facts about themselves.

What has been said so far is surely obvious. It is also obvious that the most important connection between doing something in private and doing a private kind of thing is that persons typically do private things only under circumstances in which they have reason to believe that they are doing them in private, that is, in situations where they believe confidentiality obtains in respect to the information that is being disclosed. The assurance that they are doing something in private in this sense is often a condition that must be satisfied before they are willing to disclose intimate facts about themselves or to engage in intimate activities in the presence of others. It should be evident, too, that there are important similarities, as well as some differences, between the first and third cases—between knowledge of one's own mental states and the disclosure of intimate information about oneself to selected persons.

A thought-experiment can illuminate much of what is involved in the special concerns persons have that personal information of certain sorts not be disclosed without their consent. Suppose technological advances made it somehow possible for an outsider to look into or monitor another person's mind. What, if anything, would be especially disturbing or objectionable about that?

First of all, we all have far less control over when we shall have certain thoughts and what their content will be, than we have over to whom and to what degree we shall reveal those thoughts. Because our inner thoughts, feelings, and bodily sensations are largely beyond our control, we would doubtless feel appreciably less secure in our social environment than we do at present, were it possible for another person to "look in" without our consent and see what was going on in our heads. This is so—at least in part—because many of our uncommunicated thoughts and feelings concern very intimate matters. Our fantasies and our fears often concern the very matters that in our culture we would least choose to reveal to anyone else. At a minimum, we would suffer great anxiety and feelings of shame if the decisions regarding where, when, and to whom to disclose were not wholly our own. Were outside access to our thoughts possible in this way, we would see ourselves as creatures who are far more vulnerable at the hands of other persons than we are now.

Second, we must consider the more straightforward worry about accountability for our thoughts and feelings. As has been mentioned, these are often not within our control. For all of the reasons that it is wrong to hold people accountable for behavior not within their control, we would not want the possibility of accountability to extend to our uncommunicated thoughts and feelings.

A third reason why retaining control over intimate facts and behaviors might be of appreciable importance to individuals is that our *social* universe would be altered in fundamental and deleterious ways, were that control to be surrendered or lost. This is so because one way in which we mark off and distinguish our most important interpersonal relationships is by the kinds of intimate information and behavior that we are willing to share with those persons. One way in which we make someone a close friend rather than an acquaintance is by revealing certain things about ourselves to that person—things that we do not reveal to the world at large. One way in which persons often enter into a special relationship is by mutually engaging in sexual behavior that they do not engage in with the world at large. Knowledge about ourselves has been called "moral capital," which is exchanged and otherwise used to create and maintain relationships of intimacy and closeness. In this view, privacy is a logically necessary condition for the existence of many of our most meaningful social relationships.[2]

Finally, one plausible concept of what it is to be a person involves the idea of the existence of a core of thoughts and feelings that belong to the individual alone. If anyone else could know all that one was feeling, except in the form one chose to filter and reveal what one was and how one saw oneself—if anyone could be aware of this complex of personal information at will—individuals might cease to have as complete a sense of themselves as distinct and separate persons as they have now. On this view, a significant and perhaps fundamental part of what it is to be an individual person is to possess the capability of being exclusively aware of one's own thoughts and feelings.

Considerations such as these help to explain why it is important that individuals be able to retain exclusive control over communications concerning private or intimate matters. Because of our social attitudes toward the disclosure of intimate facts and behavior, most people would be extremely upset were they to learn that these facts had been made known to persons other than those to whom they chose to disclose them. For example, if people engage in intimate behavior and believe that they are doing so in private, they may very well be hurt or embarrassed if they learn subsequently that they were observed without their knowledge or consent. The belated knowledge that they were observed will cause them distress both because their expectations of privacy were in-

[2] This important argument has been developed by Charles Fried (Privacy. *Yale Law Journal* 77:475, 1968; *An Anatomy of Values: Problems of Personal and Social Choice.* Cambridge, Mass.: Harvard University Press, 1970.).

correct and because their concerns about their own vulnerability were made plausible by the fact that they were observed while engaged in intimate behavior. People are entitled perhaps to have situations be what they appear to be, especially in those cases in which they regard privacy as essential to protect them from increased vulnerability.

PRIVACY, CONFIDENTIALITY, AND SEXUAL INFORMATION

The most direct application of the foregoing theory to the area of sexuality arises from the fact that for many persons in our culture, matters relating to sex are paradigmatically private in all of the senses described above. This is so for a variety of reasons. In the first place, during sexual behavior involving another person the participants are vulnerable in the straightforward physical sense: They are individually vulnerable because they are fully engaged in the activity. They are vulnerable to attack in much the same way in which persons who are asleep are vulnerable. The participants are also vulnerable vis-à-vis one another: Sexual activity brings persons into close physical contact with each other, and mutual trust in the security of this environment is a simple dictate of prudence.

In the second place, sex and vulnerability are linked psychically in our culture. As has been indicated, sexual intimacy is one means by which individuals can create, maintain, and confirm special relationships of closeness. To select another person as a sexual partner is a way of setting that individual apart from the host of other persons with whom one interacts. In addition, our culture teaches individuals to attach great significance to their sexual competency —their ability to achieve and bestow sexual satisfaction. Hence, many persons see their success or failure as individuals bound up in many ways with their sexual abilities or problems. These persons tend to regard information about their sexual behavior as relating directly to an area of great vulnerability and as potentially very damaging.

Many individuals in our culture are taught that all matters pertaining to sex are shameful. One strain of this culture teaches that it is wrong to have any interest in sex for its own sake or for the pleasure it provides. In this view it is wrong to have most of the sexual fantasies, motivation, desires and longings, and interest in sexual matters that almost all persons experience. Another strain of the culture teaches that there is a sharp and important difference between sexual activity that is normal and appropriate (for example, heterosexual intercourse between persons who are married to each other) and all other sexual activity, which is considered abnormal, unnatural, or perverse. Although there is disagreement about precisely where to draw the line between these two kinds of sexual activity, this school of thought teaches that it is wrong to have the sorts of sexual fantasies or desires—let alone to engage in the kinds of sexual conduct—that fall outside the bounds of the normal and appropriate. As a result, individuals who have been socialized in these ways will regard virtually any disclosure about their own sexual beliefs and sex lives as reflecting discreditably upon them.

Finally, of course, our culture also teaches almost everyone that activities involving sexual thoughts and behavior should be conducted in private, even if there is nothing wrong or shameful about the content of the thoughts or behavior in question. For this reason, persons will be rendered uncomfortable—will suffer discomfort and even pain—whenever the environment is altered so as to contain either contemporary observers to acts of sexual intimacy or after-the-fact confidants to whom descriptions of past sexual behavior are disclosed.

There is still another consideration concerning the presence of observers of intimate sexual acts: The presence of such observers, even when their presence is made known in advance and agreed to by those being observed, can alter the behavior of the individuals involved. This can happen in at least two ways. Given the way persons have been socialized to think about sex, they may be prevented in quite a direct way from engaging in an act of sexual intercourse. The inhibitions may simply be too great to permit the individuals to proceed. In such circumstances, of course, therapy or research involving an observer will not be helpful. It is important that the persons involved not perceive their inability to proceed as an added reason for regarding themselves as inadequate or as having failed in any way.

In addition, there is a metaphysical aspect of the situation that is less obvious and more complex. Even if the individuals involved are ready, willing, and able to proceed with an observer present, the presence of an observer may inevitably alter the character of the experience to make it different from the experience it would have been in the absence of an observer. Having someone watch or listen may necessarily so alter the character of the interaction that it is simply not the same kind of interaction that it was before there was an observer. In particular, the presence of the observer may remove a dimension of the spontaneity that is characteristic of some extremely satisfying sexual activities. Aware of the observer, the participants will be engaged in part in "spectatoring"—viewing or imagining what is going on from the observer's perspective. Thus, they cannot "lose" themselves in the activity as they could if they were alone. This ability to lose oneself in the sexual experience may be central to the nature of the experience itself, as well as significant for the value of the experience from the participants' standpoints and desirable from a therapeutic standpoint.

The point to be made here is a very general one. One consequence of subjecting sexual behavior and personal sexual beliefs to therapeutic and research observation may be that the individuals who are observed will find that the sphere of private thought and behavior that constitutes or reinforces their sense of self and individuality has been substantially eroded. Another consequence may be that the essential character of sexual intimacy as it has existed in our culture will be altered so that it both becomes and is viewed as something very different. This is not so much an argument against observation as it is a reason to be concerned about observation—even observation accompanied by consent. That is to say, even if consensual observation can be justified on some grounds, there may be important and (in some cases) undesirable consequences that are worthy of recognition, attention, and careful consideration.

APPLICATIONS TO SEX THERAPY AND SEX RESEARCH

The cases in which there are special problems concerning confidentiality in respect to sex therapy or sex research can be divided into several distinct kinds. These are as follows: (1) situations in which it is both theoretically possible and desirable to obtain consent from the person concerned (namely, the client or subject) before any disclosure of information is made about that person's sexual beliefs or sexual actions; (2) situations in which it is not always possible for the therapist or researcher to obtain consent from the individual about whom disclosure of information is made; (3) situations in which, whether consent was present or not, the therapist or researcher may have strong reason to consider making a subsequent disclosure of confidential information to a person or persons not directly involved in the therapy or research.

CONSENSUAL DISCLOSURES

Because of the strong de facto claim individuals have to retain control over sexual information about themselves and because of the special injuries that they perceive as resulting from a loss of that control, research subjects and clients in therapy have a right to know—in advance of any disclosures concerning their sex lives— exactly what degree of confidentiality will be maintained, and they have a strong claim to have any assurances of confidentiality respected. This means that they and not the professionals involved in the research or therapy should have the power to decide to whom else the information acquired will be communicated—if to anyone—including, specifically, other members of the professional community.

At this point it is worth mentioning that the practice of viewing sex therapy as taking place within the dominant medical model may act in a way counter to the claims of confidentiality. It is common in medicine for the physician to perceive the patient as something like an object to be acted upon and as a collection of symptoms, behaviors, and physical signs to be discussed freely with other professionals (more freely, in fact, than with the patient himself or herself). In an environment of this sort, it will be difficult for a patient to preserve his or her sense of autonomy and individuality. It will be easy for those who are *not* patients to see themselves as different in important respects from patients in this environment. In such a context, the professional personnel have a tendency to become manipulative and paternalistic toward their patients. As a result, the patients' special claims to privacy, confidentiality, and sensitivity in respect to sexual matters may be given insufficient weight or may even be entirely neglected or ignored.

If the therapist or researcher acquiring sexual information anticipates that subsequent disclosure will be made, the patients or subjects involved should be told specifically and unequivocally, in advance of any disclosures by them, what the limits of confidentiality will be. In the typical private therapeutic setting, this usually creates no difficulties. But some patients and subjects are not seen in that setting. For example, therapists sometimes treat persons who are in custody for having committed sex crimes. In such cases the therapist may be inclined to view issues of confidentiality somewhat differently, claiming that the client is the employing institution rather than the individual who is being treated. There may be good and sufficient reasons not to accord information acquired in such settings the same degree of confidentiality normally provided in other settings. But consideration of whether that is so ought to proceed from analysis of all the relevant issues, not by recourse to the pseudosolution of determining who is really the client. The claims of individuals to retain control over sexual information about themselves remain virtually identical, irrespective of the setting. The chief difference is that in many institutional settings, genuine consent even to the initial disclosure of such information by the confined person is not obtainable.

Similarly, given the plausibility of the theory developed earlier in this paper, individuals have a strong claim to be fully informed about the precise nature of any research in which they participate and about the precise degree of control that they will exercise over any publication of the research data if they are or can be identified as having been connected with the research in any way.

There are any number of cases in which it may not be either possible or desirable to maintain complete confidentiality. In such cases the individual involved should be advised at the outset of the limits that may apply to the degree of confidentiality that can be assured. One such possible case would concern a person seeking a transsexual operation. For example, if the person seeking the operation were married, the spouse would have a strong claim to be informed about the proposed sex change before its occurrence. If there were children, they too would arguably have such a claim. It may be reasonable and proper for physicians and surgeons to refuse to perform any sex-change operation until after communication of the contemplated change to the subject's spouse and children, if any.

Analogous considerations apply to problems of confidentiality as they relate to the training and licensing of sex therapists. This is so both because there are strong policy considerations favoring knowledge about a therapist's own sexual practices and attitudes and because persons who wish to become sex therapists are in a good position to decide whether or not they are willing to make such disclosure as a condition to becoming a therapist. Supposing that it is relevant to the training or licensing of a sex therapist for authorities to know what the prospective therapist's own sexual practices have been, it may be important to verify the person's account of his or her own sexual practices. This might require some degree of disclosure to others (either directly or inferentially) of information the person had transmitted about his or her practices. Similarly, if a prospective therapist is denied certification by authorities on the ground that he or she is not suited to be a sex therapist, that person may wish to contest that determination. In such a case, information that was otherwise held confidential would have to be made public in the interest of providing adequate due process to all concerned.

DISCLOSURES WITHOUT CONSENT

The discussion so far has assumed consent to the disclosures. It has dealt with situations in which there is no question that the individuals involved are in a position to know what information may be disclosed about their sexuality and what degree of control they and others will be able to exercise over that information. But there are many situations in which those circumstances do not apply. When they do not, special problems emerge that have particular implications for sex research and therapy. One feature peculiar to this area is that much if not most intimate sexual activity occurs between individuals (rather than singly or in groups). It is in the nature of sexual behavior that each partner comes to acquire a substantial amount of information about the other's sex life and sexual attitudes. As a result, especially in the therapeutic setting, the therapist may be placed in a situation in which he or she becomes the recipient of information concerning the sexual behavior and attitudes of a person or persons other than the client in therapy.

For example, suppose only one of the two persons in a marital unit seeks sex therapy. Whatever other reasons may exist for thinking it desirable that both parties to the marriage participate jointly in the therapy, the foregoing situation provides an additional one, for it is hard to imagine that sex therapy with one partner in a married couple would not at some point involve disclosure and discussion of sexual information about the absent partner. To some degree, of course, this is a problem generic to all therapy—but it is often given insufficient attention even in the nonsexual setting. The point here is that when sex therapy is involved, special considerations apply. That is to say, given the theory of privacy and its relationship to sex as outlined above, there are special reasons to support individuals' claims that there not be any unconsented-to disclosures of their sexual attitudes and practices.

The question is whether those claims are sufficiently strong to make it wrong *in all cases* for the therapist to proceed with the therapy, if he or she receives sexual information from the client concerning anyone but the client. The question cannot be answered unequivocally, but to take it seriously is at least to suggest the need to explore some alternative strategies as possible solutions to the problem. One suggestion is to encourage the active participation of the other partner, especially where a continuing relationship is involved; a second possibility is to solicit the consent of the other partner to disclosure by the client of such information as is necessary to the client's treatment; a third possibility is to discourage the client from disclosing any unnecessary information about the nonclient partner. Finally, a fourth possible solution is to discourage the client from revealing the identity of the nonclient partner, if the person's identity is not obvious (that is, the spouse) and if personal identification is not central to the success of the therapy.

JUSTIFIABLE BREACHES OF CONFIDENTIALITY

Another set of cases involve situations in which the therapist is inclined to break confidentiality because of what he or she learns in the course of therapy. It might be argued that it is never permissible for the therapist to do this—that there are simply no circumstances in which it is ever proper for a therapist to divulge information acquired from a client in the therapy situation. But it is hard to defend such a view. If the argument is that a breach of confidentiality would always be impermissible because the therapist has *promised* confidentiality, promise-keeping has been elevated to the highest of all values—a most implausible hierarchy. (It is a weaker but more plausible view that all breaches of confidentiality are wrong in the sense that something 'bad' is done by breaking the confidence: This is a weaker argument because it can be countered by the claim that this particular breach of confidence was the 'right' thing to do on the whole and in the individual circumstances.) If one argues that a breach of confidentiality would always be wrong because any breach would so impair the needed trust relationship that the practice of therapy could no longer be undertaken successfully, the argument is theoretically defensible but in fact implausible. Therapists have at times disclosed the confidential communications of their clients, this has become known, and the institution of therapy has both survived and flourished despite this.

Still, if the foregoing theory of privacy is accepted, it suggests that very great care be exercised before confidentiality is ever broken in respect to sexual matters. The most obvious candidate for an exception to this rule is the case in which disclosures made during therapy lead the therapist to believe that the patient will in the future engage in unconsented-to harmful behavior toward others (for instance, the case of a patient who is considered likely to commit a rape or sexual assault). Here, more than in any other situation, the injuries caused by a breach of confidentiality are likely to be less severe—both to the practice of therapy and to the client himself—than those caused by a decision on the part of the therapist to remain silent.

This problem is not limited to the therapeutic setting. The sex researcher as well as the therapist can inadvertently acquire or be given access to information that indicates the likelihood of harmful behavior on the part of the subject. For example, a person engaged in sex research may learn from the answers to a questionnaire that a certain research subject inflicts (and by inference intends to continue inflicting) sexual violence on others—or that the subject engages children too young to consent in sexual activity. Here too there are certainly cases in which any injuries caused by a breach of confidentiality may be less severe than those caused by the researcher's or therapist's decision to keep this information to himself or herself.

It should be noted that the criterion proposed here—risk of serious harm to another individual—is different from two other (less weighty) criteria with which it might be confused. One is the criterion of the illegality of the behavior per se. The other is the criterion of possible or probable harm to the *patient*. The former is a weaker consideration because much sexual behavior is illegal even though it is not harmful to the participants (for example, consensual sodomy). The latter is a weaker consideration because the client can always be presented in advance with an explanation of the consequences of choosing to act in ways deleterious to himself or herself.

There are less serious situations in which the patient's claim to confidentiality conflicts with the anticipated realization of some good or the prevention of some evil. One such case is created by the institution of medical insurance. Given the plausibility of most people's desire to keep very tight control over sexual information about themselves, it is not surprising that many persons want to keep secret the fact that they are receiving sex therapy. But if their health insurance covers the cost of sex therapy, they also want to take advantage of the coverage. In this dilemma there is probably no way to avoid making limited disclosure of the fact of the therapy, if the insurance is to be invoked. Nonetheless, insurance companies and sex therapists should work together to develop special protective measures to prevent unnecessary disclosure to others of any information concerning the fact or nature of the treatment.

SOME ASSUMPTIONS OF THE FOREGOING THEORY OF PRIVACY AND AN ALTERNATIVE TO IT

The arguments presented in the first part of this paper are not necessarily arguments for the intrinsic desirability of privacy and confidentiality in respect to sexual behavior and sexual beliefs. It may be that very different attitudes and practices would be in some ways preferable to those currently prevailing in our society. This point will be discussed shortly.

Most of the arguments already presented turn on the empirical but not logically necessary fact that persons in our culture and in most other cultures are socialized in certain ways in respect to sexual matters. Given this socialization, an array of arguments can be developed to show why privacy and confidentiality in respect to sexual matters will be of great importance to these individuals and to explain why these persons will be distressed or feel threatened if they must surrender control over the right of access to any information concerning their sexual behavior or their sexual thoughts, attitudes, and beliefs. Given this socialization, it can be demonstrated that the character of the sexual experience itself may even be altered when others are permitted to enter into the participants' sexual world as observers.

It is important to recognize that all individuals in our society will have been socialized to some degree in the prevailing cultural attitudes toward sex of the sort described above. There will be individual differences, to be sure, and the differences may be substantial. Still, given the ideology of the culture, both in respect to gender socialization and in respect to more specific attitudes and "rules" concerning sexual behavior, it seems likely that all individuals will share to a substantial degree in the perception of sex as specially connected with privacy in setting, with vulnerability, and with intimacy.

Conceding all of this, it is nonetheless worth asking whether it might not be preferable for individuals to be socialized differently. Nor is this merely an abstract intellectual inquiry—for among those who would have reason to favor an alternative mode of socialization concerning sexual matters are many persons directly involved in providing sex therapy or conducting sex research (especially, perhaps, those who identify themselves as committed to the practice of humanistic psychology). An alternative theory is possible. Although seldom made explicit or argued for, it is worth taking seriously. One possible reconstruction of such a view would go something like this:

Persons have made themselves excessively vulnerable because

they have accepted the idea that certain activities are shameful unless done in private. There is no reason to accept that convention.
Of course people are embarrassed if others observe them engaging
in sexual intercourse—just as they are embarrassed if others see
them unclothed. But that is because our culture has taught them
to have those attitudes, not because the attitudes are intrinsically
right and proper. Indeed, our culture would be a healthier, happier
culture if persons would revise their thinking about the kinds of
activities they now feel comfortable doing only in private and
about the kinds of thoughts they now feel comfortable disclosing
only to those with whom they have a special or intimate relationship.

In the first place, there is no good reason why privacy is essential
to these activities. Sexual intercourse could be just as pleasurable in
public—if persons grew up unashamed—as is eating a good dinner
in a good restaurant. Sexual intercourse is 'better' in private only
because our society has told us so.

In the second place, a change in our attitudes with regard to sex
and privacy would make individuals more secure and more at ease
in society. If persons were as indifferent to the presence of outside
observers when they were having intercourse as they are when they
partake of a meal, they could not be injured by others watching
them (regardless of whether the fact of observation was known to
them).

In the third place, interpersonal relationships would be improved
if there were less concern for privacy. Forthrightness, honesty, and
candor are considered virtues, for the most part, while hypocrisy
and deceit are not. Yet the current emphasis on the maintenance of
a private side to life tends to encourage hypocritical and deceitful
behavior. Individuals tend to lead (and to see themselves as leading) dual lives: a public life and a private life. They present one
"self" to the public—to casual friends, acquaintances, and strangers
—and a different self to themselves and to a few intimate associates.
This way of living is hypocritical because it is designed to camou-
flage the real, private self from public scrutiny. It is a dualistic,
unintegrated life that renders its devotees needlessly vulnerable,
shame-ridden, and lacking in a clear sense of self. It provides a stark
contrast to the more open, less guarded life of a person who has

little to fear from disclosures of self because he or she has nothing that requires hiding.

A set of views and arguments such as the above is worth taking seriously. As previously suggested, it is likely that the ideology of many sex therapists and researchers is closer to this set of views than to the dominant and more traditional sexual ideology of our culture, although the details of this position are seldom explicitly formulated. If this *is* the view that many persons within the field advocate, it is important that it be fully and explicitly stated and that it be carefully and critically examined to determine whether it is ultimately defensible.

Any attempt to consider seriously a view such as this should begin by considering more precisely the respects in which it departs from the more conventional view of privacy, confidentiality, and sexuality outlined earlier. There are at least three issues that have not been explored sufficiently. First is the question of the value that the alternative theory attaches to those characteristics of spontaneity and individuality that play such an important role in the more traditional view as it has been described. On at least one interpretation, both theories prize spontaneity and individuality equally highly, with the alternative theory viewing openness in interpersonal relationships as a better way of achieving those ends. However, on another interpretation, autonomy, spontaneity, and individuality are replaced as values in the alternative theory by the satisfactions that attend the recognition of the similarities inherent in all human experience and the sameness that characterizes all interpersonal relationships. The question of which theory allows more options concerning the kind of life one will fashion for oneself is a central issue that would have to be settled—assuming that maximizing options for living is an important consideration.

Another issue that would have to be explored is the question of what would be gained and what would be lost in regard to the character of interpersonal relationships. One of the principal arguments for the conventional theory put forward earlier is that the sharing of one's intimate thoughts and behaviors is one of the primary media through which close, meaningful interpersonal relationships are created, nourished, and confirmed. In that view, one defining characteristic of a relationship of close friendship is that friends are willing to share with each other information about themselves that they are unprepared to reveal to the world at large. One characteristic that helps to define and sustain a relationship of sexual love is the willingness of the parties involved to share with each other sexual intimacies that they are unprepared to share with the world at large. If this reasoning makes sense, either as a conceptual or as an empirical truth, then perhaps acceptance of the alternative theory would mean that these kinds of relationships would no longer be possible or would at least be less likely. But perhaps the conventional view is equally unsatisfactory in this area: Perhaps friendship and love both can and ought to depend on some other, less proprietary, less commercial conception than the mutual exchange of commodities. Perhaps the prevailing cultural view of intimate interpersonal relationships is as much in need of alteration as is the attendant conception of the self.

Finally, as a corollary to this, one would have to examine more closely some other features of the alternative theory. For example, even if persons no longer thought it important to mark off and distinguish their close friends from strangers (that is, by the conventional means of sharing intimacies), might not the ideal of openness and honesty—if applied to *all* interpersonal relationships —make ordinary social interaction vastly more complex and time-consuming? If this proved to be true, then these daily interactions, rather than the other tasks of living, would become the focus of our waking hours.

These are among the important issues that require further exploration. They are certainly among the issues that any fully developed theory of privacy, confidentiality, and sexuality must confront and try to resolve, whether seeking to perpetuate or to alter the cultural institutions, attitudes, and practices that currently prevail in respect to sex therapy and sex research.

4

ETHICS OF SEX RESEARCH INVOLVING CHILDREN AND THE MENTALLY RETARDED

ALBERT R. JONSEN

JAY MANN

The title of this essay embraces two topics that have been embroiled in ethical controversy: sex research and research with children and the retarded. The ethical controversy surrounding the first is the general subject of this congress. It is our task to report the basic contentions of the ethical controversy surrounding research involving children and retardates and to relate these to sex research. It is our hope that we can illuminate the problems and perhaps even resolve some of them.

Although our report is concerned specifically with children and the retarded, it also raises issues about other groups that might be considered special populations and in need of special protection. Our colleagues on the Ethics Congress task force agreed that children and mental retardates constitute two categories that must be designated as "special" for purposes of participation in sex research. However, some members pointed out that additional groups might merit inclusion under this rubric. It was suggested that the following groups be considered: prisoners, disabled persons (both institutionalized and noninstitutionalized), the mentally ill, homosexuals, and the elderly. The commonality among these groups is that the participation of their members in sex research presumably exposes them to greater risks or takes advantage of a more restricted freedom than is the case with the average adult. We suggest three concepts that might be useful in determining whether a particular individual or class of individuals is disadvantaged in these respects and therefore requires special treatment.

The first concept, *diminished capacity*, would apply to those individuals whose mental state—for example, senility, immaturity, or mental impairment—prevents their making reasoned judgments about the nature or consequences of their participation. These individuals are presumably incapable of giving consent that is truly informed. Moreover, if their mental state is such that their response to participation is difficult to predict, the investigator is faced with the additional problem of making an accurate risk-benefit assessment.

The second concept, *diminished autonomy*, applies to children under the control of parents or parent surrogates and to institutionalized subjects. The use of "captive" populations is common in behavioral research. The college student—the traditional "guinea pig" of the psychology researcher—is an example: Although participation in college-based research is ostensibly voluntary, the student may experience covert pressure to participate. In the case of less autonomous groups, such as prisoners or other institutionalized subjects, the pressure may be more intense. A prisoner, for example, may believe cooperation will influence his parole or his treatment. The issue with captive samples is again informed consent. In order to ascertain whether it exists, one would have to determine whether groups whose power to make independent decisions has been restricted are given adequate information about their participation and are under no coercion, however covert, to participate.

The third concept, *increased vulnerability*, applies to those individuals whose participation in research makes them exceptionally vulnerable to social reprisals. For example, individuals who prefer homosexual partners or who are involved in variant sexual practices such as mate swapping would fall into this category. The major issue here may be confidentiality—a concern in all sex research, but a more crucial consideration in studies dealing with information that, if disclosed, might be damaging to the subjects' status in the community.

It is clear that other groups share with children and retardates the need for special ethical guidelines. However, we believe that a comprehensive detailing of the issues in research with children and retardates will provide some suggestions for formulating guidelines appropriate to the needs of other groups whose participation in research entails exceptional risks or impairment of the conditions necessary for informed consent.

RESEARCH INVOLVING CHILDREN

Throughout history, children have been subjects of research. A legendary Persian prince is said to have isolated newborn babies from all human speech in hopes of discovering whether language was natural and spontaneous. Queen Caroline of England recruited children from a foundling hospital in order to test Jenner's vaccination on them before it was applied to her own royal progeny. The modern controversy over research with children and the retarded can be traced to events at Willowbrook State Hospital for the Mentally Retarded where, during the 1950s and 1960s, healthy mentally retarded children were infected with mild hepatitis in order to study the natural history of the disease. That research aroused great public controversy, and its merits and faults are debated even today. It initiated discussion within and without the medical profession over whether any invasion or manipulation of the body or person of a nonconsenting subject could ever be ethically justified apart from expectation of benefit to that very subject [1].

The prevailing codes of ethics governing the use of human subjects for experimentation are curiously ambivalent about children. The progenitor of these codes, the Code of Nuremberg, would—if taken literally—exclude children as subjects, for it requires the voluntary consent of the subject "as absolutely essential," without any provision for proxy consent [2]. On the other hand, the World Medical Association's Declaration of Helsinki states that "the consent of the legal guardian should be procured" for nontherapeutic research involving legally incompetent subjects [3]. A similar position has been adopted by the American Medical Association:

Minors or mentally incompetent persons may be used as subjects only if (i) the nature of the investigation is such that mentally competent adults would not be suitable subjects; (ii) consent, in writing, is given by a legally authorized representative of the subject under circumstances in which an informed and prudent adult would reasonably be expected to volunteer himself or his child as a subject [4].

This position, permitting nontherapeutic research on the basis of proxy consent of the legally authorized representative, was tacitly accepted by the first DHEW regulations [5].

It is not an unchallenged position. Beecher cited (and disagreed with) the purported British position that any medical intervention on a normal healthy child (or on a sick child without the intent to provide therapy) was ethically and legally unacceptable [6]. A case currently sub judice seeks to establish this position in an American jurisdiction, arguing that parents have no legal right to consent to any intervention not directed to their child's benefit.[1] Philosophers and theologians continue to debate the question: Princeton's Paul Ramsey and Georgetown's Richard McCormick take opposing views. The former repudiates any ethical justification for research with a normal child; the latter claims that even children bear a certain obligation to benefit society, which responsibility justifies a presumption of their consent to experiments involving minimal risk [7, 8].

At the heart of the legal and ethical controversy are two central issues: proxy consent and the relevance of risk-benefit assessment. The National Commission for the Protection of Human Subjects of Biomedical and Behavioral Research, established by Congress in 1974, has been charged with an investigation of these issues with regard to research involving children and the institutionalized mentally incompetent. The recommendations of the Commission, of which one of the present authors[2] is a member, have been presented to the Secretary of Health, Education, and Welfare. These recommendations will doubtless influence federal policy governing the conduct and support of research involving children. They will therefore serve as the framework for our analysis of ethical issues in sex research involving children and the retarded.

First, we shall survey the history of sex research in order to show

---

[1] *Nielson* v. *Regents of University of California* (Cal. Sup. Ct., Civil Action No. 665–049, filed December 19, 1973).

[2] A. R. J.

how sex research with children fits into the development of the field and to reveal some of the problems that have propelled and restrained research; second, we shall state several modalities of social research in general that pertain to the ethics of research with children in particular; third, we shall detail the areas of research with children that seem particularly important; finally, we shall attempt to fit together the scientific and the ethical imperatives regarding research with children.

We write this essay with an audience in mind. That audience is not one of researchers or ethicists, nor is it one of parents and children. Rather, we have in mind a prospective audience of relative newcomers to the research world: reviewers of protocols. At present and for the foreseeable future, the ethics of research will be judged primarily by those members of the professions and the public who are appointed to institutional review boards wherever biomedical and behavioral research is being done. We must assume that most such persons, while highly motivated and knowledgeable in their own fields, know very little about sex research. We shall try to provide them with a perspective from which they can fairly and intelligently judge proposals to conduct such research. Of course, their judgment will rest on general regulations and on the specific information offered by the researcher, but between these lie many considerations that strongly influence judgments—considerations about the nature of children, about the nature of sexuality, and about the nature of social research. This essay attempts to elucidate some of these considerations.

SEX RESEARCH WITH CHILDREN: HISTORY AND PROBLEMS

Questions about the ethics of sex research with children should be placed within the context of the history of sex research in general. The ways in which research problems arose and methodologies were formulated to study them follow a pattern that may be instructive when the ethical propriety of involving children and the retarded in sex research is considered. We shall briefly survey the history of sex research and, within that history, view certain proposals to study the sexuality of children and the retarded.

Sigmund Freud propelled sexuality out of prescientific darkness into scientific light. Almost a century of growing interest in the biomedical and behavioral aspects of human sexuality has followed his dramatic and heretical proclamations. It is widely known that the principal proclamation of Freud's doctrine, around which all else clustered, concerned the sexuality of childhood. He wrote,

It is part of popular belief about the sexual instinct that it is absent in childhood and that it first appears in the period of life known as puberty. This, though a common error, is serious in its consequences and is chiefly due to our ignorance of the fundamental principles of the sexual life [9].

Curiously, despite that central proclamation, ignorance of childhood sexuality remains profound. Today, 70 years after Freud wrote those words, John Money labels childhood sexuality "a research frontier, unopened to empirical and operational study" [10]. In another recent article, Warren Johnson notes a dearth of "much needed research to obtain basic scientific knowledge on the subject of childhood sexuality"; he also describes formidable opposition to any effort that might be construed as encouraging childhood sexuality [11]. And Dr. William H. Masters, in response to the question "When will your type of research be done with children?", had to reply, "Not in my lifetime" [11].

However, the fact that Dr. Masters has in his lifetime seen and effected an immense expansion of the old frontiers of sex research reminds us that sex research in general has proceeded—though with extreme circumspection. At each point in its cautious progress, it encountered obstacles in the form of social attitudes, moral prohibitions, and legal proscriptions that seemed insurmountable at the time. The same discreet exploration may or may not be possible with regard to childhood sexuality. Still, the history of research into adult sexuality shows that it has advanced by virtue of gradual changes in mores and morals as well as the deliberate design of studies and selection of subject matter by the researchers. Public attitudes do not impose the sole constraint upon sex research with children. Other constraints are imposed by the ethics of the researchers themselves, by the ethical standards of the profession, and by the laws and regulations governing the ethical conduct of research. Many potential studies have been shelved before being put to the test of public acceptance because their sponsors were unable to assure themselves that these studies met criteria for ethical research; some studies that meet ethical standards are inevitably repudiated by public attitudes. Perhaps a time will come when public attitudes will be so relaxed as to tolerate even research that thoughtful persons deem ethically inappropriate.

Byrne has noted that scientists initially approached the socially proscribed area of direct investigation of human sexual behavior by studying "animal sex, native sex, and crazy sex" [12]. Studies of the mating habits of species other than man, cross-cultural research into sexual behavior, and investigations of sexual anomalies or deviant and problematic sexual activities provided a more acceptable approach to the questions of sexuality than did direct investigation of human, American, and "normal" sexuality. Indeed, the policies of many funding sources sustain the focus on these areas, being less squeamish about underwriting the study of exotic or problematic sexuality than the study of modal sexual functioning.

Social scientists first undertook systematic surveys outside the clinical setting in the 1920s and 1930s. They usually employed quite indirect and nonintrusive methods and often camouflaged the real topic under study. These surveys differed from earlier investigations in two important ways: They studied samples drawn from general populations; and they were primarily taxonomic, directed toward collection of quantifiable, descriptive data from a sizable sample of subjects. These two features allowed findings to be generalized in the form of statements about normative sexual behaviors.

Sexual Behavior in the Human Male [13] opened a new era in sex research. The study was without precedent in terms of sample size and diversity, the scope of activities studied, the methods of investigation, and data analysis and reporting. In an attempt to remedy defects perceived in earlier studies, Kinsey and his colleagues designed a direct and individualized interaction between interviewer and subject "in the way friends talk to friends" [13]. This technique, a relatively free-flowing conversation recorded in a precise code, presumably yielded more accurate, verifiable, and detailed information than the previous discreet and indirect questionnaires or structured interviews. Kinsey's pioneering methods initiated the basic form of contemporary sex research: the frank, realistic, intimate encounter between investigator and subject.

Finally, sex research moved from observation and interview to experimentation, the planned manipulation of variables. In the early 1950s, experimenters moved with trepidation, as reflected in their exclusive reliance on male volunteers and the use of low-key stimuli and subjective response measures. Over a period of two decades, typical research stimuli moved from nude or seminude still photos and rather mild erotic literature to explicit film representations of sexual activity; measures of response moved from pen and pencil to the recording of physiological arousal reactions. *Human Sexual Response* [14] was the astonishing result of these methods and the harbinger of things to come.

To summarize, sex research moved from clinical origins based on reports of pathological cases, through indirect and guarded inquiry among the general population, to direct interrogation of individuals and, finally, experimental methods. This historical survey, while familiar to sex researchers, is essential information for those who must review research. The ethical issues that will be discussed are intimately related to these differences in research methodology.

The history of research into childhood sexuality is much more sparse than that of studies with adults. It follows much the same course, although progressing more slowly. Investigators have made unobtrusive, naturalistic observations of the spontaneous sexual behavior of small children [15, 16]. However, studies involving exposure of children to explicit erotic stimuli, systematic observation, or measurement of sexual response have not yet been performed. Given the many unresolved questions about the effects of intrusive interventions on children's responses and psychosexual development, researchers may find themselves hard put to predict the consequences of such research. Inability to do so prevents formulation of risk-benefit assessments and informed consent criteria requisite for ethical research. Even if public attitudes about childhood sexuality were to become more permissive, researchers might find themselves unable to devise ethical strategies for highly intrusive studies of children's sexual responses.

CLINICAL STUDIES

Most of the clinical or quasi-clinical studies in the literature of childhood sexuality report descriptive data as a byproduct of diagnostic and therapeutic procedures necessitated by the children's condition. Pediatric patients as well as children in psychoanalysis or other forms of psychotherapy have been a major source of data on childhood sexual behavior [17, 18]. Children with problems of gender identity and sexual identity related to endocrine or psychosocial influences have also been studied. These children usually have been brought for treatment to medical clinics where investigators have relied on clinical methods of data collection, interview, and behavioral observation, but physical examinations and laboratory tests such as endocrine assays have also been used [19]. Children brought to clinicians because of sexual involvement with adults have been studied in a similar manner. Typically, these children are interviewed by the clinician; they may also receive a genital examination if trauma is suspected. Often these children have been interrogated by law enforcement authorities seeking evidence for prosecution of the alleged offender [20].

A few researchers have studied individual normal children or small samples of normals, using observational methods similar to those used with clinical subjects. For example, Kleeman reports that he began collecting data on children's masturbatory activity over 25 years ago, beginning with his own children and children in Edith Jackson's Rooming-In Project [21, 22]. Kleeman later reported additional single-subject observational studies of the masturbatory activity of normal young children [15, 16]. He cites five major sources of data on masturbation, based on clinical observation [21]: (1) reconstructions from the psychoanalytic treatment of adults and children; (2) case reports of individual children incorporating histories from parents and observations of the child by the therapist; (3) reports from pediatricians [17]; (4) observations of institutionalized children by trained observers, with comparison data from observation of normal children in the home setting [23–25]; and (5) observations of children in clinic or public nursery settings away from their homes [26, 27]. Of necessity, observation is the major quasi-clinical means of collecting data on the behavior of infants and very young children. With older children, additional procedures used in diagnosis and treatment can be employed, including doll play, interview, and projective tests. The use of dolls and projective tests as stimuli can be viewed as quasi-experimental intervention to the extent that these measures manipulate the child's responses.

Single- or multiple-subject studies in which medical or psychological treatment of the child is a major component raise a number of separate issues in addition to those raised by other types of research. These issues will be discussed in a later section.

TAXONOMIC STUDIES

The transition from studying clinical samples to studying normals and from collecting data on individual cases or small groups of cases to surveying larger samples was cautious and deliberate.

One early study of boys ranging from 8 to 18 years of age was conducted by Merrill in 1918 [28]. Although it differed from the clinical case studies in that it collected interview data from a large group (N = 100) and was performed outside a medical setting, it could legitimately be classified as a quasi-clinical study because it investigated a deviant sample: delinquent boys. The investigator, a probation officer, interviewed boys who were passing through a juvenile court in Seattle. The author's findings included data on preadolescent masturbation to orgasm and oral-genital homosexual contact. This early study exemplifies the license granted to the investigator reporting on childhood sexual activity when the children in question are labeled as deviant. It is doubtful that an American researcher during the same period would have been able to publish comparable data on nondelinquent normal boys.

Some 30 years later, Ramsey studied a nonclinical group of 291 preadolescent and young adolescent males representing all the boys in a seventh- and eighth-grade group (and some others) in a medium-large city in Illinois [29]. Using personal interviews, the author collected data on masturbation and other sexual activities.

One other early study is also noteworthy because it broke with tradition by surveying a nonclinical sample. Hughes, a state health officer–biologist in North Carolina, used a group-administered questionnaire to survey a cross-section of grade-school and high-school rural and urban boys who were mostly between the ages of 15 and 20 [30]. Because of its predominant focus on boys over 15, this study does not qualify as a study of preadolescent sexual development. However, it serves as an approximation of later nonclinical research with younger children. The study was hardly a model of scientific objectivity. Many items in the questionnaire were embedded in moral judgments (for example, "Has anyone ever tried to give you the mistaken idea that sexual intercourse is necessary for the health of the young man?"). Although the author's reasons for injecting moral bias into the questionnaire items are a matter of conjecture, these items may have served to counter accusations that Hughes's questions "put ideas in the heads" of his young subjects.

Kinsey and his colleagues collected detailed interview data from 212 preadolescent boys [13]. Their method as adapted to this age group will be described in a subsequent section. In addition to interviewing preadolescent boys, these investigators collected data on preadolescent sexual activity from retrospective self-report interviews with adults, from reports of parental observations, and from interviews with older subjects who had had sexual contact with preadolescents. The survey reported data on sexual and nonsexual sources of erotic arousal and detailed descriptions of orgasm (based in part on data from the previously cited study by Ramsey [29]) and included observational reports on the speed of reaching orgasm in 1,888 boys, aged 5 months to adolescence, who were timed with a stop watch. In a few cases, observations of young preadolescents were continued over a period of months or years, until the individuals reached an age at which it could be established that true orgasm was involved [13].

Kinsey and co-workers also reported data on 147 preadolescent females ranging in age from 2 to 15 years [31]. These authors mentioned that they had conducted a detailed study of younger children (in particular, children between 2 and 5 years of age) to investigate the sources of their sex education, but that the study needed to be carried further before the results were ready to be reported in detail. Some of the results were subsequently published [32]; the remaining data are recorded on computer tape in the archives of the Institute for Sex Research [33].

STUDIES OF PROCREATIVE INFORMATION

In the past, investigators studying young children's acquisition of procreative and related sexual information have relied on retrospective interviews with adults as major sources of data. Only a very few researchers have interviewed children directly in order to assess their knowledge and beliefs about sexual anatomy, conception, and procreation. Researchers undertaking such studies must contend with a dispute that has long embroiled sex educators and the general public: a dispute about what children should be taught and what they already know [34]. It is often assumed that asking the child questions about sex and procreation is tantamount to giving the child new information. Researchers sensitive to this issue have generally selected samples of children whose parents approved of their children's receiving some basic information about sex and procreation. One study, based on interviews with 30 boys and 30 girls aged 3 to 12, reports that, "given the hesitance of many parents to have their children questioned about sexual matters, random sampling was not attempted" [35]; the study sample was recruited from upper middle-class Caucasian families in Berkeley, whose attitudes toward sex education were assumed to be more liberal than those one would encounter in most communities. Another study in which children were interviewed directly about procreative and sexual knowledge used a select sample of boys and girls aged 3 to 5.5 who attended a university nursery school [36]. This study employed a twelve-item questionnaire derived from a similar instrument used by Kreitler and Kreitler [37] to study the concepts of sexuality and birth held by Israeli children. The questionnaire covered knowledge of excretion, including names of the functions, organs, and products; the mother's and father's respective roles in conception; and the process of birth.

Some interviewers used more circumspect methods in preference to direct questioning. Conn [38] used doll play as a technique in interviewing 100 children aged 4 to 11. Levy [39], anticipating the realistic products currently produced by toy manufacturers, used a doll with a clay penis in order to study young children's awareness of sex differences. Interviewers at the Institute for Sex Research used another play technique with their young subjects: asking them to draw pictures, which were then used as the basis for questioning by the interviewers about the child's own behavior [40].

One source of data requiring no interaction of the investigator and the child is content analysis of children's stories. One study that analyzed the spontaneous stories of a group of boys and girls aged 2 to 5 revealed little sexual content [41]; a similar study using another sample of boys and girls in the same age bracket reported that their spontaneous stories contained a high proportion of violent themes and a low proportion of sexual themes [42].

An ingenious study by the E. C. Brown Center for Family Studies [43] surveyed children's knowledge of gestation by having classroom teachers in California and Oregon ask young children to draw pictures that answered the questions "Where was I before I was born?" and "What did I look like before I was born?"; the 1,100 drawings received from respondents were then subjected to content analysis.

SEX ROLE STUDIES

The profound influence of sex role socialization on the enactment of one's sexuality has been described by numerous authors [44]. The study of sex-typed behaviors in young children appears to be a special case in sex research.

Parents often manifest concern about sex-inappropriate behaviors of their children, especially their sons [45]; however, they do not usually translate that concern into fear that sex role research will negatively influence sex role behavior. (In contrast, these fears frequently surface with research focused on genital sexuality or its procreative results.) This suspension of concern has permitted researchers to conduct experiments in sex role socialization without encountering parental opposition, even to the extent of devising experimental situations in which sex-role behaviors are manipulated through modeling or other processes [46]. Experiments in which children's sexual knowledge or specific "sexual" behaviors (such as genital exploration) were dependent variables would undoubtedly evoke much more opposition from parents than have experiments focused on their socialization—although sex role socialization is at least as crucial to the development and expression of sexuality as is children's knowledge of procreation or their early interest in one another's genitals.

Research studies in the area of childhood sexuality begin to lose their immunity to parental censure as they draw closer to genital sexuality. For example, Broderick [47] studied the development of heterosexual socialization in preadolescents, with particular attention to the formation of relationships. He questioned children about their feelings of attraction to other children, about their "girl friends" and "boy friends," and about dating, kissing, and other dimensions of interpersonal activity prevalent in the age group. Questions about genital sexual behavior were not a part of the study. Nonetheless, the study elicited an irate response from many parents [48].

METHODOLOGY AND MORALITY

This survey of the movement from the clinical to the nonclinical, from observation to interrogation and experimental manipulation, reveals some methodological considerations that are directly relevant to the ethical problems. We will argue that the reactivity of a given study is the key variable in assessing its ethical implications.

The term *reactivity* refers to the probability that a given method of investigation or exposure to a specific body of content or class of stimuli will influence the subject's attitudinal, emotional, or behavioral responses. Reactivity sometimes characterizes a random effect inadvertently elicited by a measurement technique: For example, in a study done by one of the present authors [49], the daily checklist that served as an inventory of subjects' sexual behavior, fantasies, and urges was demonstrably more effective in shaping sexual behavior than were the explicit erotic films used as experimental stimuli. However, we also use the term *reactivity* with reference to a calculated effect resulting from an experimental manipulation: For example, it is common practice among social psychologists to design experiments so as to have a maximum impact on subjects [50].

Three variables, characteristics of the stimulus, presumably contribute to reactivity. We shall use these as referents in evaluating specific research approaches in terms of the probable impact on the subject. Each variable describes an essentially discrete dimension of research methodology or content; however, there may be a degree of overlap in some instances. The variables are as follows:

1. *Intrusiveness.* This term describes the degree of investigator-subject interaction dictated by the design of the study. For example, an interview requires more investigator-subject interaction than a questionnaire, which can be mailed out or group-administered; thus, the interview would be relatively high in intrusiveness. At the negative end of the intrusiveness continuum are so-called unobtrusive measures, which require neither co-operation nor interaction from the subject [51]. Content analyses of children's classroom drawing, cataloguing and describing graffiti, and inspection of library catalogue cards for signs of activity are examples of unobtrusive measures.

2. *Inquisitiveness.* This term characterizes the nature and extent of the information elicited from subjects. Procedures designed to elicit information about behavior generally deemed private would rate high on the inquisitiveness continuum.

3. *Explicitness.* This term describes the nature of the experimental manipulations and the content of measuring instruments such as tests, interview schedules, and other protocols in terms of their sexual explicitness. For example, the use in an experiment of films vividly depicting coitus would rate high in explicitness. Although usually applied to sexual material, the term could also be used to describe one dimension of other emotionally charged themes (for example, violence).

It is apparent from our historical survey that sex research has progressed toward methodologies that are higher in reactivity. More recent studies, in contrast to earlier ones, rank higher in intrusiveness, inquisitiveness, and explicitness, and would be expected to elicit more noticeable change in attitudes and behavior. It is pre-cisely this reactivity or tendency to bring about change in attitudes and behavior that constitutes the central ethical problem of sex re-search with children. Researchers consistently encounter parental opposition when they attempt to recruit children for sex research. This parental opposition is apparently based on fear that the re-search will effect changes in their children's sexual attitudes, in-formation, and behavior.

In general, three different beliefs seem to prompt fear in parents. First, they believe that children cannot make critical judgments that would enable them to resist or reject information. Second, they believe that sexual information is emotionally overpowering and will arouse children physically or titillate their curiosity, which may in turn trigger precocious sexual behavior. Finally, parents consider sex education their exclusive province and see themselves as responsible for imparting it to their children in terms of their own cultural and religious convictions. If these beliefs are well-founded, children will presumably be changed by sex research in ways that are beyond their own control and the control of their parents—assuming that sex research is in fact highly reactive. The more intrusive, inquisitive, and explicit the research methodology, the more it will offend traditional beliefs about the psychological, social, and moral dimensions of childhood sexuality.

When researchers propose to act in ways that are beyond the control of their subjects or their subjects' guardians and when their activities appear likely to effect changes that are considered risky or dangerous, they face the two central ethical issues of research. These two familiar ethical issues—informed consent and risk-benefit assessment—are thus linked to the *reactivity* of a given research study. Whether or not the dimensions of intrusiveness, inquisitive-ness, and explicitness do in fact bear a direct relationship to reac-tivity in every instance is an empirical question. Some studies high in these three dimensions might conceivably effect less change than other studies that are relatively low in these dimensions. But in general, studies using methodologies characterized by high intru-siveness, inquisitiveness, and explicitness are likely to be viewed as having a high potential for reactivity by adults concerned with the subjects' welfare.

RECOMMENDATIONS OF THE NATIONAL COMMISSION FOR THE PROTECTION OF HUMAN SUBJECTS

Before discussing the problems reactivity poses for risk-benefit assessment and consent, we shall summarize the recommendations recently delivered to the Secretary of Health, Education, and Welfare by the National Commission for the Protection of Human Subjects of Biomedical and Behavioral Research, concerning research involving children [52]. The result of extensive review of the problems involved in research with children, these recommendations suggest new avenues for exploring the ethics of research with children.

The Commission defines children as "individuals who have not attained the age of consent for medical care or for research activities in the jurisdiction in which the research will be conducted." (We shall comment later on this definition, both in itself and in its application to the specific problems of sex research.) The Commission defines research activities as "all procedures performed in a formal investigation designed to contribute to generalizable knowledge; they include, but are not limited to, diagnostic, prophylactic and therapeutic interventions that are the focus of systematic investigation, and other interventions or modifications of procedures, observations, comparisons, measurements, the use of questionnaires and surveys, and the analysis of data, undertaken for the purpose of obtaining specific information" [52].

The first recommendation is a general commendation of research, stating that research is valuable and necessary for the health and well-being of children, that it can be done ethically, and that it should be supported by the Secretary of Health, Education, and Welfare under certain specific conditions. Those conditions are set forth in the recommendations that follow.[3]

The second recommendation states the conditions that must be fulfilled if research is to be judged ethical: scientific soundness;

---

[3] Only the salient points are cited here. Each of the ten recommendations is highly nuanced and is followed by explanatory comments. The full text is available (see reference [52]).

prior animal and adult studies; safest possible procedures; protection of privacy and confidentiality; equitable selection.

The third recommendation states that research "that does not involve greater than minimal risk" may be conducted, provided an institutional review board is satisfied that the general conditions for ethical research are met. (The Commission defines minimal risk as "the probability and magnitude of physical or psychological harm that is normally encountered in the daily lives, or in the routine medical or psychological examination, of healthy children." Research involving more than minimal risk is justified only by the demonstration that the research offers some direct benefit to the subject or, if it does not, that it represents a "minor increase over minimal risk" and "presents experiences to subjects that are reasonably commensurate with those inherent in their actual or expected medical, psychological or social situations" [Recommendation 5]. In the latter case, the research must promise knowledge "of vital importance for the understanding and amelioration of the subject's disorder or condition.")

The seventh recommendation states that assent of children should be sought (in general) and *must* be sought when the children are over the age of seven. The term *proxy consent* is discarded in favor of "permission of parents or guardians," which permission should "reflect the collective judgment of the family that an infant or child may participate in research." In addition, close parental involvement (in some cases even parental presence) is required for certain sorts of research.

The eighth recommendation recognizes that for certain types of research, parental permission may not be a reasonable requirement to protect the subject. The types of research included in this category are (1) research designed to identify factors related to the incidence of certain conditions in adolescents for which in certain jurisdictions they may legally receive treatment without parental consent; (2) research in which the subjects are "mature minors" and the procedures involved entail essentially no more than minimal risk that such individuals might reasonably assume on their own; (3) research designed to understand and meet the needs of neglected or abused children, or children designated by their parents as "in need of supervision." In such cases, review boards may waive the requirement of parental permission, provided that some alternative mechanism is utilized to protect the children's rights.

ETHICAL EVALUATION
OF RESEARCH

When a protocol is presented, reviewers must first judge whether it affects human subjects and, if it does, whether those subjects are put at risk of detriment to their welfare or rights by the research. Clearly, the probability and magnitude of the risks vary according to the nature of the subjects. Should a researcher propose to use children as subjects in sex research, the characteristics of the prospective population must be carefully delineated in terms of age, gender, status (that is, whether they are patients, institutionalized, school children, juvenile offenders, etc.) and, if possible, social and economic class. One immediate problem with such designation comes from the Commission's definition of children as "individuals who have not attained the age of consent for medical care or for research activities in the jurisdiction in which the research will be conducted." Since no jurisdiction has established an age of consent for research, the age of consent for medical treatment would appear to be the most relevant criterion. This varies from jurisdiction to jurisdiction: In some areas there is a statutory age of consent; in other areas there are exceptions to the statutory age for certain types of medical treatment, such as obstetrical care, abortion, contraception, and addiction.

It is interesting to note that these legal exceptions are allowed primarily for matters having to do with sexuality. It might be presumed that research into these matters might be carried out as if the subjects were "mature minors" capable of consent regardless of parental consent. The Commission's recommendation provides for this:

If the Institutional Review Board determines that a research protocol is designed for conditions or a subject population for which parental or guardian permission is not a reasonable requirement to protect the subjects, it may waive such requirement provided an appropriate mechanism for protecting the children who will participate as subjects in the research is substituted [Recommendation 8, p. 17].

In commenting on this recommendation, the Commission notes:

A number of states have specific legislation permitting minors to consent to treatment for certain conditions (e.g., pregnancy, drug addiction, venereal diseases) without the permission (or knowledge) of their parents. If parental permission were required for research about such conditions, it would be difficult to develop improved methods of prevention and therapy that meet the special needs of adolescents. Therefore, assent of such mature minors should be considered sufficient with respect to research about conditions for which they have legal authority to consent on their own to treatment [Recommendation 8, p. 18].

Thus, for certain types of research in certain localities, persons otherwise legally defined as children can be considered adults. (However, for purposes of the remainder of this paper, children shall be considered as individuals prior to puberty in whom neither the psychological nor physiological maturity required for the foregoing exception has been attained.[4])

Several points of importance for sex research involving children emerge from these recommendations. First, the definition of minimal risk as risk not surpassing that encountered in children's normal daily lives might apply to much sex research. Second, the allowance of more than minimal risk where therapeutic benefit might result would apply to a broad range of sex research associ-

[4] Adolescents (postpubertal individuals under the age of 18) are not viewed as children for the purposes of this paper because their physiological maturity, their potential for sexual activity, their relatively greater autonomy, and their legal status set them apart from younger (prepubescent) children. However, we recognize that adolescents comprise a heterogeneous group whose members are located on a twofold continuum with characteristics ranging from full emancipation, both de facto and de jure, to stringent parental control and from sexual activity and experience to sexual inexperience and naiveté. We suggest that the positions of any individual adolescent on both continua might serve as referents for the considerations applicable to his or her participation in research. Thus, the right of an adolescent to volunteer for research might be assimilated to his or her legal right to medical treatment for sexually related conditions in certain jurisdictions. Beyond legal considerations, researchers and review boards who are sensitive to parental and community response might ensure that selection procedures take into account the individual subject's level of maturity as a sexual being and his or her degree of autonomy within the family. Anyone who proposes to do either therapy or research involving adolescents must inevitably walk a narrow legal and ethical line between the gradually increasing autonomy of the young person and the gradually diminishing authority of parents.

ated with treatment of sexually related conditions. Third, the insistence on parental permission, involvement, and participation poses formidable problems for sex research with children. Finally, the categories of research for which parental permission may be waived, mentioned in Recommendation Eight, apply clearly to certain types of sex research, such as inquiries into social or economic circumstances surrounding adolescent pregnancy, investigations of sexual conduct leading to venereal disease, or studies of sexual abuse of children by parents.

In all these recommendations, the determination of risks and benefits and the suitable manner of obtaining assent of children and permission or participation of parents remains largely at the discretion of the institutional review board (IRB), an entity established in 1966 for all institutions where research is supported by the Department of Health, Education, and Welfare. The discretionary power of the IRB poses a major problem to those who wish to conduct research in areas that are either unknown from the scientific viewpoint or controversial in terms of values. Sex research involving children is both. The remainder of this paper will suggest ways in which an institutional review board might interpret the recommendations when judging a protocol for sex research using children as subjects.

The first specific question to be asked about the proposed research is "whether it entails risks or discomforts to the children greater than those normally encountered in their daily lives or in routine medical or psychological evaluations." The Commission expands on this by referring to "modest changes in diet or schedule, immunization, physical examination, obtaining blood or urine specimens and developmental assessments. Many tools of behavioral research, such as most questionaires, psychological tests or puzzles, may also be considered of minimal risk" [52].

Can the "tools of behavioral research" be so easily considered of minimal risk when the behavior under investigation is sexual behavior? It is important to review the available literature on this controversial point.

Let us first summarize children's responses to research. There appears to be little risk to the child subject from research involving unobtrusive measures, including discreet observation. Observational data might pose some risk if it were used to embarrass the child or to impose constraints on behavior that might not be in the child's best interests. One might also argue that individuals of any age are entitled to know when they are being systematically observed and when their behavior is being recorded.

Investigators who have interviewed child subjects or administered questionnaires to children report very few responses indicative of distress. Children in the Moore and Kendall study of reproductive concepts

did not appear anxious in the interviewing situation; some did appear disheartened that they did not have responses to the questions asked. As students in an experimental school, they had all experienced testing previously and many were either sufficiently bright or competitive or both that they wanted to perform well [36].

The minor distress experienced here appears unrelated to the sexual content of the study. The concept that asking questions will "put ideas in their heads" was not supported by the work of Bernstein and Cowan, whose results "suggest strongly that children actively construct their notions about babies; they don't wait to be told about procreation before they have an idea of how it occurs. What may be taken as misinformation may largely be a product of their own assimilative processes at work on materials with too complex a structure for them to understand" [35]. The consensus of investigators who have worked with prepubescent children of various ages is that children tend to gloss over questions that they do not understand and screen out material that is not relevant to their current interests or compatible with their level of development. Given the extensive use of erotic material in advertising and in the media, including television, the average child is exposed to a spate of stimuli that could conceivably elicit erotic responses. In order to determine whether questions or procedures used in a given study would produce additional stimulation, one would have to have some idea of what the child encounters in everyday experience. The experience of children would vary from one subcultural milieu to another, from one family to another, and as a function of the individual child's age and level of maturity. In general, it is reasonable for a review committee to consider nonintrusive research as posing minimal risk, even when it involves direct questioning.

What of novel procedures, such as new modes of observation or new levels or types of explicitness? Is it possible to make an assessment of risks of procedures for which there is little or no precedent? One could, of course, adopt the position that no procedures or content be used beyond those already proven innocuous by previous studies. But this would produce a stalemate—new information is needed in order to expand the boundaries of acceptable research, and the boundaries of research must be expanded in order to provide new information. A somewhat more open attitude would be to test new procedures by small increments. For example, if a given questionnaire or procedure has produced no untoward results with a sample of children, subsequent investigators might feel secure in increasing the explicitness, the intrusiveness, or the inquisitiveness of the procedures by some small increment or by one "just noticeable difference." Another position—which could be combined with the second attitude—would be to avoid procedures that have been demonstrably harmful to child subjects in the short term and to avoid any methodology that incorporates experiences substantially beyond those to which the child would presumably be exposed in the natural environment.

The natural environment varies according to social class and economic status, among other factors; it differs for healthy children and those who suffer chronic disorders. It is strikingly different in different cultures. In order to determine the normal experience of a given group of children, it is necessary to look carefully at the structure of their environment. One can identify natural environments in which there is treatment of children (for example, those with chronic disorders, the institutionalized, and those whose sexual behavior has brought them into contact with law enforcement or judicial agencies). The normal experience of such children might surpass in stressfulness any methodology contemplated by researchers. On the other hand, the experiences of children who have been traumatized by medical investigative procedures can serve as caveats for investigators.

An instance of the use of diagnostic procedures that proved harmful to children with endocrine disorders is reported by Money and Walker [53]. Because of the principle involved, it appears useful to describe this study in some detail. Fifteen girls, initially examined at a Johns Hopkins pediatric endocrinology clinic because of precocious pubertal development, were subsequently referred to a psychohormonal research unit. The girls were interviewed at the research unit, and those old enough to respond were given questionnaires to complete. Both parents of each study subject were also interviewed. The girls, none of whom was younger than age 10 at the time of the last interview, were followed for periods of up to 18 years. During the course of their interviews with these girls, Money and Walker discovered that previous diagnostic procedures had produced severe adverse reactions, which they describe in the following excerpt:

Reactions to nudity for medical photography and vaginal examinations were explicitly recorded in 6 cases. In the other 9 cases nudity was not an explicit issue. Unconcern over nudity for medical photography was overtly indicated once. In five cases—33% of the sample—reactions to nudity and vaginal examinations ranged from distress to extreme phobic avoidance. One girl, aged 8-4/12, refused to undress in the presence of anyone. Another girl, aged 6-11/12, refused to allow her mother to bathe her or her gynecologist-father to take nude photographs of her. Nude medical photography was a source of embarrassment and severe stress for another girl, aged 7-1/12, who was also "disgusted" over her pediatrician's attempt to conduct a vaginal examination. Vaginal examinations and vaginal smear tests were responded to by two girls, aged 4-6/12 and 6-7/12, as violently upsetting. The origin of intense phobic reaction to nudity and vaginal examinations, when it occurs, has not been traced. When it does occur, however, it is so powerful that it may result in refusal, defiance, and determination to escape that completely negate the physician's endeavors on the child's behalf. Such a reaction is a psychologic danger signal not to be taken lightly. Its resolution requires collaboration of both the mother and the daughter in a program of case management. It may require that the child be examined only by a female physician, and the same one on each return visit. It also requires that the child be helped to comprehend why, whereas the doctor's words say that she is normal except for growing too fast, his actions convey the message that she is a curious creature, if not a freak, to be poked at, examined, X-rayed, and photographed. Children, like adults, are helped by understanding the rationale of what is done to them, and why, in a medical examination. Otherwise they are too susceptible to overconcern with their physician's insistent attentiveness to their genitalia [53].

Children with psychohormonal abnormalities or gender identity conflict unquestionably encounter childhood experiences quite different from those of their normal peers. If they are diagnosed and receive counseling or treatment, they will necessarily experience some highly reactive procedures. However, they constitute a population for whom relatively intrusive research might prove to be *less* stressful than the results of being allowed to develop without professional treatment or counseling. Nonetheless, as Money and Walker have stated, it is incumbent on the clinician or researcher to mitigate the adverse effects of his or her procedures insofar as possible. Callous responses by the researcher can exacerbate the distress of a child who is already implicitly labeled "misfit" or "freak" by parents, peers, and clinicians. In contrast, the concerned and sensitive clinician or researcher can make the investigative environment safer and more supportive than the natural environment. Green, who has worked extensively with children with gender problems, describes some of the measures taken by his group to minimize the possibility of trauma to his subjects [54]:

1. Spell out the risks to the child and to the parents, including the possibility that the study will increase the child's attention to his or her gender identity conflict and aggravate parent-child dissension.
2. Obtain informed consent of both parents and children (after risk factors have been elucidated).
3. Provide the child with a card enabling him or her to make collect calls to the investigator or directly to the Human Experimentation Committee. (This committee is prepared to handle grievances, if any, from children or parents.)
4. Make therapeutic interventions during interviews, when therapy appears indicated because of the child's stressful reactions to current life events. (Such interventions should be made when necessary, even at the cost of confounding or losing research data from a subject.)

The foregoing example illustrates the principle that measures for minimizing risks can be incorporated in those studies in which potential benefits must be weighed against a high potential for adverse effects. It also calls attention to an important dictum in using child subjects whose ordinary experience is stressful or atypical as a result of physical, emotional, or sociocultural disadvantages: namely, that the researcher not regard the child's disadvantaged situation as license to ignore the child's personal welfare. Rather, within the boundaries imposed by the child's condition, the investigator should make every effort to avoid procedures that are likely to produce stress, even though comparable stress might be a common element of the child's ordinary experience.

The reactions of the girls with precocious pubertal development in the study described above [53] provide some basis for assessing the risks one might encounter in performing a study of the genital anatomy and physiology of children (for example, an approximation of Masters and Johnson's study of adult sexual response [14]). One would expect comparable reactions to any procedure that offended the child's sense of modesty or propriety or that encroached upon the integrity of the child's body. However, it is noteworthy that some of the children in Money's sample did not appear to have reacted negatively to nudity, medical photography, and vaginal examinations (in contrast to those who reported severe distress). It is important to consider individual differences both in the children themselves (and their backgrounds) and in the personal characteristics and research strategies of the investigators. There may be children—perhaps from families with accepting attitudes toward nudity and sexuality—who would not react adversely to genital examinations conducted under conditions designed to minimize anxiety. (Pediatricians do, in fact, examine children's genitals when such examinations are indicated.) It seems plausible that children who have not been taught to view themselves as freaks would be less likely to register a phobic reaction to such examinations.

Although a few sex educators [11] have suggested that parents might facilitate later adult sexual health by encouraging their children's sexuality and Money [10] has suggested the value of sexual rehearsal play, it is unlikely that studies in which children are asked to stimulate their own genitals (or allow them to be stimulated by others) would pass public scrutiny. Even if an investigator were to find parents who would agree to their children's participation and children who were willing to participate, many years would have to elapse before the effects of participation on adult sexual adjustment could be assessed. The risk factor of such a long-term study cannot be evaluated.

Cross-cultural studies permit some evaluation of children's reactions to sexual stimulation in situations in which it is socially sanctioned [55, 56]. Observations of children in preliterate societies in which sex play is permissible before adolescence indicate that there is nothing inherently traumatic in such activity; rather, trauma occurs when childhood impulses collide with adult disapproval. In many societies there are societally prescribed rituals for initiating prepubescent children into sexual practices, often under the tutelage of adults.

Children in our own society who engage in prepubertal sexual activity meet with powerful cultural taboos. Studies reporting reactions of children who have been sexually involved with adults provide evidence of this [57–59]. Further evidence is found in the Kinsey data collected from adult males who had had sexual contact with prepubescent children [13]. Such reports may provide a basis for assessing the response of children in our own society to sexual stimulation and for estimating the range of variation in children's capacity to accommodate to research designs that are relatively high in intrusiveness and explicitness.

A moderate proportion of women in our society have had some preadolescent sexual contact with adult males: Kinsey [31] found that 24 percent of his sample of 4,441 women reported such contact. Some children register severe reactions to such contact, but it is unclear whether such reactions follow from the behavior itself or from adult reactions to it [60]. A number of researchers concur in the belief that children with adequate ego strength can undergo potentially damaging sexual experiences, even repeatedly, without sustaining long-term emotional trauma or impaired sexual adjustment in adulthood [61–65]. These researchers concur in identifying extreme adult reactions after the event as a major source of emotional disturbance for the child. Another research finding relevant to the capacity for sexual experience manifested by some children is the observation that children involved sexually with adults may have played a cooperative or initiatory role in the interaction [63, 65, 66]. Gebhard comments on the ethical implications of this finding as follows:

The "victim" is often a willing sexual partner and even sometimes a seductive one, but if the person is under a certain age our social ethics definitely necessitate legal protection of the "object-victim" in such a situation [67].

One group of children who usually sustain trauma as a result of sexual contact with adults are those who have been raped or otherwise subjected to force or duress [20].

PERMISSION OF PARENTS

Children can be enrolled as subjects of research with consent of their "legally authorized representatives." We cited earlier the dispute among ethicists over this point: Some maintain that it applies only to beneficial activities, while others contend that it encompasses activities that are not directly beneficial but involve no risk or minimal risk to the subject. The Commission for the Protection of Human Subjects relies heavily on parents and family as the child subject's primary protective agents. It departs from the "thin" notion of proxy consent to a richer concept of parental permission and participation, involving not only a detailed knowledge of what the research will entail but also a close involvement and sometimes even physical presence during the conduct of research. However, the Commission recognizes that some children do not dwell within a protective familial unit and that some types of research that might be highly desirable, such as study of child abuse, cannot be carried out with strict adherence to the mandate of parental permission. Such research is allowable only if some effective mechanism can be devised to protect the child's interests.

The strong insistence on parental permission and participation poses a particular problem for sex research. There is some evidence pointing to a more general acceptance of sexuality as a natural part of childhood [11]. This attitude is accompanied by increased parental concern for teaching children concepts of time, place, and responsibility as means of directing sexual behavior into socially approved channels. The encouraging trend toward parental acceptance and attendant concerns may in time modify an attitude that has seriously hampered research into childhood sexuality: the notion that sexual ignorance preserves the innocence of the child. Despite the weight of evidence that repression of childhood sexual interests and condemnation of early sexual behavior has exacted a high toll in sexual dysfunction among adults [68], many parents still prefer to keep their children uninformed about sex. The parental concerns encountered by Sorensen [69] in his survey of adolescent sexuality reflect the attitudes of many parents toward the presumed innocence of their young and adolescent children. Sorensen's research team initially selected 839 adolescents aged 13 to 19 for interviews about their sexual behavior. Only 508 parental units gave permission for their children to participate in the study; one might expect that the rate of consent would decline sharply for a comparable sample of younger children. Parents who were opposed to their children's participation cited a variety of ostensible reasons for demurring (for example, "It wouldn't matter to me, but she wouldn't want to"; and "My 14- and 12-year-old are either at school or at home where there is no opportunity for sex play. If they don't have sex, you don't need to talk about it with them"). Others were more forthright in expressing their opposition (for example, stating apprehension that the interview "might put some ideas in her head she don't know"). One Texas mother was reported as saying, "They don't need to know, talk, study so much about sex. Leave it alone, and they will be better off" [69].

The arguments advanced by parents for withholding permission for sex research with children are familiar ones, echoes of the long-standing controversy over sex education in the schools [34] and of polemics against eroticism in films [70]. The convictions of these parents are sometimes rooted in absolutes acquired from their religious training or from early family teaching; often they are reinforced by strong feelings of anxiety about the erosion of parental control and values and by powerful mistrust and anger directed at the amorphous adversary. These assumptions, because of their tenacious emotional taproots, are unlikely to yield readily to logic or to empirical data. For example, opponents of sex education have remained unconvinced by evidence that promiscuity, unplanned pregnancy, and venereal disease appear to be less prevalent in school districts with sex education programs than in districts without such programs. However, in fairness to parents who hold conservative views on sex education, definitive evaluations of the effects of sex education with various age groups have yet to be made. Detractors have also claimed that the sexual ideologies propagated by many sex researchers contain biases reflecting white middle-class notions about what sex should be, rather than representing the broad spectrum of sexual mores in our society [34].

The willingness or unwillingness of parents to give proxy consent for their children to participate in sex research is closely tied to their assumptions about the benefits and risks of providing children with information about sex. There is some evidence that the alternative to providing sexual information is not necessarily blissful ignorance, even in the case of very young children. An information deficit in an area of human experience creates a vacuum that is liable to be filled by myth and superstition more damaging than the facts. For example, Kreitler and Kreitler [37], found that a high percentage of children in their sample, lacking accurate information, had confabulated their own concepts of gestation and birth. They frequently pictured the embryo as frightened and sad in the dreary confines of the womb. Many of the children believed that the baby was liberated from its uterine prison by cutting open the mother's abdomen. It is difficult to believe that these concepts are more reassuring to the child than accurate information.

Children who are denied factual information often obtain their sex education from the garbled accounts of peers, from locker-room vulgarity, or from pornography. Investigating the sex education of matched samples of adult sex offenders, other offenders, and controls, Goldstein and Kant [71] found pornographic materials encountered during adolescence to be the major source of sex education for a high proportion of their respondents.

The data further suggest that children readily reinterpret any information given to them. Sex researchers, sex educators, and others who provide children with information about sex should attempt to discover whether the message received is the same as the message sent. Review boards might ask investigators to comment on this disparity of information as one of the possible risks of their studies.

Irrespective of the arguments for or against providing the child with sex information, researchers have had little choice but to restrict their sampling to children whose parents were willing for them to participate. As a consequence, studies using biased samples have yielded results that could not readily be generalized to other groups. This is another potential hazard that researchers face when they encounter parental opposition.

Parental opposition, even when based on massive distortion of the actual details of the study, has been known to spread through a community and infect an entire sample. The parents of one child accused Broderick of "Communism" and "Kinseyism" for trying to conduct a relatively low-key survey designed to solicit information from fifth- to twelfth-grade students about dating, falling in love, and kissing [72]. The child's parents enlisted the support of the local press and launched a successful telephone campaign to discourage other parents in the community from granting permission for their children's participation. As a result, the heterogeneity of the sample was reduced.

One strategy that is used to allay parental anxieties about their children's participation is to invite the parent(s) to be present at the interview [13, 31, 36]. Kinsey's research team interviewed children aged seven and younger in the presence of their parents; this age group appeared more comfortable with their parents present. By contrast, children over seven years of age were interviewed alone because the older children as a group appeared less comfortable with their parents present [73].

The age of the child is an important consideration in the parents' decision to grant permission. Sorensen found some parents initially reluctant to allow their 13- to 15-year-old children to be interviewed for a survey of adolescent sexuality [69]. Sorensen's researchers were themselves concerned about the possibility of disturbing the sensitivities or naiveté of subjects in this age group. After much deliberation, the research team decided to include them because of the importance of the information to be gained from younger adolescents.

The nature of the research also may influence parental decisions. Studies incorporating research procedures that could be described as relatively low in intrusiveness, explicitness, and inquisitiveness would probably elicit more parental cooperation than studies high in these dimensions. Additional factors that would be reassuring to parents are the established reputations and academic affiliations of the investigators and the use of an academic or other "respectable" physical setting for the research.

In order to understand the nature of parental concerns, researchers must appreciate the family as a rule-governed system. When the family is viewed in this light, parents may be seen as regarding sexuality as an area over which they wish to retain control. They may regard regulation of their children's sexual behavior as a mechanism for maintaining homeostasis within the family system. They may recognize, explicitly or implicitly, that rules concerning sexual behavior are closely linked to parental authority in general, to religious values, and to the family's established life-style. If parents believe research will introduce into this system information antithetical to their own values, they may consider their children's participation as a threat to family solidarity. In some instances, parents may permit an older child to participate, while refusing the researcher access to younger siblings.

The concerns voiced by parents may also reflect uneasiness lest their own privacy be invaded or their own beliefs challenged by the research. Broderick [72] encountered parental opposition related to the following specific points: (a) parents' objections to the inclusion of questionnaire items asking for names and parents' occupation(s); (b) the question of whether students and faculty at a nearby university would have access to the data; and (c) parents' concerns that the subjects' responses would consist of either common knowledge or "tall tales," because "any good parent knows whether his child is involved in any of those things." Implicit in these concerns is the common assumption that the child is an extension of the parent. In this context, the issue of risk to the child may be subsidiary to parents' concern for their own well-being, as they perceive it.

If consent from parents is to be truly informed, the parent would need to know the subject matter of the study, the method of investigation, and the possible consequences for the child. In addition, if the child's right to privacy is to be respected, the parent would require reassurance that the content of a given child's responses will not be divulged. Although ethically sound, providing parents with advance information about the details of the study may create a methodological dilemma for the investigator: In at least one instance that can be documented [72], advance information resulted in the invalidation of one block of data. In the previously mentioned study, Broderick purposely refrained from informing parents that questionnaires would be distributed in their children's classrooms, because he feared that parents would bias responses by coaching their children. His apprehensions were realized when students in one classroom provided clear evidence that they had been coached by their teacher; the entire classroom gave an identical response to every projective question: "I do not know. I have not had the *experience.*" Even the underlining was uniform [72].

An interesting ethical issue would arise should a parent refuse to let his or her child participate in a study involving a group of which the child was a part (for example, a school class). If only a few children are excluded from a group study because of parental unwillingness, they may feel deprived of an experience that has been presented as fun or they may be distressed by their parents' inexplicable behavior. At the least, they would feel discriminated against as having been excluded from a group activity, perhaps without understanding the reason for their exclusion. Therefore, it appears important for investigators to design selection procedures that would minimize the excluded child's distress.

When parents acquiesce to the child's participation, the researcher is faced with the need to obtain informed assent from the child as well. The protocol for obtaining assent will vary according to the age and level of comprehension of the child involved. In order for the child to assess his willingness to cooperate, the child is entitled to know what to expect—what the research participation will entail. The description of the subject matter of the project should be given in terms that the child can understand. The child should also be informed of the provisions for maintaining confidentiality. It is conceivable that in some instances, parents may grant consent for the participation of children who themselves are hesitant or unwilling to participate. Children may also feel coerced by group pressure to participate. In order to preserve the child's autonomy, the researcher must be alert to any signs of reluctance or ambivalence in the child and must make the child fully aware that nonparticipation is an acceptable option.

The device of project monitor or ombudsman may be employed to deal with many of these problems. Parents may be reassured and more cooperative if they know that someone whom they trust (and who is not otherwise associated with the research) is acting as "overseer" for the project. Children who are reluctant to refuse to participate or embarrassed to withdraw might be encouraged to present their difficulties to this monitor. The monitors themselves might be on guard for signs of distress or lack of cooperation in subjects. They may also assist the researcher in assessing risks and benefits and in soliciting assent from subjects in a manner that is fair, honest, comprehensive, and comprehensible. A monitor should have the authority to withdraw a child from a project and even to recommend to an institutional review board that a project be modified or terminated, for valid reasons.

We have attempted to show that the risk-benefit calculation required for any ethical judgment about research involving children might be converted into an estimate of the reactivity of sex research. The more intrusive, inquisitive, and explicit the research methodology and tools, the higher the risk of effecting changes in attitudes about sex and sexual behavior. Since the possibility of effecting changes over which parents have little or no control is probably the principal deterrent factor in securing parental permission for children's participation in research, the judgment of investigators and institutional review boards regarding the reactivity of a study should be communicated fully to parents or guardians. For most types of research, parental fears of loss of control can be assuaged or even eliminated by informing them of the index of reactivity of the project and attempting to involve them in the actual conduct of the investigation in ways compatible with the research design. When this is not possible, the active involvement of a project monitor may accomplish the same end. In sum, it is our judgment that most forms of sex research with children can be performed in a manner that meets ethical standards in research.

TREATMENT-RELATED RESEARCH

An examination of the ethics of sex research involving children would be incomplete without some consideration of the implications of research in which treatment of sex-related problems in children is the principal object of study. In some instances, sex-related problems in children may be treated by psychotherapeutic, behavioral, medical, or surgical procedures as part of a formal study; in other instances, treatment of an individual child or a few individuals may result in generalizable knowledge that is subsequently published as research, although the original objective was solely therapeutic change. Thus, whether or not it is so designated at the outset, any case in treatment has the potential for becoming the subject of published research. It is important, therefore, to view treatment not only within its own context but also from the perspective of research.

Children under the age of puberty and postpubescent nonemancipated minors constitute two groups who might be involved in treatment-related research under either of the conditions described above. It is clear from the clinical literature and from unpublished reports of practitioners who treat children and adolescents that psychodynamically oriented psychotherapy, behavior modification, and medical and surgical procedures comprise the major methods used to treat young people for a variety of sex-related problems. Some of the patients (usually the older ones) are self-referred; others are brought to treatment by parents, institutional or agency personnel, or other adults in authority. The problems for which these young patients are being treated include psychohormonal, gender, and sexual identity disorders; sequelae of incest, rape, and other sexual contact with adults; sexual behaviors offensive to adults in authority (for example, public masturbation or sexual advances to peers by institutionalized retardates); venereal and other sex-related diseases; problems associated with contraception and pregnancy; and emotional or behavioral problems diagnosed as symptomatic of sexual conflicts. In addition, there are reports from practitioners at family planning clinics and adolescent clinics that young patients are presenting with complaints of sexual dysfunction—even though the treatability of these problems and the appropriateness of seeking treatment for them has not yet gained full acceptance among adults. It is obvious that contraceptive and pregnancy-related services and treatment for sexual dysfunction would be sought only by those who are already sexually active or who intend to become so; however, pregnancy statistics for girls aged 10 to 13 suggest that the incidence of sexual activity among young children is increasing significantly. As a result, the treatment of newly pubescent and even prepubescent children for sex-related problems may become much more common, accompanied by a corresponding need for research to evaluate the effects of treatment.

The recommendations of the National Commission for the Protection of Human Subjects relevant to research with children have been summarized in a previous section. These recommendations outline suggestions for minimizing risk and criteria for determining whether the potential benefits outweigh potential risks to the child, as well as measures for gaining the informed consent and assent of the child and of parents (or of other adults *in loco parentis*). These recommendations apply to all types of research involving child subjects, including clinical or treatment-related research. But when treatment is an issue, the interpretation and application of the Commission's recommendations require more complex decision-making, more attention to the nuances of each individual case, than is necessary in nonclinical research. For example, failure to be accepted as a subject in survey research may have only minor consequences for a child; but the child under consideration for treatment of a severe sex-related disorder has much more at stake. Either decision—to treat or not to treat—has profound implications for the child. The possible consequences of treating the child may be only partially predictable. Treatment is intended to be highly reactive—its objective is change (this is in sharp contrast to survey research, for example, which incorporates measures designed to minimize reactivity). One expects treatment procedures to act upon the child to produce change—although not necessarily the change that was intended. Given the multitude of variables that impinge upon the child within his or her complex ecological system, the individual differences among children, and the paucity of adequately validated treatment procedures, it is not yet possible to predict consistent and precise outcomes.

Even if specific change could be consistently programmed, simply deciding what constitutes therapeutic change poses a formidable dilemma. It is important to remember that the selection of a specific treatment objective for a child with a sex-related problem reflects a specific set of beliefs about what is healthy or normal or "best for the child." Yet such decisions are being made in a cultural milieu in which sexual mores and practices are themselves changing at an unprecedented rate. It is not unlikely that two sets of experts evaluating a given child's sexual behavior might find themselves polarized. One group might label the behavior an aberration calling for drastic change; the other group might regard it as a natural and allowable option in a pluralistic society. In view of the high degree of variability in the area of sexual values and beliefs, many conflicts are likely to occur regarding the necessity for treatment of sex-related problems in children. Parents may object to children's requests for treatment (for example, a young woman who wants to take oral contraceptives); children may resist parents' attempts to treat them for conditions that the children do not define as problematic; investigators may disagree with child or parents or both about the necessity for treatment.

Given that the risk-benefit ratio may be exceptionally difficult to assess in treatment-related research and that informed consent and assent of both parent (or parent surrogate) and child may be difficult to obtain, what are the implications for investigators and review boards? In summary, the principles to be used in making decisions appear to be identical to those enunciated in previous sections of this paper. However, their implementation is more difficult. In contrast to the basic researcher who may simply abandon a project if he or she cannot make a precise determination of risks, the clinician-researcher cannot resolve a dilemma merely by deciding not to treat. The decision not to treat a patient who may be experiencing severe distress is a decision with serious ethical implications. There are no simple formulas that can be applied to decision-making, either by clinician-researchers or by clinicians in general.

It is important for the clinician-researcher to be able to combine both the clinical and research roles. If, in making clinical decisions, he or she were to function primarily as a clinician, the clinician-researcher would then be justified in doing what clinicians must do routinely: deciding to treat or not to treat on the basis of clinical acumen and the best available data, with full awareness that treatment implies some element of risk. It is important also that clinical needs take precedence over research needs when the well-being of the patient-subject necessitates some deviation from the research design. On the other hand, the role of the researcher would prevail with respect to obtaining informed consent, protecting the privacy of the patient-subject, and instituting all possible measures (such as requesting the appointment of a project monitor) that might alleviate or circumvent potential problems arising from the patient-subject's participation in the project. Finally, one additional area of responsibility rests with the clinician-researcher: the responsibility of persuading the hesitant or recalcitrant patient-subject or parent when the clinician is convinced that treatment is strongly indicated. In other words, parents and participants must be informed not only of the risks and benefits of participation but also of the risks (and benefits, if any) of *non*participation.

RESEARCH WITH THE MENTALLY RETARDED

It is not uncommon to link children and the mentally retarded when questions are raised about ethical treatment of the retarded. However, the linkage may be less than helpful. Of course, prepubescent retarded persons *are* children, and the same ethical considerations would apply to both groups, for the most part. But considerations that would approve some intervention in the life of a normal child on the basis of its anticipated contribution to maturation may not obtain in the case of a retarded child.

Once the retarded individual has entered puberty, the comparison is even less apt. While intelligence may be measured in ways that make the older retarded appear similar to children, many genuine differences separate the two groups. In considering the retarded as a potential research population—in particular, for purposes of sex research—physical maturity, awareness of sexual activities, emotions and attitudes related to sex, and readiness for masturbation and sexual contact with others are all variables that cannot be disregarded (despite the unfortunate tendency to consider the retarded as being sexless). Finally, since many retarded persons live in institutions or under supervision, the effects and influences of institutionalization must be taken into account.

Questions concerning the sexuality of the retarded and, a fortiori, questions related to research about their sexuality, deserve much more ample treatment than a few pages at the end of a long essay. Unfortunately, the National Commission for the Protection of Human Subjects does not provide the same guidance with regard to the retarded as it does in the case of children. Its mandate required it to study the problems of research with the "institutionalized mentally infirm." This omnibus category—so designated more by de rigueur style of legislative language than by the dictates of psychology or psychiatry—includes the retarded, the senile, and the psychotic, but excludes persons (even persons in these three groups) who do not live under the authority of an institution. This essay, on the other hand, considers only the retarded, both institutionalized and living independently or with family. Thus, the Commission's recommendations are only partially relevant to our topic. We must conclude that a complete and satisfactory treatment of the subject of sex research with the retarded is hardly possible at this time. We therefore confine ourselves to a statement of some considerations that might serve as elements of a more adequate future treatment of the topic.

A number of studies of the sexual knowledge, attitudes, and behavior of the retarded have been published [74]. However, there remain massive gaps in our empirical knowledge of the sexuality of retarded persons. Doubtless, research proposals to remedy this informational deficit will be forthcoming. Edgerton suggests the following areas as having high priority for research in the field [75]: (1) the relationship between sexual behavior and self-esteem; (2) self-control of sexual behavior among the retarded; (3) the ability of the retardate to use contraceptive devices; (4) the right versus the ability of the retardate to marry and have children; (5) public attitudes toward the sexual behavior of the retarded and their influence on the retardate; and (6) new methods of sex education for and about the retarded.

Mental retardation has been defined as

subaverage general intellectual functioning which originates during the developmental period and is associated with impairment in one or more of the following: (1) maturation, (2) learning, (3) social adjustment. Subaverage refers to performance more than one standard deviation below the population mean [76].

This definition is very broad. Any diagnosis of mental retardation invokes complex and controversial criteria for intellectual, emotional, and social functioning. Moreover, the mentally retarded are not all alike: Not only are there a variety of forms of retardation based on different medical and psychological criteria, but within these different forms there are individual differences in cognitive ability, emotional stability, social skills, and sexual behavior. In particular, the sexual behavior and attitudes of retarded adults are as heterogeneous as those found among groups of nonretarded adults. By no means do retarded individuals match the two polar stereotypes—sexually naive (or asexual) and promiscuous (or impulse-ridden) [77, 78]. Investigators conducting sex research with children find that parents consistently underestimate the level of sexual knowledge and liberality of attitude of their normal children; the same judgment appears to be true of those charged with care of the retarded. A study of 61 noninstitutionalized mildly and moderately retarded adolescents found subjects to be significantly more liberal in their sexual ethics than their parents predicted (although parents did accurately predict their children's sex knowledge scores) [79].

It is imperative for those who propose to do sex research involving the retarded (and those who must make judgments about the ethical acceptability of such research) to recognize the equivocal nature of the diagnosis and the great diversity of personal characteristics of persons so diagnosed. The National Commission does this in its recommendations on research involving the institutionalized mentally infirm. The Commission asserts that some persons who fall into this category may be quite capable of giving informed consent. It introduces the concept of assent by acknowledging that some persons, though intellectually or emotionally impaired, have the capacity to understand and to direct their lives in certain ways. The Commission affirms that for research involving no more than minimal risk, the assent of the subject is sufficient [80].

The foregoing recommendation leads to a second consideration relevant to sex research. It is quite difficult to determine what might constitute "no more than minimal risk" for persons designated as mentally retarded. In the case of the institutionalized mentally infirm, the Commission defines minimal risk as "the risk (probability and magnitude of physical or psychological harm or discomfort) that is normally encountered in the daily lives or in the routine medical or psychological examination of normal persons" [Recommendation 2] [80]. This means that the impact of a procedure should be no greater for a person who is mentally infirm than for any normal person undergoing the procedure. However, if we return to the concept of reactivity introduced earlier in this paper, we may wonder whether the impact of sexual information might not be significantly different on a retarded person than on either a normal child or an unimpaired adult. If so, would provision of (or deliberate exposure to) such information constitute more than minimal risk for a retarded person?

The physical maturity of retarded persons who are not chronologically children makes possible overt behavior that is unlikely to occur in children. The provision of sex-related information could be harmful to those whose understanding of self and of social relationships is impaired. One potentially dangerous situation is the possibility of unplanned impregnation and pregnancy. Another risk is the possibility of socially inappropriate behavior, which could even lead to criminal charges: The research might provide information that subjects, because of diminished capacity to interpret it or to integrate it into behavior, could translate into inappropriate activities. (Obviously, *inappropriate* will mean different things to different judges—but it is clear that an unforeseen and unintended instigation to sexual overtures in public would create more alarm than an unintended inducement to masturbation in private.) Even more serious would be the possibility of sexual exploitation of the retarded person as an unintended consequence of participation in research. In sum, review boards must scrutinize most thoroughly the latent potential for reactivity in proposed research. If the above cautions are observed, persons conducting sex research with the mildly or moderately retarded—particularly those living with parents or parent surrogates—can generally consider their subjects as normal in all respects except those in which they exhibit deficiencies. Invitations to participate in research must be designed to respect those deficiencies, rather than taking advantage of them.

The assessment of risk can lead both the research and the reviewers of research in a vicious circle: One cannot judge the reactivity of providing sex-related information without studying the
actual reaction of subjects to whom it is provided; yet, one cannot
study their reaction without first estimating the risk. Researchers
and reviewers must proceed with caution, scrutinizing the nature
of the information, attempting to find analogies, utilizing the
technique of the "just noticeable difference" to test new procedures. In general, however, it can be said that when mentally retarded subjects are judged capable of informed consent or assent
and when the research involves no more than minimal risk—and
when both the capacity of the subject and the risks of the research
are evaluated by cautious and prudent persons—the involvement of
these subjects in sex research would be permissible.

Clearly, the researchers and the reviewers must make the requisite evaluation; they will presumably be cautious and prudent persons. However, it may sometimes be necessary to request the judgment of someone who is more impartial than the researchers and
more intimately acquainted with the subjects than are the reviewers. The Commission suggests that a "consent auditor" be appointed whenever the subject's capacity to consent or assent is in
question; it requires the presence of such a person when the research involves more than minimal risk and does not hold out
promise of direct benefit for the subject. Sex research with the retarded is likely to qualify on both counts: doubt about capacity
and uncertainty regarding risks. In such situations, the reviewers
would be well advised to appoint a consent auditor. This role
should be filled by someone who is independent of the research
team, responsible only to the institutional review board, and familiar with the physical, psychological, and social needs of the prospective subjects as well as their legal status [Recommendations 2,
3] [80].

A final set of considerations concerns the benefits of sex research
to the retarded individuals or to the class of persons designated as
retarded. The Commission requires full justification for the use of
the retarded population for research. In general, that justification
would turn on prospective benefits of the research to the members
of that population (whether they be the individuals on whom the

research is to be done or other, future members). It would be difficult to offer as justification prospective benefits to normal persons; it would be impossible to accept this reasoning if the research involved more than minimal risk.

For the most part, any proposed research that involves more than minimal risks should hold out promise of therapeutic benefit to the subject. It is conceivable that sex research might include experimental techniques of behavior modification aimed at reducing harmful or unacceptable sexual behavior. In such cases, risks somewhat more than minimal could be tolerated in prospect of individual benefit. Certain other types of research (for example, attempts to discover whether retarded persons can utilize contraceptives) may be intended to benefit the subject, but may also be quite risky—in the example cited, failure to achieve responsible contraception might result in unwanted pregnancy. Such benefit-oriented research should not be undertaken without effective reduction of the risks.

Finally, the relevance of any sex research with the retarded might be questioned. The Commission does not require that all research involving the mentally infirm be "significant" or "relevant," since it is unlikely that any general definitions or measures of these qualities could be devised to act as criteria. However, it insists that for research with more than minimal risk involving subjects with impaired capacity to consent, "the anticipated knowledge (1) be of vital importance for the understanding or amelioration of the type of disorder or condition of the subjects, or (2) may reasonably be expected to benefit the subjects in the future" [Recommendation 4] [80]. Should sex research involving a retarded population ever require such stringent justification, the involvement of a legally appointed guardian is mandatory. If the risks appear to be more than small increments to the minimum-risk criterion, the research must be reviewed by a national ethical advisory board (which the Commission recommends be established) [Recommendation 5] [80].

In conclusion, one final consideration about the relevance of research must be mentioned, although it involves major value assumptions. Research into the sexuality of children is justified by the intent to understand, correct, and improve sexual development in order to promote the eventual state of satisfying and responsible adult sexuality. In contrast, it might be thought that research into the sexuality of retarded persons, particularly those who are unlikely ever to be able to enter into responsible sexual relationships, has little or no purpose other than satisfying the curiosity of the researcher. Clearly, this objection can be refuted in cases where the research is aimed at aiding persons suffering from behavior disorders harmful to themselves or to others. Response to the broader challenge depends on more thoughtful reflection about the place of sexuality in the lives of those who suffer severe limitations in their intellectual and emotional capabilities. That thoughtful reflection lies beyond the bounds of this essay.

REFERENCES

1. Katz, J. *Experimentation with Human Beings.* New York: Russell Sage Foundation, 1972. Pp. 1007–1010.
2. Trials of War Criminals before the Nuremberg Military Tribunals. *United States* v. *Karl Brandt.* Washington, D.C.: U.S. Government Printing Office, 1949. Vol. 2, p. 181.
3. World Medical Association. Declaration of Helsinki, 1964. In H. Beecher, *Research and the Individual: Human Studies.* Boston: Little, Brown, 1970. P. 277.
4. American Medical Association. Ethical Guidelines for Clinical Investigations. In H. Beecher, *Research and the Individual: Human Studies.* Boston: Little, Brown, 1970. P. 223.
5. U.S. Department of Health, Education, and Welfare. *The Institutional Guide to DHEW Policy on Protection of Human Subjects.* DHEW Publication No. (NIH) 72–102 (Washington, D.C.: U.S. Government Printing Office, 1971). P. 71.
6. Medical Research Council, Great Britain. Responsibility in Investigations on Human Subjects. In H. Beecher, *Research and the Individual: Human Studies.* Boston: Little, Brown, 1970. Pp. 262–265.
7. Ramsey, P. The enforcement of morals: Non-therapeutic research on children. *Hastings Center Report* 6(4):21–30, 1976.
8. McCormick, R. Proxy consent in the experimental situation. *Perspectives in Biology and Medicine* 18:2–20, 1974.
9. Freud, S. Three Essays on Sexuality. In S. Freud, *Standard Edition of the Complete Psychological Works.* London: Hogarth, 1953. Vol. 7, pp. 135–245.

10. Money, J. Childhood: The last frontier in sex research. *The Sciences* 16(6):12–15, 27; 1976.
11. Johnson, W. R. Childhood sexuality: The last of the great taboos? *SIECUS Report* 5:1–2, 15; 1977.
12. Byrne, D. Social psychology and the study of sexual behavior. *Personality and Social Psychology Bulletin* 3:3–30; 1977.
13. Kinsey, A. C., Pomeroy, W. B., and Martin, C. E. *Sexual Behavior in the Human Male*. Philadelphia: Saunders, 1953.
14. Masters, W. H., and Johnson, V. E. *Human Sexual Response*. Boston: Little, Brown, 1966.
15. Kleeman, J. A Boy Discovers His Penis. In *The Psychoanalytic Study of the Child*. New York: International Universities Press, 1965. Vol. 20, pp. 239–266.
16. Kleeman, J. A. Genital Self-Discovery During a Boy's Second Year. In *The Psychoanalytic Study of the Child*. New York: International Universities Press, 1966. Vol. 21, pp. 358–392.
17. Levine, M. Pediatric Observations on Masturbation in Children. In *The Psychoanalytic Study of the Child*. New York: International Universities Press, 1951. Vol. 6, pp. 117–124.
18. Furman, R. A. Excerpt from the Analysis of a Prepuberty Boy. In I. M. Marcus and J. J. Francis (Eds.), *Masturbation: From Infancy to Senescence*. New York: International Universities Press, 1975.
19. Green, R. *Sexual Identity Conflict in Children and Adults*. New York: Basic Books, 1974. P. 35.
20. Hayman, C. R., Lewis, F. R., Stewart, M. S., and Grant, M. A public health program for sexually assaulted females. *Public Health Reports* 82:497–504, 1967.
21. Kleeman, J. A. Genital Self-Stimulation in Girls. In I. M. Marcus and J. J. Francis (Eds.), *Masturbation: From Infancy to Senescence*. New York: International Universities Press, 1975.
22. Olmstead, R. W., Svibergson, R. I., and Kleeman, J. A. The value of rooming-in experience in pediatric training. *Pediatrics* 2:617–621, 1949.
23. Spitz, R. A., and Wolf, K. M. Autoerotism: Some Empirical Findings and Hypotheses on Three of Its Manifestations in the First Year of Life. In *The Psychoanalytic Study of the Child*. New York: International Universities Press, 1949. Vols. 3, 4, pp. 85–120.
24. Freud, A., and Burlingham, D. Infants without Families: Reports on the Hampstead Nurseries. In *The Writings of Anna Freud*, Vol. 2. New York: International Universities Press, 1973.
25. Provence, S., and Lipton, R. *Infants in Institutions*. New York: International Universities Press, 1962.
26. Roiphe, H. On an Early Genital Phase. In *The Psychoanalytic*

Study of the Child, Vol. 23. New York: International Universities Press, 1968.

27. Sperling, E.   Research in Early Genital Arousal: An Overview of Theory and Method. Paper presented at the meeting of the American Psychoanalytic Association, San Francisco, December 18, 1970.

28. Merrill, L. A.   A summary of findings in a study of sexualism among a group of one hundred delinquents. *Journal of Juvenile Research* 3:255–267, 1918.

29. Ramsey, G. V.   *Factors in the Sex Life of 291 Boys*. Madison, N.J.: Published by the author, 1950.

30. Hughes, W. L.   Sex experiences of boyhood. *Journal of Social Hygiene* 12:262–273, 1926.

31. Kinsey, A. C., Pomeroy, W. B., Martin, C. E., and Gebhard, P. H. *Sexual Behavior in the Human Female*. Philadelphia: Saunders, 1953.

32. Elias, J. E., and Gebhard, P. H.   Sexuality and sexual learning in childhood: Research and possible implications for education. *Phi Delta Kappan* 1:401–405, 1969.

33. Pomeroy, W. B.   Personal communication.

34. Breasted, M.   *Oh, Sex Education*. New York: New American Library, 1971.

35. Bernstein, A., and Cowan, P. A.   Children's concepts of how people get babies. *Child Development* 45:77–91, 1975.

36. Moore, J. E., and Kendall, D. C.   Children's concepts of reproduction. *Journal of Sex Research* 7:42–61, 1971.

37. Kreitler, H., and Kreitler, S.   Children's concepts of sexuality and birth. *Child Development* 37:363–378, 1966.

38. Conn, J. M.   Children's awareness of the origin of babies. *Journal of Child Psychiatry* 1:140–176, 1947.

39. Levy, V. M.   Studies of children's responses to differences in genitalia. *American Journal of Orthopsychiatry* 60:755–762, 1940.

40. Pomeroy, W. B.   Personal communication.

41. Pitcher, E. G., and Prelinger, E.   *Children Tell Stories*. New York: International Universities Press, 1963.

42. Ames, L. B.   Children's stories. *Genetic Psychology Monographs* 73:336–396, 1966.

43. Miles, F. F.   *Children's Art and Human Beginnings* (pamphlet). Eugene, Oregon: E. C. Brown Center for Family Studies, 1971.

44. Safilios-Rothschild, C.   *Love, Sex and Sex Roles*. Englewood Cliffs, N.J.: Prentice-Hall, 1977.

45. Lansky, L. M.   The family structure also affects the model: Sex role attitudes in parents of preschool children. *Merrill-Palmer Quarterly* 13:139–150, 1967.

46. Wolf, T. M.   Response consequences to televised, modeled sex-inappropriate play behavior. *Journal of Genetic Psychology* 127:35–44, 1975.

47. Broderick, C. B.   Sexual behavior among pre-adolescents. *Journal of Social Issues* 22:6–21, 1966.
48. Broderick, C. B.   Personal communication.
49. Mann, J., Sidman, J., and Starr, S.   Effects of Erotic Films on Sexual Behavior of Married Couples. In *Technical Reports of the Commission on Obscenity and Pornography*, Vol. 8. Washington, D.C.: U.S. Government Printing Office, 1970.
50. Aronson, E., and Carlsmith, J. M.   Experimentation in Social Psychology. In G. Lindzey and E. Aronson (Eds.), *The Handbook of Social Psychology* (2nd ed.), Vol. 2. Reading, Mass.: Addison-Wesley, 1968.
51. Webb, E. J., Campbell, D. T., Schwartz, R. D., and Sechrest, L. *Unobtrusive Measures: Nonreactive Research in the Social Sciences.* Chicago: Rand McNally, 1966.
52. National Commission for the Protection of Human Subjects of Biomedical and Behavioral Research. *Report and Recommendations: Research Involving Children.* DHEW Publication No. (05) 77–0004 (Washington, D.C.: U.S. Government Printing Office, 1977).
53. Money, J., and Walker, P. A.   Psychosexual development, maternalism, nonpromiscuity, and body image in 15 females with precocious puberty. *Archives of Sexual Behavior* 1:45–60, 1971.
54. Green, R.   Personal communication.
55. Malinowski, B.   *The Sexual Life of Savages in Northwest Melanesia.* New York: Harcourt Brace Jovanovich, 1929.
56. Ford, C. S., and Beach, F. A.   *Patterns of Sexual Behavior.* New York: Harper & Row, 1951.
57. Weiss, J., Rogers, E., Darwin, M., and Dutton, C.   A study of girl sex victims. *Psychiatric Quarterly* 29:1–15, 1955.
58. Bender, L., and Blau, A.   The reaction of children to sexual relations with adults. *American Journal of Orthopsychiatry* 22:825–837, 1937.
59. Halleck, S. L.   Emotional Effects of Victimization. In R. Slovenko (Ed.), *Sexual Behavior and the Law.* Springfield, Ill.: Charles C. Thomas, 1965.
60. Gagnon, J. H.   Female child victims of sex offenses. *Social Problems* 13:176–192, 1965.
61. Schachter, M.   Apropos de pretendus dommages psychiques consecutifs à une agression sexuelle commise par un adolescent sur la personne d'un petit garçon. *Acta Paedopsychiatrica* 32:191–195, 1965.
62. Barry, M. J.   Incest. In R. Slovenko (Ed.), *Sexual Behavior and the Law.* Springfield, Ill.: Charles C. Thomas, 1965.
63. Halleck, S. L., and Hersko, M.   Homosexual behavior in a correctional institution for adolescent girls. *American Journal of Orthopsychiatry* 32:911–917, 1962.

64. Finch, E. Sexual activity of children with other children and adults. *Clinical Pediatrics* 6:1–2, 1967.
65. Bender, L. Offended and Offender Children. In R. Slovenko (Ed.), *Sexual Behavior and the Law*. Springfield, Ill.: Charles C. Thomas, 1965.
66. Gibbens, T. C. N., and Prince, J. *Child Victims of Sex Offenses*. London: Institute for the Study and Treatment of Delinquency, 1963.
67. Gebhard, P. H., Gagnon, J. H., Pomeroy, W. B., and Christenson, C. V. *Sex Offenders*. New York: Harper & Row, 1965.
68. Masters, W. H., and Johnson, V. E. *Human Sexual Inadequacy*. Boston: Little, Brown, 1970.
69. Sorensen, R. C. *Adolescent Sexuality in Contemporary America* (The Sorensen Report). New York: World Publishing, 1973.
70. Link, W. C. (statement). In *The Report of the Commission on Obscenity and Pornography*. New York: Bantam, 1970. Pp. 448–451.
71. Goldstein, M. J., and Kant, H. S. *Pornography and Sexual Deviance*. Berkeley and Los Angeles: University of California Press, 1973.
72. Broderick, C. B. Personal communication.
73. Pomeroy, W. B. Personal communication.
74. Gebhard, P. H. Sexual Behavior of the Mentally Retarded. In F. F. de la Cruz and G. D. La Veck (Eds.), *Human Sexuality and the Mentally Retarded*. New York: Brunner/Mazel, 1973.
75. Edgerton, R. B. Some Socio-Cultural Research Considerations. In F. F. de la Cruz and G. D. La Veck (Eds.), *Human Sexuality and the Mentally Retarded*. New York: Brunner/Mazel, 1973.
76. Heber, A. A Manual on Terminology and Classification in Mental Retardation (monograph). *American Journal of Retardation* (Supp. 64), 1959.
77. Whalen, R. E., and Whalen, C. K. Sexual Behavior: Research Perspectives. In F. F. de la Cruz and G. D. La Veck (Eds.), *Human Sexuality and the Mentally Retarded*. New York: Brunner/Mazel, 1973.
78. Edgerton, R. B., and Dingman, H. F. Good reasons for bad supervision: Dating in a hospital for the mentally retarded. *Psychiatric Quarterly* 38 (Supp.): 221–223, 1964.
79. Hale, J. E., Morris, H. L., and Barker, H. R. Sexual knowledge and attitudes of mentally retarded adolescents. *American Journal of Mental Deficiency* 77:706–709, 1973.
80. National Commission for the Protection of Human Subjects of Biomedical and Behavioral Research. *Report and Recommendations on Research Involving Those Institutionalized as Mentally Infirm*. DHEW Publication No. (OS) 78–0006 (Washington, D.C.: U.S. Government Printing Office, 1978). Recommendation 4, p. 16.

5

VALUE IMPERIALISM
AND EXPLOITATION
IN SEX THERAPY[1]

H. TRISTRAM ENGELHARDT, JR.

Having an orgasm is not like taking a breath. Sex is vested with special values that influence and reflect the basic organization of societies. Respiration is neither as immediately social nor as intrusive as sex in its significance. This is true in part because sexual activities are rarely as necessary for an individual as breathing and are usually much more pleasurable. Studying reproductive physiology is thus of a different character than studying respiratory physiology. As a consequence, treatment of sexual dysfunctions also has a different valence than the treatment of respiratory dysfunctions. After all, the existence of two genders bears in many ways on almost all, if not all, human institutions. The human race is dimorphic, and differences in form and biological function can have a strong influence on human relationships. This is to say the obvious: Sex is powerful, provocative, evocative, and much more interesting than many other human activities. It offers unique possibilities for abuse in the context of therapy.

As intrusive as sexuality is, its meaning is ambiguous. That is, sexuality (being sexual, having a sex) may refer to one or more of the following states: (1) being able to reproduce; (2) possess-

[1] I am indebted to many persons who contributed in various ways to the development of this paper. Patricia Blakeney, Daniel Creson, Edmund Erde, John Moskop, Ruth Walker Moskop, Paul Walker, and Stephen Wear have read and criticized earlier drafts. Others have unknowingly contributed through arguments on other subjects that were suggestive in the preparation of this paper—though they themselves may disagree strongly with the arguments and conclusions presented here. Among these individuals I must acknowledge Joseph Margolis.

ing the chromosomal bases of sexual differentiation; (3) possessing sexual dimorphism (with or without the usual chomosomal basis of sexuality; consider transsexuals); (4) being able to engage in activities capable of producing sexual pleasure among partners (that is, including both heterosexual and homosexual activities); (5) being attractive to members of the opposite or of the same sex; and (6) being able simply to be the subject of sexual sensations (including all sexual activities, even solitary sex). Sexuality in all these senses involves values that vary with the different senses: For example, compare the value of the sexual success of sex for reproduction versus sex for recreation. Here, as in all areas of disagreement regarding values, some individuals are likely to force their values on others (concerning how much one should reproduce, whether recreational sex should exist only within marriage, etc.). Sex therapy in particular affords many circumstances in which the therapist can impose his or her values on the patient or client—especially in terms of defining what is normal or abnormal, deviant or proper sexual activity.

There is also a special problem of exploitation in sex therapy. This is true in part because of variations in levels of interest regarding sexuality. One person can often induce in another interest in engaging in sexual activity with the goal of being the sexual partner of the individual whose interests have been aroused. This is again to state the obvious: Seduction is possible. Moreover, the level of desire for sexual relations is often higher than, for example, the desire for food that treatment for a gastrointestinal dysfunction might arouse in a patient—unless the individual concerned was extremely hungry (and in any case, food is usually more easily available than sex in our culture). Further, in the study of gastrointestinal physiology and respiratory physiology, the subjects will eat and breathe in any event. But with sexuality there is not an inescapable need to engage in activities leading to relief. That is to say, seduction is possible in the area of sexuality in ways that are not possible in the area of gastronomy. In addition, because of the special authority of their role, therapists may be able to influence unduly the acceptance of sexual activity in the treatment context. Because of the values associated with sexuality in our culture, therapist-patient sexual relations are given a significance not imputed to physicians taking patients out for a meal (our sexual taboos might be compared with Hawaiian taboos against meals amongst members of the opposite sex[2]). In short, in our culture most sexual experiences are more intense and freighted with more personal significance than are most meals.

Accordingly, I will address two topics in this paper: (1) the possible intrusion of the values of therapists into the context of treatment; and (2) the possible sexual exploitation of patients by sex therapists. I shall discuss these topics with regard to ethical issues and from a philosophical and historical perspective. The first section of the paper will set out basic philosophical presuppositions and the second section will provide some historical illustrations. Once this background is available I will advance some suggestions regarding the intrusion of sexual values in treatment and will assess the ethical implications of sexual exploitation by therapists. In conjunction with the last set of issues, the question of the propriety of sex therapists having sexual relations with their patients will be explored.

IMPOSITION OF VALUES: PHILOSOPHICAL ASSUMPTIONS

All medicine imposes values; all therapists are partisans. When this seems not to be the case and when it appears that medicine is only describing reality, it is simply that some values are more widely shared than others. Because of their generality they may appear to be brute facts rather than values. But labeling a particular state of affairs a disease is not simply to describe the world:

[2] These differences are given a charming description in Captain Cook's journal: ". . . the women never upon any account eat with the men, but always by themselves. What can be the reason of so unusual a custom, it is hard to say; especially as they are a people in every other instance, fond of Society and much so of their Women. They were often asked the reason, but they never gave no other Answer, but that they did it because it was right, and expressed much dislike at the custom of Men and Women eating together of the same Victuals. . . . more than one-half of the better sort of the inhabitants have entered into a resolution of enjoying free liberty in Love, without being troubled or disturbed by its consequences. . . . both sexes express the most indecent ideas in conversation without the least emotion, and they delight in such conversation beyond any other. Chastity, indeed, is but little valued . . ." [1].

Rather, to call a condition an improper state of suffering (consider, for example, that the suffering of teething is not a disease state, but "proper" [2]), to term a state of affairs a pathological state, is to make a value judgment [3]. Some pains are "normal" and to be expected; others are "abnormal" and to be treated. Thus, once a state is seen as pathological, it becomes a condition to be remedied. Medicine has a therapeutic imperative [4]. Medicine characterizes some conditions as improper, in medical terms *abnormal* or *deviant*, and others as proper, that is, normal or nondeviant [5]. Medicine then acts in an attempt to restore normalcy. It also functions as a technology with the goal of applying the medical sciences toward the end of restoring or preserving health. Medicine acts to restore normalcy or to create normalcy as defined within certain physical and psychological limits by a particular culture. Thus, physicians in our culture generally approve of mammoplasty to enhance a woman's attractiveness, but they do not endorse altering the shape of the feet for the same reason.

One should note here the scope of the meanings of the word *therapy*. In English, *therapy* preserves many of the meanings of the original Greek. The Greek (θεράπεια) includes many meanings: a waiting on; a service (as in a divine service); a fostering or giving of nurture; a tending in sickness; medical treatment; paying court. The Engish sense of therapy retains the meanings of both care and cure. A similar ambiguity exists with respect to the word *treatment:* One can give therapy (treatment in the sense of care) to decrease difficulties associated with a sexual life-style, without aiming at eliminating (in the sense of curing) that life-style. Such distinctions are implicit in many medical contexts. Thus, one may give therapy for the pain of teething though not for the teething itself. In contrast, one may seek not only to treat the pain of a headache but to cure the underlying cause. Such levels of therapeutic imperatives occur as well with respect to sexual problems. If one terms a condition a disease, the implication is that one should if possible extirpate it, root and branch. On the other hand, "sexual distress" (perhaps captured by some appropriately stipulated meaning of *sexual dysfunction*) can identify a state somewhat analogous to the pain of teething: One can seek to treat the distress without any judgment about the abnormality of the underlying condition. Medical treatment for a condition thus invokes a disapproval of that condition, though the extent or depth of that disapproval varies.

In terms of these evaluations, medicine structures social interactions. It legitimizes certain social structures and behaviors as wholesome and normal. Medicine determines the roles of the abnormal, the defective, the diseased, and the sick. One can here only remind the reader of the various meanings of *abnormal, defective, diseased, dysfunctional, ill, sick,* and other such terms. Here we are forced to be stipulators rather than mapping out all the meanings of these terms in their natural habitats. As Talcott Parsons has indicated, among the features of the sick role are (1) exemption from some or many usual obligations (for example, if seriously ill, one is excused from work); (2) blamelessness for being in a state of illness (for example, a truly ill individual, unlike a malingerer, is held not to be blameworthy for failing a physical examination; the ill person, however, may bear responsibility for becoming disabled); (3) responsibility for seeking remedy for the condition (that is, the ill person ought to pursue treatment, is held responsible for not having done so, and can be held responsible for remaining ill); and (4) recognition of certain individuals as expert in treating illness [6–10].

Value judgments thus play a wide-ranging role in medicine. Moreover, they have force, authority, and power. Consider, for example, the social impact of diagnosing syphilis, schizophrenia, leprosy, or smallpox in an individual. Consider as well the social function of such diagnostic categories as *inadequate personality.* The *Diagnostic and Statistical Manual* of the American Psychiatric Association (*DSM-II*) defines *inadequate personality* as a behavior pattern

characterized by ineffectual responses to emotional, social, intellectual and physical demands. While the patient seems neither physically nor mentally deficient, he does manifest inadaptability, ineptness, poor judgment, social instability, and lack of physical and emotional stamina [11].

Under this rubric, an individual who is generally incompetent may receive a medical diagnosis marking his or her social problem as a medical problem. Of course, this may be beneficial as well as detrimental—after all, medicine has the ability to give social and often therapeutic aid to patients and clients (for example, by explaining that homosexuality is not a disease or not unnatural; or by curing impotence).

One must note as well that value judgments intrude into all medical practice in varying ways and in varying measures. One can appreciate this by remembering that diseases or dysfunctions nearly always presuppose an environmental context. Thus, while sickle cell trait may have neutral or only minor detrimental consequences in a modern urban society [12], it may have distinct advantages in environments that have falciparum malaria but no antimalaria drugs [13]. In addition, the cultural ambience is also an important part of the environmental milieu. That is, what will count as disease or nondisease will depend not only on the physical but also on the cultural environment (which is not to deny that there will be a large degree of cross-cultural coincidence with regard to what will count as states of illness). There is thus a strong element of arbitrariness or freedom in shaping disease concepts ranging from leprosy to schizophrenia, on the one hand, to vitiligo and inadequate personality on the other. Value judgments increase or decrease in their degree of general acceptance as they are made along this spectrum, thus allowing for greater disagreement or divergence of opinions.

Characterizations of human sexual function and dysfunction tend in great measure to display the problems of the more arbitrary definitions of medical normality and abnormality. Even basic sexual functions such as reproductive ability do not have a single universal value. Given the present overpopulated condition of the world, marked fecundity is no longer generally accorded a positive value. As arguments against increasing population become stronger, arguments against alternative life-styles such as homosexuality are correspondingly weaker if those arguments are based on homosexuality being unnatural in the sense of nonreproductive: Why should it be considered disadvantageous or dysfunctional if homosexuals fail to contribute to population growth—unless they carry especially advantageous genes? In fact, our changing estimate of the value of reproduction has been tied to many current attitudes about sexual activity. As will be discussed below, current interest in treating premature ejaculation and anorgasmia would not have received widespread support, at least in official circles, in the Middle Ages, when sexual intercourse was viewed as existing for reproduction, not for pleasure.[3] Our ideas about which capacities all humans must have, have changed.[4]

An understanding of the propriety or impropriety of therapists importing their values into the therapeutic context will depend on recognizing the necessary intrusion of value judgments in general in all medical contexts. In assessing the probity of such intrusions of values into sex therapy, one develops strategies for coming to terms with the value-laden nature of medical discourse in general. Moreover, this will be the case not only with regard to the use of the languages of disease and health, normality and abnormality, but also with respect to issues in sexual ethics.

MORAL CHOICES

In developing a sketch of the ethical considerations bearing on therapists importing their value judgments and presuppositions into sex therapy and research, I am presupposing what can be termed a secular theory of values. This involves two fundamental assumptions: First, ethical conduct refers to a general strategy for interpersonal relations based on eschewing the use of force or coercion, relying instead on appeals to free choice for and against various lines of conduct [15]. Respect for free choice as such is not one goal to value among others, but a side-constraint or necessary condition for the possibility of the ethical enterprise [16]. Insofar as one acts in ways inconsistent with mutual respect for freedom by appealing to force or coercion, one departs from the ethical enterprise and instead makes a power play in decisions among lines of conduct. The move from an ethical interpersonal context to a co-

---

[3] For example, St. Augustine indicated that the purpose of intercourse is reproduction and that intercourse for pleasure alone, even in marriage, is sinful [14].

[4] That is, we no longer consider it a norm of health that all humans be reproductive. It is also important to distinguish the issue of socially constructed biological norms from other social norms. Thus, even if homosexuality were a disease, one could decide it was socially advantageous. This is analogous to getting an excellent pension for a lame leg: The lame leg is still considered dysfunctional, though perhaps worth it.

ercive context is the move from allowing others to choose their own values, to imposing instead one's own values on others. Such impositions may be made either out of self-interest (that is, a sort of value imperialism) or out of what one takes to be the best interest of others (paternalism). According to this account, to take the ethical enterprise seriously is to take freedom seriously. It requires letting each individual act on his own values as long as such actions do not directly and significantly restrict the freedom of others to choose freely.

This leads to my second assumption: Choices among ways of life are not basic ethical choices as long as they are not choices between those life-styles that presuppose coercion and those that do not. Choices among life-styles are more like aesthetic choices—they are made in terms of which life-style is richer, more beautiful, and more supportive of the values that humans esteem. Such choices are not moral choices in the strong sense unless they bear on the protection of free choice.

Some characteristics of these two assumptions must be noted. First, in the arguments that follow, freedom is made the cardinal value or condition in considerations of morality. This is so because respect for freedom is the sole consistent basis of an alternative to the use of force (with force construed broadly to include controlling others through activities such as deception) in interpersonal relations. Only if respect for persons as self-determining entities is established, does reason-giving irrevocably replace the use of force as the basis for the community of persons. This involves eschewing force even to the point of not forcing others to choose their own values freely. (Again, note that freedom functions as a side-constraint, as a necessary condition for the possibility of a community of persons based on reason-giving rather than on attempts at mutual domination [16].) One can thus consistently decide freely not to be free (to cite a medieval example, one may decide rationally to cloud one's freedom and rationality by engaging in sexual intercourse with great ardor and abandon, until one is compelled by passion and unable to choose freely[5]). Freedom, as such,

---

[5] Note here the medieval concern, as St. Bernadine of Sienna put it, not to have intercourse "too frequently, with inordinate affection, or with dissipation of one's strength" (Seraphic Sermons 19.3) and, as St. Thomas Aquinas put it, not to have

is not the basic value in that it must be preferred over all other values in choices among lines of conduct in order to maintain the moral life. It may be so valued, but it need not be valued that highly as a basis for morality (for example, one can decide to get drunk). The point is that freedom is a necessary presupposition for a sphere of conduct even before it is considered as a value. Only if freedom is presupposed does the practice of holding individuals worthy of blame or praise make sense.[6] An experience of an obligation to act morally is justified, not simply caused, only if one presumes that moral agents are free. Only then would one's actions be responsible, worthy of blame or praise, rather than simply lamentable or admirable. In short, to live in a sphere of action where one can have obligations to others and speak of respect for oneself and for others (and not simply be covertly pressing the pursuit of some particular goods) requires presupposing freedom in action. It requires also recognizing that freedom is the condition for the possibility of a community of persons held together not by force, but by reason. Freedom makes possible respect for persons and obligations to persons beyond mere interest in the use of persons.

In addition, moral arguments based on respect for freedom tend to be more decisive and more clear-cut than arguments based on ranking good, values, purposes, and consequences or outcomes. Thus, rape is wrong—even if in a particular case more people were pleased by it than displeased and even if the aggregate amount of joy in the world was thereby increased. Equally, rape would be wrong even if it turned out in the long run to have been good for the person who was raped. It remains wrong, as unconsented violence, even if the person raped enjoyed the act and somehow bene-

---

reason "absorbed by the vehemence of delight so that it can not understand anything during this delight" (On the Sentences 4.31.1.1) [translations by J. T. Noonan] [17].

[6] The presupposition of freedom is necessary not only in the sphere of ethics but also in the sphere of science. Truth claims can make sense only if individuals are presumed to be free. Only then do they reflect a choice to forward a claim made on the basis of reason, not past conditioning. If all behavior is treated only and simply as *caused* (as opposed to *chosen* on good grounds), then the statement "all behavior is only and simply caused" is itself caused: It is not asserted because it is true, but because it is caused. The self-conscious assertion of the truth of the causal claim must be treated as asserted by a knower who is free in the sense that he or she is not being caused to make such an assertion, but chooses to do so on the basis of good grounds or reasons.

fited from it (for example, her long-standing anorgasmia was cured). On the other hand, oral-genital sex with consent and sexual experimentation with consent are licit even if they outrage public sensibilities, as long as these acts do not take place on the property of others or in public so as to annoy or intrude upon others (that is, constrain the freedom of others). In fact, oral-genital sex would be licit even if it led to bad teeth and poor marriage, as long as the persons involved were not *forced* to engage in this activity.

This is not to say that one should always decide—or in fact, *can* always decide—to be moral. There may be circumstances in which any decision will be wrong to some extent. The world may not have the coherence that allows for an unambiguous moral choice in all circumstances. For example, if one has promised absolute confidentiality to a patient who then reveals that he is going to rape and murder 20 persons, one could justify breaking confidentiality by giving reasons that moral persons would recognize as reasonable grounds for disclosure—though they might still recognize that such a decision is regrettable and in a real sense evil. Either choice would involve an element of immorality (that is, acting in disregard of a promise and thus not respecting others as free agents; or knowingly losing a great moral good, the dignity and lives of others). If one chooses to break confidentiality, one should recognize oneself as blameworthy; if one chooses to keep confidentiality, one should feel regret at the loss of the dignity and lives of others. One could not justify breaking such a promise on the basis that by keeping silence one would hurt others or be responsible for their deaths. If absolute confidentiality had not been promised, one may never have known of the risk; one's knowing, as such, does not increase anyone's jeopardy. In fact, if anything, a practice of absolute confidentiality would in general decrease danger to the public by allowing people with such dangerous inclinations to seek help earlier without fear of being reported. That is to say, a general practice of violating confidentiality could not be justified. One might be able to justify making certain exceptions in restricted cases, especially if such exception-making did not become well known. But insofar as one's regard for promise-keeping was founded on respect for the freedom of other persons, such a breach of confidentiality would always in a real sense constitute a moral evil.

That is, one would be acting immorally—having simply declared that in some cases other considerations are more important than morality (that is, morality in the strong sense of commitment to a community of persons based on mutual respect). However, since respect for freedom is cardinal to the moral life, one should allow few exceptions to it in the strong sense. Or, rather, society should at most tolerate minor immoralities of this sort. Consider, for example, someone promising at 18 to live with another "until death do us part" and then at 30 seeking a divorce against the wishes of the other party. Such an action has an ineradicably immoral element (unless one holds that the 18-year-old did not understand the significance or meaning of such a promise, or one had good arguments against personal identity over that period of time—contentions that are fraught with problems of their own). There may simply be good reasons for a certain amount of immorality at certain times (for example, seeking happiness for oneself and one's children)—reasons that most other moral persons in fact acknowledge as sufficient. Moreover, society may simply have little interest (if not a negative interest) in enforcing such promises.

MORAL-AESTHETIC CHOICES

In order to contrast this type of moral consideration (that is, respect for persons as free agents) with considerations of the pursuit of particular values, I offer a distinction between (1) decisions among lines of action where the basis of the decision is regard for persons as free moral agents, and (2) decisions among lines of action on the basis of the goods they make available, the life-styles they enhance. I term the first type, moral decisions *in the strong sense*; the second type, *moral-aesthetic* decisions (I continue to call moral-aesthetic decisions "moral decisions" out of regard for the usual employment of the term *moral*). Arguments in the first mode are likely to be more decisive (for example, the conclusion that it is wrong to have sexual intercourse with persons without their permission will receive widespread support), while arguments in the second mode carry less force or conviction (for example, the statement that married life is better than celibate life is apt to arouse dissent, at least in some quarters).

Many moral choices, though not moral choices in the strong sense, are more economic than aesthetic. Teleological theories of conduct, especially utilitarian accounts, usually involve economic theories of various kinds: They concern the distribution of goods. Insofar as the choice among schemata for the distribution of goods is not based on considerations regarding the freedom of moral agents, the choices are based on arguments that a life-style consequent upon a particular economic system (that is, involving goods in the broadest sense) will tend to be richer, more enjoyable, or more beautiful than others. One should note that *economic* is here used broadly to characterize a scheme for exchanging various goods in order to maximize the aggregate or average amount of goods, to achieve a preponderance of certain goods, or to achieve a certain form of distribution of goods (or some combination of the above). Such choices among rules for behavior can be made on utilitarian grounds without violating the side-constraint of respect for the freedom of moral agents. For example, one might properly forbid abortions late in pregnancy because of a general revulsion at destroying fairly well developed human life (with the objective of maximizing the general happiness)—but only after sufficient time had been made available for women to choose freely whether or not to have their pregnancies terminated. Or, one might forbid public lewdness, but not private sexual acts among consenting partners.[7]

In the sphere of sexual activity, I will argue that there are no peculiarly sexual ethics, only general ethical principles concerning respect for individual freedom. One should not coerce others, lie to others, or break promises to others in the area of sexual relations. One should encourage modes of sexual activity that are likely to maximize the general happiness and discourage those that are likely to diminish the general happiness. But one may do so only within the limits of two constraints: (1) the recognition of the right of

---

[7] Because I am advancing a modified Kantian position, I must note that Immanuel Kant would not have agreed to the proposition that there are no moral rules against sexual activities as long as the freedom of others is not violated—though he should have, given his general theory of the role of freedom in ethics. Kant, in fact, disapproved of all sexual activity outside of marriage, even masturbation. The problem stems from Kant having falsely held (primarily because he conflated freedom as a side-constraint and freedom as a value) that one has a moral duty to oneself [18].

persons to do as they choose as long as their activities do not directly diminish the similar rights of others, and (2) the recognition of our woeful lack of knowledge concerning which sexual activities or life-styles are likely to maximize the general happiness.[8]

Thus, there appear to be no grounds, in the strong ethical sense, for determining how or with whom one should have sexual relations (as long as all directly involved are agreed). Choices regarding the number, kinds, and frequency of sexual partners are choices among life-styles. They are more aesthetic than ethical choices. This is not to belittle such choices; whether one values more a poor supermarket wine or a good Margaux, a crude painting or a fine Renoir, a quick meal at a hamburger stand or a dinner at a fine restaurant, a conversation with rude strangers or with refined close friends, casual sex with strangers or sex in the context of friendship, reveals important elements of one's character. But the character failing of preferring a poor supermarket wine over a good Margaux is not a moral character flaw, or at least not a flaw in the strong moral sense. It may, nevertheless, still be a serious matter. One could imagine an ethical system in which such matters were taken seriously and were held to be of moral moment.

This way of approaching ethical issues means that the only strong cases of moral degeneration or degradation are those that involve the use (or abuse) of others without their consent. Thus, rape is clearly immoral while urolagnia is not. What would count as degrading or improper in the weaker, moral-aesthetic sense turns upon cultural norms and institutions, social roles and practices.

---

[8] These arguments are not meant to discount religious claims of knowing what are in fact proper human sexual life-styles. On the contrary, the arguments in this paper are meant to provide a framework within which religious viewpoints can be protected. For unless all agree to the truth of a particular religious revelation, we will have either to tolerate opposing views or to impose values on others by force (as with the Inquisition). To refer to views about proper human sexual life-styles as "moral-aesthetic" or "weak moral" issues is meant to signal the fact that these are issues about which there is likely to be little agreement. It is in matters of this kind that we had best be prepared to be tolerant, for few are likely to wish to accord others the right to impose on them sexual life-styles that they take to be wrong or misguided. This paper proposes a framework of pluralism for negotiating moral intuitions about sexual life-styles. It does not disparage particular religious views concerning sexual morality. Rather, it encourages such views as matters of private conviction. Finally, calling choices of sexual life-styles weak moral choices from a secular ethical viewpoint is not meant to deny that they may be strong choices in religious terms.

Consider, for example, that drinking cow urine is a pious and edifying act within the context of the Hindu religion.[9] What will count as affronts to human dignity or as proper ways of self-actualization will also be context-dependent and will ultimately turn on judgments regarding those life-styles. From a secular-ethical viewpoint one would have to judge whether living as (for example) a pious Hindu or a devout Baptist or an atheist increases or decreases the general goods of life. In like manner, the cultural milieu will influence one's choice, insofar as such a choice is possible, among the life-styles of a heterosexual, homosexual, or bisexual.

IMPOSITION OF VALUES: HISTORICAL OVERVIEW

History enlightens the present by—inter alia—exposing the folly of the past, thus alerting us to the likelihood of the equal folly of current beliefs and customs. The history of attitudes toward human sexuality can be helpful in this way by confronting us with the beliefs that our immediate forebears held with certainty and that we at present would reject. The realization of the precariousness of judgments regarding sexual mores need not lead us to a complete sexual relativism (that is, deciding that such choices are matters of indifference). But it should suggest that opinions regarding sexual mores must be advanced with great caution to ensure the rights of others to choose their own life-styles. Given an appreciation of the force with which sex therapists in the past advanced "false" views regarding sexuality, one may wish to assume a studied neutrality. If one moves beyond such neutrality, it is necessary to inform patients that one's suggestions on behalf of a particular sexual life-style are more aesthetic than moral in a strong sense. There is a moral obligation to give such warnings in order to avoid the possibility of coercion of patients or clients by the therapist, whose particular opinions or suggestions regarding sexual life-

9 "The water [the cow] ejects ought to be preserved as the best of holy waters—a sin-destroying liquid which sanctifies everything it touches, while nothing purifies like cow-dung" [19].

styles are likely to be interpreted as medical "facts." The history of medicine is replete with examples of therapists pressing their own values on others. A brief survey of some of the vicissitudes of sexual attitudes in medicine should teach restraint, caution, and even diffidence in advancing opinions about the probity of different sexual life-styles.

Since Plato sang the praises of Eros in the *Symposium* and *Phaedrus* and speculated that the word *hero* was derived from *Eros* [20], the estimation of *eros* has fallen on bad times. As Nietzsche put it, Christianity gave Eros poison to drink; it did not kill Eros, but only degenerated him into a vice [21]. Though one can consider this an overstatement, once one enters the Christian age, it is difficult to find works containing the freedom and openness of discussion of sexuality, including homosexuality, that one finds in the *Symposium* and *Phaedrus*. Instead, European attitudes reflect their contact with Pauline and Neoplatonic ascetic views regarding sexuality. Celibacy is preferred to marriage (Corinthians 7:9), and homosexuality is condemned (Romans 1:24–27). The New Testament (Galatians 5:20) and early Christian (Didache 5:2) condemnations of medicine (that is, *pharmakeia*) came to be applied only to contraception and abortion. Sexual intercourse was freighted with a special, morally problematic character. During the eighth to the twelfth centuries these attitudes developed into frequent condemnation of sexual intercourse, even in marriage, if engaged in for other than reproductive goals (or to prevent adultery).

Medical opinion tended to maintain this general distrust of the erotic. The eighteenth- and nineteenth-century view of masturbation as a disease illustrates how moral values are translated into medical values [22]. "Morally right" was interpreted as medically normal or natural, while "morally wrong" came to mean medically abnormal, unnatural, or deviant. One sees a chain of value transformations (at least in the case of some conditions): A moral judgment about sin is transformed into a medical judgment about abnormality or disease. These medical values can in turn lead to moral judgment (that is, assertions that one ought to avoid X for the common good, since X is a disease). Consider, for example, the remarks of Dr. Joseph Howe concerning the deleterious influences of masturbation:

'The sins of the father shall be visited on the children, even unto the third and fourth generation.' Nowhere in the category of disease is the truth of this saying so manifest as in the case of masturbators. The evil that they do lives long after them. Their vicious habits, continued as they are through the period when nature is endeavoring to create a vigorous condition which will resist the wear and tear of active adult life, leave an indelible impress on the whole structure. All the tissues and secretions of the body are affected, and the seminal fluid partakes of the general deterioration. It is thinner, more watery, of a pale yellowish white color, and contains fewer spermatozoa than it does in a healthy condition. The movements of the spermatozoa as seen under the microscope seem to have much less activity than the spermatozoa from a healthy, vigorous man. Pus and epithelial cells are likewise present in variable quantities. This defective seminal fluid is sure to give to the fetus the seeds of weakness and decay which are ready to germinate with the first exciting cause. There is no more potent factor in the development of disease. The child of masturbating parents enters the world with vitality so impaired that there is a constant invitation to the attack of every affection. The child commences life with a highly organized nervous system, morbidly sensitive to every external impression. The muscular and osseous tissues are much softer than they are normally. I have never yet seen a case of rickets in a child whose parents did not give some voluntary or involuntary evidence of a pernicious habit, or of sexual excess of some description [23].

The values of a particular way of life are thus imposed under the cloak of medical authority.

Consider also the intrusion of moral judgments into "medical" advice given to nineteenth-century Americans regarding sexual intercourse. Dr. Dio Lewis argued as follows, in one manual:

It is right then, to exert the sexual function when children are desired, and rightly desired, and only then—i.e., at times when both man and woman are in good health and spirits, and in thorough loving harmony; when moreover, conception will probably ensue and the best qualities of its parents be embodied in the resultant offspring. . . . Passionate enjoyment must be made wholly incidental; never pursued as an end. . . . Intercourse not designed to be productive is unholy; and children who, when begotten, are not wished for by both father and mother, are 'conceived in sin' whether in or out of wedlock [24].

Or consider the statement by Theophilus Parvin in an article on sexual hygiene, that "not one bride in a hundred, of delicate, educated, sensitive women, accepts matrimony from any desire of sexual gratification; when she thinks of this at all, it is with shrinking or even with horror, rather than with desire" [25]. In short, the history of medical attitudes toward sex therapy documents the importation of the therapist's approval or disapproval of certain sexual activities and life-styles into the therapeutic context. This has generally taken the form of outright condemnation, often under the rubric of disease, abnormality, or deviance.

INTRUSION OF THERAPISTS' VALUES DURING TREATMENT

In the circumstances of treatment there are many avenues for the imposition of values upon patients. This is particularly true of sex therapy. Sex therapists can introduce their values into the treatment situation (1) by terming particular forms of sexual activity abnormal, deviant, unnatural, or pathological (versus normal, healthy, etc.); (2) by labeling such activity immoral; or (3) by suggesting that some sexual life-styles are better or more successful (for example, more satisfactory, more enriching, more pleasurable) than others. As the foregoing discussion indicates, therapists will be justified only rarely in the first case, more so in the second, and most often in the third.

The view that the choice among sexual activities is primarily a choice among life-styles (regarding which there are rarely clear-cut considerations) has arisen at least in part in reaction to the general failure of traditional arguments, based on notions of natural law, which assert that particular forms of sexual activity are unnatural or abnormal. Such arguments fail because no general agreement can be reached about the nature of normal or natural sexual function (at least with any normative force for *normal* or *natural*, that is, as meaning more than a statistical fact or being useful in characterizing the behavior of a particular species). Natural-law arguments depend on one or more common prior assumptions such as (1) we can discover the goals of nature, and God wishes us to act in accord with these goals;[10] or (2) the survival of the species (or

[10] Arguments of this kind characteristically condemn or approve of particular sexual activities not because those activities are widespread or rare, but because they

some other goal) is the overriding good, and we therefore term
pathological all states that impede the realization of that survival
or other goal (for example, the strengthening of heterosexual
bonds).[11] Because of the general failure to establish such assumptions, persons tend—with good grounds—to have varying ideas

conform to or violate an ideal view of man. Thus, natural-law opponents of masturbation would not be persuaded to call such activity natural merely by virtue of the
fact that it is usual (indeed, nearly universal):

> . . . where there is an especial ugliness making sex-activity indecent there you
> assign a determinate species of lechery. This may crop up in two ways. The first
> is common to all sins of lechery, namely that they are in conflict with right rea-
> son. The second . . . is that they are in conflict with the natural pattern of
> sexuality for the benefit of the species. . . .

It may happen variously. First, outside intercourse when an orgasm is procured
for the sake of venereal pleasure; this belongs to the sin of self abuse [26].

The difficulty of showing what God has in mind for humans—which is necessary
in order to sustain this type of natural-law argument—tends to weaken its general
acceptability. Absent a notion of God wanting nature to be a specific way, there
could always be good grounds for going against nature (that is, what evolution had
established—if that could be determined). Part of the value of being human is to be
free of "natural" constraints.

One can perhaps detect a humorous appreciation of purported natural-law proscriptions in the note concerning bestiality "Raro fit cum tigribus," reputed to exist
in an early edition of Genicot's *Institutiones theologiae moralis*. In fact, during my
research for this article I was given the following verse, composed by a number of
priests, to be sung to the tune of a medieval hymn:

Raro tantum fit cum tigri
Raro cum leonibus
Sed interdum non frequenter
Fit cum elephantibus
Sed vix umquam, imo nunquam
Fit cum scorpionibus.

Far from being meant blasphemously or irreligiously, this is a continuation of the
High Middle Ages tradition of taking such things seriously—but only up to a point:
probably one of the major elements in the health of the medieval church.

[11] This position is difficult to hold as well, since we term individuals *diseased* on
the basis of their suffering, even if their condition is part of species adaptability (as
in the case of sickle cell disease). We do not regard sickle cell disease as simply the
purchase price of sufficient species adaptability to ensure adequate survival in the
presence of falciparum malaria and in the absence of antimalaria drugs. Moreover,
such an attitude would often collide with the ethical requirement to respect individual persons. Nor would natural-law arguments of this kind be decisive in the
labeling of sexual activities as normal or abnormal, because different activities contribute in roundabout ways to the survival of the species. For instance, it has been
suggested that homosexuality may have evolved because the existence of a certain
number of homosexuals in a community confers survival advantage upon the group
as a whole [27]. Finally, it is not clear why one *need* value species survival. Arguments for goals other than the survival of the species have proven even more
inconclusive.

about the purposes of sexuality (and, as a result, about sexual dysfunction).

As a consequence, what counts as sexual health or dysfunction will depend not on natural-law considerations or even on what is usually the case. Compare the following conditions, for example, with regard to the use of the language of health and disease: impotence in a 30-year-old male versus impotence in an 80-year-old male; or impotence in a 30-year-old priest versus impotence in an 80-year-old married man. Or compare the following: exclusive homosexuality in a member of a nearly extinct tribe struggling for survival—in a tribal society that usually does not approve of homosexuality—versus exclusive homosexuality in a person living in San Francisco; or the homosexuality of a devout member of a Hassidic community versus the homosexuality of an atheist living in an overcrowded Japanese city. Or, finally, compare the condition of a homosexual in Athens in the fifth century before Christ versus that of a homosexual in the High Middle Ages [28, 29]; or a person who prefers oral-genital sex living in Rome in the second century A.D. versus someone of the same preference in eighteenth-century Puritan America. In each case, what is defined as disease or dysfunction will depend in large measure on the context or environment in which the condition occurs, and the context or environment is culturally determined, for the most part. There is no standard (that is, universal and invariant) human environment or culture (and cultures are always part of human environments) [30].

Approaching the definition of sexual dysfunction or disease in this fashion presupposes that we apply the terms *disease* and *dysfunction* only if the following two conditions are satisfied: (1) The person is constrained to be in such a state by force of physiological or psychological processes beyond his or her direct voluntary control (for example, compare inability to achieve sexual intercourse because of impotence to inability due to lack of trying); (2) the state in question is judged to be incompatible with goals held as proper to human life, or the state produces pain without contributing to the goals considered proper to humans (compare a twentieth-century woman who considers anorgasmia a dysfunction, to a nineteenth-century woman who believes—in agreement with her society—that lack of female response is normal). It follows from this view of disease that an exclusively heterosexual individual could be termed diseased in a culture structured in terms of bisexual relations. Still, because of this very plasticity, there are good reasons to eschew "disease" language with respect to sexual functions, except in cases where there is likely to be general agreement (for example, absolute impotence during the reproductive years).

One alternative to the use of disease language is the moral condemnation of particular activities. Yet, just as there is little ground for agreement with regard to which sexual activities are normal or natural, there is little ground to command strong moral agreement for condemning some sexual activities as immoral—aside from those that fail to respect other persons as free agents, such as rape. Given the lack of strong general grounds for such condemnation, therapists who wish to make specific moral judgments should declare their presuppositions in advance (for example, "I am a Roman Catholic sex therapist and believe that the following activities are immoral . . .").

Even if a sex therapist agreed to restrict the use of disease language and outright moral condemnation in conducting sex therapy, a more modest form of persuasion would remain open, namely, arguments on behalf of particular sexual life-styles.[12] The therapist could properly point out the advantages of a heterosexual life-style over one of voyeurism, exhibitionism, or the pursuit of a shoe fetish [31, 32]. One could also suggest the advantages of a heterosexual life-style over an exclusively homosexual life-style, given the general character of our culture, the pleasures of having and raising children, and so forth. Arguments of this sort would be in the

---

[12] One should remember that the terms *therapy* and *therapist,* as noted earlier in this article, are broader in meaning than "curer of disease." Therapy includes actions directed toward alleviating the suffering and dissatisfaction associated with physiological and psychological processes beyond one's direct control, even when such processes themselves are not abnormal and thus do not require a "cure." One can provide treatment even where there is neither disease nor abnormality. Thus, one can "treat" the complaints of a healthy woman during a normal childbirth by using both drugs and reassurance.

One must also note that sex therapy involves developing new patterns of physiological and psychological responses. It is not simply education in the sense of providing new information to increase patients' awareness and pleasure in sex. Rather, like most health-care interventions, it is aimed at altering the patterns of involuntary lineaments of physiological and psychological processes (for example, impotence, premature ejaculation, and anorgasmia).

aesthetic mode; that is, they would maintain that one life-style is richer, more beautiful, or more pleasurable than another.

But how is the therapist to know a priori what is best for the patient? One can make general recommendations regarding most cases in advance and regarding particular cases as one encounters them. Nevertheless, for all that any of us (who do not happen to be shoe fetishists) know, some particular pursuer of a shoe fetish may have developed his way of life to a particularly august height—in defiance of predictions to the contrary. One must recognize that an argument for one sexual life-style over another does not have the strength of, for example, the argument that melanoma is a disease or the argument that killing the unconsenting for sexual pleasure is immoral. Arguments forwarding the virtues of a particular life-style turn on the moral character they encourage, the virtues they allow to flourish, and the human abilities they draw out. Such arguments are important, but they are also both difficult and tentative. They are neither purely scientific or factual arguments nor strong ethical arguments (that is, based on preserving the freedom of others). Consequently, the opinions of the therapist(s) either should not enter into the treatment context or should be expressly acknowledged by the therapist as an argument for a particular sexual life-style.[13] However, the therapist need not agree to help a patient adjust to a sexual life-style of which the therapist does not approve (whether or not the therapist has strong moral considerations against such a life-style). In other words, the need to respect individual freedom to choose one's sexual life-style is bilateral, even in the therapeutic context.

There are also special problems with regard to the attitudes of therapists toward the sexual life-styles imposed by parents, guardians, and institutions upon their wards (for example, children, the mentally retarded, and the severely ill). Out of regard for these authorities' rights to freedom of expression, there is a justifiable reluctance to outlaw such impositions. Thus, the American states are not empowered to prevent parents or religious institutions from teaching children, for example, that all sexual pleasure is a sin, as long as children are free of such influences once they reach ma-

[13] The general point that physicians should acquaint patients with their moral viewpoints is made by Alastair MacIntyre [33].

jority. After all, small children and the severely incompetent tend to be less fully persons in their own right (in the sense of free moral agents) and can be seen as extensions of the person of their guardians. It is for this reason that it is proper for guardians to decide for their wards what lies in their best interests. It is the guardians, not the incompetent wards, who are unambiguously self-determining and therefore have freedom worthy of the respect of others.

From a moral point of view, there are obvious limitations to the control of guardians over their wards. For instance, guardians may not do to their wards what is clearly not in the best interests of their wards. But since there is little unanimity concerning a given person's sexual best interests, few direct interventions can be justified in the prerogative of guardians to educate (or refuse to educate) their wards in sexual matters. At best, one could justify compulsory sex education in public schools regarding physical and psychological facts about reproduction, sexual functioning, birth control, and venereal diseases on the basis that this was a basic prerequisite for social functioning (in consideration of the good of the children, apart from any benefit to society). Granted that there is a need to avoid advocating particular religiously based sexual life-styles in public schools, there could still properly be an endorsement of the general outlines of secular sexual life-styles (for example, that the use of contraception has good social consequences).

It follows that sex therapists who have not identified themselves as partisans of particular religions and who have not made prior promises to the parents of the children they are treating, could properly recommend certain attitudes toward sexual activities. The therapist should be candid with parents and indicate that he or she is advocating a particular sexual life-style. The degree of candor to be used with the child depends on the maturity of the child. As children approach majority, they can be treated more as patients or clients in their own right, rather than simply as wards of certain guardians, which is to say, as children become more able to understand the nature and significance of decisions with regard to sexual activities, they can on moral grounds demand respect for those decisions—including candid help in appraising the merits of various sexual life-styles.

SEXUAL RELATIONS BETWEEN
THERAPIST AND PATIENT

The taboo against patient-therapist sexual relations is deep and widespread. One finds it, for example, in the Hippocratic oath, which forbids the physician to take advantage of the therapeutic context in order to engage in either homosexual or heterosexual relations:

Into whatsoever houses I enter, I will enter to help the sick, and I will abstain from all intentional wrongdoing and harm, especially from abusing the bodies of man or woman, bond or free [34].

The question is whether such a restriction should be absolute, and in particular, whether the prohibition should apply to sex therapy. The answer to this question turns on four issues of conditions: (1) whether the client (patient) is clearly apprised prior to the commencement of therapy that sexual relations are likely to be a part of the therapeutic context and has freely consented; (2) whether therapist-patient sexual relations provide particular therapeutic advantages in the treatment of certain sexual problems; (3) whether such advantages, if they exist, would outweigh the potential for coercion and exploitation consequent upon the removal of the prohibition against therapist-patient sexual relations; and—if the two preceding conditions are met—(4) whether one could employ special sexual partner surrogates to achieve the good results sought, while lessening the potential for exploitation.

First and most important, individuals should not enter unknowingly into a situation within which sexual relations will be proffered as a part of treatment. Considering patients' perceived need for treatment, their frequent willingness to accept without question what the therapist judges best for them, and the awe with which some patients regard therapists, therapists may have an unfairly manipulative advantage over patients. Thus, at the very least, any anticipated use of sexual relations as a part of therapy (even via sexual partner surrogates) must be disclosed in advance. Such disclosure does not necessarily eliminate the possibility of manipulation or coercion, however.

The second issue (the question of therapeutic advantage) is empirical and requires research to determine what is, in fact, the case. Since it is reasonable to assume that the potential for coercion or exploitation is significant in therapist-patient sexual relations, it would be necessary to engage in such research only with great care, interpreting any findings with considerable caution. The burden of proof would fall on those persons who wished to approve patient-therapist sexual relations. The onus would be particularly heavy because of the available alternative of using sexual partner surrogates (thereby dividing responsibilities and diminishing the conflicts of interest and possibilities for exploitation[14]). Obviously, complete separation of roles would not be possible with the use of sexual partner surrogates (that is, both the therapist and the surrogate would presumably be on the same "team"); special precautions would be in order. As long as one has no general grounds for opposing sexual relations prior to or outside of marriage (and thus, for example, would not oppose treating an individual with sexual dysfunction in conjunction with a nonspouse partner of the patient's choosing), one should not oppose absolutely the use of sexual partner surrogates.[15] Still, there are numerous areas of concern, including (1) avoiding the exploitation of sexual partner surrogates (here special issues arise regarding the moral status of prostitution[16]); (2) disclosing fully to prospective sexual partner surrogates the possible social and psychological effects of their profession; (3) obtaining—when applicable and feasible—the consent of the spouse (or established sexual partner) of any patient with whom a sexual partner surrogate is to be used;[17] and (4) having

[14] This is often done in medicine. For example, in the case of the transplantation of kidneys and other organs from brain-dead patients, the physician pronouncing the patient dead should not be the transplant surgeon [35]. He or she should not even be a member of the transplant team [36].

[15] In fact, there would be no strong moral grounds against supplying male sexual partner surrogates for females or against supplying homosexual sexual partner surrogates, if the other questions regarding the use of surrogates can be resolved. However, one might decline to provide such services for prudential reasons (such as local legal sanctions).

[16] As long as individuals are not coerced to be prostitutes, the foregoing arguments regarding choice among life-styles would apply. One may not wish to forward prostitution as an optimal career choice, yet one need not have strong moral considerations against it.

[17] The consent of the spouse would be desirable as a recognition of the marriage covenant, but not as a necessary condition (just as the consent of one spouse for the other's sterilization or abortion is a desirable but not a necessary condition). The

good indications that the benefits are likely to exceed the harm accruing to patients incident to the use of sexual partner surrogates.[18] In short, the interest is, as it should be in any medical context, to avoid coercing or harming the patients involved.

In summary, one should attempt to avoid the coercion that is likely to accompany therapist-patient sexual relations, as well as similar difficulties that might be encountered in sexual relations between patients and professional partner surrogates. Beyond these admonitions, the level of concern that should be voiced is as yet unclear, given the sparse data available concerning the effects of such practices. In the absence of reliable information to the contrary, one should always move conservatively: First, do no harm [37].

CONCLUSIONS

Given the foregoing discussion, four general points can be advanced regarding the intrusion of therapists' values into the treatment context and the probity of therapist-patient sexual relations. These points are here summarized in order to indicate rubrics under which general guidelines for sex therapy can be developed:

1. Disease language should be restricted to those conditions acknowledged as impeding a function generally held to be proper to humans (for example, impotence in a male during the reproductive years). One may extend the scope of disease language (for example, deciding to term impotence in an 80-year-old male a disease), provided that a significant number of

---

value of adequate sexual functioning would then be recognized as a 'good' that one spouse could not deny another; after all, one would not want to force a divorce in order to allow sex therapy. The same considerations apply with regard to the consent of the spouse (or established sexual partner) of the partner surrogate. One should recognize the possible legal dangers of using married surrogates without the consent of their partners, or of providing a surrogate to a patient without the consent of the patient's spouse.

[18] This condition is prudential. In the strict sense there are no strong moral grounds against allowing an individual, ceteris paribus, to choose to assume a risk. However, the therapist should discourage undue risk-taking on the part of the patient.

individuals within the particular culture experience distress from the condition in question (for example, a group of 80-year-old males arguing that impotence is inappropriate for their age group). But if there is disagreement regarding the appropriate use of the disease idiom, the therapist should speak rather of "distress" specific to those who have not achieved physiological or psychological goals they hold to be proper for themselves (for example, impotence in those 80-year-old males who are interested in sexual intercourse).[19] One should indicate to patients that the meaning of such terms is relative to particular circumstances and that there is no clear standard or definition of successful adaptation or health (and therefore of dysfunction or disease).

2. Particular sexual practices should not be condemned as immoral as long as they do not violate the individual freedom of other persons. If the therapist disapproves of a particular sexual practice from his or her own moral or religious viewpoint, he or she should announce this fact to prospective patients prior to the inception of therapy (for example, "I am a devout Methodist therapist . . .").

3. The therapist may properly solicit a patient's agreement regarding the virtues of a particular sexual life-style only if the therapist informs the patient that he or she is not simply stating medical facts.

4. Therapist-patient sexual relations should be avoided unless there is good evidence that, in particular cases, such practices have special benefits not provided by other forms of treatment. In such cases, the use of sexual partner surrogates is preferable, if feasible, with special provisions to avoid coercion and harm to either the patient or the surrogate. Informed consent to the attendant risks should be obtained from all parties involved.

Finally, in all these considerations the therapist should remember the special values of intimacy and love that our culture teaches us to nurture. The therapist should be attentive to helping those who

[19] This tactic also circumvents the problem of causing unwarranted anxiety by forcing the sick role (with the special opprobrium of deviancy) upon individuals who are not in fact diseased.

come for aid with the awareness that sexual activities can help those values to grow and prosper, thus enobling human life.

REFERENCES

1. Cook, J. *Captain Cook's Journal 1768–71*. Edited by Capt. W. S. L. Wharton. London: Elliot Stock, 1893.
2. Engelhardt, H. T., Jr. Human Well-Being and Medicine: Some Basic Value Judgments in the Biomedical Sciences. In H. T. Engelhardt, Jr., and D. Callahan (Eds.), *Science, Ethics, and Medicine*. Hastings-on-Hudson, N.Y.: Hastings Center, 1976. Pp. 120–139.
3. Engelhardt, H. T., Jr. The Concepts of Health and Disease. In H. T. Engelhardt, Jr., and S. F. Spicker (Eds.), *Evaluation and Explanation in the Biomedical Sciences*. Dordrecht, Holland: D. Reidel, 1975. Pp. 125–141.
4. Engelhardt, H. T., Jr. Explanatory models in medicine: Facts, theories, and values. *Texas Reports on Biology and Medicine* 32: 234–248, 1974.
5. Engelhardt, H. T., Jr. Ideology and etiology. *Journal of Medicine and Philosophy* 1:256–268, 1976.
6. Parsons, T. Definitions of Health and Illness in the Light of American Values and Social Structure. In E. G. Jaco (Ed.), *Patients, Physicians and Illness*. Glencoe, Ill.: Free Press, 1958. Pp. 165–187.
7. Parsons, T. Illness, Therapy and the Modern Urban American Family. In E. G. Jaco (Ed.), *Patients, Physicians and Illness*. Glencoe, Ill.: Free Press, 1958. Pp. 234–245.
8. Parsons, T. The Mental Hospital as a Type of Organization. In M. Greenblatt, D. J. Levinson, and R. H. Williams (Eds.), *The Patient and the Mental Hospital*. Glencoe, Ill.: Free Press, 1957. Pp. 108–129.
9. Parsons, T. *The Social System*. New York: Free Press, 1951. Pp. 428–479.
10. Siegler, M., and Osmond, H. The "sick role" revisited. *Hastings Center Studies* 1:41, 1973.
11. Committee on Nomenclature and Statistics of the American Psychiatric Association. *Diagnostic and Statistical Manual of Mental Disorders (DSM-II)* (2d ed.). Washington, D.C.: American Psychiatric Association, 1968. P. 44, § 301.82.
12. McKenzie, J. M. Evaluation of the hazards of sickle trait in aviation. *Aviation, Space and Environmental Medicine* 8:753–762, 1977.
13. Livingstone, F. B. The distributions of the abnormal hemoglobin

genes and their significance for human evolution. *Evolution* 18: 685, 1964.

14. Augustine. *De bene conjugali I.* Vienna: Corpus Scriptorum Ecclesiasticorum Latinorum 41:227.
15. Kant, I. Grundlegung zur Metaphysik de Sitten. In *Kants Werke* (Akademie Textausgabe). Berlin: De Gruyter, 1968. Vol. 4, pp. 433–435.
16. Nozick, R. *Anarchy, State and Utopia.* New York: Basic Books, 1974. Pp. 3–35.
17. Noonan, J. T., Jr. *Contraception.* Cambridge, Mass.: Harvard University Press, 1966. Pp. 250, 253.
18. Kant, I. Metaphysische Anfangsgrunde der Tugendlehre. In *Kants Werke* (Akademie Textausgabe). Berlin: De Gruyter, 1968. Vol. 6, pp. 422–426.
19. O'Malley, L. S. S. *Popular Hinduism.* London: Cambridge University Press, 1935.
20. Plato. *Cratylus* 398d.
21. Nietzsche, F. *Beyond Good and Evil.* § 168.
22. Engelhardt, H. T., Jr. The disease of masturbation: Values and the concept of disease. *Bulletin of the History of Medicine* 48:234–248, 1974.
23. Howe, J. W. *Excessive Venery, Masturbation and Continence.* New York: E. B. Treat, 1887. Pp. 92–93.
24. Lewis, D. *Chastity: Or, Our Secret Sins.* Philadelphia: George Maclean, 1874. P. 316.
25. Parvin, T. The hygiene of the sexual functions. *New Orleans Medical and Surgical Journal* 11:607, 1884.
26. Aquinas. *Summa theologiae* 2–2, 154, 2. Translated by T. Gilby. McGraw-Hill, 1968.
27. Wilson, E. O. *Sociobiology.* Cambridge, Mass.: Belknap Press, 1975. P. 555.
28. Gooditch, M. Sodomy in ecclesiastical law and theory. *Journal of Homosexuality* 1:427–434, 1976.
29. Gooditch, M. Sodomy in medieval secular law. *Journal of Homosexuality* 1:295–302, 1976.
30. Engelhardt, H. T., Jr. Ideology and etiology. *Journal of Medicine and Philosophy* 1:256–268, 1976.
31. Ruddick, S. Better Sex. In R. Baker and F. Elliston (Eds.), *Philosophy and Sex.* Buffalo, N.Y.: Prometheus Books, 1975.
32. Nagel, T. Sexual perversion. *Journal of Philosophy* 66:70–83, 1969.
33. MacIntyre, A. Patients as Agents. In S. F. Spicker and H. T. Engelhardt, Jr. (Eds.), *Philosophical Medical Ethics: Its Nature and Significance.* Dordrecht, Holland: D. Reidel, 1977.
34. Hippocrates. *Oath.* In W. H. S. Jones (Trans.), *Hippocrates.* Cambridge, Mass.: Harvard University Press, 1962. P. 301.

35. Kennedy, I. M.   The Kansas statute on death: An appraisal. *New England Journal of Medicine* 285:946–950, 1971.
36. Ad Hoc Committee of the Harvard Medical School to Examine the Definition of Brain Death. A definition of irreversible coma (special communication). *Journal of the American Medical Association* 205:337–340, 1968.
37. Jonsen, A. R.   Do No Harm: Axiom of Medical Ethics. In S. F. Spicker and H. T. Engelhardt, Jr. (Eds.), *Philosophical Medical Ethics: Its Nature and Significance.* Dordrecht, Holland: D. Reidel, 1977. Pp. 27–41.

6

ACCREDITATION AND TRAINING IN SEX THERAPY

HAROLD I. LIEF
LORNA J. SARREL
PHILIP M. SARREL

In 1970 Masters and Johnson published *Human Sexual Inadequacy*, in which they described the basic psychophysiological sexual dysfunctions that plague men and women [1]. Their approach to treatment of these problems failed in less than one-fourth of the couples who had received therapy in St. Louis, a remarkable outcome since no other comparable results had been reported at that time. In a sense, they gave birth to a new field.

In 1971, in a personal communication, Dr. William H. Masters stated that he believed sex therapy would be a rapidly developing and somewhat chaotic field over the next decade. He felt chaos was unavoidable since, in the absence of any formal standards in the field, anyone could declare himself or herself a sex therapist and such persons could do anything they wanted under the rubric of sex therapy.

This prediction has proved to be accurate. In the early years of the seventies there were a few dozen sex researchers and therapists working full-time in this field. Today there are literally thousands of practitioners who present themselves to the public as sex therapists. Sex therapy now includes a variety of approaches to treatment, some of which appear to be quite effective; however, reliable evaluation of treatment outcome remains a challenge to researchers and therapists alike [2]. In addition to the problem of self-styled sex therapists who may have no relevant capabilities, there is another problem in that otherwise competent professional people who have minimal or inadequate training in the fundamentals of sexology can and do declare themselves to be sex therapists.

Sex therapy is an infant field. Without standards, it is liable to become ridden with charlatans and professionals who are incompetent—at least in sex therapy. Indeed, the nature of the field makes it peculiarly vulnerable to abuse. The dual temptations of sex and money appeal to the greedy quack or fraud who wishes to "make a fast buck" or to satisfy other needs via sexual exploitation of his or her clients. These temptations may also apply to otherwise well-meaning, self-styled therapists who, thinking they are already experts in human sexuality, believe that by reading a book or two and attending one or two short workshops they automatically become competent. Because of such practices, the public may become so suspicious and hesitant about seeking help for sexual problems that the entire field will be damaged severely.

Unlike other professional fields, sex therapy has no professional training schools, no well-accepted standards of behavior for professionals, and no system for licensing or certification. There is but one fledgling organization, the American Association of Sex Educators, Counselors, and Therapists (AASECT), which has begun to bring some order to the field through its statement of standards, its process of certification, and its listing of certified therapists. AASECT's efforts are an important beginning, but not a full solution.

Where do we go from here? What are the pros and cons of regulating sex therapy through certification or licensing? In particular, what are the ethical issues? Can we agree on a core curriculum for training and identify the ethical issues involved in setting up training programs? These are the subjects we address in this paper.

PROFESSIONAL REGULATION AND ACCREDITATION OF SEX THERAPISTS

PROFESSIONAL MONOPOLIES: FREEDOM VERSUS ORDER

Why are professions organized and regulated at all? It was Max Weber's view that "men prefer to legitimize their privileges and benefits and so give to institutions a justification for existence absent in a mere constellation of interests" [3]. The historical process by which medical care, for example, has become organized in this country has been the result of complex interacting forces: the enlightened self-interest of doctors, the pressure of health-care consumers, the lobbying efforts of other powerful interest groups (insurance companies, unions, nurses, and others), and the remarkable growth in knowledge and technology. Whatever the system of organization, it must find political acceptability if it is to become institutionalized and endure.

Perhaps the most important impetus behind professional regulation is the desire to create a degree of monopolistic control over practice. The professionals involved may deny this intent because *monopoly* has bad connotations, but in fact there are important gains both for professionals (at least those on the inside) and for society: The gains are basically in the direction of increased order and smoother functioning in a complex world. For example, consumers are already asking, "How can we select a qualified sex therapist?" Young people who want to enter the field are exerting pressure for established routes to assuming a professional identity as sex therapists. But the problem with organizing a professional monopoly is that it limits freedom. It limits the freedom of practitioners who are not inside the system, and it limits the variety (as well as the amount) of service available to consumers. Monopolies also tend to create rather fixed definitions of concepts such as *health* and *therapy*, which may inhibit innovation in the field. The tension between the desire for freedom and the desire for order is thus a fundamental philosophical and practical issue.

Another important ethical issue that touches on the matter of professional regulation is the problem of delivery of services. Berlant states that "the development of the medical profession has been closely tied with the development of stratified relationships between social groups, so that quality medical care has tended to be a prized scarcity and an object of class behavior" [3]. Despite some societal controls, health care has been largely directed by professionals, mostly physicians. Societal well-being and professional benefits and rewards may coincide, or they may not. (To paraphrase a cliché, what is good for the AMA may not be good for the country.) To offset the danger of professional interests controlling the availability and delivery of health-care services, democratic processes must be utilized. Dyck puts it this way:

The whole purpose of democratic processes from a moral point of view is to achieve a higher measure of disinterestedness, dispassionateness, and vivid imagination on how various parties are affected by one policy or another. To accomplish this, democratic processes seek to maximize participation of diverse interests, at least to achieve representation of those diverse interests and to establish procedures by which persons and groups are guaranteed due process [4].

But even if physicians and other health-care professionals are morally conscientious and patients are highly sophisticated, social policy may still result in inadequate health care to certain disadvantaged members of the population. It may not be sufficient to achieve adequate representation of diverse groups in the community on boards of agencies that control health care, unless larger health policy issues are dealt with appropriately. What is appropriate is not always obvious; there are often conflicts between claims to health care and there are inequities in the distribution of services. Although "the enjoyment of the highest attainable standard of health is one of the fundamental rights of every human being, without distinction of race, religion, political belief, economic or social condition"—according to the World Health Organization (WHO) [5]—this ideal state has not yet been attained.

We believe that at this stage in the history of sex therapy, regulation of the profession and the establishment of some generally accepted standards for training are likely to have the effect of making sex therapy more widely available to all income groups. Within five or ten years this desirable effect could reverse itself, although other trends within health care (consumer representation, some form of national health-care system, health maintenance organizations, etc.), if they continue, may lead to a more just and democratic process. We are not necessarily fated to repeat the process of organization and institutionalization of the medical profession.

The issues of monopolistic control and delivery of services are clearly interrelated. If the professional group in power defines appropriate care in a narrow, elitist way, emphasizes the need for rigorous training, and excludes all unorthodox approaches, sex therapy could become an elitist field available almost exclusively to the well-to-do. This development can and should be prevented. On a purely practical level we have observed many sex therapists engaging in antimonopolistic and nonelitist behavior. They have offered their knowledge and expertise to groups of paraprofessionals and volunteers so that these people could engage in "front line" sex counseling. They have served as consultants to schools and colleges to advise them in setting up sex education programs and sex counseling services. They have set up workshops for groups of adults and families to promote sexual health. To the extent that these goals—namely, the dissemination of knowledge and sharing of expertise—can be established as a part of the professional role of sex therapists, the field can help its practitioners to avoid the elitist trap and serve all the people, not just the privileged few.

ADVANTAGES OF REGULATION

1. We are living in a time in which health professionals will be increasingly accountable to the public for both the quality and the cost of services provided. To the extent that a field can demonstrate satisfactory self-regulation, it may be less subject to outside control.
2. Ensuring a basic level of professional competence assures the consumer (patient or client) that he or she will receive at least minimally adequate care. If there is a fee for services, the patient or client should receive services commensurate with the fee. Even if the monetary transaction is indirect (through tax dollars or third-party payment), receipt of fair value for a fee paid remains an ethical issue. However, it is unclear at present exactly how to measure the value of such services: by time and motion alone, by comparison with other types of health care, or by extrinsic guidelines (which have not yet been developed) reflecting the special skills and competencies of sex therapists?
3. Regulating training practices and setting standards of performance and ethical behavior should help to ensure that the patient or client will not be exploited, harmed, or misused by the practitioner. (This is a major purpose of this meeting.)

4. Licensing or certification of practitioners makes it more difficult for a practitioner to make false claims about his or her training, experience, or competence.

5. Certification or licensure would help to delineate levels of competence, making it easier for inadequately trained professionals to recognize their own limitations. (An example from medicine is the physician who, though not surgically trained, could legally practice surgery, but refrains because of possible censure by his or her peers, the threat to courtesy privileges at the hospital, and the possible threat of malpractice suits.) Furthermore, standards of competence in the field would provide additional motivation for those who wish to become sex therapists to undertake appropriate training. Delineation of standards would also tend to upgrade those training programs that are deficient in some fashion.

6. Where training is carried out with the highest professional and ethical standards, practitioners are more likely to incorporate a manner of professional behavior that will protect patients and clients.

7. Publicly recognized standards would enable the consumer to select a sex therapist more wisely and would make it easier for professionals making referrals to choose someone competent.

8. It will be in the interests of accredited practitioners to inform the public. For this reason, any form of accreditation or certification short of total licensing by the government is likely to promote consumer awareness and educate the public.

9. A professional organization or certifying or licensing board might serve as a vehicle for consumer complaints—a possible alternative to malpractice litigation. Fellow practitioners could also lodge complaints about ethical violations by peers or incompetence of colleagues due to incapacity with a board or organization having power to revoke a certification or license.[1]

10. Regulation is likely to make sex therapy more accessible to persons in lower income brackets. At present, sex therapy is avail-

[1] Thirteen states have enacted legislation making it mandatory for a doctor to report any instance of a colleague's professional misconduct, whether it be an ethical violation or the result of incompetence due to the physician's functional impairment.

able mainly to those who can afford to pay private practitioners. Economically less advantaged people would be able to receive sex therapy if there were more clinics with free care or sliding scale fees and if third parties (including Medicaid) would agree to pay for sex therapy. Indeed, the adoption of more uniform training standards and certification would be likely to promote a better dissemination of sex therapy into all levels of the population:

a. Certification or licensing is likely to lead to a greater acceptance of sex therapy as a legitimate area of health practice, which would in turn exert pressure on third-party payers.

b. Granting agencies that fund training programs are likely to encourage selection of trainees who are not in private practice and who plan to use their training in a public setting or become teachers or trainers of others.

c. Public and social agencies are more eager to support their staff members' seeking training if there is some certification or license to be obtained from the process.

d. Hospitals, agencies, and clinics are more likely to hire a professional to do sex therapy if there is some reliable way of judging the person's level of competence, such as proof that he or she has completed an established training program and is certified or licensed.

DISADVANTAGES OF REGULATION

1. Any field—but particularly a new field—is enhanced by keeping options open, by examining new ideas and techniques, and by encouraging outcome research; premature adoption of standards may maintain certain perspectives and therapeutic methods and eliminate others before sufficient time has elapsed for adequate study.

2. Certain important questions remain to be resolved in the area of training. For example, how thorough must training be in terms of duration, mastery of theoretical and practical knowledge, and supervised clinical experience? Can people be trained for sex counseling and sex therapy, respectively, at different

levels? To what extent is medical training (or at least medical supervision) necessary? Premature closure imposed by regulation could jeopardize satisfactory settlement of these issues.

3. Establishment of official standards for training and practice in sex therapy could discourage or prevent physicians, marriage counselors, and other professionals from carrying out sex counseling or therapy in their practices.

4. Setting standards and providing regulation necessarily involves regulatory bodies, politics, power struggles, bureaucracy, and red tape. Benefits that may accrue from regulation are liable to be outweighed by these concomitant impediments.

5. Licensing or certification of practitioners can lead to the creation of a monopoly in the practice of sex therapy. This can be used by the few on the "inside" as a self-serving tactic to exclude the many on the "outside."

6. Regulation may predispose to acceptance of a mediocre order of competence—a move toward a "lowest common denominator" set of criteria. (Such effects have been noted in other fields that are currently regulated: For example, a person with an M.D. degree and a state medical license can call himself or herself a psychiatrist and engage in the practice of psychiatry—including the administration of electroshock therapy—with impunity and without benefit of legal sanction, even though this person has no postgraduate training in the field.)

WEIGHING THE ADVANTAGES AND DISADVANTAGES OF REGULATION

The arguments in favor of some form of regulation of sex therapy as a profession appear to us to be somewhat stronger than the arguments against regulation. However, the solution does not lie merely in the act of choosing to adopt regulation, but rather in developing a schema for regulation that minimizes and guards against its potential liabilities while maximizing its positive elements. The experiences of other professions such as psychology, marriage counseling, and medicine can assist in this difficult task. In this perspective, it appears that regulation—despite its shortcomings—offers the best course. Without the safeguards provided by some form of voluntary regulation organized by the members of the field, the eventual likelihood of a less desirable alternative, externally imposed regulation, is greatly increased.

VARIOUS FORMS OF
ACCREDITATION FOR PRACTITIONERS

Membership in a Professional Organization for Sex Therapists

While membership in a professional organization generally implies at least a minimal level of training and experience, there are too many exceptions to make this an absolute criterion of competence and integrity. All too often, organizational membership reflects whom one knows rather than what one knows. Furthermore, there is some question as to whether there should be several professional organizations or only one. A single organization avoids confusion and overlap, but there is not enough uniformity of thought within sex therapy at the moment for a single organization to speak for all practitioners. A degree of pluralism may help to maintain flexibility in the field. (For comparison, we might note that in the field of psychoanalysis the American Psychoanalytic Association and the American Academy of Psychoanalysis have different standards for admission to their organizations. Membership in either group indicates attainment of a level of training sufficient to qualify one to be recognized as a psychoanalyst.) On the other hand, too much pluralism can be very confusing.

Certification of Specialists by a Superordinate Organization

At some point in the history of the development of most specialties, a superordinate organization has been established to set standards for training and practice. An example of such a board is the American Board of Internal Medicine. In the recent past these have been salutary developments, but excessive control and the inhibition of innovation and creativity remain potential dangers. There is further damage in the creation of a multiplicity of specialty or subspeciality boards, which would splinter the field too greatly and might prove confusing to the public and professionals alike. There is also the problem—not addressed in this paper—of the criteria by which certification or licensure is achieved.

Licensing versus Certification or Accreditation[2]

Clearly, government licensing would provide the strictest form of regulation for practice. This has both advantages and disadvantages. Licensing is the most monopolistic approach because anyone not licensed is legally constrained from practicing. On the other hand, licensing is also the most effective way of eliminating quackery, although certification also appears promising in this regard. In the field of marriage and family counseling, three states now limit practice to persons who are licensed and three have adopted certification. In all six states, there has been "a demonstrated reduction in quackery and fraudulent practice" [6]. Evidence of this can be demonstrated quite objectively in states where licensing laws were enacted: The yellow pages of the telephone book show a marked reduction in the number of persons listed as marriage counselors, and the types of announcement and credentials presented are more uniform and appear to be more genuine. It is interesting to see how quickly the effects of state licensing were felt. They were not the result of legal prosecution of offenders—in fact, insufficient time had elapsed for such action to be completed. This supports the contention of Myles Johnson:

Clearly, licensure and regulatory acts of all types have been inadequately and even capriciously enforced in this country. If the impact of such regulations depended on a "body count" of persons convicted of violating them, the acts would have to be considered a fraud. The truth is that the impact of such regulatory legislation is not measured in its enforcement but in the *lack* of enforcement [7].

Licensing by the state may be particularly disadvantageous in the field of sex therapy. Because intense feelings and attitudes are associated with sexuality, it may be especially dangerous to place the field in the hands of potentially misguided civil servants (possibly self-serving bureaucrats of politicians; possibly bigots or authoritarian officials). For example, if state licensing placed control over

[2] All fifty states license psychologists, and a few states license or certify marriage counselors. As of 1977 no state had yet licensed or certified sex therapists.

sex therapy within a state department of health and the head of that department happened to be either ill-informed or emotionally unprepared (or both) to accept the idea of sex therapy, the consequence could be disastrous both for the professions and for the public. Licensing at the state level might also lead to fossilization of the field, codifying tenets of practice into law, which would make needed change and updating extremely difficult.

It is also possible for state governments (or even the federal government) to undertake the task of accrediting practitioners via certification. This lessens the degree of control over who is entitled to practice, since lack of certification simply prevents a person from advertising himself or herself as certified. With or without certification, one is free to practice and advertise as one chooses. The principles of a free marketplace of services would thus prevail.

RECERTIFICATION OR RELICENSURE

If some form of regulation of sex therapy becomes operational, procedures for periodic review leading to requalification of practitioners are likely to follow. At the present time, physicians throughout the country participate in continuing medical education programs to update their professional skills and meet recertification standards. Some specialty boards are also beginning to require periodic recertification. Two states now require evidence of continual upgrading of knowledge and skills for relicensing.

Periodic requalification in sex therapy would be likely to involve an examination process. It could also include peer review of actual therapy cases as summarized by the therapist(s) or screened directly by way of audio- or videotapes. Such peer review would add to the scant supply of data providing direct evidence for what constitutes effective sex therapy. It could also provide feedback on the success of our criteria for selecting trainees and the success of our training programs.

RECOMMENDATIONS
REGARDING ACCREDITATION

It is our belief that some form of control over who practices sex therapy and how that practice is conducted is necessary at this time. We do not favor licensing of sex therapists because of the disadvantages listed above (in particular, the tendency toward total monopoly, the increased probability of establishing inflexible standards of practice, and the drawback of bureaucratization). We favor some type of certification, whether administered through a government body or through one or more professional organizations. As an ancillary measure, professional organizations such as the American Psychological Association, the American Psychiatric Association, the American College of Obstetricians and Gynecologists, and the National Association of Social Workers should be encouraged to set up sections dealing with sex therapy. This would be likely to encourage recognition of the need for high-quality training and standards of practice in the field.

TRAINING FOR PROFESSIONALS IN THE FIELD OF SEXUAL HEALTH

Before turning to our second major topic, issues in the training of practitioners of sex therapy, it is appropriate to try to differentiate among the three levels of competence—sex education, sex counseling, and sex therapy—described in the 1975 WHO report:

Education, counseling, and therapy may be regarded as inseparable parts of the total effort in sexual health care. First, the provision of sexual health *education* to the community, to the physician, and to other health workers has the highest priority because this can be done with the least amount of training and will affect the greatest number of people. While sex education should be a basic part of preventive medicine, it has also been shown to be effective in assisting individuals and couples to overcome sex problems. Second, there is a need for *counseling* of individuals and couples with slightly more complicated problems: This can be carried out by a nurse, midwife, the general practitioner, the gynecologist, and others. Third, there is a need for in-depth sex *therapy* by specially trained professionals who see the people with the most complicated problems. Health and other community workers require more specialized training to undertake sex counseling and sex therapy [5].

Table 6-1 indicates the hierarchical system of professional tasks and roles in response to patients' sexual problems and primary

TABLE 6-1. *Classification of Professional Tasks and Roles in Response to Sexual Problems*

Level of diagnosis of sexual problem	Patient need	Professional task	Professional role
Sexual ignorance	Need to know	To provide accurate information	Inquirer-educator
Situational discomfort/anxiety	Need to relax	To reduce or to eliminate immediate causes of sexual dysfunction	Counselor
Interpersonal distance/conflict	Need to reorient the relationship	To reshape dyadic system	Marital therapist
Historical intrapsychic conflict	Need to explore tension between intrapsychic and interpersonal systems	To explore the interface between historical conflict and sexual discomfort/dysfunction	Psychotherapist
All of the above	Flexible use of new repertoire of sexual behaviors	Formulating hierarchy of patient needs and incorporating those into a sequence of treatment	Sex therapist

Source:: From N. Vines and H. I. Lief, The Physician's Roles and Tasks in Sex Counseling and Therapy, presented at a workshop of the American College of Physicians, April 1976, Philadelphia; also in H. I. Lief, Sex Education in Medicine: Retrospect and Prospect (in Rosenzweig and Pearsall [9]).

needs. The sex counselor should be a competent sex educator; the sex therapist should be a competent sex educator and counselor and, in addition, must have attained a minimum level of competence as a marital therapist and psychotherapist and must be familiar with the specialized skills (such as graded behavioral tasks) usually employed to facilitate effective sexual communication and to overcome sexual inhibitions.

All levels of sexual health care require the ability to conduct an interview competently; increased skill is required as the complexity of the case increases. The skillful interviewer is able to interact with patients by means of "exploratory" responses (which are designed to elicit additional information) as well as "understanding" responses (which allow patients to identify the interviewer's thoughts and feelings). By using these methods the interviewer can provide a relaxed atmosphere in which patients feel understanding and support—and feel they have obtained the interviewer's permission to express themselves honestly. The interviewer may also give tacit or explicit permission for patients to experiment with sexual behaviors that heretofore have been inhibited or associated with guilt or anxiety.

An ethical issue of considerable importance occurs in conjunction with the therapist's efforts to reduce or remove sexual inhibitions. Clients' beliefs or attitudes often stand in the way of improved sexual functioning and increased pleasure. What happens when a new behavior, which the client believes to be wrong or shameful, is deemed a necessary step in overcoming a sexual dysfunction? One example is the recommendation to masturbate (often suggested to a woman who is totally anorgasmic). Although most women will undertake this assignment, many will have reservations and some will be unable to accept this prescription because of strong feelings of guilt or revulsion. The judgment about whether masturbation or other inhibited behaviors can or should be recommended is one that requires empathy, tact, and appropriate timing on the part of the therapist.

At the level of sex education, the sexual health caretaker may provide information, correct misinterpretations and misconceptions, and abolish sexual myths (for example, mistaken notions about the effects of aging, the importance of penis size, the need for simultaneous orgasm, or the dangers of oral sex). Education can often be combined with medical treatment such as changing medication (for example, prescribing a higher-dose birth control pill when a low-dose pill seems to provide insufficient estrogen for maintenance of vaginal health) or treating vaginitis. The opportunity to combine sex education with direct medical therapy is of course unavailable to a therapist who lacks medical training, unless he or she collaborates with a physician.

Sex counseling is a method of working with individuals or couples that utilizes education but goes beyond education; it includes offering advice, allowing ventilation of feelings, promoting communication, and—on occasion—employing behavior therapy techniques such as sensate focus [1]. Sex counseling may be practiced by a wide range of persons, from the doctor in office practice to the social worker in an agency setting or a nurse in a family planning clinic. When sex counseling involves assigning behavioral tasks and attempting to change attitudes that may be blocking clients' sexual responses, it approaches a form of sex therapy. Persons who offer this type of counseling require specialized training of some kind, but it is unclear how and where they should get such training. Perhaps the best training available at present is via workshops in human sexuality, which are being offered around the country (some under the auspices of AASECT, others by sex therapists who work privately or are affiliated with universities or medical schools). One of the most important skills in sex counseling is knowing when to refer a client to a sex therapist, psychiatrist, or marriage counselor. Each counselor must be aware of his or her own limitations and must be alert to those situations in which immediate referral should be made.

The sine qua non of sex therapy is flexibility. The sex therapist should be flexible enough to use a variety of techniques, with the choice of technique depending on the circumstances. In addition, sex therapists should be equipped to do either conjoint marital therapy or individual psychotherapy in sufficient depth to allow effective use of behavior modification techniques such as sensate focus. Timing is a critical factor in using specific behavioral techniques to overcome sexual dysfunction; in many instances conjoint or individual therapy must be carried out prior to the use of sensate focus. On the other hand, many therapists use sensate focus as a diagnostic tool in the hope that resistances will be minimal and behavioral therapy will thereby be facilitated. If strong resistances are encountered, it should be recognized that these provide clues to the underlying psychodynamics of the client or client couple. Therapists who can respond flexibly with a variety of treatment methods must have much more intensive and prolonged training than sex educators or counselors. They must depend on clinical experience to select appropriate methods or to initiate changes in strategy and technique as the circumstances suggest. In keeping with their increased sophistication, they must be relatively free from untoward biases and blind spots that might create nonproductive countertransference reactions. The skillful sex therapist should be able to work either with a cotherapist or alone (since cotherapy is not always available or practical).

After the initial phase of evaluation and history-taking, the therapist(s) and client or client couple should reach an agreement (often loosely referred to as a contract) about the goals of treatment. Will the goal be removal of the sexual dysfunction or dysfunctions? Will it be to help the couple deal with their marital interactions, including their sexual dysfunction(s)? Might it also involve efforts to remove any nonsexual maladaptive behavior that one or both partners may exhibit? In general, the best therapy is the least therapy necessary to attain the stated goals. The therapy "contract" negotiated at the start may be renegotiated at any point along the way. When patients actively participate in setting goals, the therapist is less likely to fall into the trap of defining goals based on his or her own value system. (A common example is the therapist who defines sexual health in terms of coitus and coital orgasm, even if these goals are not shared by the client or clients being treated.) Clear definition of the goals of therapy will lessen the likelihood of clients having unrealistic or grandiose expectations.

TRAINING FOR SEX EDUCATION AND COUNSELING

All health-care professionals should possess the basic knowledge and skills needed to deal with sex education and sex counseling within the context of their practices. However, those persons who lack interest in or have inhibitions about carrying out sexual health care should not undertake this aspect of health care delivery. The fundamental courses in human sexuality now available in over 100 medical schools provide a basis for physicians to become proficient sex educators. Most of these courses do not yet provide sufficient opportunity to conduct sex counseling under supervision; the majority of physicians in practice today, unless they have had postgraduate training in this area, must settle into roles as sex educators rather than counselors. Since about one-half of the medical schools now have established sex therapy clinics, there may well be a marked improvement in the competence of physicians to move to the level of sex counseling in the decade ahead.

Curriculum changes similar to those that have taken place in the medical schools should be incorporated in the training of social workers, psychologists, and nurses. Workshops or courses in human sexuality should also be included in the training of community mental health workers and staff members of family planning clinics, rehabilitation and geriatric facilities, and other specialized clinical services in which sexual function and dysfunction are relevant concerns.

TRAINING FOR SEX THERAPY

While training does not ensure competence, it greatly increases the probability of competence. The training of sex therapists is now so variable that the situation verges on chaos. Those who are interested in learning requisite skills are bewildered: They take courses and attend workshops that overlap in some areas but leave gaps in other areas. It is difficult for many trainees to find an opportunity for supervised practice. There is a crying need for agreement among professionals in the field as to what constitutes an adequate background for entry into training programs and what should form the core curriculum essential to training. This could serve as a guide for trainers and trainees alike.

Selection of Trainees

ETHICAL CONCERNS. Ethical concerns in the selection of trainees begin with consideration of their responsibility toward future clients. This includes (1) selecting those trainees who are most likely to provide competent therapy; (2) selecting those trainees who are least likely to exploit or harm clients through unethical behavior or (unconscious) coercion; and (3) selecting a certain number of trainees who are likely to work in public agencies and clinics rather than entirely in private (fee-for-service) practice. In addition, there are ethical responsibilities on the part of the trainer or supervisor toward applicants and trainees. These include a respect for the individual's privacy; selectors must weigh this carefully in cases where it conflicts with the need to solicit specific personal information in order to evaluate an applicant's character or potential for competence. Selection boards also have an ethical obligation to conduct a careful and objective assessment of each applicant.

There is also a general ethical responsibility toward the field of sex therapy itself. This is a potential area of controversy. Since sex therapy as a discipline is especially vulnerable to criticism, some might argue that it is advisable to select only those trainees who are not likely to cause embarrassment or call undue attention to the field through their personal behavior. We have some concern that such a policy could lead to unwarranted prejudice against applicants merely on the basis of their life-style.

THE RELEVANCE OF A PROFESSIONAL DEGREE. What does it mean if an applicant for training has already earned an advanced degree (for example, M.D., Ph.D., M.S.W., or a master's degree in a behavioral science)? In terms of skills, it may mean much or little. Persons with some years of clinical experience may have already acquired the basic skills in history-taking, interviewing, and psychotherapy. Such persons may also have learned much about the nature of the therapist-client interaction, how the therapist's own feelings and attitudes influence treatment, and the types of patient with whom they work well or with whom they have difficulty. On the other hand, it is possible that the professional degree may not have been accompanied by much clinical experience or training (or, for that matter, by any experience at all); in this case the degree may mean next to nothing in terms of skill development. The situation is even more complicated in the case of certain clinicians who are so "locked in" to a particular mode of treatment that they have difficulty in learning new approaches (such as couple-oriented therapy or cotherapy) or new roles (such as the egalitarian inquiring role of a psychotherapist, in contrast to the directive approach of the typical physician). At the other extreme are the psychoanalysts who have difficulty in learning the more directive style of the behavioral therapist; sex therapy, at least for the more difficult cases, usually requires a combination of psychotherapy, marital therapy, and behavioral therapy.

Regardless of the academic degree earned by the applicant, several years of counseling or experience in the conduct of psychotherapy should be a requirement: Otherwise the trainees have to learn the basic fundamentals of psychotherapy, interviewing techniques, and history-taking at the expense of time and attention devoted to the conduct of sex therapy per se. The applicant's counseling experience should be carefully scrutinized, since it is likely to be a better indicator of suitability for training than the specific degree. A professional degree carries the possibility of professionalization and its concomitant advantages and disadvantages (cited above). A doctorate usually indicates a greater degree of professionalization and persistence, not necessarily an increase in levels of skills.

PERSONAL CHARACTERISTICS, INCLUDING TRAINEE SEXUALITY. In the long run, personal characteristics of trainees are probably more important than their previous experience. Yet it is difficult to select candidates with the characteristics of good therapists, in part because there is no general agreement about what those characteristics are. A study involving a three- to four-year follow-up of candidates for training in psychiatry and psychoanalysis clearly demonstrated the inability to predict accurately which applicants would become good therapists on the basis of the personality characteristics gleaned from their initial screening [8]. Nevertheless, some form of screening should be carried out to eliminate those applicants with psychoses or sociopathic personalities.

How relevant are applicants' or trainees' personal sex histories to their competence as sex therapists or to their future professional ethics? If a candidate's personal sex life is relevant, to what extent and in what manner can inquiry be made while protecting the individual's right to privacy? These are serious and complex ethical questions that cannot be answered definitively here, partly because of the lack of any data on this point. We may all believe that there are some important ways in which a person's sex life and sexual attitudes influence his or her professional behavior and competence, but we cannot at this stage be scientific in our judgments. We know that some celibate nuns and priests can offer adequate sex counseling and that heterosexuals can effectively counsel homosexuals (and vice versa). There are no simple formulas, and each person must be evaluated as an individual. Yet, in order to establish ethical standards for selecting trainees, we must make some general decision based on present knowledge.

It is necessary to distinguish between personal sexual behavior that is pathological (perhaps even criminal) and sexual behavior that reflects personal life-style. If we think of sexual behavior as a continuum it is less difficult to make decisions regarding behavior at either end of the continuum, keeping in mind that what appears to be a variant life-style to one person may be a serious moral issue to another person. At one extreme, if a trainee has a criminal record involving sexual assault or has exhibited ongoing paraphiliac behavior, he or she should not be considered as an acceptable applicant except under the most unusual circumstances (which are rather difficult even to imagine). At the other end of the continuum, it would be unethical to reject a trainee because he or she has an "open" marriage or lives with a sexual partner without benefit of matrimony. The majority of difficult decisions will lie toward the middle of the continuum. There is a need for flexibility here, since ideas about how personal sexual activities and attitudes influence professional behavior are likely to change over time, as data accumulates. Flexibility is also needed to allow for regional (geographical) variation in social attitudes. It would be a mistake to have a long and detailed list of specific "forbidden" private sexual activities for trainees.

Are an applicant's philosophy, attitudes, and feelings about sex relevant to his or her future performance as a sex therapist? We would like trainees to be "sexually healthy"—but this is a concept that is itself a value judgment. Virtually all trainees, at least initially, have some areas in which they are uncomfortable or prejudiced. One of the purposes of training is to help the trainee to recognize these areas and perhaps to change. Certainly we would not

want to train prospective sex therapists who are rigid and judg-
mental or who think sex is dirty and disgusting; but such persons
are not likely to apply for training in the first place.

Proposed Core Curriculum

Having selected trainees, one would want them to be involved in
planning their curriculum. There will inevitably be individual differences among curricula developed by different groups in different
localities. These differences are valuable, and no centralized body
should dictate details of curricula. However, there is a need for a
basic and unifying core. The following is one proposal for this core
curriculum.

A. Areas of Knowledge
1. Sexual and reproductive anatomy and physiology of sexual
   response
2. Psychosexual development from infancy through old age
3. Dynamics of interpersonal sexual relationships
4. Sociocultural factors in sex value systems
5. Medical factors that may influence sexual function: illness,
   handicaps, medication, estrogenic factors, pregnancy, contraception, fertility, and their relevance to sexual functions;
   the use of medication in sex therapy
6. Sex therapy concepts and specific techniques, including a
   variety of therapy models such as cotherapy, group treatment, and so forth
7. Recent research in the field of sexuality
8. Marital and family dynamics
9. Evaluation and referral
10. Prevention of sexual problems through education, influ-
    encing social policy decisions, and so forth
B. Experiential Learning
Trainees should have an opportunity to become comfortable
with the subject of human sexual behavior in all its variety.
They should become aware of their own sexual values, attitudes, feelings, biases, and blind spots, and should be aware of
how these may affect their work in sex therapy. Because sexual
behavior carries with it a strong emotional charge, there are

many aspects of sexual health care that may elicit strong feelings and set up inappropriate countertransferences. Therefore, the need for attitudinal experiential learning remains a sine qua non of training at all levels of sexual health care.[3] Training should also include instruction in the complex interpersonal dynamics of cotherapy, with particular emphasis on the influences of sex-role stereotypes on cotherapy.

C. Skills

1. Case material learned passively

The trainee should have the opportunity to hear (and perhaps to see) actual cases by audio- or videotape, through a one-way mirror, or in the capacity of a relatively silent cotherapist. This experience should include discussion of these cases with the therapist(s) involved.

2. Supervised experience

Training should always include supervised experience in the conduct of sex therapy. A trainee should have at least 200 hours of *supervised* clinical experience; the optimum would be 500 hours of clinical experience, with 100 hours of individual supervision and 100 hours of group supervision. As part of their supervised clinical experience, trainees should have the opportunity to work alone, to be part of a cotherapy team, and to conduct group sex therapy. A method whereby the trainee conducts therapy as an active and equal cotherapist with an experienced therapist probably provides the greatest protection for patients or clients. Long-distance clinical supervision of trainees by videotape may be a useful technique in some settings.

Completion of a specified number of hours in clinical experience and under supervision does not automatically create a skilled therapist, since personal factors often interfere with the acquisition of knowledge and skills or with their appropriate utilization. Nevertheless, minimum standards should be established and maintained.

[3] There are many ways of accomplishing this [9]. Some of the standard methods are sexual attitude restructuring (SAR), which makes use of erotic films and small group discussions; individual and group supervision; working in tandem with a more experienced cotherapist; Kagan's "interpersonal recall system" [10]; and supervised role-playing.

D. Ethics

Trainees should participate in discussions of the major ethical issues in sex therapy—one of which is the conflict of interests and values inherent in the dual role of the student therapist.

E. Personal Growth

Training should provide for personal growth as well as professional growth. Personal growth during professional training is a step-by-step process in which attitudinal teaching and experiential learning are as important as the acquisition of information and the development of skills [11].

Evaluation and Accreditation

We recommend that an evaluation process for training programs be instituted, using the methods of the American Association of Marriage and Family Counselors as a model. Each training program would be carefully scrutinized in order to determine whether the stated criteria for staff, curricula, clinical experience, library, and other components of training are being met. Levels of approval can be established, ranging from "not approved" to "fully approved" and including provisional approval stipulating any deficiencies that must be corrected before full accreditation is given. Each program should be reevaluated every three to five years.

Evaluation of the individual applicant for certification as a sex therapist depends in part on successful completion of training; in part on assessing the extent to which clinical skills acquired in training are being applied in practice; and in part on scrutiny of letters of recommendation. Specific tools for evaluation might include written examinations; applicants' responses to videotaped case histories; and tapes of applicants interviewing actual or simulated patients.

Whatever methods are employed, some established form of evaluation of training programs and of individual applicants is essential if accreditation is to be recognized by potential consumers or by referring professional and agencies. A full discussion of these issues is beyond the scope of this paper.

One additional point merits attention. Potential conflicts of interest arise if a single agency or organization fulfills the dual function of accrediting training programs and certifying individual practitioners, or if the accrediting agency also conducts training programs designed to prepare individuals for certification. To ensure objectivity and credibility, the accreditation process should be carried out by an independent and autonomous group.

CONCLUSION

We have explored many but not all of the issues related to the training and regulation of sex therapists. It is clear that each issue merits further consideration. The discussion of a curricular model for training is deliberately brief and requires elaboration. We have omitted a discussion of the relationship between sexual health and health in general. This paper reflects our own emphasis on the medical component of sex therapy; future dialogue on the subject of training and accreditation should allow time for persons with different approaches to respond and add to our ideas. The possibility of medical monopoly versus the appropriate role(s) of other professionals in the delivery of sex therapy must be considered in the light of the need for medical knowledge and medical skills in order to attain therapeutic excellence.

REFERENCES

1. Masters, W. H., and Johnson, V. E. *Human Sexual Inadequacy*. Boston: Little, Brown, 1970.
2. Reynolds, B. S. Psychological treatment models and outcome results for erectile dysfunction: A critical review. *Psychological Bulletin* 84:1218–1238, 1977.
3. Berlant, J. L. *Profession and Monopoly*. Berkeley: University of California Press, 1975. P. 307.
4. Dyck, A. J. Ethics in Medicine. In S. J. Reiser, A. J. Dyck, and W. J. Curran (Eds.), *Ethics and Medicine: Historical Perspectives and Contemporary Concerns*. Cambridge, Mass.: MIT Press, 1977. P. 121.
5. World Health Organization. *Education and Treatment in Human Sexuality: The Training of Health Professionals*. Technical Report Series 572 (1974). Geneva, Switzerland: 1975.
6. Fowler, R. C. Personal communication.

7. Johnson, M. Missing the point of licensure. *Social Work* 22(2): 140, 1977.
8. Holt, R. R., and Luborsky, L. B. *Personality Patterns of Psychiatrists: A Study in Selection Techniques*, Vol. 2. Topeka, Kansas: Menninger Foundation, 1958.
9. Lief, H. I. Sex Education in Medicine: Retrospect and Prospect. In N. Rosenzweig and P. Pearsall (Eds.), *Sex Education for the Health Professional*. New York: Grune & Stratton, 1978. Pp. 22–36.
10. Kagan, N. Influencing human interaction: Eleven years with IPR (Interpersonal Process Recall). *Canadian Counsellor* 9(2):74–97, 1975.
11. Seashore, C. In grave danger of growing: Observations on the process of professional development. *Social Change Quarterly* 5(4): 36–45, 1975.

I I
DRAFT OF ETHICS GUIDELINES

DRAFT OF ETHICS GUIDELINES FOR SEX THERAPISTS, SEX COUNSELORS, AND SEX RESEARCHERS

This set of guidelines represents a systematic attempt to delineate the ethical responsibilities of professionals working as sex therapists, sex counselors, sex educators, or sex researchers, regardless of their disciplinary background. The intent is to provide, within the framework of these principles, guidance both for professionals and for the public regarding standards of ethical conduct.

These guidelines are designed to be adopted by institutions, organizations, governing bodies, or agencies for whom they may be applicable. There is no discussion of certain topics such as professional etiquette, the process of investigation of grievances, enforcement of these standards, or types of disciplinary action that might be appropriate, since these are properly within the jurisdiction of any group that adopts these guidelines.

Because not every situation that may present an ethical dilemma can be foreseen or specifically addressed, it is important to realize that the omission of a subject in these guidelines does not imply either endorsement or condemnation of related conduct: Such situations must be judged by the application of general standards of ethical conduct. It is hoped that these guidelines will serve as a flexible instrument, since unanimity of opinion rarely exists in the interpretation of what is ethical or unethical.

SECTION I: COMPETENCE
OF SEX THERAPISTS[1]

It is the ethical responsibility of every sex therapist to maintain high standards of professional competence and integrity. Competence and integrity are interrelated qualities that are both requisite to the responsible provision of service to others: Competence without integrity or integrity without competence is an unsatisfactory compromise of professionalism. It is important to protect the public and other professionals from persons who represent themselves as sex therapists but in fact are lacking in competence. Because this is a relatively new field of professional practice, some established and recognized practitioners of sex therapy do not meet all educational and training requirements that can now be recommended for the field. Such individuals, however, should be able to demonstrate their competence to the satisfaction of their peers.

1. Sex therapists describe their education, training, experience, professional affiliations, and competence in an honest and accurate manner.
   a. Educational degrees are cited by a sex therapist only when they have been received from an accredited institution that is recognized by a regional or national agency.
   b. Educational programs, including workshops, seminars, symposia, colloquia, and undergraduate or graduate courses are not to be regarded as clinical training in sex therapy unless they specifically include faculty supervision of the conduct of sex therapy by the student or participant or a practicum in sex therapy under appropriate supervision. It is inaccurate and dishonest to claim that one has received clinical training in sex therapy by attending a lecture, demonstration, conference, panel discussion, or other similar teaching presentation, unless such activities are designated by an institution as a formal part of its training program, in which case actual supervised experience in sex therapy must also be a part of this program.

[1] This section on competence applies equally to sex counselors, sex educators, and sex researchers in most points. Points that have variable applicability to these other professionals are designated by a double asterisk.

   c. Experience in sex therapy is not the same as giving advice about sexual problems in the course of providing professional services to clients. Sex therapists or sex counselors should represent themselves accurately and fairly by describing their experience in terms of the time they practice sex therapy or sex counseling, rather than claiming their entire time in the practice of their primary discipline (for example, psychology, social work, psychiatry, obstetrics and gynecology) as equivalent to experience in sex therapy.**

   d. Sex therapists should claim affiliations only when formal faculty or staff appointment or employment exists or when membership or fellowship in a professional organization has been approved. It is unethical to misrepresent the degree and nature of one's professional affiliations.

   e. Competence in another primary discipline such as psychology, psychiatry, or marriage counseling is not equivalent to competence in sex therapy.

2. Sex therapists should possess adequate knowledge of the following areas:

   a. Sexual and reproductive anatomy and physiology

   b. Developmental sexuality (from conception to old age) from a psychobiological perspective

   c. Dynamics of interpersonal relationships

   d. Sociocultural factors in sexual values

   e. Medical factors that may influence sexual function, including illness, disability, drugs, pregnancy, contraception, and fertility

   f. Techniques and theory of sex therapy, including more than a single model

   g. Techniques and theory of psychotherapy**

   h. Marital and family dynamics

   i. Psychopathology

   j. Principles of evaluation and referral

   k. Ethical issues in sex therapy

This does not mean that a sex therapist must be able to provide a full range of treatment services for problems in each of these areas: Recognizing the limits and extent of one's professional competence and making appropriate referral when needed is an integral part of professional competence.

3. Sex therapists have earned an educational degree equivalent to a master's degree or doctorate in human sexuality or in a field related to the practice of sex therapy, such as psychology, social work, medicine, nursing, or counseling.**

4. Sex therapists should receive specific training in the field of sex therapy in addition to their educational background. This training should always include supervised experience in the conduct of sex therapy.**

5. Sex therapists should recognize the necessity and benefit of professional growth by participating in continuing education, reading professional journals, and attending scientific meetings. Sex therapists should maintain knowledge of current developments in their field.

6. Credentials alone do not give evidence of full competence. The proof of competence is the ability to provide objective and responsible services to clients. If the therapist, because of emotional or physical impairment, cannot provide objective and responsible services, he or she should seek competent professional consultation or treatment and refrain from professional activities while necessary.

7. Sex therapists should only recommend persons for admission to a training or educational program or for employment if they are known to be qualified in matters of education, training, and personal character. Persons who refuse to follow accepted principles of ethical conduct that apply to the field of sex therapy or to their primary discipline should not be recommended for training or employment.

8. Sex therapists should aid in preventing unqualified or incompetent persons from the practice of sex therapy.

   a. Sex therapists should not enter into association for the practice of sex therapy with unqualified or incompetent persons.

   b. Sex therapists should not make referrals to unqualified or incompetent persons. When making a referral, it is the responsibility of the sex therapist to verify the competence and integrity of the person to whom clients are referred.

   c. Sex therapists should only practice in a location where doing so would not be in violation of licensure or certification laws regulating professional practice.**

d. Sex therapists who possess knowledge of violations of ethical principles of conduct or evidence of professional incompetence should notify the appropriate authority (certifying or licensing boards, organization ethics committee, etc.), unless constrained by legal or professional considerations of confidentiality.

SECTION II: CONFIDENTIALITY IN SEX THERAPY

The intimate, personal nature most people attach to information about their sexuality requires the sex therapist to exercise extraordinary precautions in protecting the confidentiality of knowledge gained in the course of evaluation, treatment, and follow-up of clients. The following considerations apply to the area of confidentiality in the sex therapist–client relationship:

1. There is a general responsibility on the part of sex therapists to treat all information received in a therapist-client relationship as confidential, even if some portions of information appear trivial, irrelevant, or not requiring confidentiality. The client should be fully informed in advance of establishing a therapist-client relationship of the circumstances under which confidential material may be divulged.
2. The very existence of a therapist-client relationship is a confidential matter, since there are circumstances under which the identification of such a relationship would imply the presence of sexual problems or difficulties on the part of the client.
3. Information received by the sex therapist from a client or prospective client or from diagnostic evaluation, treatment, or follow-up of a client may be divulged to the extent required only under the following circumstances:
   a. When the client provides written consent (except when the information has been obtained from another person whose privacy would be violated by unauthorized disclosure). Special precautions should be taken when the release of con-

fidential information has a high risk of being harmful to the client.

b. When there is clear and imminent danger to an individual or to society. In such an instance, disclosure should only be made to appropriate family members, public authorities, or professional workers (in assessing the necessity for such an action, it is permissible for the therapist to consult with other professionals, including a lawyer, as long as the consultation protects the identify of the client involved).

c. When required to defend the sex therapist, employees or associates of the sex therapist, or the institute or employer of the sex therapist against formal accusation (for example, court proceedings or hearings of an organizational ethics committee) by the client of wrongful conduct.

d. When necessary to establish or collect a professional fee.

4. In cases in which a subpoena is served to obtain confidential information about a client, sex therapists should protect their material by claiming a privileged relationship in jurisdictions where this privilege is recognized. When such privilege is not clearly recognized, the sex therapist may obtain legal counsel and attempt to resist the subpoena. A sex therapist who believes that an unjustified violation of the confidentiality and trust of the therapist-client relationship would occur if such material were divulged under legal edict in response to subpoena may properly refuse to comply and will not be viewed as acting in other than an ethical manner.

5. If a sex therapist wishes to use information about a client or materials related to the evaluation, treatment, or follow-up of a client for purposes of education, training, research, or publication, the express free and informed consent of the client must be obtained.

6. A sex therapist may discuss in a professional manner information about a client or matters related to the evaluation, treatment, or follow-up of a client for purposes of consultation with professional colleagues.

7. Since the normal functions of an office, clinic, agency, or institution where sex therapy may be conducted include exposure of confidential information to persons who are neither sex therapists nor health-care professionals, particularly secretaries,

students, trainees, and assistants, it is important that the degree of this exposure be minimized insofar as possible and that careful methods be used to select employees, students, and trainees. Sex therapists should specifically instruct such persons in areas related to confidentiality.

8. Sex therapists are responsible for planning and maintaining the confidentiality of all client-related records, including (but not limited to) correspondence, evaluation notes, results of diagnostic testing, notes about therapy sessions, tape recordings (audio or audiovisual), and case summaries. This responsibility extends to the ultimate disposition of such confidential records.

9. It is permissible for sex therapists to provide such information about a client to an outside agency as is necessary for matters of accounting, bookkeeping, data processing, banking, duplicating, microfilming, printing, or other legitimate purposes. Care should be exercised in the selection of such an agency, and the agency should be notified of the strict need for confidentiality.

10. When sex therapy involves one or more therapists working with a client couple, whether married or not, unusual circumstances pertaining to confidentiality may arise. In such instances, the following considerations apply:

   a. Disclosure of information that one client has requested be kept confidential from his or her partner should not be made without the express consent of the person providing the confidential information.

   b. When only one client of a client couple provides consent to the release of confidential records or information, the sex therapist is responsible for releasing only information about the consenting client and must protect the confidentiality of all information deriving from the nonconsenting client.

11. When sex therapy is done in a group therapy format, special and complex circumstances pertaining to confidentiality may apply. It is important for sex therapists to recognize this risk and inform prospective clients of it. Group therapy leaders should remain alert to the potential loss of confidentiality when other clients, not bound by professional ethics, may learn information of a private, intimate, or secret nature.

12. All considerations related to confidentiality in the sex thera-

pist–client relationship continue after the termination of this relationship.

SECTION III: WELFARE OF THE CLIENT

The client is in a unique position of vulnerability in respect to the sex therapist for a variety of reasons. These may include uncertainty about the differences between propriety and impropriety, the criteria for efficacy or harmfulness, and what constitutes common, accepted practice as compared with irresponsible or unusual therapy. Clients' abilities to make judgments about their welfare are potentially lessened by the wish to succeed in therapy, the belief that the therapist(s) will always act in the clients' best interests, and the assumption of competence, knowledge, and high ethical standards on the part of the therapist. Therefore, the sex therapist must be constantly mindful of the responsibility for protection of the client's welfare and rights and for the rigorous maintenance of the trust implicit in the client-therapist relationship.

1. Sex therapists should recognize the limitations of their personal and professional competencies and should undertake evaluation or treatment of clients only in areas where they are qualified.
2. Sex therapists should not make false or exaggerated claims of efficacy in regard to their past or anticipated results.
3. Treatment should not be undertaken without the free and informed consent of the client or prospective client. Sex therapists should discuss the methods and techniques they employ with prospective clients, as well as the reasons for their use.
4. Fees and costs should be discussed freely and openly with prospective clients. Arrangements for payment should be completed at the beginning of establishing a client-therapist relationship.
5. Sex therapists are encouraged to provide services to clients who are able to provide little or no financial compensation.
6. Sex therapists are vigilant in providing services solely for the

benefit of the client and in avoiding situations with a potential for conflict of interest, impairment of professional objectivity, or abuse of the client's trust. Thus, sex therapists should generally avoid treating their employees, relatives, business associates, close friends, or their own sexual partners.

7. It is unethical for the therapist to engage in sexual activity with a client.

8. Sex therapists should not observe clients engaging in sexual activity. In addition to the invasion of privacy inherent in such observation, there is a considerable risk of activating undesirable elements of transference and countertransference of a sexual nature by such practices.

9. Nudity of the client or sex therapist or both during treatment sessions is unethical, since the potential risks outweigh the potential benefits in our contemporary cultural milieu. Client nudity during a physical examination by a licensed physician or nurse is not prohibited or unethical.

10. Sex therapists may be confronted by marital or relationship problems of varying degrees. The sex therapist has a professional obligation to make objective assessments of such situations and to inform clients of such assessments. However, sex therapists should indicate to clients that the ultimate decision to alter or terminate a relationship, such as by separation or divorce, is solely the responsibility of the client. Because clients extend considerable trust to the therapist, and because clients consider therapists to be both knowledgeable and acting in the clients' best interests, therapists should be cautious in giving advice regarding the termination of relationships.

11. In treatment of a couple, when neither client has requested that any matters be held confidential or kept secret from the other, but when the therapist(s) judges that there is a significant risk to discussing jointly information not known to one client, it is the responsibility of the therapist to point out this fact to the relevant person and to obtain his or her consent before disclosure of such information.

12. The therapeutic relationship should be terminated when it is reasonably apparent to the therapist that the client is not benefiting from it despite the use of alternative therapeutic

strategies and techniques. In such instances it is the responsibility of the sex therapist to suggest appropriate referral when it appears warranted.

13. When research or training is being done in the context of providing therapeutic services, a potential for conflict of interests exists. In circumstances when it appears that the benefit to the client(s) is being compromised due to such practices, it is necessary to modify or terminate the research or training in order to maximize the objective benefit to the clients from therapy, even though the clients have consented to participation in research- or training-related therapy.

14. Although controversial, the use of partner surrogates in sex therapy may be an ethically permissible way of establishing a therapeutic environment, when conducted in a responsible manner. If partner surrogates are to be used at all, clients should understand that the partner surrogate is not a sex therapist; surrogates should understand that their role is not that of either sex therapist or psychotherapist; and sex therapists working with partner surrogates must exercise diligence and concern for protecting the dignity and welfare of both the surrogate and the client.

    a. Persons functioning as partner surrogates should receive special education in matters related to client confidentiality.

    b. If use of a partner surrogate is contemplated, the sex therapist should be highly sensitive to the client's values.

    c. Sex therapists working with partner surrogates have a strong responsibility to discuss in depth with these persons the possible social, psychological, physical, and legal risks pertaining to their roles.

    d. In some jurisdictions, the use of partner surrogates may be counter to existing laws. In these circumstances test cases may appropriately be sought or sex therapists may work toward changes in the law.

15. Sex therapists should be aware of the personal value system that they introduce into the therapy context and should disclose these values to the client when such information is relevant to treatment. Moreover, therapists should avoid gratuitously enunciating opinions or prescribing values that reflect

their personal biases rather than being responsive to the perceived needs and well-being of the client. In this regard therapists should not condemn certain types of sexual practices, except those that are coercive or involve deceit.

SECTION IV : WELFARE OF STUDENTS AND TRAINEES

Sex educators, researchers, and therapists respect the rights and dignity of students and trainees. The maintenance of high standards of scholarship, including the accurate and objective presentation of educational information, is a responsibility of all sex educators, researchers, and therapists. The preservation of academic freedom, with the checks and balances imposed by appropriate ethical standards, is recognized as necessary for growth of the scientific and humanistic study of human sexuality.

1. Students and trainees are accorded confidentiality in regard to information of a personal or intimate nature obtained by a teacher or training supervisor. This provision of confidentiality does not preclude the following:
   a. Objective evaluation of students and trainees by their teachers, including evaluation by committee
   b. Recommendations about students and trainees for their personal or professional purposes
   c. Pursuit of disciplinary action involving students or trainees in matters pertaining to scholarship, personal conduct, or violations of ethical standards
2. Students and trainees are entitled to periodic evaluation of their performance, with advance knowledge of the timing and mechanism of the evaluation process.
3. It is unethical for teachers or training supervisors to abuse their position of authority by compelling or enticing students or trainees into sexual activity with them.
4. Although it is recognized that individual privacy may be somewhat compromised, persons seeking training in sex therapy, sex research, or sex education may be queried about their personal

sexual histories and attitudes, since these may materially affect the competence and objectivity of professional performance. When such information is obtained, it must be treated in a highly confidential manner. However, it is important that students be informed that *both* personal and academic or professional data relevant to competence and appropriateness for a prospective position may be included in recommendations for employment or additional training.

5. It is unethical to compel students or trainees to participate as subjects in research projects. Students or trainees who are asked to serve as research subjects must have freedom of choice in giving informed consent. The increased risk of conflict of interest or subtle coercion should be recognized and guarded against by educators who engage in research with their own students or trainees.

SECTION V: WELFARE OF THE RESEARCH SUBJECT

Sex researchers should conduct their investigations within an ethical framework to protect the dignity, rights, and welfare of their subjects. Research must be planned with this point in mind; ethical considerations are never solely dependent on the outcome of a study. An assessment of the benefits of the proposed project weighed against the risks involved in that project is an important guideline in making research decisions.

1. For each research project, a person or persons who will assume the ethical and scientific responsibility for the conduct and consequences of the investigation should be designated and identified to potential subjects.

2. All research involving humans should be designed to require the free and informed consent of the subjects. Simply stated, this requirement consists of the following:

   a. The procedures and details of study participation are explained accurately to the potential subject, with his or her understanding of these points.

b. The physical, social, psychological, legal, and economic risks of study participation are fully and accurately described to the potential subject. The potential subject must have adequate comprehension of these risks for this condition to be met.

c. The potential subject must be free to choose whether or not to participate, without any element of coercion, force, or deceit.

d. The potential study subject must be aware of his or her right to withdraw from the study at any time without prejudice.

3. The possibility of obtaining truly free and informed consent may be modified under certain circumstances when subjects have diminished capacity (for example, children and the mentally retarded), diminished autonomy (for example, prisoners and students), or increased vulnerability (for example, transsexuals and minority groups). In these instances the investigator has an immensely compelling responsibility to observe safeguards that preserve the rights, dignity, and welfare of subjects.

a. In the case of those legally incompetent or incapable by reason of diminished capacity (children, the mentally retarded, and the mentally ill), participation in research requires the informed permission of legal guardian(s). This permission cannot be validly granted if participation entails more than minimal risks that are not justified by anticipated direct benefits to the subjects.

b. In the case of persons whose freedom of choice is limited by circumstances, subjects may participate after giving informed consent only when adequate guarantees are obtained by the investigators that no undue inducements or elements of coercion exist that may compromise voluntary participation in the project; that subjects may withdraw without prejudice at any time; and that the subject has an opportunity for open communication with an advocate who is not the investigator.

c. In the case of populations that suffer from peculiar vulnerbility, subjects may participate in research after giving informed consent, including consent to the possibility of disclosure. The investigator is responsible for maintaining the fullest confidentiality of data available under the law.

4. Sex researchers should provide utmost protection of the confidentiality of research subjects, since information obtained in the course of research is likely to include intimate, personal, or private facts.

   a. All information obtained by the sex researcher via questionnaire, surveys, interviews, observations, laboratory tests, or other processes is confidential, even if there is no apparent risk to disclosure of this information.

   b. The fact of a subject's participation in sex research is confidential, since under certain circumstances the identification of such participation might lead to adverse legal, social, or psychological consequences.

   c. If information about research subjects is used in any publication or public presentation, there is an obligation to conceal the identity of subjects.

   d. All research-related records must be maintained with diligent and continuing attention to safeguarding confidentiality. It is the responsibility of the sex researcher to ensure this protection in regard to data collection, data processing, data analysis, and, finally, the disposition of research records. Potential research subjects should be informed of the limits that may apply to maintaining confidentiality, such as the possibility of access to research records by subpoena.

   e. All considerations related to confidentiality in sex research remain in effect on the conclusion of a subject's participation in a study and after the study has been completed.

   f. Information received from the research subject may be divulged only in the following circumstances:
      (1) When the subject provides written consent
      (2) When there is clear and imminent danger to an individual or to society
      (3) When there is need to defend the sex researcher, employees or associates of the sex researcher, or the institute or employer of the sex researcher against formal accusation by the research subject of wrongful conduct

5. Sex researchers should strive for honesty and accuracy in their

dealings with research subjects. Because of the nature of sex research, when concealment or deception is required (a determination that necessitates careful examination of all alternate methodologic strategies) potential subjects should be informed of this during the consent process. Explanation of the specific nature of the concealment or deception must be made as soon as possible after the subject's participation has ended.

6. The researcher has a dual responsibility to protect the welfare of subjects and to provide or arrange treatment for adverse physical or psychological effects that occur as a result of research participation, if the subject desires such treatment. Although this responsibility encompasses all phases of research, it applies specifically to situations of research in a context of therapy in which a subject is assigned to a no-treatment group, placebo control group, or minimal-treatment group and a determination is made that failure to receive other types of treatment is producing adverse consequences.

7. Research subjects are entitled to an explanation of the results of their participation in the study, including an opportunity to ask questions to aid in their interpretation of the data.

8. Research involving the administration of drugs to human subjects should be conducted only in hospitals, laboratories, clinics, or other research facilities that are staffed and equipped to ensure adequate medical safeguards for subjects.

9. Researchers who conduct experiments involving animals are responsible for protecting their welfare and adhering to humane methods of procedure, including adequate provision for maintenance of test animals before, during, and after study.

10. Falsification or distortion of research data is unethical.

11. In general, all sex research should be carried out in accord with the federal regulations concerning protection of human subjects, which require review of research protocols by an institutional review board. Investigators not affiliated with an institution that has an accredited review board should arrange voluntarily to have their protocols reviewed and should voluntarily accept the judgment of the reviewing body.

III
PROCEEDINGS
OF THE ETHICS
CONGRESS

WELCOME AND OPENING REMARKS

VIRGINIA E. JOHNSON

Welcome to St. Louis.

This is a very special occasion for us, as I hope it is for you. This congress demonstrates a continuity of purpose, a continuity of commitment, and, above all, a continuity of involvement in the future of our field. Our combined efforts here may help nurture and stabilize at least one phase in the growth of a very intriguing but unruly child of social change: the pursuit of knowledge about human sexuality and the use of that knowledge in ways that contribute to the alleviation of personal distress or dissatisfaction.

To place things in proper perspective, I think we might acknowledge at the outset that none of us invented sex. In fact, sexuality has been a part of human existence for quite a while. It is helpful to remind ourselves of this from time to time. Professionals working in the field of sexuality have a tendency to overlook this perspective for various reasons. First of all, the field itself seems new because the awakening of awareness and social acceptance of human sexuality are of recent vintage (I refer here only to our own society and to modern times). Secondly, we are coming of age in terms of knowledge about sexual function, sexual relationships, and sexual behavior. Finally, the impetus of a rapidly developing area of professional interest and services in a context of social change tends to obscure a broader view of relevant history.

To continue with a brief glimpse of the most recent historical threads, I want to commend three groups of people, beginning with those present who were also here in 1976 at the initial Conference on Ethical Issues in Sex Therapy and Research. That meeting may well have been a very gentle affair as compared with what this one potentially can be, because the first conference required only that we define and discuss issues—not that we make decisions or reach conclusions. While that meeting had the potential of being incendiary, since many different disciplines and viewpoints were represented and many of us disagreed on certain points, all concerned made a real effort to blend their personal feelings and attitudes to attain a consensus as to what the salient issues were. We were very pleased with that outcome, and we hope you found it productive and interesting and applicable as a starting point for this second meeting. Although all of the earlier participants were invited back, a few were unable to be present today.

I must also thank those of you who are demonstrating your commitment, your involvement, and even your curiosity by accepting our invitation to be here for the first time. I would like to emphasize that those who are new here today are no less involved and no less important to this endeavor than those present who participated in the 1976 conference.

Finally, I want to offer a special word of gratitude to the 14 members of our task force, who produced the background papers and met several times over the past 18 months devising the format of this meeting and preparing the draft of the ethics guidelines that will be considered in detail during the next three days. This task force, working with diligence, energy, and a high level of academic rigor, has provided a firm foundation for our deliberations.

One remarkable aspect of the task force and this congress should be noted. We have reached out, all of us, to people outside the profession, outside the field of the study of human sexuality. This is not only healthy and productive—as we guard against a too parochial view—but also, in my opinion, more interesting. I think we should appreciate the fact that those concerned with ethics and philosophy in a general sense, those concerned with the well-being of people in general, are willing to become involved in a field that is so controversial and to offer their contributions.

Once again, welcome. At this point, let's proceed with the congress.

9

INFORMED CONSENT

RICHARD GREEN: The subject of informed consent is problematic for many reasons. I will discuss briefly the methodological, research, and treatment issues related to obtaining informed consent in dealing with human sexuality.

Consent and the degree to which it is "informed" and freely given engages several levels. There are a variety of research strategies employed by sex researchers and sex therapists that illustrate these issues. These include questionnaire research, laboratory research, field survey research, observational studies, research in the context of therapy, research that has no therapeutic impact, counseling, research and treatment of children, and something that I call institutional consent.

First, let's look at questionnaire research. The design typically includes a controlled cognitive stimulus, a questionnaire with a series of questions. The respondent is in control of his or her response to the questions. When an individual consents to answer a questionnaire of the pattern that we typically use—"When did you first do such-and-such?" and "How often do you do such-and-such?"—the researcher's expectation is that the respondent will complete each item. However, the respondent, before beginning to answer the questionnaire, does not know every item that will be asked. There is no way that either the investigator or the respondent can know a priori the extent to which a question might be upsetting. The respondent has not given consent to being asked a given question, let alone consented to answer it.

Next, consider laboratory experiments involving physical contact. We have so-called invasive and noninvasive instruments. *Invasive* generally means that the body is penetrated by some kind of testing instrument, whether this be a needle or catheter inserted in a vein or artery or a photoelectric cell placed in the vagina or a pressure transducer placed in the rectum. Here the psychodynamics of those who volunteer for such research comes into question—the question of how their motivation, perhaps of a subconscious nature, may contribute to the degree to which they are informed. Is an individual with a strong need for sexual exhibitionism consenting to the same study as an individual with a strong need to promote the collection of scientific data? Is the symbolic meaning of their consent comparable? I suggest not.

Next, consider field survey research. Here there is the possibility of invasion of privacy and stigmatization. For example, less than systematic research has conveyed to the public the view that various behavioral problems—for example, criminal behavior—are associated with atypical chromosomal karyotypes such as the XXY and XYY karyotypes. Several problems arise here regarding informed consent, particularly with respect to longitudinal neonatal studies. What does one tell the families of children under study? Does one tell them that their children have an abnormal sex chromosome configuration? If so, what does one then tell them about its potential significance? Is it ethical to withhold either the discovery of the abnormal karyotype or information about the potential implications of the karyotype? Will alerting parents of this information so modify the parent-child relationship as to distort the research outcome?

Next, consider observational studies. These include studies conducted in private, in laboratory settings, or in the field. Such studies may or may not be conducted with the awareness of those being investigated.

First, regarding laboratory settings: Here one might be measuring psychophysiologic sexual arousal to a variety of potentially erotic stimuli. These stimuli might be of either a socially acceptable or an unacceptable nature. They might include conventional sexual stimuli or those of an illegal or atypical nature, for example, pedophilia and homosexuality. The individual consenting to participate in research in which responses to these patterns of stimuli are measured runs the risk of revealing to self and others his or her potential for erotic arousal to socially unacceptable, atypical, or illegal stimuli. Does the individual also run the additional risk of developing new erotic associations to such stimuli? Can the individual be psychologically harmed by self-awareness of the erotically arousing potential of such stimuli? Can the individual who consents to participate in such a study be truly informed of all the possible consequences? Probably not. Is it potentially more harmful to spell out these possible consequences in the informed-consent form that must be signed prior to participation? Possibly.

Next, regarding a naturalistic setting: The best example is, I believe, in Laud Humphreys's study *Tearoom Trade* [1]. Here the investigator, posing as a lookout for police in a public men's room frequented by males seeking brief anonymous homosexual encounters, was in fact recording the behaviors staged in such a setting without the awareness of the "actors." Clearly, this raises an issue of invasion of privacy. However, this study did not stop here. Surreptitiously the investigator also noted the license plate numbers of persons stopping by the men's room, checked the identity of each automobile's owner, and later, under the guise of a public survey, interviewed these persons about their sexual practices. In the dissertation and book no one was identified. However, these individuals did not consent to being studied in the first place, nor were they truly informed when they consented to the subsequent interview. Although in this case no one seemed to be harmed, were these persons' rights violated? Yes. Were they kept from harm primarily because of the investigator's genuine concern for their protection? Yes. Might they have been significantly harmed in the hands of another investigator? Yes. Can such research be carried out with adequate controls on the conduct of the investigator? I don't know. If not, should such research be eliminated? Probably.

Next, consider participant observation of another sort. Here a person or a team studying the phenomenon of group sex joins a club of "swingers" to investigate the phenomenon. Their research consideration is that paper-and-pencil instruments do not tap the vital dimensions of this experience and that a volunteer sample would not be representative of the population to be studied. Thus they argue for participant observation, perhaps without the subjects' being made aware of the fact that they are engaged in a study. While this would at first appear similar to the *Tearoom* study, consider the possibility of the investigators personally participating in the swinging activities of the club. Alternatively, the investigators might announce that they are present as scientific observers, will protect anonymity, and will not actually be participating. How would this announcement affect the research?

A reasonable argument can be made that direct participant observation without subjects' awareness is the only way to capture the genuine texture and fabric of the phenomenon under study. However, to what extent is objective evaluation contaminated by the subjective experience of being both spectator and actor? To what degree is the noninvestigator actor being victimized by the absence of either aspect of the double-barreled term *informed consent?* Here again, the actor's privacy is infringed upon and he or she is at the mercy of the ethics of the investigator.

Next, consider so-called staged events or manipulations of the environment, the goal being collection of data on behavioral change in a standardized situation. Here the use of confederates and false feedback is common. For example, the investigator may be looking at the possibilities of experimental modification of attitudes—about homosexuality, for instance—in a direction that might previously have been unacceptable to the subject. One design might be to take an individual with exclusively heterosexual arousal patterns and a given attitude about homosexuality, hook the person up to a penile plethysmograph, show him heterosexual and homosexual stimuli, and give him false feedback indicating positive arousal to homosexual stimuli; then see whether there is attitudinal change. What experimenters typically do at the completion of such a procedure is a so-called debriefing, in which subjects are told about the false feedback. This is to allay anxiety on the part of the subject that he or she does in fact have homosexual arousal patterns. However, can one assess before the study the extent to which psychological trauma may result or the extent to which such trauma might be eliminated by debriefing? Should subjects be told beforehand that deception will take place? Does such communication render this type of study meaningless, thereby precluding the value of any such research?

Next, consider research that takes place in the context of therapy. In therapy there may be randomization between treatment modes. In clinical outcome studies involving sexual behavior, several interventions may be pitted against one another. Sometimes the investigator or clinician has a hypothesis that one mode of intervention will be the most effective. Sometimes patients themselves have an idea that one or another mode will be more effective. To what extent does the therapist have an obligation to inform patients that they are in a treatment mode considered a priori to be less likely of inducing desired behavioral change? To what degree should the therapist be responsive to allocating the patients to their preferred treatment mode? Should the informed consent statement reveal to the subject the possible second-best nature of his or her treatment mode? Can one have true randomization of groups if the patient has the option to select the mode of intervention?

What about placebo intervention? Consider a study in which a variety of sexual dysfunctions are being investigated by several treatment methods and it is unclear which method is most effective. The investigator may not be convinced that any of them is particularly effective and may think it is merely the distressed couple's solicitation of help that is the active ingredient. Should patients be told that some are entering into a treatment that is not anticipated to have much likelihood of being beneficial?

Next, consider psychosurgery. There is one study in West Germany in which males who were sex offenders have been treated with stereotaxic brain surgery with parts of the hypothalamus ablated [2]. This is quite a powerful technique. To rule out the suggestion of the possible placebo nature of this intervention, it might be required that sham surgery be performed. By so doing, it would be possible to evaluate people who had had part of their hypothalamus ablated and those who had not. However, one would have to tell the patients prior to surgery that some would have a sham procedure. Is it possible that telling someone who has the real procedure that he may have had the sham procedure would work to lessen any positive effects of the surgery? Is it reasonable to subject someone to a procedure in which there is a risk of permanent damage (from the sham operation) without genuine expectation of benefit? What if the benefit is *all* placebo, but the placebo "works"? If the placebo works, should all patients be told they are having the real procedure? If so, are they informed? No. Are they helped? Yes.

Next, consider counseling. Individuals consult a clinical center for many kinds of sexual disorders. To what extent do they give informed consent to the variety of procedures that will ensue from the moment they walk in the door for their first appointment? How many centers spend the first hour describing their philosophy of treatment and preparing their clients for each stage of therapy that will follow? How many centers instruct the individuals to leave at the end of the introductory session to go home and discuss whether they wish to engage in the therapeutic undertaking? It can be argued that the nature of the therapist-patient relationship is such that from the very beginning a coercive element exists. It can be argued that the patient is under duress and thus no informed consent can be given. Can this coercion be mitigated by spending the first hour describing treatment philosophy, delaying history-taking until the second appointment?

Finally, institutions should also have the right to refuse to be studied unless truly informed consent is given. Investigators must not enter institutions under false pretenses (for instance, by masquerading as patients) in order to obtain research information. While quality control of institutions must be monitored and maintained, deceptive monitoring policies are a basic infringement on rights, whether the victim is an institution or an individual. A meaningful juxtaposition must be found for the right to be left alone and public accountability.

Informed consent—as Charles Fried will elaborate—is a deceptively simple term. When applied to the strategies of sex research and the practices of sex therapy, it engages issues of a psychologically symbolic nature that are often far more subtle than in other specialties involving *Homo sapiens*. Sex research and therapy have evolved increasingly sophisticated methodologies. With evolution, I believe, goes responsibility. Let us hope that the profession proves more equal to the task than has the species.

CHARLES FRIED: It would be a fruitless enterprise to summarize in 10 minutes a rather complex and extensive legal argument, and I won't try to do it.

Rather, what I shall try to do—on the assumption that you have read my fairly complex and, I hope, comprehensive paper—is to talk a little about the principles that motivate our obsession with informed consent.

I thought a good motto for this talk would be something that was written nearly 200 years ago. Let me just quote it for you: "The true end of man or that which is prescribed by the eternal and immutable dictates of reason and not suggested by vague and transient desires is the highest and most harmonious development of his powers to a complete and consistent whole. Freedom is the first and indispensable condition which the possibility of such a development presupposes, but there is another essential intimately connected with freedom, and that is a variety of situations" [3]. This is Wilhem von Humboldt, writing in 1791. I think this quotation, which Mill used in his famous essay "On Liberty," should serve as your motto as well; if there is one reason that your field has been so long in developing and is perhaps beginning to develop now, it is that the value of liberty, the concept of freedom, the recognition of the importance of allowing people to be confronted by a variety of situations, in Humboldt's phrase, is beginning to be appreciated more and more. Were it not for that, this conference would not be taking place and your people would all be engaged in quite different lines of work.

It is this respect for liberty that has allowed your discipline to come into being. If once again the idea were to become dominant in our society that X can tell Y what to do because X knows better than Y what is for Y's own good, then I assure you that you would all be out of work. Similarly, if the idea were accepted that some notion of the public good is justification for restricting individual liberty, then you people would be the first to go. I think you all know that. You're on the knife's edge now and it is only the principle of liberty that protects you.

The point is that it is this same principle of liberty that stands behind what a number of people have called the obsession with informed consent: The principle of informed consent is nothing but a special case of the principle of liberty. The principle of informed consent says that people are indeed able to decide for themselves what situations they will get into and what situations they will avoid. It assumes that if explanations are given patiently and fully, then not only experts but even laymen are able to decide what situations they will and will not get into. And let me remind you: If the idea were ever accepted that laymen are not able to decide for themselves—that experts must decide what is for a person's good—then you people would be the first to go.

One of the arguments that is made over and over again—in fact, it was made by my distinguished colleague at the [Harvard] Medical School, Leon Eisenberg—is that informed consent is really a fetish [4]. Dr. Eisenberg bemoans the difficulty plaguing certain kinds of clinical research because of the need to obtain informed consent. He makes the point that in a condition of ignorance, there cannot really be informed consent. Well, that is an argument that says the layman cannot decide for himself; because their knowledge is imperfect, people cannot decide for themselves what situations to get into and what situations to avoid. And that is the principle—let me remind you again—that, if accepted, would cause you to be the first to go.

Now, it is to my mind remarkable and heartening that the guidelines that have been put before you take this principle of informed consent more seriously than does any other document I have seen. This is quite appropriate, because if there is any group of professionals that ought to take the principle of liberty seriously, it is surely you. That is the lifeline on which you depend. And, of course, the principle of liberty is the principle of informed consent.

Let me contrast the conception of these very excellent guidelines with the conception of even as forward-looking a set of guidelines as those of the American Psychological Association. The American Psychological Association is by no means as clear on the principle of informed consent as are the guidelines put before you, because the American Psychological Association says that deception is permissible in research. It's permissible if the research could not be carried out in any other way, if there is no great harm done, and if there is an attempt to remove the harm afterwards. Now, that is the principle that says that if social benefit cannot be procured without imposing on people, without violating the principle of informed consent, without violating the principle of liberty, then we should weigh the benefit against the liberty. Let me assure you that once we accept the notion that liberty may be violated in a situation like this, if we permit people to be imposed upon because of an alleged social benefit—a benefit which often seems to consist of providing students with Ph.D. dissertations—and if this alleged benefit can overcome the principle of liberty, then you would be the first to go.

I'm glad that in a spirit of sensible self-protection, your group is proposing to make informed consent a necessary and inviolable principle of your work. And I was particularly encouraged to see Dick Green's suggestion that this should be true not only in research, where it's obviously necessary, but also in therapy—particularly the point that he discussed at length in his paper and summarized for you in his talk, in which an attempt is made by the therapist at the outset to describe what he is doing—to make, as it were, a contract between his client and himself and to say exactly what may or may not be expected and how it is to be brought about, and to allow the client to decide for himself. Dick Green's suggestion is very much like the suggestion put forward by the Federal Trade Commission regarding the door-to-door sale of encyclopedias. It seems to me that if liberty is important in getting yourself into a two-year contract to purchase forty-five volumes of an encyclopedia, the idea being that you have a right to cancel that contract within a certain number of weeks after you have signed up, it should be particularly true before you allow people to intervene in your sex life.

It is just sensible that your group has decided to put informed consent as the motto of its work, because that is the lifeline on which you depend. There are—to be sure—difficulties, intricacies, problems. You can treat those difficulties and intricacies in one of two ways: You can say, "This is our principle. We shall somehow try to deal with the intricacies, keeping that principle foremost in our minds." Or you can do what some segments of the medical profession have been doing for generations, namely, to bring up these difficulties and intricacies as an argument for weakening or undermining the principle of informed consent: "People can't be truly informed anyway." How often have you heard that? That is the direction in which we should not allow our deliberations to go, because if we do, then I assure you that your profession will be in the greatest peril, much greater than that of your clients or research subjects.

Thank you.

SALLIE SCHUMACHER: I wanted to start out by saying that, as usual, Dick Green left us with more questions than answers, but I think his discussion of informed consent was a very interesting approach, particularly as it relates to different research methods.

As you know, there is an increasing awareness of the kinds of bias present at all stages of the research process. For example, we are all aware that when different research methods are applied to the same problem, different questions are asked, different observations are made, different analyses are done, and different conclusions are reached.

However, just as the research design can influence the results of the study, so, too, can the extent to which an individual research subject understands the study as revealed in his participation agreement or informed consent. As noted by Professor Fried, as a result of recent emphasis on individual rights and liberties, we've been forced to look at problems that may arise for the research subject in cases where the research design requires deliberate deception of the subject by the investigator or the experimenter. Dr. Green was very careful to point out possible harmful effects on the subject inherent in different research strategies. I would like to suggest that in situations where deception is not an issue, the subject's understanding of the research and how this might affect the results of the study is as much a concern of ethics as is how the understanding may personally affect the subject. Let me give you an example of what I mean.

As some of you know, I'm affiliated with an institution where some important sleep studies are being done. One such study involves monitoring sleep EEG patterns in normal children. As part of the informed consent process in this study, the experimenter explains to the child what is going to happen and then brings the parent into the room and has the child explain to the parent what is going to happen to him. If the child has any misconceptions, the experimenter then has an opportunity to try to clarify them. One of my colleagues shared the following: In the explanation to his parents, one bright seven-year-old described the room where he would be sleeping and where he would be studied, the way in which the wires would be placed, and then stated, "And they're going to read my dreams." Well, we can wonder whether the experimenter's further attempt to explain that only the subject's

EEG record would be read had any effect on the magical world of that child. We can wonder if such a misunderstanding might be harmful to the child, but we must also be concerned with possible bias in the results of the study. For example, if the child did misunderstand this, would we really be getting a reading of his normal sleep pattern or would his dream stage be altered?

Similar misunderstandings can and do influence the results of studies in sex research involving adults as well as children, even though they may not be harmful to the subject; we must keep this in mind.

JOHN MONEY: My remarks are entitled "Consensus and Contract in the Ethics of Human Sexuality."

When I read Professor Fried's paper—and I might add Dr. Green's and also the guidelines at the beginning of the blue book [contained background papers and draft of guidelines]—I had the feeling that I had been introduced to a litany of doom. Had I read it a quarter of a century ago, I would never have had the courage to begin my clinical research and clinical service in the pediatric clinic at Johns Hopkins. My prospective career in sexological practice and research might well have been terminated before it had begun, a victim of fear of the consequences of innovation.

First, let me say that I've deliberately linked clinical practice and clinical research, because I consider it profoundly important that they should always be linked together with respect to biomedical legality and ethics. The current wave of ethical concern for the protection of human subjects should rightly be a concern not only for subjects but also for patients. We must remember that all our patients are also subjects in research, even if only in the diagnostic and treatment statistics of medical institutions. However, if medicine is practiced correctly, all patients should also be subjects in the statistics of outcome of treatment. It is the neglect of outcome studies, both short-term and long-term, that permits erroneous doctrine to triumph, simply because the evidence with which to disprove it is discarded unused. Recent information about diethylstilbestrol given to pregnant mothers is a classic example of that. The treatment of non-neuroendocrine impotence with testosterone instead of sex therapy is another example widely practiced. How does the profession get away with this? Simply because authoritarianism has long been a medical conceit, even when it entails practices that posterity will ultimately demonstrate to have been malpractice.

Because the dual role of patients as subjects is seldom recognized, we are faced with the problem that the medical practitioner today is able to prescribe a form of therapy, whether old or new, that is unvalidated, provided he does not request a review by the ethics review board of his institution. But as soon as he says that he's going to keep records, tabulate his data, and do a statistical evaluation of outcome, then he must go before the ethics review board, where there is a real possibility that under these circumstances he will not be allowed to do what he wants to do and what he knows should be done. This possibility is all the more likely if one is dealing with matters of sexuality and if the board is ultra-conservative.

In the ethical principles by which I work, there are two kinds of research, exploitational research and authenticational research. All that we hear these days about informed consent, as far as I understand it, has to do with the protection of human beings against exploitation. I believe anyone in his right mind agrees with this, for we all know what horrors of exploitation finally eventuated under the Hitler regime, for example. However, even allowing for requirements placed on pharmaceutical companies in new-drug trials, there has been no corresponding movement to protect authenticational research. We should be passing legislation and formulating rules of ethics to require that research be done, thus guaranteeing that what the patient accepts in good faith has indeed been authenticated or is being authenticated. Currently, the only redress against unauthenticated treatment is a very cumbersome judicial procedure, both time-consuming and money-consuming.

I'm afraid that in sexology, as in other biomedical disciplines, there has been no serious attempt to differentiate between the two forms of research. The necessary concern against the rank growth of exploitation is causing research into authenticity to be exterminated by the same defoliant. Of course, exploitation needs to be curbed. The rules against it are all negative, producing a negative ethics against research. But authentication needs to be encouraged with a positive ethics, endorsing research. It is too easy to be negative and to get involved in "thou shalt not," and I believe we are in great danger of doing just that.

I developed my own position with respect to authenticational research and innovation in sexological practice from Lawson Wilkins, my mentor and sponsor in hermaphroditic studies at Johns Hopkins. He was the major person in the world dealing with birth defects of the sex organs. No one had made the final decision yet as to how babies born with such defects should be assigned and treated, so sometimes he had to make decisions for which there were no precedents. In hermaphroditism, sex is not a single issue of male or female, as it is in the law. Instead, it is a multiple issue of contradictory variables. For example, a baby may be born as a normal-appearing female, except for lumps in the groin that prove to be testicular in structure and genetically of the 46,XY (male) chromosomal constitution, as are all the cells of the body. Faced with such incongruity, Lawson Wilkins knew that his decision about the sex of rearing would dictate the baby's future welfare for its entire lifetime. He had to carry the ethical and legal responsibility for the decision and for the medical and surgical procedures it would entail. For example, the decision to rear a hermaphroditic baby as a girl might entail surgical castration.

Wilkins knew that, should one of his decisions ever be contested in court, the law had no precedent to draw upon and that he might well be convicted. He attempted to open a dialogue between medicine and the law by convening an informal seminar of interested parties, including a judge whom he had known since boyhood school days. But the judge declined, protesting that such a seminar might prejudice his decision should he ever have to try a case involving hermaphroditism. That led Lawson Wilkins to declare that even though the law, abdicating its responsibility to keep in step with medicine, might have him jailed, he could not abdicate his responsibility to the babies whose lives depended on him.

That lesson has since been impressed on me by two other leading professors with whom I've worked at Johns Hopkins. It is a dictum that goes back to Vesalius, Bruno, and Galileo, namely, that there are times when the scientist or physician is so much wiser in knowledge of his own specialty than is society or the law that, in order to live up to his own moral standards, he must risk punishment as an innovator and a revolutionary until such time as society and the law come around to his way of thinking.

This is a tough assignment for many people. We live in an intellectual and social climate in which it is fashionable to attack researchers and castigate doctors who dare to be innovative. Sex researchers and therapists are not the only victims, but they are particularly vulnerable because they defy the powerful taboo against sex that is part of our cultural heritage. We are in danger of losing our professional birthright. It is slowly being eroded under the political banner of protection of human subjects and the ethics of informed consent—or rather, by those who are misusing the banner of protection and informed consent.

Let me turn now to a brief glance at history. Informed consent is a virtuous idea the proper use of which is essential to the proper regulation of human affairs with decency and dignity. Like all virtuous ideas, however, it is not an absolute. It achieves the status of absolute only because of an insidious, faulty, and covert assumption that a person who gives informed consent does so on the basis of rationality, enlightened self-interest, and voluntary choice. The theory of human nature on which this assumption is based is that of the Age of Enlightenment. It is the theory on which the United States Constitution was constructed, and it permeates much of our legal system. It is only a theory, however, and a very imperfect one that does not meet all contingencies.

Consider, for example, the case of a patient with Münchausen's syndrome. He is a medical impostor who creates his own symptoms, scrupulously conceals their origin, and masquerades as one afflicted with an undiagnosable and incurable illness. He is a self-made martyr, compulsively stage-managing his own destruction and even death. Such a person will readily sign informed consent papers by the bushel, not in enlightened self-protection (as you and I would define it) but in enlightened self-destruction. Parents may do the same on behalf of their children: It is a bizarre form of child abuse—Münchausen's syndrome by proxy—and may indeed lead to the child's death.

Such cases provide a critical test of the responsibility of the professional person who prepares the informed consent papers and administers the various diagnostic tests and therapeutic trials. Whereas he acts in complete good faith, unless he makes the correct diagnosis he is self-deceived in specifying the risks for which informed consent is signed. Thus he is vulnerable not only to disciplinary action by the ethics review board, but also to possible charges of malpractice by, say, a next of kin.

This type of case should serve to remind us that in biomedical science and service, human sexuality included, we, the "experts," can as yet predict very little concerning the risks or lack of risk associated with our diagnostic tests or methods of intervention. What we can do, however, is to be fair and impartial in apprising a patient of the complete range of current knowledge concerning the issue for which informed consent is being sought. Lawson Wilkins could not prophesy the long-term risks attendant on some of his decisions when they were still at the innovative stage. But he could share his knowledge so that he and the parents of a newborn hermaphroditic baby might arrive at a consensus on the basis of this shared knowledge. They were then in a position either to sign a joint contract—despite the risks of innovation—or not to sign it. A joint contract between researcher and subject (or doctor and patient) does away with secrecy and deception. This is so even if the contract is to participate in a double-blind study which, by definition, requires that some information be kept secret until the study has been completed. A joint contract permits innovation instead of stifling it. It creates a partnership of moral equals. It serves the purposes of both parties and, when documentation of the outcome is systematic and published, it serves also to benefit posterity. Systematic documentation and statistical evaluation of clinical service—let me again remind you—is synonymous with clinical research. In human sexuality, the ethical issues of sex therapy and sex research are unitary, not divided.

In October of 1977 I made my way for the first time to the Himalayan kingdom of Nepal. There, in the valley of Kathmandu, I visited the great Buddhist temple in the former imperial city of Patan. Fresh from the blinding sunlight, it took a few moments for my vision to adjust to the shadows of the innermost shrine where the golden Buddha sat with his golden attendants. They were half hidden behind piled-up offerings of flower petals, incense, coins, and little mounds of grains of rice. A movement startled me. I looked again. Yes, my first impression was correct: There they were, dozens of sleek and glossy-coated temple rats, safely monopolizing their god's rice. Today I have a parallel image of a monopoly of sleek and glossy-coated human-sexuality experts monopolizing the rice offered at the shrine of their idols. They will be protected by and have a vested interest in legal certification and a code of ethics that maintains the status quo at the expense of innovation in research and practice.

Research and practice both need innovation. If you think I am exaggerating in my fears about these matters, consider the widespread federal and state legislation in 1977 concerning child pornography, so-called kiddy porn. The new laws are intended to prevent sexual exploitation of juveniles; yet, for the most part, they are formulated on the totally faulty assumption that juvenile sexuality does not exist—indeed, that sexuality begins de novo at age 16. These laws constitute a ready-made legal instrument for the prevention of all research into childhood sexuality. Not for one second do I doubt that they will one day be so used. Thus will be stifled all investigation, desperately needed, of the juvenile origins and determinants of both normal and abnormal psychosexuality. We will be forbidden to conduct research into pedophilia or incest; instead of attempting to understand these conditions and learn more about their origins, we will be obliged to betray the participants to the police. The same problems would arise in sex therapy with regard to the use of surrogates, for example, and with regard to any kind of participant-observer research.

Whether we are patients, subjects, researchers, or deliverers of health care, we have an ethical obligation as individuals in the interest of the commonweal to foster medical research and documentation. This obligation cannot be stressed enough. We as members of society must realize that just as inexorably as we pay taxes, so also must we pay our research dues to our descendants in return for the research benefits that we have inherited from our forebears. Certainly there must be restrictions and safeguards for the protection of individual rights, but we also have an ethical obligation to the future. There must be safeguards to ensure that we pass on to our children and grandchildren the same rights, privileges, and benefits of research that we ourselves have been heir to.

We in sex therapy and sex research are committed to not upholding sexual prudery and taboo. At heart we are not self-serving and self-seeking people. We are not primarily concerned with legal or financial protection for ourselves or our own generation alone. So, let us be articulate: Let us make a big noise demanding new laws that will allow us to be judged both ethical and honorable in what we have done for generations as yet unborn.

SAMUEL GOROVITZ: Having read two substantial and thought-provoking papers and having listened to two insightful commentaries, I have been asked to provide general comments on the whole, including some discussion of the issue of deception, and to do so in 10 minutes. I will have to limit my remarks to just a few points.

Dr. Green's discussion of staged events raised two important issues with respect to the use of deception. He described for us both therapeutic and experimental settings in which deception is or at least seems to be an essential part of the protocol. How are we to assess the propriety of such deception? Dr. Green holds, plausibly enough, that we must assess the risk-benefit ratio—but on reflection, the adequacy of that suggestion seems to diminish. It is easy enough to make such an assessment in regard to the purchase of a lottery ticket. It is hard but still possible to arrive at some determination of a risk-benefit ratio in regard to more complex situations such as exploration for minerals or for oil. But where the benefits and risks are primarily psychological, it is not obvious to me that any kind of quantification is really possible. Either discussion of risk-benefit ratios is a metaphor, deceiving us with the illusion that it refers to an applicable method, or else we must be given some account, however approximate, of how such ratios are to be calculated.

A second point is closely related to the first. How are we to measure the negative value of an assault on a person's dignity? How are we to assess the possibly silent rage or torment or shame that the deceived can know as a result of seeing himself as having been ill-used? To deceive in the course of an experiment is, at least in

part, to treat the subject as an instrument employed in the furtherance of one's own objectives. That is true no matter how noble
those objectives are. Here we should recall the Kantian dictum:
Treat others always as ends unto themselves, never as means only.
The word *only* is crucial here. It is fine to use another in pursuit of
one's own objectives so long as that use is also adopted by that
other in pursuit of his objectives. Otherwise, that use constitutes
an assault on the dignity of the person. The moral weight of such
an assault is not readily measurable.

Dr. Green himself suggests a way out: the use of what Professor
Fried calls second-order consent. I see nothing wrong with the use
of deception, as long as it is made plain in seeking consent that deception—perhaps of an unspecified sort—will be involved. Of course,
some subjects may be lost as a result, some treatments may be im-
peded, and some research may be thwarted utterly. But all that
seems little enough price to pay for moral integrity.

Professor Fried pointed out that the principle of informed consent relies heavily on the view that people are able to decide for
themselves what situations they will and will not get themselves
into. He did not confuse that with a different point of view, one
from which I want to distinguish it explicitly, that is often closely
associated with it in discussions of informed consent: namely, the
belief that people know best what is best for them. John Stuart
Mill, in "On Liberty," made much of that claim. Fried, in his remarks, did not, and quite properly. The point of informed consent
is that people can decide, not necessarily what will be best for
them, but simply what they will and will not allow to happen to
them. Even if it is not true that individuals know best what is best
for them, it does not follow that those others who do know best
should make the decisions. This, I take it, is very much a part of
the meaning of respect for freedom, for if we respect another's
freedom to choose only insofar as his choices correspond to our
perceptions of correctness, it is a hollow sense of freedom indeed.
That is why we must be prepared to accept situations in which,
for example, therapeutic interventions are suboptimal, in which
more effective treatment might have resulted had the patient not
decided in his or her own behalf. That is part of the price we pay
if we respect freedom in a serious way.

Professor Fried rightly reminds us that the usual standard for determining what is acceptable procedure in medical therapy is the standard of the profession. Will this model help us in thinking about sex-related therapy? Dr. Money talked about some of the deficiencies that he had perceived in medical practice—in particular, the failure to make good use of potentially available evidence about what has and has not worked in regard to therapeutic intervention. That point is closely related to the issue I am about to address.

Even in medical therapy it is often unclear what the standard really is in a given situation. One example is in regard to a type of surgery known as the portacaval shunt, in respect to which the "standard" depends on whom you ask, which section of the literature you choose to read, and what subspecialties are addressing the question. What happens when we try to transfer this notion of the standard of the profession to sex-related therapy?

First, the standards of the profession are not well established, in part because the profession itself is quite new and is not well established. Second, the establishment of standards is particularly difficult because the profession is not well defined; it lacks a clearly specifiable population of practitioners. Third, any attempt to establish a clear demarcation of the population of the profession will, I suspect, be difficult. Interactions that have a therapeutic effect on sexual problems are of many kinds and can come from many quarters, and sex therapy seems to shade into other forms of social interaction much more naturally than medical therapy does. In the formulation of our sexual identity and in the gaining of maturity as sexual beings, we learn much from our friends and perhaps especially from our lovers, including much about ourselves; in the process, we undergo changes of the sort that could reasonably be seen as therapeutic successes. What is the mark of a sex therapist? Who should be on the roster and why? Before we could possibly become clear about the standard of the profession in regard to modes of therapy, we would have to have a reasonably clear identification of the members of the profession. There is a risk here of defining the profession itself in terms of some independently selected standard called therapy; but if we do that, we trivialize the claim that the profession has certain standards, for then it has them by definition—perhaps by quite arbitrary definition—and not by a substantive decision of the profession.

Professor Fried expressed his discomfort at the notion of allowing the researcher's standards to govern, because the researcher's motives are not necessarily in the best interests of the patient or subject. He contrasts this situation with a purely therapeutic setting where the standard of the profession is the usual legal standard, about which he expresses no discomfort—though perhaps he has some. But the contrast is too starkly drawn. The practitioner's motives, like those of the research scientist, are many and are not necessarily dominated by considerations of the patient's welfare. For example, a clinical decision can be influenced (perhaps dramatically) by a physician's desire to use his hard-earned skills—simply to use those skills, to practice the art of medicine—which may be interesting or challenging to the physician but which is not necessarily in the patient's best interest. I am not comfortable about the standard of the profession even in regard to traditional medical therapy; hence, it does not provide me with a very comforting model for standards in newly emerging branches of therapeutic intervention.

Regarding research, Professor Fried claims to believe rigidly in the right to pursue knowledge freely and without restraint. I know him too well to think for a moment he can mean that. Indeed, he goes on to explain the basis for the view that restraint is essential because of the necessity to respect the rights of others. His way of expressing here his enthusiasm for research—an enthusiasm that I share—is unfortunate because it tends to tarnish the clarity with which elsewhere he argues most persuasively that a sense of restraint based on a respect for the rights of others is itself an integral ingredient of that right to pursue research.

Finally, I want to call special attention to the most interesting feature of Professor Fried's paper. In a span of ten pages, discussing the legal grounds for claims and for defenses against claims, he invoked these concepts: reasonable belief, good faith, fear, ignorance, emotional distress, embarrassment, and alarm. This was not a psychologist's essay discussing the purposes and techniques of therapy and research in sex-related areas. This was a lawyer's presentation of grounds for claims and defenses against claims. If ever there were elusive notions resistant to measurement, to quantification, or to incontestable confirmation, they are these. Here, once again, we are reminded most vividly of the dependence of the law itself on judgment, insight, and considerations of taste. It should be obvious that no understanding of law and no set of guidelines can ever eliminate that dependence in such a sensitive area as that of sex-related therapy and research.

CHARLES FRIED: There is only one point I simply can't refrain from replying to, and that is the question of the right to pursue research. Of course, I put that in a most provocative way. The point is that there is a right to pursue research free of all restraint except the restraint of infringing on the liberty or rights of others. What that right asserts is that there should be no constraint on research because some people find the conclusions uncomfortable, because some people find that the conclusions undermine the moral fabric of the society, or because some people consider that the research would foster inappropriate attitudes toward the poor or toward racial minorities or whoever. That's what I meant—that there should be no restraint on research simply because someone doesn't like what the research might reveal or indicate. That's research as free speech. On the other hand, where the function of the research is to constrain the liberty of others, that's when we do indeed run up against a barrier, as I said.

Having exercised only moderate self-restraint, I'd like to open the floor to the other members of the group.

R. CHRISTIAN JOHNSON: I'd like to follow up on some remarks made by Dr. Green.

The question of the informed consent of an institution is, I think, a rather tangled one, because it is not clear (for most institutions) who is authorized to give consent on behalf of the institution.

I'd like to expand the question of the institution to include the family, the friends, the associates, in fact, everyone concerned who might conceivably object to the research or be affected by its outcome. If you go beyond the individual research subject in securing consent, you get into a tangle of conflicting obligations and may prevent the research altogether. I think the question of informed consent is a very personal issue involving the respondent and the investigator; I would like to suggest that we give careful attention to the question of informed consent secured from institutions rather than from individuals per se.

I would also like to comment on Dr. Schumacher's remark

about the possibility that complete disclosure might interfere with the validity of the research. If that does happen, then the research itself is not well conceived. If the researcher finds that the research outcome is invalidated by the necessity of giving the potential subject a detailed description of the research, then it is hard to see how the research could be justified.

CHARLES FRIED: I wonder if Dick Green would like to respond to that particular point. My guess is that the remark involved a slight misunderstanding of what Dick was talking about. I think Dick meant the situation where the institution itself is the research subject.

RICHARD GREEN: Right. For example, the reporter surreptitiously entering the institution as a patient while actually doing an exposé of the institution—where the institution itself, like a patient or research subject, has a right to informed consent as to the circumstances of that individual's presence. That was the issue.

ALBERT R. JONSEN: There is an issue of informed consent in therapy and research that hasn't been directly addressed, and I'd like to put it into the record even though I'm sure we can't develop it at much length. I have to give credit to Jay Katz—who would have been here had he not been prevented—because what I'm going to say arises from some recent conversations I had with him.

The issue is this: When speaking about informed consent to medical therapy, we have to remember that the therapeutic effects are not the result of a happy conjunction of the biochemistry of a drug plus the physiology of a person, but that a great deal has to be attributed to the human interaction, the dynamics between the therapist and the patient. Some ways of interpreting informed consent seem to require that a good deal of the uncertainty of the therapist has to be revealed to the patient. If we're to be truly honest about almost any therapeutic procedure, we have to admit a considerable lack of certainty about its effects. As most of us are aware, that lack of certitude may have a detrimental effect on those who come for therapy, precisely because they are coming to find some certitude. The development of confidence in the therapist is as important as the development of confidence in the therapeutic procedure. Therefore, the revelation of lack of certainty on the part of the therapist may have a detrimental effect on the ensuing therapy. I think that problem needs a good deal of exploration, both theoretically and empirically. In the field of sex therapy, where the development of self-confidence may be extremely important, it may be counterproductive to have a truly thorough informed consent disclosure. It may have the opposite effect in the research area, however, because the revelation of uncertainty about the research outcome may elicit the cooperation of the subject as one who wishes to play a part in the process of achieving greater certainty—while perhaps benefiting personally by the result.

MIRIAM F. KELTY: I would like to follow up Al Jonsen's point about lack of certitude. In my prepared comments about the guidelines, I recommended that the researcher does have an ethical obligation to share his or her uncertainty with the research participant. I feel that this should be the situation in therapy as well. We live in a society characterized by an increasingly rapidly changing technology and by changing social values (though at a much slower rate). Our knowledge base is changing rapidly, with the result that the efficacy of treatment as well as the efficacy of research may rapidly become obsolete. The responsibility to communicate uncertainty must extend beyond the delivery of services and the conduct of research to continuing education, so that people who have been trained not to express uncertainty, but rather to communicate their competence and confidence in what they are doing, are encouraged to share some of their inevitable uncertainty with the patient or the research participant.

RALPH SLOVENKO: On the issue or ethics of giving placebos, let me call attention to Sissela Bok's splendid article in *Scientific American* [5], in which she suggests that it would be adequate to inform subjects of the nature of the experiment and the fact that placebos will be administered. If they then consent to the experiment, the use of placebos cannot be considered surreptitious. Although the subjects in a blind or double-blind experiment will not know exactly when they are receiving placebos or even whether they are in fact receiving them, the initial consent to the experimental design including the possibility of placebo administration removes the ethical problems having to do with deception.

On the issue of liberty underlying informed consent in law, Professor Fried is quite right philosophically, but there might be a footnote to that in the sense that as a practical matter, informed consent as it has evolved is really a ploy used by lawyers to avoid the problems in proving negligence where it was necessary to bring in an expert to establish standards of care. Lack of informed consent in the legal sense was used to show that there was no consent. But then the concept spun off on a course and life of its own and now, as implemented by practitioners, it has the mark of high tragedy and low comedy. The consent process involves information, comprehension, and voluntariness. As there would be no check on a patient who says that he did not comprehend what the doctor told him, the most important criterion (assuming the patient is competent) is information. So the physician plays it safe by providing the patient with more information than any court would require.

Informed consent leaves much to be desired as a regulatory tool in ongoing therapy of a psychiatric nature [6]. Such therapy is different from medical care involving a one-time technique or surgical procedure. How does one tell a patient about the risks that may be encountered in the course of ongoing therapy? What are the *potential* risks that must be communicated to a patient in psychotherapy? In informing patient about alternative treatments, is it necessary to spell out the 200 different types of therapy that are available and the specific techniques that are employed?

CHARLES FRIED: If I understood Professor Slovenko correctly, he is suggesting that somehow the courts, whatever the historical basis of their using the concept of informed consent, would not adhere to it to the extent that all the speakers here or the general discussions require. That seems to me to be incorrect. It seems to me that the courts are requiring it all the time.

RALPH SLOVENKO: May I restate the proposition? Sir Thomas · More's *Utopia* had no lawyers, for they are "a sort of people whose profession it is to disguise matters" [7]. The doctrine of informed consent arose during the last decade or so to avoid the evidentiary problems in proving a case of negligence. To establish negligence it was the task of the plaintiff to procure an expert, which was next to impossible because the expert had to have practiced in the defendant's community. Of course, in that strict form, the rule virtually immunized physicians who were the sole practitioners in a community. Subsequently, the courts stated the rule in terms of "the same or similar locality." The problem then became that of defining similar localities. It was difficult indeed to prove standard of care.

However, under a different route of the law, if the consent were "uninformed," the procedure would be an unpermitted touching—in legal terms, a battery. Under this theory, it was simply necessary to allege that the patient did not have sufficient information concerning the risk. It was a much easier task for the plaintiff. Using this approach, the standard of care is irrelevant. Let me refer to an article on this topic by Professor David Louisell [8]. People—particularly in the mental health field—have become rather rigid in their thinking as to what is the necessary information, not recognizing that a ploy lies behind it all.

SAMUEL GOROVITZ: The discussion has suggested that informed consent is primarily a legal notion, a legal requirement. That is not correct. The concept of informed consent arises out of our respect for one another in regard to interpersonal dealings. It is a concept that is reflected in the law, but it is not in any *essential* way a legal artifact or a legal concept. In a society without law, one could still have an important place for the notion of informed consent as a criterion that must be met before certain kinds of interpersonal transactions would be justifiable. It is important to remember that insofar as informed consent appears in the law, it is a reflection of the importance of a certain kind of interpersonal respect that extends far beyond the law.

A second point—quite an obvious one, perhaps a trivial one—is one that we nonetheless need to be reminded of from time to time: Informed consent is never a sufficient condition for anything. We focus so much attention on the problems of obtaining informed consent that sometimes we tend to think that informed consent is the only condition that must be met before proceeding. But in fact, it is only one test that must be passed. For example, just imagine a sex therapist and a patient who agree that a little adventure in the patient's life might increase the patient's capacity for arousal, and together they agree to rob a bank. Now, there may be informed consent present, but robbing a bank is still an unwarranted activity.

REFERENCES

1. Humphreys, L. *Tearoom Trade: Impersonal Sex in Public Places.* Chicago: Aldine, 1970.
2. Rieber, I., and Sigusch, V. Psychosurgery on sex offenders and sexual "deviants" in West Germany. *Archives of Sexual Behavior* 8: 523–527, 1979.
3. Von Humboldt, W. *The Limits of State Action.* Edited by J. W. Burrow. Cambridge University Press, 1969.
4. Eisenberg, L. Social imperatives of medical research. *Science* 198: 1105–1110, 1977.
5. Bok, S. A. Ethics of giving placebos. *Scientific American* 231(12): 17–23, 1974. [See also S. A. Bok, *Lying: Moral Choice in Public and Private Life.* New York: Pantheon, 1978.]
6. Slovenko, R. Psychotherapy and Informed Consent: A Search in Judicial Regulation. In W. E. Barton and C. J. Sanborn (Eds.), *Law and the Mental Health Professions.* New York: International Universities Press, 1978. Pp. 51–70.
7. More, T. *Utopia.* London: W. Bulmer, 1808.
8. Louisell, D. W. "Informed Consent": Does It Have Meaning? In G. H. Morris and M. L. Norton (Eds.), *Intersections of Law and Medicine.* Ann Arbor: Institute of Continuing Legal Education, 1972. Pp. 119–131.

PRIVACY AND
CONFIDENTIALITY

RICHARD WASSERSTROM: I remember that when I finished my Ph.D. dissertation in philosophy, I was requested by university microfilms or someone to write a 150-word abstract of my dissertation. I was horrified to discover that I could do it.

To avoid that embarrassment again and in the interest of staying on schedule, I have decided that since you all have my written paper and—I hope—read it before you came, I am not going to make any introductory remarks. I doubt that a 10-minute summary would contribute much to your understanding of the paper if you haven't read it. So, we shall start off by hearing from the panelists.

I will ask Professor Slovenko to begin.

RALPH SLOVENKO: Professor Wasserstrom in his scholarly paper makes many interesting and provocative observations. In the brief time allotted for my response, it is not possible to comment on the full range of his observations. Wasserstrom's inquiry proceeds initially on the assumption that there is a special connection felt by many persons to exist between sex and privacy. Yet, in the final part of his presentation, Wasserstrom questions settled notions about the developed theory of privacy, confidentiality, and sexuality. He suggests that the need for privacy is a fallout of an imperfect society. He further suggests that it may be desirable for individuals to be socialized differently and that ours would be a healthier, happier culture if there were not so many actions that people now feel comfortable doing only in private, or thoughts that they now feel comfortable in disclosing only to those with whom they have special relationships. In short, Wasserstrom advocates a substantial diminution in the private or secret areas of our lives, especially our sex lives.

According to Philippe Ariès, the French historian, the origins of the social concept of privacy are closely linked to the breakup of large households [1]. There was little room for privacy in the days of communal living. The concept of privacy developed during the industrial age and reflects the alienation and isolation of that style of life. The breakup of communal living imposed privacy on people, which was then used as a protective device and later became a treasured value.

In the post-Watergate climate of suspicion, all secrets are presumed to be bad secrets. Since disclosure is salutary in the political arena in order to maintain representative and accountable government, the justification of secrecy in other areas is perhaps naturally questioned as well. It is time, it is said, that we are shown for what we are—warts and all. One laundry soil and stain remover is even called Shout: "It will get out stains you couldn't get out before." "Let us abolish private life," says Suzanne Brogger of Denmark in her angry book, *Deliver Us From Love* [2]. Bruno Bettelheim suggests that what we must strive for, as in so many other matters, is the right balance between what should be respected and protected as private and what should be part of our public or communal life. He would not recommend keeping things private because they are shameful—which merely exacerbates the shame—but he would recommend privacy for providing solitude, which (he suggests) is essential for human personality [3].

Wasserstrom says that the emphasis upon the maintenance of the private side of life tends to encourage hypocritical and deceitful modes of behavior. This way of living is hypocritical, he says, because it is in essence a life devoted to camouflaging the real, private self from public scrutiny. It is, he says, a dualistic, unintegrated life, which renders the individuals who live it needlessly vulnerable, shame-ridden, and lacking in a clear sense of self.

This view, though there is something to be said for it, is overstated. One can be true to oneself and to others without divulging one's fantasies and private thoughts. Everyone knows people who do not lead a double life, though they do not reveal all their fantasies. In science, whenever there is an exception, the theory has to be modified to take the exception into account.

Wasserstrom forgets the need for a private domain. The thoughts and fantasies in one's private life are essential in psychological development, and they are helpful in times of stress. The nighttime of life has its therapeutic purposes—"Wrap your troubles in a dream," sang Bing Crosby. A person may not wish to discuss or analyze away a fantasy because of the need for it. Thus, in the face of objective and obvious evidence, a man may believe he is pregnant and hold on to that fantasy as long as he needs it. Adults, like children, are in some measure cruel to one another. Put to the public light, a needed fantasy may thereby be crushed.

There are fashions and trends in how, where, and what we keep secret or hope to keep secret. In the upper-middle-class society of eighteenth-century Europe, people would talk about their mistresses much more freely than is done today, although that appears to be changing. The so-called sexual revolution has removed compulsions of secrecy in regard to many aspects of sexual behavior; homosexuality, for example, is now more openly acknowledged. Kinsey's researchers, after eliciting intimate details of some housewife's sex life, would then ask about her husband's salary, and often the answer was, "That's rather personal, isn't it?" A woman, after performing coitus on stage, is mindful about her dress covering her knees later that evening. A girl on the beach may wear next to nothing, but she requires full regalia in the center of town. Thus, the claim to secrecy or privacy is often specific to location and instance.

Wasserstrom says, "Sexual intercourse could be just as pleasurable in public—if persons grew up unashamed—as is eating a good dinner in a good restaurant. Sexual intercourse is 'better' in private only because society has told us so." Wasserstrom here fails to distinguish dining in public from sharing a private meal in the privacy of the home. One does not open the family dinner table to the public, but limits it to family and cherished friends. While one does not oppose the presence of strangers in a restaurant while dining out, the presence of strangers in one's home (or even at the same table in a restaurant) is hardly encouraged. Dining with one's spouse or lover in a restaurant is a public admission of a certain degree of intimacy with that person, but not with every other person in the restaurant. When dining in public, people behave differently because they react to the potentially critical scrutiny of the public eye by dressing more elegantly than they would at home, by sitting at a separate table, and by speaking in a low voice so as not to be overheard. Similarly, sexual relations with one's lover or spouse are publicly acknowledged but not totally exposed. A couple might exchange rings, purchase a marriage license, change surnames, or simply hold hands to publicly demonstrate their intimacy. But, as in the case of public versus private dining, the most relaxed and vulnerable behavior, namely sexual intercourse, is reserved for the privacy of the home.

Moreover, I would say that having a good dinner in a good restaurant is *dining*, not merely eating. The difference between dining and eating is elegance; Wasserstrom seems to overlook this important distinction as well. Be it in Africa or the United States, the civilized or nonpsychotic individual follows rules and rituals in regard to fornication, defecation, and consumption of food. Said Chekhov, "Everything about a human creature should be beautiful—face, clothes, spirit, thoughts" [4]. In his writings, Chekhov expressed strongly the view that tact brought people closer to real, as opposed to imaginary, understanding. "Letting it all hang out" neither makes for beauty nor enhances intimacy.

By the way, we may recall the age-old observation that language is actually incapable of expressing one's most cherished and deepest thoughts. One's most personal thought is speechless, subterranean, unconscious. Sometimes humming or whistling is more expressive than words. George Groddeck, noting the limitation of language, says we should indeed be delighted by it:

Even the most marvellous poet can express no more than a fraction of his thought in words. His best ideas remain as mute as with everybody else, and he would be committing a sin if he revealed them. It would amount to being unchaste. He would lose himself and cease to exist as an individual if he could completely expose himself. . . . Language acts as a fetter which wisely holds us back. Nature shies away so much from showing itself as it really is that it does not allow the inner life to be conceived in words, not even in silent words. . . . When something has to be communicated from the innermost soul as happens particularly in relationships between men and women, then it is done by gesture, touch, by the light of the eyes, perhaps by a louder sound, perhaps even by music, but never by language. The barrier is insurmountable [5].

Undressing the mind, or attempting to do so, is no more a panacea than undressing the body. Social nudity has seemed for some a panacea for the social problems affecting modern civilization; hence, the endorsement of nudist colonies and nude therapy. Nudity came to be regarded as a curative act: It would free the mind as well as the body. It became a fad, but never the prevailing view.

That baring everything on one's mind is not essential for intimacy is reflected in Dr. Karl Menninger's admonition to one patient: "Your fantasies are none of your wife's business." Marriage counselors are increasingly agreed that an individual ought not to feel obliged to tell his or her spouse about previous love affairs, as this might only lead to needless strain. Revealing them may indeed be counterproductive to intimacy. In Ibsen's *Wild Duck*, everything is revealed and the family is torn asunder. Even the whale knows that it is more likely to be harpooned if it stays on the surface spouting too much.

There is a special connection between sex and privacy, just as there is between one's wages and privacy. Both involve matters of potency and virility. In a row of public urinals, it is the height of indiscretion for a man to look sideways; he must look straight ahead, up, or down. The fear that the development of technology may make it possible to look into or monitor another's mind is age-old. Indeed, some of the fears of the psychiatrist stem from the belief that he can read minds. Sex and vulnerability are indeed linked psychically, and so the maintenance of trust and confidentiality is imperative in sex research and therapy.

In his discussion of unconsented-to disclosures, Professor Wasserstrom refers to the situation in which one of two persons in a marriage seeks therapy and reveals intimate facts about the other to the therapist. Professor Fried in his paper also refers to this situation. While it is often considered desirable that both parties to the marriage participate jointly in the therapy, all too often the concern about confidentiality of the uninvolved party is lightly regarded. His or her concerns are often dismissed as paranoid. When a therapist sees one partner alone, the other partner may feel that his or her most intimate confidences are being divulged to the therapist. To a greater or lesser degree, we all have a sense of pride and none of us wants to be made a cuckold. Trust is a crucial factor in the development of a relationship, and when one partner knows that the other is revealing his or her confidences to a third person, albeit in therapy, he or she feels an impact to pride. It is often claimed that total secrecy is necessary for the conduct of psychotherapy and therefore the law should never subpoena the psychiatrist as a witness. But the husband-wife relationship, too, requires confidentiality. When we have a triangle of husband-wife-therapist, the uninvolved spouse begins to censor that which he or she does not want the therapist to know. Wasserstrom offers several fair recommendations to this problem in his paper. It might also be suggested that a therapist be selected who is unknown to the nonclient partner; one is less concerned about a divulgence when he does not encounter the therapist in daily life.

But the nonclient partner in any event may be righteously indignant that he or she is being discussed by the other in a therapy situation; the nonclient naturally feels that privacy is being unfairly invaded. This is particularly true in the group therapy situation. One therapist tells of a wife who reveals in group therapy the embarrassing fact that her husband is having sexual relations with the family dog and watches porno films. Another illustration, given by another therapist, is about an executive, a married man, who is having an affair with his secretary; the secretary enters group therapy, where she divulges all, and the information reaches his wife. Good practice may dictate that both partners should be in therapy: It always bodes ill for a relationship when only one of the partners is in therapy. To what extent does the injury to the relationship result from the breach of confidentiality? It is my understanding that Masters and Johnson's sex therapy is directed at the dysfunction of a couple, not of the individual.

In his book *The Spaniard and the Seven Deadly Sins*, Fernando Diaz-Plaja notes that however Catholic the Spaniard may be, he has a great dislike of confession. He explains, "The Spaniard always disliked permitting another what he most appreciates, the intimacy of his home. Many violent and serious bedroom quarrels are due to the disgust with which the husband sees his conjugal life regulated, or at least advised, by his wife's confessor. From this, the extreme suspicion of the psychiatrist follows logically" [6]. The fact that Roman Catholics are now in the minority of Christian denominations requiring confession may confirm the unpopularity of such practices generally.

Another set of cases involves possible or justifiable breaches of confidentiality by the therapist. If the argument is that a breach of confidentiality would always be impermissible because the therapist has expressly or implicitly promised confidentiality, then, as Wasserstrom says, this elevates confidentiality to the highest of all values—a hierarchy that would put the value of confidentiality above even life in some cases. But certain disclosures have always been accepted by the law and the medical profession. In Jewish law, a secret not only may but must be broken if it stands in the way of saving a life. The physician is bound by ethics and law to notify authorities whenever he has a patient afflicted with any one of a range of infectious and other diseases, and he cannot be held legally liable for passing on such information even though it may rebound to the disadvantage of the patient.

When is disclosure by therapists in order? Should—or may—a therapist or physician tell the patient's wife or the authorities that the patient is committing incest with his daughter, or that the patient has a venereal disease? That the patient, a physician, is engaging in sex with his female patients? That the patient, a teacher, is taking indecent liberties with his young students? That the patient has made a false complaint of rape that resulted in prosecution? The illustrations are limitless.

An improper disclosure may result in a legal judgment for damages for defamation, invasion of privacy, or breach of confidentiality. An action for defamation is subject to the defense of truth, but a breach of secrecy, even if the statement is true, may result in a suit in tort for invasion of privacy or a suit in contract for breach of confidence. It is the promiscuous nontestimonial disclosure of information that leads to liability. The one who discloses has the burden of justifying the disclosure.

To illustrate, in one case, a complainant was allowed recovery on a theory of breach of contractual relation against her physician for his disclosure to her husband of her diagnosis and of certain statements made by her while in psychotherapy.[1] It sometimes happens

[1] *Barry v. Moench*, 331 P.2d 814 (Utah 1959).

that a counselor or therapist will give warning, directly or indirectly, about a patient's suitability for marriage or parenthood. A girl, for example, may fail to tell her boyfriend that she has had feelings of bodily detachment or has made suicide attempts. Should the physician make a disclosure or otherwise attempt to disrupt the relationship? In buying a car, particularly a used one, a prospective purchaser will have a mechanic look it over, but in social relationships, it may be sheer folly to have the assessment of a third person or a computer. Nonetheless, it happens, and it has resulted in liability.[2]

In an oft-cited case, a telephone company employee who was registered at a hotel was treated by a local physician for sores. The physician informed him that he believed his disease to be syphilis and advised him to leave the hotel. He refused, and the physician warned the hotel owner that he thought the guest was afflicted with a "contagious disease." The hotel owner placed the guest's belongings in the hall, fumigated his room, and forced him to leave. The guest sued the physician, contending that the disclosure of any confidential communication at any time or under any circumstances was a breach of the physician-patient relationship and gave rise to a cause of action in damages. The court, holding against liability, stated, "No patient can expect that if his malady is found to be of a dangerously contagious nature he can still require it to be kept secret from those to whom, if there was no disclosure, such disease would be transmitted."[3]

In the much-publicized recent case of *Tarasoff* v. *Regents of the University of California,* a young man confided a murderous plot to his psychotherapist at the university clinic. He threatened to kill a girl who had jilted him. Upon her return to college, he carried out the threat. Her parents brought a wrongful-death suit against the university for failure to have the patient committed or to warn them about the threat. In a 5–2 decision, after a year's deliberation, the California Supreme Court ruled that a doctor or psychotherapist who has reason to believe that a patient may injure or kill another must notify the potential victim, his relatives, friends, or

---

[2] *Furness* v. *Fitchett* [1957] New Zealand L. Rep. 396.
[3] *Simonsen* v. *Swenson,* 104 Neb. 244, 177 N.W. 831 (1930).

the authorities.[4] Traditionally, the priest eschewed reporting a penitent, but the secular priest of today—the psychiatrist—is obliged to make a disclosure (for the reason that cynical materialism has today engulfed the healing arts).

Naturally, the case prompted considerable controversy. The decision has given rise to a number of questions: How is an idle or remote threat to be distinguished from an immediate one? Must the psychiatrist report every homicidal fantasy? Would a doctor be liable if he failed to report a vague threat which the patient eventually acted upon? What constitutes danger? In which of the illustrations mentioned should the psychiatrist make a report? To whom? To the family, the school superintendent, the police? In the aftermath of the *Tarasoff* case, the following notice appeared on the bulletin board of one clinic: "As per usual the court has established a vague middle ground with no well-defined rule for making a legal judgment. For the time being, it is probably better to err in the favor of over-caution. It is a state ruling, that of California, but it can be used as a precedent for rulings in other states." There has been a move to put the *Tarasoff* decision in statutory form; the proposal would require "professionals treating mentally ill persons to notify any intended victims of threats of harm the mentally ill person makes."[5]

There are some things with which one person has no moral right to burden another, and the latter must decide for himself when the former has overstepped the boundaries and cannot expect the right of confidentiality. Consider one of James Thurber's cartoons, in which a woman says to her new beau, "If you can keep a secret, I'll tell you how my husband died." None of the testimonial privileges in law (including even the highly regarded attorney-client privilege) shield communications relating to planned or future criminal conduct. At best, they cover past history. By analogy, there are some out-of-courtroom situations in which one is not justified in holding a confidence. As Wasserstrom suggests, it is not possible to draw a line—as it is a matter of good judgment—

---

[4] *Tarasoff* v. *Regents of the University of California*, 17 Cal.3d 425, 551 P.2d 334, 131 Cal. Reptr. 14 (1976) (*Tarasoff II*), *vacating* 13 Cal.3d 117, 529 P.2d 553, 118 Cal. Reptr. 129 (1974) (*Tarasoff I*).
[5] Michigan House Bill 5010 (1975).

and it may be misleading to give specific examples, but it seems that one can accept in confidence a communication from another that he has a history of child-molesting, but on the other hand, if he confides that he is going to kill someone and has obtained a gun for that purpose, then it would seem to be a tenable position for any therapist or group member to make a divulgence in a proper manner, such as in seeking civil commitment. Indeed, in all likelihood, the young man in *Tarasoff* regrets that his murderous impulses were not controlled. Decisions to avert harm must be dictated by common sense and by strong conscience as well as by standards of professional ethics.

It is unfortunate that Wasserstrom chooses to emphasize the need for a general reduction in confidentiality rather than an increase in the conscientiousness with which those entrusted with such confidences handle their responsibility. There are levels of confidentiality, and they mean something. There is positive value in privacy; it is not entirely a fallout of an imperfect society. Privacy is an essential ingredient in the emergence of humanity. Privacy has therapeutic value in personality development, in the nurturance of imagination, and in the making of close relationships. Wasserstrom recognizes that friends in a close relationship are willing to share thoughts about themselves with each other that they are unprepared to reveal to the world at large, and that these relationships would be impossible or at least less likely without confidentiality.

The law at least seems to recognize a certain value in keeping secrets, but it balances that value against the public's need to know. It seems unproductive to bemoan the negative effect of secrecy on sex therapy and research if that very secrecy is a fundamental need of the people whom the therapy or research is supposed to benefit. Wasserstrom might consider first investigating the psychological and corresponding sexual need for the intimacy of secrets between sexual partners before advocating a total razing of the walls of confidentiality. If the law is an accurate indicator of people's wishes, he may find that people want both their own privacy and all the knowledge they might conceivably need about others. Thus, the public need to know and the private need to keep secret must be balanced against each other, rather than either one entirely displacing the other. Groddeck is correct in saying that nature protects us, at least in some measure [5]. When it is "you and me against the world," to quote Helen Reddy, it really seems better than revealing all of my secrets to make it "me against the world and you."

We are indebted to Professor Wasserstrom for his thoughtful and provocative paper. I am grateful for the opportunity to respond.

JUDITH LONG LAWS: The papers that formed this morning's session have concentrated on the protection of the client or subject in research. I want to broaden the focus a bit and return to general issues of research ethics. In so doing, I would like to emphasize, first of all, constraints on research; second, matters of design; third, the question of validity; and fourth, variations on the subject role, the experimenter role, and their role partnership.

The generally accepted constraints on research with human subjects include the following: (1) limitations of the alternative means of obtaining the desired information; (2) methods of compensating the subject; and (3) the overall value of the proposed project in terms of its contribution to knowledge. I mention these considerations in order to emphasize the similarity or continuity between the ethical requirements of sex research and those of other psychological research. In terms of validity, if not in terms of ethics, we need to be wary of projecting our assumptions about sex onto our subjects in research.

Whether the emphasis on personal integrity (Fried's concept) or privacy (Wasserstrom's concept) is seen as fitting in with the accepted constraints on research depends on your models of subject and experimenter roles. In the traditional paradigm, the experimenter role is a personification of Science. His power—I am talking about a "he" that is not generic, in this instance—his power derives more from this attribute than from any power he has to determine consequences for the subjects, at least outside the experimental situation. He is also a stranger. He is an expert. He is impassive, objective, and nonwarm. In fact, he models the denial of feelings that is one of the hallmarks of the experimenter-subject relationship. He is nonresponsive and may be evasive. Neither the instruction, consent, or manipulation stages of the experiment nor the usually optional debriefing stage involves any meaningful dialogue between the experimenter and the subject. An unexamined feature of the unreality of this type of experimental situation—which has been extensively researched only from the subject's side—has ethical implications. It seems very likely that the situation is not real to the experimenter either. Hence, he does not take responsibility for what happens as a consequence of the experimental interaction. I might cite here Rokeach's findings on the surprisingly long-lasting effects of the standard experimental manipulation on self-concept—effects that were still apparent a year after the experiment [7]. I venture to say that most of us save our consciences by neglecting to follow up the subjects in our research. That's a sobering thought. I think it relates to a general structural feature of the experimenter-subject relationship, that is, lack of parity. This lack of parity permits a lack of reciprocity. Even though the consequences of participation in the experimental situation may be very different for subject and experimenter, the subject has no way of forcing the experimenter to be responsible should he not be so inclined. It will be obvious that I am here skipping over the thorny issues of the privilege of the various professions to regulate themselves and the questions of professional ethics that are not subject to challenge. (I find, by the way, that Professor Fried's comments about the liabilities of experimenters are hanging over my head like a black cloud as I make these remarks; I won't do justice to them, but I'm sure you are aware of them, too.)

Now, the subject role: There are two competing scripts that can be found in the published research literature. The first is the ideal role partner for the experimenter role that I just described: a captive responder, actually an empty vessel who is to be filled with the experimenter's cleverly conceived manipulation. In this script, *subject* is entirely a misnomer. The role is really that of an object. I need not remind this audience that it is standard practice to throw out the data from any subject who refuses to believe the experimenter's manipulation; when we do debriefing, we commonly do it to find out whether the subject has bought a line or not. We don't normally exploit the many other potentials in the debriefing situation. (I'm talking as a social psychologist here.) The endless search for the ideal, receptive, impressionable, naive subject underlies the characteristics of the subject-experimenter role relationship in this script. The spineless, docile, acquiescent subject is the appropriate complement to the inhuman, godlike experimenter.

There is an alternative script that casts the subject as an ingenious problem solver who exploits his past learning and the cues present in the experimental situation. The subject's flexibility and persistence in striving to enact the good-subject role defeat the experimenter's ingenuity in constructing tasks and cover stories. Although I am glossing over issues of validity without adequate attention to detail, the acquiescence of the subject in either script appears to be an intractable problem, whether we consider him to be ignorant or to have a history of past learning.

Those who are familiar with social-psychological research will recognize that deception is central to the conceptualization and design of most research in this field. Nothing I have said so far challenges the central role of deception nor promises any protection from the liability discussed by Fried. Moreover, the situation that I am describing poses nowhere near the threat to the subject's integrity that is to be found in situations of diminished autonomy, diminished capacity, or experimenters controlling major life outcomes for subjects. Clearly, the situation in which the researcher is also a therapist is infinitely more complex than the simple research situation that I address.

Furthermore, I am not at all convinced that consent is the sole or sufficient protection for a subject's autonomy, well-being, or self-enhancement. (I might just say parenthetically that one of the issues I wish I had time to deal with is the question of negative versus positive compensations or goals for the subject participating in research. As a survey researcher I have learned that in order to induce cooperation, one has to offer a respondent—as we call them in sociology—something other than the glory of serving science; but as Green points out, there are some problematic issues—though I think Green overstates them—in our offering other inducements, such as money, to subjects. The issue of the means of obtaining consent is one that will continue to concern us. We're aware of many means of influencing consent at present; it stands to reason that researchers will become more ingenious in "selling" participation to subjects as consent standards become more stringent.)

Some of the speakers this morning raised the issue of who decides what is in the subject's best interests. I am sensitive to that issue because it is relatively easy for people in positions of authority, such as professors and therapists and certainly social psychologists, to know better what is really good for the subject. And without offering an answer to that problem, I'll just say it depends on your model of the person.

Besides the analysis of varieties of subject and experimenter role, there is also a typology of experimental situations. Some types of situations render the subject much more vulnerable than others. I don't have time to run through such a typology, but let me just suggest that certain ways of structuring the information-getting situation reinforce the passive subject role and dampen the active problem-solver role. I might also remind you that the widespread use of deception in our experiments—I won't tar anyone else with this brush—is motivated by twin desires: on the one hand, the desire for consent, and on the other hand, the desire for validity.

A feature of a typology of situations would be the different gradients in variables that have been mentioned in this morning's discussions. For example, the subject's need for confidentiality should be examined in terms of the consequentiality of sharing of relevant information beyond that privileged initial dyad. What difference does it make if research assistants deal with coded questionnaire or interview material? I'm not dismissing the question, but I think it defines a different kind of situation. A point that was overlooked in this morning's discussion is something that I will call, for want of a better term, an indifference gradient. People actually are indifferent to the sharing of a good deal of information, and we want to be sure we know which kinds. Anybody who reviews all the research about television will be astonished at the kinds of things Americans are indifferent to having done to them and being communicated to or about them.

I'd like to make one point under the headings of *in vitro* and *in vivo* research, which is that the model of the subject may or may not correspond to the model of the person that an experimenter or researcher is working with. For psychologists this can be critical, and Wasserstrom's somewhat unexpected reference (at the end of his paper) to basically humanistic models of the person should be taken as a reminder that there are other options besides the circum-scribed ones that I have identified here. With respect to models of the person, let me urge on you my own strong suspicion that limits of experimenters' and subjects' or therapists' and clients' responsi-bility is a very critical dimension. There appears to be a zero-sum model operating here in the sense that the farther the therapist or experimenter extends the responsibility he takes for consequences to the subject or patient, the less responsibility is left for the sub-ject or patient. That only matters if you are taking at all seriously the family of basically humanistic models of the person.

I will have to just tantalize you with a list of alternative methods that have been employed as ways of breaking down the role defini-tion of subject, the role definition of experimenter, or the script that binds both of them together. First of all, there are many vari-ants of role taking. One option is that, instead of exposing the sub-ject to a deception and running him through the experiment like a rat, the subject is simply invited to give the responses that a subject would give in the version of the experiment that involves decep-tion. This is the most extensively researched of the alternatives. Second is the use of unobtrusive measures; I think Dick Green and others would argue that what the subject doesn't know can't hurt him, and that the limits of our ethical responsibility are not ex-ceeded by the fact that we may be collecting data of which the subjects of our research are unaware. Another possibility—which social psychologists don't do as much, but other psychologists des-perately want to do—is to so constrain the subject's behavior that even if the deception isn't working, the subject cannot mislead the experimenter, cannot outflank or outwit the experimenter. An-other possibility is the screening of subjects, as Dick Green sug-gested. I don't particularly like this alternative because of the threat to validity that restricting the sample would inevitably in-troduce. I think some very exciting possibilities are involved in ex-panding the idea of debriefing (a canon of good procedure that is more honored in the breach—at least for social psychologists—as I have already mentioned); Wasserstrom suggests some possible de-velopments that I'll just mention now. One would be that, rather than using the debriefing situation only to check the manipulation or to give information that corrects any misinformation deliber-

ately given in the instruction stage, there be a cathartic or an af-
fective component of debriefing as well as a cognitive one. Wasserstrom suggests that there could be a relatively disinterested person
who would give the subject information about the experiment and
perhaps solicit consent; this might remove some of the elements of
lack of freedom that are of concern in this type of situation. A further development of this would be to conceive of the research enterprise as basically a process, rather than an episode, and one in
which experimentation that maximizes control could be one phase,
but in which both experimenter and subject would be well versed
in all phases and would be willing and able to exchange roles at
various stages of the process. That, of course, would take research
out of the realm of capitalistic production and put it back into the
realm of humane letters, which would be an undesirable outcome,
but it's worth considering as a theoretical possibility.

One final point without a specific programmatic suggestion: I
think we could be more creative about the question of positive inducements for participation in scientific inquiry by offering subjects or clients inducements that really pay off and really have consequences for self-enhancement. I think I will just leave you with
that point.

ROBERT J. BAUM: Professor Wasserstrom's paper covers a broad
range of topics and suggests some important connections between
a general theory of privacy and the ethical issues confronted by sex
researchers and therapists. There are two critical issues that he fails
to address as explicitly and in as much detail as seems necessary for
the task at hand, namely, the formulation of ethics guidelines for
the profession. I shall only have time to begin an elaboration of
these two topics.

First and most important, it is essential to consider explicitly
and desirable, if possible, to arrive at a consensus as to whether privacy—that is, control over information about and access to oneself—has value in and of itself, or has value only as a means to
some other end. In the terminology of classical philosophy, is privacy of intrinsic value or solely of instrumental value? Professor
Wasserstrom recognizes the instrumental value of privacy when he
points out that it is essential to the diminution of an individual's
vulnerability insofar as invasion of privacy can result in hurt, em-

barrassment, and distrust. But I am unable to determine from his essay whether he believes privacy to have any intrinsic value. This is particularly critical to his treatment of the problem of breaching confidentiality, where he seems to be applying a utilitarian criterion to the effect that confidence may be (and perhaps ought to be) breached if the breach will result in less harm being done overall than if the confidence had been maintained. If the only value of privacy is its utility in protecting its subject from harm (psychological or physical), then to determine which way to go in a given case, the sex researcher or therapist would only have to weigh the possible harm to others against the possible physical or psychological harm to the subject or client (with perhaps a little extra weight on the subject/client side to account for a minimal weakening of the institution of researcher-subject/therapist-client confidentiality). But if privacy has intrinsic value as well, the situation becomes more complicated.

I want to suggest, although time does not permit me to present a full defense of this position, that privacy is valuable in and of itself. I believe Charles Fried has argued this point eloquently in his book *An Anatomy of Values* [8], although I am somewhat distressed to see that subsequent journal articles by other authors seem to have missed or misinterpreted his point here [9, 10]. The intrinsic value of privacy is significantly greater than the instrumental value it possesses in most situations.

Professor Wasserstrom seems to accept the general definition of *privacy* as the control over certain information about and access to oneself as distinct from the withholding of such information. But he does not indicate clearly that he believes that this control, this autonomy or self-determination of the individual, is an essential part of the individual's personhood and that her or his personhood is diminished in proportion to the expropriation of this control by others. This erosion of an individual's personhood results even if the violation of her or his privacy does not cause her or him any immediate hurt, embarrassment, or discomfort. Indeed, Professor Wasserstrom seems to be denying this fact about privacy when he asserts that "absent special or unusual circumstances, individuals have no particular interest in retaining control over the disclosure of many facts about themselves" [see Chapter 3 under PRIVACY AND CONFIDENTIALITY].

Although it may be a debatable *empirical* question whether or not most people are in fact interested in retaining control over information about themselves, this is not particularly relevant to the *ethical* question of whether it is important to them as persons and as moral agents to retain such control. It is important to make as clear as possible the distinction between the control of information and the information itself. (In this regard, I feel that some of Professor Slovenko's comments were somewhat misdirected in that he was concerned with the goodness or badness of withholding information and keeping it secret. It seems to me that that decision is up to the individual and that one can argue on either side what the advantages or disadvantages are of revealing certain types of information.) The point that must be argued here is the question of who has control over that information, who has the right to release that information—not simply whether or not it should be released or taken in a given case. This does not imply anything at all about the amount of information that the individual ought to release or to whom one should release it under specific circumstances. I tend to agree with Professor Wasserstrom's recommendations that social values in institutions be changed so as to decrease substantially the kinds of actions and information many people now choose to keep to themselves. But even if the world is changed in such a way as to encourage people to reveal more of themselves to others, each person must still retain the right to control the release of this information. That is, even if there is no potential harm that might result from the release of specific information, harm is being done if it is released against the will of the subject, namely, the harm of the violation of the right of the individual to retain control over that information.

If privacy is valuable in and of itself, then in the context of research and therapy the confidence of subjects or patients should be broken—that is, their right of privacy should be taken away—*only* when the same or a more important right of others is being violated. Thus, I would agree with Professor Wasserstrom's assertion that breach of confidence is justifiable to prevent rape, but not for the reason he offers (his reason being that the injuries caused by any breach of confidentiality would probably be less severe than the consequences of maintaining the confidentiality). The critical offense in rape is not the infliction of pain, physical or emotional.

What distinguishes it from common assault and battery is precisely its invasion of the "zone of privacy," the forcible usurpation of the individual's right to control access to her or his body; it is therefore justifiable in some circumstances to breach one person's confidence to prevent that person from invading another person's privacy. The really difficult problem in the case that Professor Wasserstrom raised in his essay, is that of weighing the *probability* of a future rape (or some other invasion of privacy) against the *actuality* of the therapist's or researcher's breach of the patient's or subject's confidence.

The second critical issue that requires attention is that of the distinction between public and private behavior. This is especially important for determining whether or not informed consent must be obtained in various research and therapy situations. If an act is unquestionably public, then consent to observe and report on it is not necessary. But which acts are public, and what makes them public?

A partial answer to this question is contained in Professor Wasserstrom's discussion of private communication, but his account must be expanded to deal with behavior other than communicative behavior. Certainly, any acts performed under the circumstances specified in his essay as essential for private communication will also be private to the same degree. Whatever occurred in that setting is directly knowable only to the participants.

It appears to be consistent with Professor Wasserstrom's theory of private communication to hold that an act is private if that act cannot be seen or heard by any person other than the participants *and* there is an understanding, tacit or explicit, that none of the participants will reveal what occurred without the consent of the other participants. But this is not adequate for dealing with a variety of situations that can arise in the areas of both sex research and sex therapy. For example, does a person have a right to see a sex therapist without anyone else knowing about it, even if this requires that the therapist take steps to protect the patient's privacy beyond the steps normally taken by physicians and other professionals? Does a researcher have a right to observe individuals' behavior as long as it occurs in a public place? These are not easy questions, but they cannot be avoided.

I now have time only to point out one or two ways in which an expanded theory of privacy might be developed: First and perhaps most important, the definition of a private act must be sharpened to include unequivocally all acts which are such that it is reasonable within the cultural and physical context to assume that no one other than the participants can see or hear what is going on. This qualification makes wiretapping and surreptitious observation, for example, clearly invasions of privacy, but it is not adequate for dealing with problems such as accidental intrusions, assignment of responsibility for providing guarantees of such privacy, or the kinds of questions and problems that Professor Gorovitz raised in his comments earlier today.

Another critical issue for a comprehensive theory of privacy is an adequate analysis of the concept of anonymity. Alan Westin, in his discussion of privacy as it relates to computer data banks, has argued that anonymity can provide an effective shield of the privacy of individuals [11]. Thus, many of our acts that are performed in public are essentially private if no one who observes them knows us personally. For example, I observed the actions of many persons on the airplane that brought me to this meeting, but since I personally knew none of the persons whom I was observing, my observations did not violate their right to privacy. On the other hand, if I had made an effort to learn the identity of any of these persons and thus break down their shield of anonymity, I might have violated their privacy in significant ways. This kind of restriction applies clearly to cases like the *Tearoom* study.

I have tried to show, in the brief time available, that the concept of privacy is extremely complex. Professor Wasserstrom's paper provides an excellent starting point for discussion, but many critical questions remain unanswered and some may even be unanswerable. Nevertheless, it is important for the establishment and maintenance of ethical standards in the profession to continue the search for answers to these difficult questions. It is as important to do this as to enforce standards strictly in the more clear-cut cases.

RICHARD WASSERSTROM: I'd like to take two minutes just to made a little clearer what my methodology was in doing the paper.

In the first part of the paper I tried to construct all the arguments that I could for why—if they were inclined to give reasons—people might claim that they ought to have control over information about themselves. I thought the reasons they might give were rather a mixed bag in terms of being somewhat utilitarian and somewhat nonutilitarian. Some of them had to do with an idea of what it was to be a person, for example; I don't think that would be considered utilitarian. Then I thought about the implications that this view—which I think might be a dominant view in the United States—might have for why it would be important to respect privacy in a variety of contexts.

This is where I think the biggest source of possible misunderstanding is, and I apologize for not having made it clear enough in the paper. In the last part of my essay, I simply wanted to say that all the reasons and arguments I had presented earlier seem to depend on certain assumptions. Thus, if someone didn't want to accept those arguments and their underlying assumptions, what alternative arrays of arguments are available? I regret that the paper left people with the impression that I was offering a point of view that people ought to adopt. I don't have the foggiest idea of what view people ought to adopt, but I thought an alternative view was worth taking seriously, particularly in this context, for two reasons: First of all, it seems to me that what sex therapists and sex researchers do, whether they want to or not, is to change people's attitudes and beliefs to some degree about the strength of the connection between sexual information about themselves and privacy. You get people to talk about things that a more traditional view would have said they almost never talk about. The second reason that I thought it was worth considering was that I had the impression—perhaps an erroneous one—that a fair number of professionals in psychology (and perhaps also in sex therapy) come closer to holding this alternative view than do other members of our society, and that it's important to try to make as explicit as you can the view that you hold and to see what arguments it depends on and what implications it has for privacy. So, look at it as an invitation to think about a topic, not a nailing of some theses on the therapist's door.

With that, we ought to open the floor to general discussion.

JOSHUA S. GOLDEN: Let me say that I agree wholeheartedly with Dick. As I understood it, the purpose of the paper was to present a variety of views for our examination.

Let me proceed to say as a qualification that it is very dangerous to attribute motives to people. They are probably in a better position than we are to understand and explain what their motives are. But Dr. Money raised the point this morning that maintenance of the status quo is something in which many of us have an investment and that to change the status quo may be a very provocative thing. I sense that perhaps Professor Slovenko's response was the kind of response that one might expect from attempts to change the status quo. It's important, however, as Dick Wasserstrom reminds us, to present arguments to support our points of view. For example, Professor Baum suggests that there is an intrinsic value to privacy, but he didn't have time to tell us exactly why that was so. It would be interesting to know.

To go back for a moment, Professor Slovenko's argument against the notion of an alternative view of the value of privacy cited a variety of kinds of evidence. One example with which I am familiar is the book by Professor Diaz-Plaja, *The Spaniard and the Seven Deadly Sins*, an impressionistic study by a Spaniard particularly directed toward educating Americans and other non-Spanish people about the unique and idiosyncratic characteristics of the Spaniard. To generalize this author's observations about a specific ethnic subculture and apply them to anyone who holds different values and different attitudes would be, I think, misleading, and it would call into question the nature of the evidence upon which the contention was based.

FRITZ REDLICH: I gather from this morning's discussion that under certain circumstances, the random clinical trial and the double-blind method may be considered ethical. To be a candid observer is not ethical under all circumstances, however.

The question I would raise is, Why are we under such a compulsion always to be ethical? In this conference, the overwhelming majority seem to be on the side of God and the angels. But there is room for disagreement and even for actually being unethical for possibly constructive purposes. I think that to some extent life and progress take place as a result of an interplay between these forces. Of course, one then has to face the consequences of being unethical. To be a candid observer under certain circumstances has such consequences. But I think we should not eliminate the possibilities. I think sometimes one has to have the courage to risk a certain kind of behavior and face the consequences. If this were never done—and I think I follow the thinking of Dr. Money in this, to some extent—a great deal of research would stop altogether, and this would be a pity (or maybe a lack of pity) for future generations.

RALPH SLOVENKO: Of course. But—as Harry Truman said—if you can't stand the heat, you stay out of the kitchen. You have to know the consequences.

PATRICIA SCHILLER: There seems to be a good deal of discussion of the operational definition of research, but I was wondering whether anyone would like to elaborate on operational definitions concerning sex therapy. What items or methodologies would you incorporate in a written contract for sex therapy? What methods would you recommend to give the patient a sense of freedom? In other words, what would the dialogue be? It's so personal. It's so much a matter of style and of individual value systems. How can we ensure some consistency and continuity in terms of following through on some of these very important value judgments?

RICHARD WASSERSTROM: Tomorrow people will be divided up into groups that will spend most of the day focusing on the different issues and their relationship to the proposed guidelines. It seems to me something like that would be an appropriate topic of discussion in the group considering informed consent.

REFERENCES

1. Ariès, P. Centuries of Childhood. New York: Knopf, 1962.
2. Brogger, S. Deliver Us from Love. New York: Delacorte, 1976. P. 49.
3. Bettelheim, B. Some Comments on Privacy. In Surviving and Other Essays. New York: Knopf, 1979. Pp. 399–411.

4. Chekhov, A. P. *Uncle Vanya.* Edited by O. Magarschack. London: Harrap, 1962.
5. Groddeck, G. Language. In *The Meaning of Illness: Selected Psychoanalytic Writings.* New York: International Universities Press, 1977.
6. Diaz-Plaja, F. *The Spaniard and the Seven Deadly Sins.* New York: Scribner's, 1970.
7. Rokeach, M. Long-range experimental modification of values, attitudes, and behavior. *American Psychologist* 26:453-459, 1971.
8. Fried, C. *An Anatomy of Values.* Cambridge, Mass.: Harvard University Press, 1970.
9. Thomson, J. J. The right to privacy. *Philosophy and Public Affairs* 4:295-314, 1975.
10. Rachels, J. Why privacy is important. *Philosophy and Public Affairs* 4:323-333, 1975.
11. Westin, A. *Privacy and Freedom.* New York: Atheneum, 1967.

RESEARCH WITH
SPECIAL POPULATIONS

JAY MANN: Our colleagues on the task force are in complete agreement about the paper that Al Jonsen and I wrote. They all agree that it's the longest paper in the blue book. So, out of compassion, I won't use my 10 minutes to expand on the points that were covered in the paper; rather, I shall try to boil the product down and skim off the principal issues that we addressed.

The codes of ethics governing the use of human subjects in research derive from three basic assumptions, which have been alluded to by previous speakers. First, that the knowledge acquired through research holds potential benefit for the category of individuals being studied as well as for the larger society. Second, that such benefits must be balanced against potential risks to research subjects. And finally, that subjects must be adequately and fully informed of the possible consequences of participation.

Our paper explores an additional assumption, namely, that the use of children and other groups presumed to be exceptionally vulnerable to risks as research subjects requires that extraordinary ethical safeguards be invoked. Our first task was to identify and define the groups to be labeled special populations. In addition to children, these might include the aged, the retarded, the disabled, and other groups presumed to be especially vulnerable to exploitation or social strictures. We would classify as a special population any group exhibiting one or more of the following characteristics: diminished capacity for making informed decisions; diminished autonomy; or increased vulnerability to exploitation or social strictures. We have chosen to focus on children as best exemplifying the issues raised by research populations exhibiting the foregoing characteristics. However, in applying the statements about children to other special groups, especially to groups of adults, it is of course necessary to take into account the ways in which the needs and capacities of a given group differ from those of children, in addition to considering the commonalities among groups.

Our purpose in this paper was to delineate some of the issues faced by review boards having the responsibility of evaluating proposals for sex research involving children or other special groups. Since the Commission for the Protection of Human Subjects had already drafted a set of guidelines reflecting the issues relative to participation of children in general research, we decided to build on the commission's guidelines and focus our discussion on the specific dimension of sex research, which raised questions not fully covered by the more general commission guidelines.

These issues cluster around the following prevalent assumptions: first, that sex research is potentially reactive and has the potential for changing the behavior and attitudes of research subjects; second, that the consequences of such change may be harmful to the child or unacceptable to the child's parents. Implicit in these two assumptions are some widely held beliefs, for example, the belief that children cannot resist or reject information; that they will be emotionally overpowered or stimulated to precocious sexual behavior by sexual stimuli; and finally, that sex research encroaches on the parent's prerogative as sex educator and arbiter of family mores.

The validity of these beliefs is arguable. The tenacity with which they are held may be changing, along with other attitudes relative to sex. However, at this point they are still articles of faith with heavy emotional overtones for large segments of the public. The child as a sexual being is not an image that most adults can react to calmly. Therefore, these beliefs must be taken into account as predictors of public response. Also, they raise questions about the nature of changes likely to result from sex research with children and the consequences of such changes in a society that is still ambivalent about the sexual interest or activity of the child.

Along with issues related to the nature of change, one must consider which elements of research procedure are most likely to prove reactive, that is, to produce unscheduled change in child subjects. We argue that reactivity is largely a function of three characteristics of a stimulus or procedure: first, intrusiveness (that is, the extent to which the research design requires the child to interact with the investigator); second, inquisitiveness (a dimension characterizing the nature and extent of the information elicited from the child); and third, explicitness (a dimension that describes the content of the stimuli or measuring instruments such as tests or interview schedules).

Within the context of the commission's guidelines, the purpose of judging research procedures by criteria such as these is to determine whether they pose risks greater than those that the child would encounter in daily life. Admittedly, this judgment is a difficult one, given the wide variation in the social environments of children as well as in their capacity to accommodate to experiences. Furthermore, there is little agreement as to the sorts of change that might occur and the degree to which these might constitute risks. These uncertainties might be reduced by the very sort of sex research with children that researchers are currently constrained from performing because of these uncertainties; this, then, is an instance in which the solution has become the problem.

A final issue is that of informed consent. Informed consent by whom? If the consentor is a parent or other caretaker, as in the case of institutionalized subjects, it is important that the person act in the best interests of the child or other subject. However, even if it were possible for the consentor to determine the subject's best interests, the question of the subject's understanding of participation remains unanswered and unresolved. To what extent can young children or subjects with greatly diminished understanding fully comprehend the consequences of participation, when the adults are themselves operating on assumptions that have not yet been systematically explored or tested? Another issue relative to informed consent raises complex questions. On the one hand, the Commission for the Protection of Human Subjects sets guidelines that make a strong argument for parental permission for children's participation in research. This requirement vests considerable authority in parents, who themselves may be fearful that by consenting they are relinquishing control over their children's sexual attitudes and behavior and compromising their own privacy and the integrity of the family system. Obviously, this poses problems for sex research involving children. On the other hand, in recognition of the limitations imposed by requiring parental consent, the commission's guidelines tempered this requirement by allowing an exception: the right of the child to bypass parental control in seeking medical treatment, especially in sex-related conditions. This exception can be viewed as supporting the child's right to volunteer for sex research without first obtaining parental permission.

These are the major issues addressed in our paper. Thoughtful consideration of these issues requires that we reexamine prevailing assumptions about the nature of childhood and the autonomy of the child, about the nature of the parent-child relationship, and about the realities of childhood sexuality.

IRA L. REISS: I read this paper expecting to find much that I would disagree with. Although this proved incorrect, I do have a few comments that might be of some value. I thought the paper was well conceived and well reasoned. Many alternatives were discussed, except in one area—the area that is of the most concern to me as a sociologist. My concern is the tendency to evaluate the importance of safeguard procedures as if all the research being done were of one type. I think the risk inherent in research that involves drilling into someone's brain to affect their future sexual behavior or the risk involved in sex therapy is of a much higher order than the risk of asking someone, "What's your attitude toward premarital intercourse?" I'm sure the authors of the paper are aware of that. In fact, the paper deals with a special type of group whose needs for protection are different from the needs of other groups. But they don't address this general issue, and it needs to be discussed.

One other point related to this: There is a political aspect involved in obtaining consent, at least in sociological research. I think I can best illustrate this by relating what happened to me when I started one of my first research projects, almost 20 years ago. I wanted to get permission to interview high school students in a black high school and in a white high school. (This was in the late fifties, when high schools were still segregated in Virginia.) I sent my research assistants to both schools, but their requests were refused. Then I went myself. In the white school, I got permission by talking to the principal—who had turned down the research assistants' request. I asked him, "How many people get pregnant in this school in a year?" He replied, "Fifteen." I then asked, "Well, don't you think we ought to find out something about student attitudes towards sexuality?" He said, "I'm afraid we'll give them ideas" (a typical reaction). I countered this by asking, "Aren't you afraid that you will be accused of not caring about them if you don't endorse this research?" That was admittedly a semiblackmail procedure; but I was merely verbalizing a possibility that the principal already realized.

Then I approached the principal of the black high school—who was black himself—accompanied by a friend of mine (who, like myself, was white). I asked permission to administer our questionnaire to his students. The principal was evasive and would give no reply. As the conversation kept returning to the governor of the state, I began to see that the principal was probing to determine what my attitude on segregation was: The governor was part of the Byrd machine and had taken a firm stand against integrated schools. There was a joke going around that the Byrd machine had inbred so much that it finally produced an idiot: the governor. I repeated that joke in front of the black principal, who then turned around and said, "When do you want to give out the questionnaire?"

I think that's part of the research procedure. Research doesn't occur in a vacuum, where you can just tell people, "This is a valuable piece of research, and science will benefit." There is a political aspect to it. People who—like the black principal—ask for an indication of where you (as researchers) stand are forcing you to show your good will, to give some sign that you won't abuse the information obtained (from the point of view of the person granting permission); they are simply concerned about the welfare of the group with which they are aligned. I say this to remind you that we can get hung up on the issue of informed consent, believing that if we obtain consent we have solved all the ethical issues. But the ethical issues really go far beyond the problems of merely getting someone to sign a sheet of paper.

One other point connected with the political aspect is that you have to know the values of the group you're researching. I'm sure therapists are aware of the importance of this in dealing with their patients. We found, for instance, that the perception of the risk of answering questions about sex varies according to what the potential respondent's own attitude is toward sex: That is, if people are very permissive and open-minded regarding their own views of sex, they won't think there is any risk at all in the procedures and they will be quite willing to entertain the idea of answering questions, whereas subjects who are more conservative and more traditional in their attitudes toward sex tend to view the potential risks as being much higher. A different approach is needed with each group. In some groups, you couldn't even ask certain questions. Yesterday, for instance, before I left Minneapolis, one of my students told me he was planning to go back to his native country—Iran—and use the questionnaire that we have developed on premarital sexual attitudes. He said he knew it would be very difficult in that cultural milieu, because if you asked an unmarried woman in the presence of her brother whether or not she were virginal, you might well be attacked by the brother. One had to be aware that if he went into that culture as a naive researcher and tried to administer a questionnaire, he might never return. These considerations apply specifically to research, but I imagine they might also apply to therapy.

One or two other points struck me on the subject of informed consent in sex research. I think Dick Green pointed out in his paper that one might lose a large portion of one's sample by making a general statement to the effect that questions would be asked about the respondents' intimate sex life. Some people have proposed using a different procedure, namely, obtaining informed consent for each question separately. You could just say, "You can stop at any point and you are free to refuse to answer any question. You will know what I am going to ask, because there will be a set of questions covering a single topic." Using this system, you would avoid sensitizing your respondents to refuse before you had a chance to establish rapport; thus, you might get a better series of results. I don't think such a procedure is necessary in all research of this sort, but it would be helpful in much of the research that we have been involved in.

A portion of sociological research involves deception of some sort. I fail to see any harm in the use of deception in certain cases. For example, we asked people their attitudes about male sexuality and their attitudes about female sexuality. Our intention was to find out whether they were egalitarian. We never asked the respondents if their views were egalitarian; we simply asked gender-oriented questions and then compared the attitudes reflected by their answers. That is deception of a sort, but I find it difficult to see what harm was done in that particular case. I think there are a lot of situations, at least in sex research, where it seems fairly clear that we don't have to provide complete information to the respondents and can still justify to ourselves that we are not doing them any apparent harm.

My last comment concerns the commission's proposal to set up a national ethics advisory board. My gut reaction to that is one of fear and trepidation. I hate to think that one small group of people would have the responsibility of making decisions on difficult cases. If there were to be such a board, I would favor a policy of a continually rotating membership to avoid the possibility of a group of people with one set of values getting into a position where they had veto power over some of the more innovative research that would come to their particular attention. I would like to hear others' thoughts on how that control might be avoided.

ALBERT R. JONSEN: I just want to assure you that the National Commission's proposal for an ethics advisory board is intended to bring together a group of ideal observers, all of whom have perfect knowledge and perfect virtue.

RUTH MACKLIN: When I agreed to be a panelist discussing the Jonsen-Mann paper, it was the the understanding that I would be talking about what the Jonsen-Mann paper addressed, but the task assigned to me instead was to talk about research on prisoners. Thus, I am going to raise for your consideration this question: Under what conditions, if any, in light of the Jonsen-Mann paper, is it ethical to use prisoners as subjects of sex research? As background material I have before me and will read brief portions of the National Commission's report on research involving prisoners [1]. I spent some time reading the background papers that form part of the appendix, so while I am by no means expert, I can bring in a little of the background and the considerations that the National Commission brought into its deliberations in preparing the report.

First of all, what are the ethical problems that arise in using a special population of prisoners as research subjects? Are they in fact the same considerations that arise with the other special populations to which this session is devoted, or are there some unique or different considerations that arise with prisoners? I believe there are some unique and different considerations.

The chief ethical issue with regard to research on prisoners, both generally and in sex research, is whether or not prisoners are capable of granting informed consent that is fully voluntary—that is to say, freely granted, uncoerced. This suggests a different emphasis from the bulk of the Jonsen-Mann paper. The chief issue that arises out of research on children and the retarded and the other populations, such as the emotionally disturbed, the senile, the elderly, and so on, is the question of their capacity to grant informed consent—that is, whether or not people have a diminished capacity for understanding, for remembering, for reasoning, for processing the issues, for being able to project the issues into the future and assess the possible consequences of their participation in research of any sort. These, however, do not seem to be the major concerns with prisoners, since I think it's safe to assume, unless shown otherwise, that prisoners do not suffer from those particular diminished cognitive capacities that we attribute to the other special populations. The main issue with prisoners is the question of the *voluntariness* of their consent: Can incarcerated individuals grant truly free or uncoerced consent?

The conclusion as stated in the National Commission's report— I mean the brief answer to the question—is no. But here is what the Commission said in particular in its conclusion:

In the course of its investigation in review of evidence presented to it, the Commission did not find in prisons the conditions requisite for a sufficiently high degree of voluntariness and openness, nothwithstanding that prisoners currently participating in research consider in nearly all instances that they do so voluntarily and want the research to continue ([1], p. 12).

There is evidently a difference in perception between the prisoners themselves and others about prisoners' desire to participate in research. In my view, the conclusions drawn by the Commission are too strong. I would support continued research on prisoners, especially in the area of sex research, under certain conditions.

I will return to some of the specific points raised in the Commission's report in a moment, but first let me turn briefly to the concepts and principles articulated in the Jonsen-Mann paper: (1) the question of diminished capacity; (2) the issue of diminished autonomy; and (3) the question of increased vulnerability. Do all these considerations—which apply to other special populations—apply as well to prisoners? My answer is no. In fact, Jonsen and Mann themselves make a qualifying statement that seems to be operative as a background consideration:

A prisoner, for example, may believe cooperation will influence his parole or his treatment. The issue with captive samples is again informed consent. In order to ascertain whether it exists, one would have to determine whether groups whose power to make independent decisions has been restricted are given adequate information about their participation and are under no coercion, however covert, to participate [see Chapter 4].

With respect to the question of diminished capacity, unless it can be shown that some prisoners have diminished capacity in ways that the mentally retarded or children or psychiatric patients do, I think that one would have to provide evidence to prove that prisoners suffer diminished capacity to understand, reason, and make decisions about their own well-being. One of the background papers prepared for the National Commission by Roy Branson included in it a quotation from the now infamous Detroit psychosurgery case, known as the Kaimowitz case. Let me relate briefly what the court said in that case and see whether it applies. The excerpt from *Kaimowitz* v. *The Department of Mental Health of the State of Michigan* reads as follows:

Although an involuntarily detained mental patient may have a sufficient I.Q. to intellectually comprehend his circumstances, the very nature of his incarceration diminishes the capacity to consent. . . . Involuntarily confined mental patients live in an inherently coercive institutional environment. They are not able to voluntarily give informed consent because of the inherent inequality in their position [2].

The issue of psychosurgery in itself raises separate questions—as my colleague at the Hastings Center put it when he testified before the Senate Health Subcommittee—in that "the consenting organ is the damaged organ" [3]. It might be more appropriate to leave aside or bracket the issue of psychosurgery and look instead at other forms of sex research conducted on prisoners, particularly the use of antiandrogens and other chemicals, to see whether or not consent granted by prisoners might be viewed as sufficiently voluntary under certain conditions, namely, conditions where there is a reasonable hope or expectation that those same prisoners or others like them might benefit from the research.

I have discussed diminished capacity very briefly. It is the question of diminished autonomy that engenders most of the controversy surrounding the use of prisoners in research generally as well as in sex research. Here there is more overlap, I think, between the considerations that apply to prisoners specifically and to other special populations discussed in the Jonsen-Mann paper. This seems to be the principle that most directly applies to the ethics of sex research involving prisoners. The issue of autonomous consent is clouded by the fact that prisoners who are candidates for such research—for example, sex offenders—are suffering from compulsion: Although consent may not be totally voluntary and autonomous in this context, many letters from prisoners seem to contain a rather passionate plea for such experimental treatment.

Concerning increased vulnerability, the third concept in the Jonsen-Mann paper—I'm not sure if that applies to prisoners. Do prisoners suffer from increased vulnerability? In a sense, yes, and in a sense, no; it depends in part on what happens when they're released. This is a very complex issue that will vary according to the particular case, and it probably would benefit from social science research.

There is one remark about children in the Jonsen-Mann paper that does apply to prisoners. Let me draw your attention to it:

Nonetheless, as Money and Walker have stated, it is incumbent on the clinician or researcher to mitigate the adverse effects of his or her procedures insofar as possible. Callous responses by the researcher can exacerbate the distress of a child who is already implicitly labeled 'misfit' or 'freak' by parents, peers, and clinicians [see Chapter 4 under ETHICAL EVALUATION OF RESEARCH].

I think it is worth pointing out that this observation on children might equally apply to prisoners who are sex offenders, specifically as regards the perception of those prisoners by society at large.

Now, let me say a few words about the National Commission's report. The big difficulty that must be resolved is the question of the diminished autonomy of prisoners. Assuming that there is such a thing as diminished autonomy in what might be viewed as an inherently coercive environment, our question is, What is implicit in that assumption about the ability of prisoners to participate voluntarily in research? The Commission's general conclusion suggests that in most cases, research on prisoners should be proscribed, that is, there should be a moratorium on research involving prisoners. Nevertheless, when one looks at the Commission's specific recommendations, one finds a number of conditions that might well be met by sex research on prisoners.

First, let's look briefly at Recommendation 2:

Research on practices, both innovative and accepted, which have the intent and reasonable probability of improving the health or well-being of the individual prisoner may be conducted or supported, provided the requirements under Recommendation 4 are fulfilled ([1], p. 15).

The point here is that one has to assess the reasonable probability of improving the health or well-being of the individual prisoner, which may be hard to do in the case of innovative therapy and research. That's precisely what is at issue—that's why research is done, namely, to determine whether there is a reasonable probability of improving persons' well-being. But at least that intent might well be present if indeed it is a question of sex offenders and the choice is between continued (perhaps lifelong) incarceration, on the one hand, or using innovative or experimental forms of therapy that might possibly serve the end of gaining an earlier release from imprisonment, on the other hand. So I take that recommendation as one that is compatible with performing sex research on prisoners.

To recapitulate, given the National Commission's report and recommendations on research involving prisoners, and given the concepts and principles articulated by Jonsen and Mann in their paper, the question is, How does sex research on prisoners fare as compared, say, with ordinary drug research performed on prisoners? As I said, I would argue that sex research on prisoners can be ethically justified on the basis of the careful wording used in the Commission's report as well as in the Jonsen-Mann paper. The issues revolve around the exchanging of freedoms. What are people worried about? They're worried about potential coercion of prisoners. They're worried about the coercive environment. The question I want to raise is this: Are we trading one set of freedoms for another? Is it an enhancement of prisoners' freedom to bar their participation in research? Or is it rather a *restriction* of prisoners' freedom to deny them the opportunity to serve as research subjects, particularly in an area where they have some reason to believe that the results of the research will be beneficial to them?

If freedom—freedom versus coercion—is the main issue here, we have to ask which course of action gives prisoners more freedom and perhaps serves to enhance their dignity. Why should one notion of freedom, namely, that arising out of the so-called coercive environment of prisons, take precedence over another notion of freedom, namely, the right of prisoners to choose what they may do within the confines of an extremely restricted environment? Given a set of individuals whose freedom is already severely restricted by society, which of these two alternatives would make the prisoners freer? My answer would lean toward allowing prisoners to volunteer for sex research on the grounds that if there is both the intent and the reasonable probability that continued research would help them or others who are caught in the grip of the conditions that sex offenders describe, then it can be ethically justified using the very same concept that is used to argue against it: freedom of choice.

ALBERT R. JONSEN: I might mention that [HEW] Secretary Califano last week issued recommendations on research involving prisoners that differ considerably from the Commission's recommendations. Those are now available for public perusal and comment, and anyone who is particularly interested in this field should look for them in the *Federal Register*.

DAVID H. BARLOW: I agree with Ira Reiss that the background paper was particularly well thought out and well written. I can't say that I disagree substantively with any part of it.

What I can do, however, is react to it from my position as an active clinical researcher doing sex research, and present one or two examples or case studies and see how they might apply. I also have the task of making a few comments on these guidelines specifically as they might apply to adolescents.

The Jonsen-Mann paper, as Jay summarized it at the beginning, explores the view that sex research methods and procedures are likely to vary along the threefold continuum of intrusiveness, inquisitiveness, and explicitness. The authors make the point that in sex research involving children who are retarded, these three concepts can be considered the equivalent of risk, since the more intrusive and explicit the procedures involved in the research, the greater the chance that these procedures will have an effect on the subject outside the influence of the parent or guardian—an axiom that would seem to apply to all research involving children, whether retarded or not. The logical conclusion is that many parents are going to shun research activities that would involve their children as these dimensions—intrusiveness, inquisitiveness, and explicitness—increase. These ideas are important to me personally, since our research at Brown would certainly be categorized as highly intrusive, highly inquisitive, and extremely explicit.

In our research we are trying to develop new clinical treatments for various sexual problems. We are also looking at patterns of sexual arousal and variables that affect those patterns. Most of the research is characterized by direct genital measures of sexual arousal, including the vaginal probe technique; these arousal patterns are generated by very explicit visual, auditory, or cognitive stimuli derived from cues given by the patients, and certainly the techniques can be considered inquisitive to the extent that we are determining specific arousal patterns. One procedure involves making an initial audio tape based on the subject's or patient's report of what is sexually arousing to him or her. This audio tape is then played back, and the various physiological indices of arousal are correlated with segments of the audio tape that produced the highest response. The parts of the tape that produced the greatest arousal are then elaborated on and replayed, and this procedure is repeated until eventually we have a tape that is highly erotic to a given patient.

A recent case in point involved a man who complained of a

strong fetish regarding open-toed white sandals worn by women. Since he lived in the South, this proved to be a problem for about nine months of the year. We used the audio-tape method with this patient and found that he was not, in fact, aroused by open-toed white sandals; rather, he was aroused by women's feet when held in very specific positions. The sandal was not a part of the arousal pattern at all. This may seem like a minor point, but it was very important to the patient, who had not been aware of the precise distinction he made (even though it was part of his own sexual arousal pattern).

Regarding the guidelines for inquisitiveness mentioned in the background paper, I can't think of any procedure that is more directly inquisitive than identifying objectively some arousal pattern that has escaped the awareness of even the subject under study. I think Professor Wasserstrom would cite this as an example of the essence of invasion of privacy, in that the thoughts of a person are that person's private domain. I think you would all agree that not only are these procedures inquisitive, but—inasmuch as we use the vaginal probe measure when we work with women—they are also very intrusive measures. Finally, the stimuli we use are very explicit by definition.

As I related the anecdote about our audio-tape method, I expect most of you agreed that it was intrusive and explicit in a procedural or methodological sense. But as Jonsen and Mann imply, at least in some parts of their paper, a definition that includes consideration of the effects of the procedure seems more pertinent. For instance, the paper cites a study by Money and Walker on children who reacted with avoidance and distress to procedures involving nudity or vaginal examinations [4]. Now, these are certainly necessary aspects of a very common medical examination in adults—but since there were noticeable adverse consequences, it became an ethical issue. But another question could be asked: Were the adverse effects lasting? Diving into cold water certainly has some immediate adverse consequences, but the more long-range consequences might be a pleasurable swim.

Contrast this Money and Walker study, in which the procedures produced some immediate adverse effects, with one of Jay Mann's own studies: the one by Mann, Sidman, and Starr, in which the self-monitoring of sexual activities was employed [5]. Now, there are a host of data to indicate that self-monitoring—a seemingly innocuous procedure—can be very reactive and might lead to undesired behavior changes that are not easily reversible. This raises the question whether there are different kinds of reactivity corresponding to different kinds of risks (that is, short-term and long-term), and whether these should be given differential consideration by institutional review boards.

Returning to the audio-tape method that we used to measure sexual arousal, is this technique "reactive" simply because it fits our definition of procedural intrusiveness? Or should its reactivity be determined rather by its effects? If its intrusiveness is determined by its effects, as Jonsen and Mann suggest, this poses a problem: The effects can be discovered only by research. The problem is that the very research necessary to determine the degree of risk might be prohibited by our estimates (or someone else's estimates) of the risks involved in the procedures. I would certainly be interested in promoting discussion of this issue and a more precise definition of these terms.

Finally, let me just bring up a few points regarding the treatment of adolescents. Jonsen and Mann dealt with problems of consent in using adolescents in sex research, and they proposed bypassing the parents in getting informed consent; this was presented as a real possibility if the adolescents were judged to be mature. Such a suggestion implies a definition of maturity, and I would be most interested in hearing your ideas on how we might arrive at such a definition. In treating adolescent transsexuals, for example, we often come up against very thorny issues in obtaining consent to use certain psychological procedures that might preclude the necessity of surgery at a later date.

In conclusion, I would like to point out that these issues are going to be very important when we get into the area of prevention. We have a new book coming out on the prevention of sexual disorders [6]; many of these issues are quite pertinent. For instance, in one chapter, Bancroft discusses the possibility of preventing rape and other sexual offenses. Well, this would be cause for rejoicing, if it could be done—but it would require research involving children. As Bancroft suggests, one promising method would be by monitoring sexual fantasies in selected children, perhaps using the intrusive measures mentioned previously. Even using such methods, it would be difficult to determine preventive effectiveness without doing longitudinal studies, which would raise additional questions concerning the ethical implications. I don't know the answers; maybe we can discuss these issues tomorrow.

ALBERT R. JONSEN: To initiate discussion, let me tell you about the genesis of our use of the idea of reactivity: Jay brought those matters to my attention as relatively common concepts within social research, his own discipline. They were not familiar concepts to me, but I seized upon them and associated them with risk evaluation because one of the major problems in reviewing research is to make the assessment of risks more concrete. That's fairly easy in biomedical research, where there are some objective measures and statistics, but it becomes extremely difficult as one moves into social and psychological research. Therefore, I thought it would be interesting to combine the idea of risk evaluation with the concept of reactivity. Could I impose on you, Jay, to explain the concept of reactivity and how we're trying to use it?

JAY MANN: In the paper we distinguished two types of reactivity: one that was scheduled or calculated on the part of the researchers, a part of the experimental manipulation; and another that was unscheduled or serendipitous, an unforeseen result of the experimental intervention. For example, in the research that Dave Barlow mentioned, my data indicated that a particular questionnaire that was intended as an information-gathering instrument did in fact strongly influence subjects' responses; that's an example of reactivity in the second sense, an unforeseen outcome of the experimental procedure. We stated in the paper that the effect of using ostensibly reactive instruments is to conjure up a notion in the minds of the public that there is likely to be resultant change. Conversely, the more low-profile and the more low-key the interventions, the less likely they are to be responded to by irate parents who are concerned about possible change. These were the concepts we were trying to get across in labeling these dimensions.

DAVID H. BARLOW: Let me just say that I thought the term *reactivity* was appropriately neutral. The terms *intrusive, explicit,* and *inquisitive,* however, seemed a bit misleading.

CHARLES FRIED: I think it's very important that we speak straight and true in this group and wherever the issue of research on special populations—I'm thinking particularly of prisoners—is confronted. Ruth Macklin was going in the right direction in her remarks; but I think the recommendations of the National Commission for the Protection of Human Subjects are a disaster, the result of a confused reaction to political pressures. Ruth said—correctly, I think— that the decision of the National Commission simply ignores the fact that, in the name of liberty not to be coerced into participating in research, liberty to participate in research is taken away or disregarded. That's one point I want to emphasize.

The second point with reference to prisoners is the contention that penal institutions are inherently coercive. That is an example of confused thinking. There is a great deal of coercion in penal institutions, of course; but it is justifiable coercion, not coercion that is directed at compelling people to participate in research. The equation of justifiable penal coercion with that coercion that prevents consent from being informed consent is the kind of equation urged by those who say, for instance, that poor people who are offered money for participating in a research project are also coerced. According to that kind of reasoning, unless society is perfect, all kinds of things that are socially useful should be stopped and people's liberties taken away without compunction. What we have is the combined views of a group of people who really don't think anybody should be in jail and a group of people who think that society is corrupt and as long as it is corrupt, liberty should be infringed. Now, those ideas are either wicked or lacking in common sense, and I think that we should resist them. I hope Secretary Califano's recommendations do indeed take a different direction than those of the National Commission, which in this instance was simply swept away by confused political or ideological currents.

ALBERT R. JONSEN: Having sweated over the Commission's recommendations for many months, I thoroughly disagree with Charles in his interpretation (although, since I have been a member of the National Commission, I have come to realize that what one means is often not clearly expressed in what one says).

The main thrust of the recommendations was, first of all, to repudiate the concept that prisons are inherently coercive, and we explicitly denied that—or thought we did. Second, we did seriously consider the liberty to participate; on balance, we found that it was outweighed by certain other considerations, which are included in the report. The Secretary of Health, Education, and Welfare rejected all our distinctions and reintroduced the idea of the inherently coercive nature of the prison; for that reason, his recommendations allow only research that can be shown to be directly beneficial to the participants and research on the nature of imprisonment itself. They will probably rule out surveys on sexual attitudes and things of that sort. There isn't time here to defend the Commission's document at length, although I'd like to. It is not a perfect document, by any means, but it's not as bad as Charles made it out to be.

RUTH MACKLIN: I'm rendered almost speechless by Charles's agreement with what I said, but perhaps some of the difficulty lies in the use of the term *inherently*. In reading background papers prepared for the Commission on this, I noticed that a distinction was made between an inherently or intrinsically coercive environment, which would refer to any authoritarian institution whatever, and on the other hand, some notion of a de facto or in fact coercive environment. To me, the report was a statement of a great many ideals—ideals that nothing short of total reform in our society might meet—which would have to be satisfied before research could be done on prisoners. The larger question for society is, Which direction do we want to take? Should we wait for total reform to occur, or should we attempt to do what we can in the interim, realizing that it may be impractical to wait for total reform? In short, perhaps the term *inherently coercive* is not quite correct. Maybe prisons are in fact coercive, but nonetheless the likelihood of changing that "in fact coercive" environment seems slim indeed.

RALPH SLOVENKO: Reference was made to the *Kaimowitz* case.[1] I think that is a good example, once again, of the court searching for

---

[1] *Kaimowitz* v. *Department of Mental Health*, Civil Action No. 73-19434–AW (Wayne County, Michigan, Cir. Ct. July 10, 1973); not officially reported but available in S. Shuman, *Psychosurgery and the Medical Control of Violence* (Detroit: Wayne State University Press, 1977), pp. 221–240.

a way to do away with a procedure with which it disagreed. That court—I was involved in the case as a member of the consent committee—was hell-bent on doing away with psychosurgery; the consent procedure was used to accomplish that purpose [7]. To focus on the consent process itself rather than on the modality or the type of experiment is to focus on the wrong problem.

ROBERT C. KOLODNY: Dave Barlow raised an interesting point in his discussion, but didn't have time to address it: I wonder if perhaps several of the panelists would like to enlarge on the differences that they perceive, if any, in approaches to sex research involving adolescents as opposed to younger children.

DAVID H. BARLOW: There were two issues I wanted to bring out; let me just enlarge on them a bit. One was the notion that possibly we might bypass parental consent as a necessary procedure when doing research with adolescents; this seemed to hinge on the judgment as to whether the adolescents were sufficiently mature. By maturity, if I'm correct, Jonsen and Mann mean sexual experience. If the research in question did not go beyond the type of sexual experience that adolescents might regularly have in their natural environment, then perhaps one might judge that they could handle the degree of explicitness inherent in the research.

The second notion that makes research with adolescents somewhat different, I believe, from research with children is that adolescents often disagree with their parents in many areas, one of which might be whether they should participate in research, particularly in a sexual context. For instance, we recently encountered a 16-year-old wig fetishist. The adolescent simply hoarded wigs in his room and used them as erotic stimuli for masturbatory purposes. This was not a particularly bothersome problem, or didn't seem so to us, but it was very annoying to the boy's mother—who periodically raided her son's room, collected all the wigs, and burned them in the garbage can. This case was complicated by the fact that the boy had begun to exercise poor judgment: He would go out on the street, approach middle-aged and older women, and stroke their hair. Then his fetish became a public issue, of course, and he eventually came to treatment. He was willing to sign almost anything in the way of consent forms, and we proceeded to test new treatments designed to increase some alternative arousal patterns—but in our judgment, the young man was not particularly interested in getting rid of his wig fetish. His mother was. Had we drawn him out sufficiently, I expect we would have outlined a classic conflict of will between a 16-year-old adolescent and his mother. Since he was obviously rather mature, the question was, Could we bypass parental consent? In this case, some treatment was indicated; but perhaps only limited intervention. Could we justifiably bypass parental consent, at the risk of further dividing the family? If parental consent is required and obtained in such a case, it is likely that the parents will not agree to limited intervention but will insist on more extensive treatment. These are some of the problems that arise with adolescents. Perhaps the best way to resolve this type of conflict would be to let an advocate decide.

ALBERT R. JONSEN: Dave referred to the idea of maturity (which we mentioned in the paper). There are two things at stake here. In many jurisdictions, there have been changes regarding the statutory minimum age for consenting to treatment for certain problems, most of them relating to sexuality (such as contraception or treatment of venereal disease). In some states there is no statutory age; in other states the age has been lowered, and the concept of the mature minor has entered the law. The Commission acknowledges that, in terms of the statutory situation in certain jurisdictions, a young person may receive medical services or treatment for sex-related conditions at his or her request without parental permission, but the same young person may be prohibited from participating in sex-related research. That legal inconsistency, however, is not directly related to the psychological concept of maturity. We intended to suggest in the paper that even where there is a statutory possibility of including a young person in research, there ought to be a judgment on the part of the researcher about the young person's psychological maturity to participate: a judgment about the particular person in the particular situation and about his or her ability to handle the specific procedures or activities that the research will entail. We were looking at both the legal concept of maturity and the psychological concept of maturity. We did not mean to equate maturity with sexual experience.

LORNA J. SARREL: One characteristic of adolescents that makes them special is the fact that at any given age there is such a tremendous variation in their psychological maturity. So much research is geared to, say, the 15-year-old, or to entering a particular grade in school. Within that grade level there is tremendous variation in the level of maturity and experience and attitudes. If you use measures of reactivity for the average 15-year-old, you will miss a large number of students in that class who would react very differently and very idiosyncratically, perhaps more so in adolescence than at any other stage of life.

IRA L. REISS: Maturity is a legal and psychological term, but it is also defined in terms of what is socially and culturally acceptable to the parents and to the young people themselves according to their peer values. For example, my colleagues and I have never been able to get permission to administer questionnaires on sexual attitudes to sixth-graders in the public schools. We've been able to administer them in the ninth grade and beyond. On the other hand, in a private school in Minneapolis last year, someone was permitted to give out a questionnaire on sexuality to the fourth-, fifth-, and sixth-grade pupils. The results were published in the weekly school paper, which went out to all the students and their parents. Now, if anyone tried to do something like that in a public school it would raise a hue and cry—and I don't think the primary reason is a difference in degree of maturity. I think the explanation is simply that the parents of the private-school pupils accepted it. It wasn't something they objected to; it fit in with their group values. There was never any mention of possible negative consequences to the young people involved, because the private-school parents had a positive attitude toward the research. The opposite was true in the public schools.

SEWARD HILTNER: You mentioned peer values. That's the first time the question of peer values has come into the discussion. Do you or Jonsen think that the peculiar kind of status that teenagers have by identifying with peer groups has ethical dimensions in terms of conducting research with them? That is, if one wanted to elicit responses from teenagers in many areas, the best way to motivate it would be by operating through their peer group. Is that coercive? Even if it is coercive, isn't this simply one example of motivating subjects to participate in research? Wouldn't failure to take advantage of such ready research opportunity produce another set of problems?

IRA L. REISS: We've never used that approach. The ethics of it would depend, I suppose, on the degree of coercion you were using. Incidentally, Alfred Kinsey and his colleagues conducted their research by first convincing the leader of a group to agree to participate, then getting the leader to persuade the members of his or her peer group.

ALBERT R. JONSEN: Paul, would you like to say anything about this?

PAUL H. GEBHARD: Well, it is definitely coercion, but I don't feel it's any worse than the coercion that is sometimes used by salesmen or Hari Krishnas or anyone else. I think a certain amount of coercion is acceptable in the interest of encouraging research participation. I wouldn't hesitate to employ that tactic again—though I might not spell it out in my proposal to the committee on human subjects.

ROBERT C. KOLODNY: This is a very tricky area. In considering the reasons that people choose to participate in research, I think it might be helpful to differentiate between motivation and coercion. On the one hand we have examples of coercion, which I'm sure will be coming up again and again. One that was recently publicized had to do with the state university system in New York and accusations that, in many departments of psychology and social psychology, students are required either to participate in various research projects or to perform some other task as compensation— or perhaps retribution—for lack of research participation [8]. On the other hand we have the use of peer groups to help motivate someone to participate in a study, that is, "I choose to participate because I see my friends around me doing the same thing; it may be interesting because subsequently we can talk about it and share our experiences." I suggest that the key to the difference between coercion and motivation may be the degree of requirement that is imposed on the situation. I wonder, Ira, if you would like to respond to that?

IRA L. REISS: The motivation should be activated by the individual's positive values. People want to talk about themselves; "Well, if you participate in this project, you'll have a chance to talk about yourself." They want to learn the results of the study; you tell them, "If you participate in this, we'll send you a summary of the study." I think that's very different from threatening them with something that might happen if they refuse to participate. In other words, I draw a distinction between positive and negative types of motivation. I feel as Paul does: I don't object to the use of salesmanship or persuasion, as long as there's no threat involved.

ROBERT C. KOLODNY: But the persuasion, the enthusiasm, and the motivation generated by the research may not constitute the reasons that the individual chooses to enter the project. There may be different operative factors having to do with peer group pressures, either positive or negative, and the teenager in particular may choose to participate so as not to be different from everyone else. Although the researcher or research team may not bring any coercion to bear, the individual's choice to participate may come through extraneous social coercion outside the researcher's control. That's the part that I think is particularly tricky to handle.

ALBERT R. JONSEN: The Commission's report on children includes a suggestion that may be helpful in dealing with this. It suggests that there are cases in which the experiences inherent in a particular life situation would be one way to judge the risks of a research intervention. For example, if one is doing research on chemotherapy for the child with cancer, the risks of certain kinds of manipulation that could be proposed to young people who are patients (and perhaps seriously ill) would be inherent in the serious nature of their illness. That would be very different from proposing the same kinds of manipulation to a well child. Although we didn't consider this in the paper, I wonder whether perhaps the inherent "coercions" in the life stage of adolescence might not be parallel to similar coercions imposed in a research situation. Perhaps the researcher wouldn't be doing anything that was outside the young person's ordinary experience, which after all is one crucial touchstone of whether a research risk is acceptable or not.

JUDITH LONG LAWS: The criterion that has been proposed for assessing risks would have the unintended consequence of designating populations most at risk in a variety of other life conditions as research fodder. That is to say, if what we propose to do to people in our research enterprise is no worse than what they would be experiencing in daily life, then is it not the case that we continue to exempt the privileged from participating in our research? Are we not then designating poor people or sick people or people who are in trouble with the law or people who are availing themselves of various social welfare programs as the people we approach for participation in research?

ALBERT R. JONSEN: That's a tough question. On the other side of it, we ought also to think of the people who are most free and uncoerced to participate freely as potential research subjects.

SAMUEL GOROVITZ: I want to respond to a point that both Dr. Hiltner and Dr. Gebhard made about coercion. Some of the discussion sounds as if it accepts implicitly the notion that it is important to ask, in connection with prospective research, whether coercion is present or absent. That is a dangerously misleading way of construing the issue. The presence or absence of coercion is not a binary choice situation. Rather, coercive elements are present to a greater or lesser degree. One of our difficulties in clarifying standards of acceptable levels of coercion is that we do not really understand very well what coercion is. We have heard some remarks about persuasion, about motivation; other related issues are incentive and the provision of opportunity. For example, the provision of opportunity may become coercive if you are dealing with a poor individual who has substantial debts and you provide him with an opportunity to earn a great deal of money in a short period of time by performing simple tasks. We need to think very hard about the various ways in which we can affect people's motivations, rather than thinking in terms of an oversimplified categorization.

Dr. Reiss identified the critical notion when he suggested that attempts to motivate potential research subjects relate positively to values that the individuals already have. This is closely related to the concept of deception that we were discussing earlier. (I refer to the Kantian distinction between treating people as ends unto themselves and treating them as means only.) If I can persuade someone to do something that I wish him to do by getting him to identify with my objectives and to share the aspiration of achieving my research objective, then that act of persuasion is likely to be noncoercive—even though it may have incorporated some rather substantial lobbying on behalf of the activity in question. However, if subjects are deceived about the real purposes of the activity, then there is no way in which they can incorporate into their own aspirations those objectives that I wish to motivate them to pursue. If we want choice to be autonomous, if we want motivation through persuasive techniques to be noncoercive, that generates pressure against using deception in the explanation of the overall research objectives.

ALBERT R. JONSEN: We have time for just one more comment.

FRITZ REDLICH: I hope the panel will make a statement about the payment of money as a motivating factor. In all other spheres of living, both in capitalistic and in communistic societies, we consider money; but when it comes to research, we have a holier-than-thou attitude, particularly insofar as prisoners are concerned. I think some clarifying statement on that would be in order. I personally think one should accept monetary compensations as a fact of life.

ALBERT R. JONSEN: Certainly research is getting more and more expensive.

REFERENCES

1. National Commission for the Protection of Human Subjects of Biomedical and Behavioral Research. *Report and Recommendations: Research Involving Prisoners.* DHEW Publication No. (OS) 76–131 (Washington, D.C.: U.S. Government Printing Office, 1976).

2. Branson, R. Philosophical Perspectives on Experimentation with Prisoners. In *Appendix to Report and Recommendations: Research Involving Prisoners*, DHEW Publication No. (OS) 76-132 (Washington, D.C.: U.S. Government Printing Office, 1976). Pp. 1-10.

3. Gaylin, W. Testimony before the Subcommittee on Health of the Senate Committee on Labor and Public Welfare, 93rd Congress, 1st Session, 1973.

4. Money, J., and Walker, P. A. Psychosexual development, maternalism, nonpromiscuity, and body image in 15 females with precocious puberty. *Archives of Sexual Behavior* 1:45-60, 1971.

5. Mann, J., Sidman, J., and Starr, S. Effects of Erotic Films on the Sexual Behavior of Married Couples. In *Technical Reports of the U.S. Commission on Obscenity and Pornography*, Vol. 8 (*Erotica and Social Behavior*). Washington, D.C.: U.S. Government Printing Office, 1970.

6. Qualls, C. B., Wincze, J. P., and Barlow, D. H. (Eds.). *The Prevention of Sexual Disorders: Issues and Approaches*. New York: Plenum, 1978.

7. Slovenko, R. On psychosurgery. *Hastings Center Report* 5:19-22, 1975.

8. Smith, R. J. Electroshock experiment at Albany violates ethics guidelines. *Science* 198:383-386, 1977.

VALUE IMPERIALISM
AND EXPLOITATION
IN SEX THERAPY

H. TRISTRAM ENGELHARDT, JR.: I have been asked to be a hard taskmaster and to restrict the comments from the panel to 10 minutes per person. I will also be brief in my summary of the paper.

In the paper I offered a number of reflections concerning ethical and other value issues raised by sex therapy and research. First, I offered suggestions for ranking ethical arguments as a means of showing which ethical arguments should be employed in developing policies regarding sex research and therapy. Some ethical arguments tend to be stronger than others, if the strength of the argument is measured in terms of the chance of getting agreement with respect to the issues at hand. Those arguments that turn out to be strongest depend on near-tautologies like "Killing the innocent for sport is immoral." When one examines such assertions, one finds that one is unpacking the intuitions that lie behind the very notion of being ethical; shooting the innocent for sport becomes clearly immoral, because it is incompatible with a community based on respect for persons instead of on force.

Most other ethical assertions are weaker because they turn on particular visions of the good life, not upon the notion of ethics itself. Assertions concerning ways of life are of the genre, "Being an exclusive homosexual is not as good as being an exclusive heterosexual," or—borrowing from the last presentation—"Wig fetishes are not good." Those conclusions don't proceed from arguments that have the same purchase on our convictions as the conclusion, "Killing the innocent for sport is immoral."

I therefore suggested that strong moral judgment must be restricted to situations that command the strength of condemnation that goes along with the statement, "Shooting the innocent for sport without their permission is immoral" (that is, statements that are particular expressions of the notion of an ethical comment as one based on respect of the freedom of persons, not on the use of force). As one moves away from that strong degree of condemnation, one moves toward judgments that turn out more and more to be advocacies of particular constellations of values, of particular ways of life.

In the paper, I then offered a short history of the development of some of our attitudes with regard to human sexuality within the field of medicine over a period of about 100 years, suggesting ways in which unacknowledged value judgments are imported into disease taxonomies or nosologies. The current controversy over the planned third edition of the *Diagnostic and Statistical Manual* of the American Psychiatric Association demonstrates how disputes about generally accepted values, and those that have a less general acceptance, can play a role in creating particular nosologies for medicine.

I suggested in the paper that the values that are imported should have a wide range of general acceptability. For example, in almost all conceivable human communities and circumstances, angina turns out to be something that is not highly valued; sexual dysfunctions, on the other hand, sometimes turn out to be virtues in a particular historical and cultural context. I illustrated the variations in views concerning the values of sexuality by a few vignettes from nineteenth-century medicine and suggested that one should exercise care in using terms such as disease, dysfunction, and distress in reference to human sexual functions, recognizing their contextual significance.

I suggested as well that therapy is a very broad concept. One can treat the pain or symptoms of something without asserting that the cause of the distress is pathological. For example, one can treat the pain of teething without holding that teething is a disease or dysfunction.

From these considerations I tried to develop a caveat concerning ways in which our values influence the psychology of discovery of most nosological categories; I ended with some remarks that returned to the issue of stronger and weaker ethical arguments, suggesting that unless one has a strong argument that all sexual relations outside of marriage are on principle immoral, one doesn't have a categorical argument against sexual relations between therapist and patient—but since there are abundant reasons for thinking that such relations would be freighted by opportunities for coercion and undue manipulation, they should probably be avoided on prudential grounds or pursued only when there is good evidence to show that such use of therapists is indeed worthwhile. In other words, the argument would turn on hard empirical data. If one had that sort of data—supporting such use of sexual intercourse—then, in fact, one could use sex surrogates instead of the sex therapists themselves, in order to avoid conflicts of interest.

So, in short, the paper serves to warn us that ethical arguments have varying degrees of purchase upon our convictions and that it is best to reserve strong moral condemnation for those actions that are coercive, that are incompatible with a community based on freedom, not on force. As a result, we should be careful with regard to the role values play in structuring our concepts of disease and our use of disease language, realizing that in the past the use of such disease language has been a way of bringing undue force to bear upon individuals in order to coerce them to accept particular views of what should count as a proper sexual life-style. Finally, the paper suggests that although physician- or therapist-patient sexual relations may not be intrinsically wrong, there are many prudential reasons for arguing against them,·providing sufficient grounds to proceed by alternate means that would divest the situation of the conflicts inherent in such a relationship (for example, use of partner surrogates where data support the need).[1]

At this point I will introduce the members of the panel. The first speaker will be Dr. Alex Kaplan.

ALEX H. KAPLAN: Dr. Engelhardt's paper contains a number of important contributions to the study of ethics in sex therapy that I feel privileged to discuss. In the time that I have, I'd like to make some general remarks based on my experience as a clinical psycho-

---

[1] However, in none of these instances are these ethical issues unique to sexuality.

analyst, not as an expert in the field of bioethics. In the first place, let me say that I am in very strong agreement with Dr. Engelhardt, that ethics are certainly not unique to sex therapy, especially as compared with psychoanalysis; I am sure the same would be true of psychiatry and other fields of medicine.

I was here two years ago at the 1976 Conference on Ethical Issues in Sex Therapy and Research, though not as an active participant. I came away with the feeling that vital issues concerning ethics, morality, and values in sex therapy and research were being discussed, issues that many professionals were unaware of or had not really begun to think about. Let me give you an example related to psychoanalysis and the American Psychoanalytic Association. It was not until the late sixties, some 53 years after our group was formed, that we suddenly became aware that we had no code of ethics. We set up an ad hoc committee to study the problem. The committee met periodically for over a year and finally produced a very long and complicated document, which was then sent to our legal counsel for evaluation. After months of study, we were advised that few if any of the suggested standards were legally binding; there was some question as to whether they were even ethical or moral standards. The gist of the criticism was that what we had set down as ethics were not really ethics, but rather guidelines, examples of what we thought an ideal psychoanalyst should do in an ideal psychoanalytic practice. We were also made aware of the fact that the ethics of psychoanalytic practice were very much affected by the constant shift in values and attitudes, not only those of the psychoanalysts themselves, but also those of the society in which those persons practiced. We concluded that every ethical action when referred would be handled on an ad hoc basis, and arrangements were made to ensure continuous reexamination of the code that was eventually adopted. Our document is now a very simple one, only one or two pages in length, and patterned after that of the American Medical Association.

As an extension of our need for an ethics code, our group went on to form more committees to deal with matters of consent and confidentiality, privacy, peer review, and relationships with third parties—all the problems that the previous as well as the present conference has been studying. I mention these facts only to point out the similarities between the ethical problems in psychoanalysis and those in sex therapy and research.

This brings me specifically to the significant contributions of Dr. Engelhardt. It was encouraging to me that he argued that "there are no peculiarly sexual ethics, only general ethical principles concerning respect for individual freedom" [see Chapter 5 under MORAL-AESTHETIC CHOICES]. He placed a special emphasis on free choice as a necessary condition for all ethical enterprise. These were points that Professors Fried and Wasserstrom also made in their papers, and I think they are most important. It follows from these precepts that imposing one's own values or attitudes upon the patient, consciously or unconsciously, would be considered immoral and unethical. This would be true, Dr. Engelhardt points out, whether such action was related to a particular sexual life-style or to therapist-patient sexual relations—unless there was "good evidence that . . . such practices have special benefits not provided by other forms of treatment" [see Chapter 5 under CONCLUSIONS (4)]. Obviously, the onus of the responsibility would be on the therapist to prove the therapeutic validity of such action.

In my opinion, the use of freedom as the basic cardinal rule in the consideration of morality attempts to remove from the discussion of ethical standards many emotion-laden arguments and value judgments, which are especially prevalent in the area of sexuality. The historical examples cited by Dr. Engelhardt and the experience of early pioneers in the field attest to the progress in discrediting value-laden arguments that have been cited as medical facts. The scientific validation of discoveries and hypotheses—which obviously encompass attitudes and values—would help to identify many fruitless avenues of inquiry concerning ethical standards in sex therapy and research. Consider, for example, psychiatrists' attitudes toward homosexuality, earlier referred to as dyshomophilia and now referred to as ego-dystonic homosexuality. The present prevailing view is that homosexuality is a problem only when it causes difficulty or distress to the individual on an intrapsychic as well as an adaptive level. In other words, if homosexuality is not a problem to the individual, it is not a dysfunction. If it *is* a problem to the individual, it's a dysfunction. The point I want to make here is that many psychiatrists' feelings concerning homosexuality were

changed by the results of a study done at Washington University
by Saghir and Robins, who compared homosexuals with matched
single heterosexuals, both males and females, and discovered that
there were no clear-cut differences between the two groups in a
variety of mental health variables [1]. Although I find myself not
in complete agreement with their conclusions, these findings at
least indicate that there may be many homosexuals who are getting
along well and are not troubled by any unusual distress. The same
is true of attitudes toward other aspects of sexuality for which up
to now there has been no validating information; if we had more
information, I think there would be fewer problems. I agree with
Engelhardt's statement that we have a "woeful lack of knowledge
concerning which sexual activities or life-styles are likely to maximize the general happiness" [see Chapter 5 under MORAL-AESTHETIC
CHOICES].

These observations may be extended to a number of other situations. When we speak of values and attitudes that the therapist
inevitably brings to the clinical or research situation, I think we
must distinguish clearly between helpful attitudes and values essential to successful therapy and research, on the one hand; and,
on the other hand, harmful attitudes that reflect a reaction to
countertransference phenomena on the part of the professional,
lack of knowledge, or conscious manipulative behavior. To cite an
example in psychoanalytic therapy, the old concept of the psychoanalyst as a neutral figure, a mirror, or a blank screen has been
greatly modified. The analyst is not a blank screen. He approaches
the psychoanalytic situation with his own values and his own judgments. But the point I want to make is that the successful therapist comes with values and judgments that are different from those
of the antecedent figures with whom the patient has previously in-
teracted in a traumatic fashion, leading to a development of pathological defenses and symptomatic behavior. In the ideal treatment
situation, when the patient is encouraged to develop a transference
neurosis it is the patient's relationship with the therapist as a real
person—with significantly different values—that initiates positive
changes in the individual's behavioral characteristics and brings the
treatment to a successful conclusion. Indeed, the differing values
of the therapist, when brought to the forefront of therapy, will en-

courage therapeutic change; I think this is equally true of sex therapy.

But of course the question arises, Who should decide what attitudes and values are helpful and integrative and what values are harmful to our patients and to the public at large? I would like to suggest that not only professionals but also the public can help in making this decision. The early pioneers suffered considerable anguish as they tried to encourage the acceptance of their own emerging values by a frequently reluctant society. Freud, Mudd, Masters and Johnson, Kinsey, and others faced hostility and opposition when they attempted to validate their hypotheses and their own values and judgments by clinical therapy and research. As I recall, the first professionals to offer Masters and Johnson an open forum for their early discoveries were psychiatrists and psychoanalysts. But prior to that encouragement, lay people had committed themselves to the support of their research: Members of the general public were interested and concerned. It is hardly a coincidence that the five scientists mentioned here have been intimately involved with problems of human sexuality.

Another aspect of this subject with relevance to our work is that our definitions of dysfunction and disease must be clarified, since— as Dr. Engelhardt points out—these are also very much affected by personal values and judgments. Who should be encouraged to seek help concerning a particular sexual life-style or a certain form of symptomatic behavior? This is not a simple matter. It involves many factors, intrapsychic as well as adaptive (that is, societal and cultural). These concerns are particularly significant in psychoanalysis and psychiatry, since so many of the categories of illness with which we deal—namely, personality disorders and neuroses— cannot be considered diseases of known etiology; rather, they are essentially dysfunctions. Confirmation of this can be found in the continual shift in psychiatric diagnostic nomenclature from one decade to another. Every 10 or 15 years we come up with different diagnoses for much the same dysfunctions. The definition of sexual dysfunction or disease as described by Dr. Engelhardt mirrors the essential features of our definition of psychoanalytic and psychiatric disorders or disabilities in that they must be deeply ingrained, inflexible, but maladaptive patterns of behavior of sufficient severity to cause either impairment in adaptive function or subjective distress. This definition is used frequently in the new statistical manual of the American Psychiatric Association [2].

In conclusion, let me say that therapy and research have too often embodied a paternalistic attitude on the part of their practitioners: namely, that the therapist or researcher knows what is best for the dependent subject or patient. I believe that by adopting and employing ethical principles that contain the concept of respect for freedom, therapy and research can move to a more mature, interdependent relationship involving a free patient or research subject as well as a free therapist or researcher.

H. TRISTRAM ENGELHARDT, JR.: Thank you very much. The next panelist will be Rev. Wilkerson.

JEROME F. WILKERSON: First of all, I would like to commend Tris for his stimulating and well-developed paper. While I feel compelled to criticize certain aspects of it, I do appreciate the thrust and truth of much of what he has to say. I could hardly agree more with his two basic conclusions: (1) that therapists should not misrepresent or impose their values on patients, and (2) that no unfair advantage of the patient should be taken in the context of the therapist-patient relationship.

Tris tells us that he is advancing a modified Kantian position. Kant tells us in his *Kritik der reinen Vernunft* that all our sense data (*phenomena*) come to us through the cookie-cutters of the mind's forms, the "categories," leaving unknown and unknowable external reality (*noumena*). This position would seem, then, to ground Tris's distrust of natural law and traditional arguments regarding sexual morality. The problem is, however, that it is at this precise point that Kant shed his skepticism and wrote a special charter for the validity of conscience, of moral judgments—in his *Kritik der praktischen Vernunft*. To Kant, conscience is the one point at which we touch absolute reality. "I ought" was to Kant what "I am" was to Descartes, and from it he went on to deduce his bedrock truths or postulates of morality: the freedom of the will, the immortality of the soul, and the existence of God. Kant never tired of saying that the two things that continually filled him with admiration were "the starry sky above and the moral law within" [3].

How, then, is Tris Kantian? Is it because he holds that choice, made freely by the will, determines morality? Kant wrote that we are obliged to act in conformity with our own wills and that in a sense we legislate the moral law for ourselves. But what this means to Tris, as outlined in his presentation, was hardly in the mind of the rigoristic sage of Königsberg. Duty, law, and obligation are Kant's watchwords. Law, to him, is independent even of human nature: It is necessary and a priori. The imperatives of morality command man to act in a certain way, whether he wants to or not. Capriciousness is hardly a part of Kant's moral system, which is summarized in his famous formula: "I must act in such a way that I can at the same time will that my maxim should become a universal law" [4]. Tris has indicated some of Kant's subsequent strict conclusions concerning sexual conduct; contrary to Tris's remarks, I do not think Kant's position—namely, that one has moral duties to oneself—is inconsistent. Whether or not one finds it so depends on what prior stand is taken on other Kantian ambiguities, a point to which I will return.

Tris's paper does reflect Kant's familiar theme that all human beings must be regarded as ends in themselves and never merely as means to an end, a teaching referred to earlier today by Professor Gorovitz. It is also Kantian of him not to look at consequences of actions to determine their morality and to speak of the moral milieu as a community of persons held together by reason. Finally, it is certainly consistent with Kant's teaching to say that moral inquiry makes no sense at all without the presumption that moral agents are free.

This last point raises an important issue. Two centuries of critical reflection reveal serious inconsistencies and problems in the themes of Kant, not the least controversial of which is his theme of freedom. Oxford scholar W. H. Walsh observes that what we cannot see, if Kant is to be believed, is how freedom is possible at all [5]. A related issue is the viability of eclectic Kantianism. Kant arrived at his ethics by a tortuous route along which he sought to defend his cherished beliefs from the onslaughts of his own skepticism; thus, he ends up by making the will, rather than the intellect, the discoverer of true knowledge. His ethical system, then, is part of an intricately interrelated and massive structure—one of the wonders of intellectual history—and as such seems truly intelligible only in that context.

In turning to Tris's criterion of freedom, the question also arises as to how free a person's actions are at any given time. How effectively do cultural presuppositions, focused on and, in a sense, legitimatized by Tris's paper, militate against actual individual freedom? In the current motion picture *Saturday Night Fever*, Tony Minero envisions freedom as escaping across the Verrazano-Narrows Bridge from the sexual and other behavioral patterns engendered by poverty and ethnic warfare in his crowded Brooklyn neighborhood. Freedom can mean different things to different persons in our society (a point also illustrated by Ruth Macklin's remarks this afternoon), and it often remains an unrealized ideal. Critics of Kantian ethics have cited its inability—as an abstract intellectual system— to deal with the factual problem of diminished freedom.

Tris himself supplies us with an example of what we must be prepared for in applying his criterion. His commitment to the one value of freedom makes him unfree to choose among values in his ethical enterprise. So it is that he is compelled to state that the man who broke a confidence to prevent twenty murders acted immorally and that there are things more important than morality. If morality is properly defined as the quality in human acts by which we call them right or wrong, the conclusions just mentioned become nonsensical statements and self-contradictory. An act cannot be right and immoral at the same time—or possibly Tris needs to employ a different vocabulary. (With reference to Fritz Redlich's remark this morning, there is, of course, a distinction between acting in a basically unethical manner and acting against specific ethical guidelines, the authentic ethicality of which may be questioned.) At any rate, I submit that the obligation to so act in this case hardly fits under the rubric of aesthetics.

I wish to acknowledge Tris's provision for special religious teachings concerning human sexuality. It is true that most religions, perhaps especially those in the Judeo-Christian tradition, are not totally dependent on reason for their moral codes and recognize instructions received by divine revelation as well. (I cannot refrain from remarking parenthetically that while this observation is supportive to most believers, it is of no help whatever to Kant and his sexual code, which Tris has reduced to aesthetics; Kant's was a religion devoid of revelation, a natural religion derived from reason alone.) The relationship between the content of revelation and philosophy, especially perhaps ethical inquiry, has been an intense one and has enlivened the history of ideas for many centuries. But seldom has this relationship been as detached and as disjunctive as envisioned by Tris. Indeed, a number of philosophical systems were given birth through the efforts of religious thinkers to reconcile the given truths of revelation with an apparently hostile system of thought. The writings of Aristotle, for example, loomed as a threat to religious thinking in the twelfth and thirteenth centuries until Aquinas, Averroës, and Maimonides accommodated his philosophy to Catholic, Moslem, and Jewish thought, respectively. And perhaps few outside the town of Königsberg would ever have heard of Immanuel Kant if the writings of David Hume had not similarly inspired him to attempt an intellectual reconciliation. And so it has been, down to Maritain, Bonhoeffer, and Buber in our own lifetime, confronting the less easily salvageable political philosophy of totalitarianism.

Considering Tris's proposed disjunctive formula in the light of this history of involvement, I suspect that theology, the systematic reflection on the data of revelation, will demand more of philosophy, that it will not be long content with a rational ethics that has so little practical guidance to offer. Perhaps at this hour, however, the modest role assigned to reason by Tris in his sexual ethics is all that would be heeded. Cultural presuppositions could be at work even here. I think, however, that the present hour is rapidly passing away. We have been through a decade of enormous change that has forced us to reexamine many of our assumptions and premises, both sexual and otherwise. This unsettling period of bold challenges and uninhibited exploration, which has generated, at least informally, a data bank of previously unknown proportions, seems to be giving way to a quieter time. There now appears a readiness, perhaps even eagerness, to review and to interpret the results of this recent intense experience. For this reason, it is my judgment that our reflections and our guidelines will be received with more interest and appreciation today than would have been true at any time in the past decade. The philosophical dynamic at work may be a corrected and updated pragmatism—Pierce, Dewey, and James revisited, especially James—an enlightened truth tested by experience combined with other outreaches to reality, a dynamic that, at a deeper level, may not be as un-Kantian as it seems.

I predict that the mood of the time, an increased and growing data base, and ongoing research will enable us to speak with greater confidence and clarity, emboldening us to say hard things. Many in the immediate past, understandably fearful either of being supportive of repressive sexual attitudes or of encroaching on individual liberty, developed a near-compulsion to be always identified with the more liberal point of view. Perhaps these compulsions are lessening and changes are coming about without the sacrifice of a wholesome respect for freedom, a value that Tris has held up to us.

Nena O'Neill, co-author of the book *Open Marriage* [6], has recently completed a new book, *The Marriage Premise*, in which she reassesses the thesis of her earlier book. The conclusions of her new research, involving hundreds of couples, are—with some oversimplification—that she was wrong and that "open" marriage does not work. She then goes on to develop one of the themes of Masters and Johnson's *The Pleasure Bond* [7]: the human rewards of commitment. Perhaps these words of hers capture something of the spirit of the times and will prove at least partially prophetic about the new era of sexual research and concern that stretches before us:

The more accustomed we become to the new freedoms and opportunities, the more open we become in our attitudes toward sex, the more couples are affirming their need for exclusivity. . . . In the process of shedding some ideas and myths, we have found that some time-honored premises are more valuable than ever before [8].

H. TRISTRAM ENGELHARDT, JR.: Thank you very much. The final panelist will be Virginia Johnson.

VIRGINIA E. JOHNSON: I think there is a subtle but real evidence in Dr. Engelhardt's paper indicating that he is not directly involved in the daily practice of sex therapy. This pleases me. It pleases me that such learned commentary and expertise on ethical issues comes from outside the field. I feel it carries a more objective impact from the consumer's standpoint—which many of us on the inside tend to ignore.

From him I can comfortably take in the phrases, "Sexual activities are usually more pleasurable than breathing" and "Sex is much more interesting than many other human activities," without wanting to shout, "That's a value judgment!" It *is* a value judgment, but it's appropriate and it's something we should recognize in terms of the interest of the people who seek us out either for information or for some form of health care.

It's easy to become academically or clinically rigid in this field, for many reasons. Some clinicians simply try too hard. Others are caught defending a position or a modality or methodology previously adopted with excessive zeal, and others limit their learning to an initial experience and close their minds to the messages that clients continue to give.

I want to emphasize the obvious: that therapy clients make value judgments. These judgments become a part of the clients' condition and thereby a very real part of the context in which they will react either positively or negatively to a therapy situation. It becomes easy to confuse the art of therapy with the value and substance of a particular methodology.

The important philosophical and religious aspects of the conduct of sex therapy, expertly discussed by our previous speakers, must be considered in the context of the real world—not just as abstract ideas. In this real world, unfortunately, sex therapists must do their work without perfect knowledge. Because important information relating to some aspects of human sexuality is currently lacking, therapists must theorize in certain domains; in the absence of knowledge, one is forced to substitute opinion, attitude, and guesswork. I expect that this facet of reality will be examined in detail in our group discussions.

At this time I will forgo further comments in order to include a contribution from Dr. Judd Marmor, Franz Alexander Professor of Psychiatry at the University of Southern California. He couldn't be here because of other commitments, but he sent us his written remarks, in which he said he tried "to touch on the main points of partial disagreement with [Tris's] otherwise superb presentation." These remarks are as follows:

Dr. Engelhardt has written a brilliant, scholarly, and provocative paper and I find myself in essential agreement with his central theses. There is no doubt, for example, that the assumption that psychotherapists can be value-free in their work with patients is a myth. The very concepts of normality or abnormality involve value judgments and can and do vary from society as well as from era to era within the same society. Indeed, I would go a step beyond Dr. Engelhardt in asserting that even the concept of freedom, which he advances as the cardinal foundation-stone of all morality, itself represents a culture-bound value. It is a value that all of us share, yet it is not necessarily a universal one.

The dominant values and mores of a society or subculture grow out of the homeostatic needs of that particular context. Freedom is a moral imperative in a democratic culture—it is the basic and necessary soil out of which all else grows. On the other hand, the concept of freedom is alien to feudal or authoritarian societies; in such settings, subservience to authority is considered a far greater good. I venture to say that to this day within the structure of the Roman Catholic church, submission to and acceptance of the authority of the presumed representative of God in the Vatican is considered a more important moral imperative than is that of individual freedom. Thus, quite apart from the question of whether or not its members have the moral right to disagree with various aspects of church dogma as propounded in Rome, even the right of a non-Catholic woman to decide freely whether or not to terminate an unwanted early pregnancy is considered by the church to be within its moral prerogative to oppose.

However, it is precisely because of our shared value—namely, that freedom is the basic keystone of our contemporary culture's ethical system—that I find myself questioning some of Dr. Engelhardt's propositions.

He seems to assume that if a sex therapist is "candid and indicate[s] that he or she is advocating a particular sexual life-style," the therapist can then properly advocate certain attitudes toward sexual activities in treating "mature" patients. This issue came up in the 1976 symposium in the course of Fritz Redlich's discussion of sexual ethics [9]. Dr. Redlich, like Dr. Engelhardt, was fully aware that the modification of values is an inevitable part of sex therapy, as it is of all psychotherapy, but he felt that there were ethical limits to the degree to which the therapist should attempt to achieve such value change and that it is inappropriate for a therapist to function as a "missionary" in working with a patient.

I suggested at that time that a criterion that might be employed in elucidating this issue was the degree to which the value change advanced by the therapist was truly essential for achieving the therapeutic objective that the patient was seeking [10]. Specifically, in terms of sex therapy, this would mean that value modification is indicated only to the degree that it will enable the couple seeking help to overcome their sexual dysfunction or problem. To go beyond this—to advocate a particular life-style, whether it be free love, group sex, homosexual or bisexual behavior, or even heterosexual behavior, if that is not what the patient or couple is seeking help for—is, I believe, going past the boundaries of ethical therapeutic behavior, regardless of how candid the therapist is in announcing his or her particular bias.

I hold to this view precisely in the interest of protecting the right of the patient to freely choose his or her particular life-style without undue influence from the therapist. In assuming that mature patients would not be particularly subject to such candid influence, I am afraid that Dr. Engelhardt underestimates the great power of transference in a therapeutic situation. To some degree all patients unconsciously become "children" in relation to the therapist in the course of the therapeutic process. It is precisely for this reason that ethical sex therapists, no less than ethical psychotherapists, must take special precautions not to abuse the psychological power with which their social and professional role endows them.

For similar reasons I take a dim view of Dr. Engelhardt's somewhat equivocal position, near the end of his paper, on the issue of sexual relations between patient and therapist in sex therapy, when he implies that such activity might be permissible if certain prior conditions were fulfilled. First, even if a patient were advised prior to the commencement of therapy that such relations were to be part of the therapy, this would not negate the considerable persuasive influence of the therapist's social role as a healing agent and the degree to which this influence hinders the ability of the patient to make a free choice. Nor does Dr. Engelhardt's position confront the ethical issue of whether such therapy is being prescribed purely in the patient's interest or to satisfy some unresolved neurotic need of the therapist. The Lowrys, among others, have pointed out the curious fact that advocates of such practices somehow never manage to include the ugly or the crippled in their clientele [11].

But quite apart from these factors, even to raise the question of sexual relations between patient and therapist as a treatment for sexual dysfunction could be justified *only* if all other forms of ethical therapy had been tried first and had failed. The fact is that those who advocate such sexual relations always consider this as a first rather than a last resort. Today, with the revolutionary methods developed by Masters and Johnson and the potential for supplementary dynamic psychotherapy where indicated, there is simply no justification for even considering such therapy. To advocate opening the door to "scientific research" of this issue as an alternate mode of therapy is to invite serious abuse and exploitation of patients.

The question of the use of surrogates is quite a different one. Given appropriate safeguards, this is something that *can* be studied and explored within ethical limits as suggested in the proposed draft of ethics guidelines being presented at this conference. Two guidelines that might be added to the existing list, however, are: (a) No married sexual surrogate should be employed without the written consent of the surrogate's spouse; and (b) No married patient should be provided with a sexual surrogate without the written consent of the patient's spouse. These two safeguards fall into the area of legal rather than ethical safeguards, but adherence to them would be a wise precaution against possible lawsuits and malpractice claims.

I might suggest that Dr. Marmor has the best of all possible worlds in that he is not present to defend his words, which in some instances are very strong and provocative. But we felt that his contribution was important, and he was a very active participant in the 1976 conference. I trust that Tris won't object to defending himself against an absent individual.

H. TRISTRAM ENGELHARDT, JR.: Thank you very much.

I am actually very much in agreement with what Dr. Marmor has said, and so I will only make a few points of clarification. First, I agree that all therapy is value-freighted. However, even to say that enjoying sexual intercourse is healthy and good is to utter a value judgment. It is because of this inescapable intrusion of value judgments into sex therapy that I suggested that therapists should try as hard as possible to signal to their patients where there might be a difference of values between the therapist and the client or patient.

As to the use of sexual relations as a part of therapy, I have the same concerns that Dr. Marmor has. It is for this reason I suggested that, should there be evidence supporting the virtues of such, those virtues should be pursued through the use of partner surrogates.

SEWARD HILTNER: With the possible addition of these final points from Dr. Marmor, I find myself very much in accord with the conclusions Dr. Engelhardt arrived at insofar as they affect sex therapy and—though he didn't talk much about it—sex research. If the final guidelines, when they are worked out, are similar to the present ones, I would be prepared to defend them with only minor modifications.

In general, I would take a more pragmatic approach than either Dr. Engelhardt or Father Wilkerson. Healers—members of the health-care professions, including sex therapists—are given a certain latitude in our society, which enables them to do with impunity certain things that they might not otherwise be permitted to do. Increased ethical responsibilities go hand in hand with this privilege. But it is simply taken for granted that any ideological or other differences that divided individuals and societies—considering the medical care of prisoners of war, for example—are set aside in the interest of more important values, such as basic medical treatment. I'm inclined to believe, in view of the pragmatic character of American culture, that a defense of the conclusions that this group may reach about the ethical implications of sex therapy and sex research does not really demand that any elaborate philosophical apparatus be advanced to support them. I don't mean to say that I want to rule out this illuminating treatment that Tris has provided. But it seems to me that a somewhat simpler argument is much more likely to appeal to our kind of society. That's really my main point.

I have a couple of subsidiary points. One has to do with Tris's use in this paper of the term *ethics* in two different senses. When he says ethics are this and not that, he is using *ethics* in an *ideal* sense, that is, in the sense in which he is prepared to defend it. But also at times he has to acknowledge that there are other kinds of ethics—or "morals"—or what other people think ethics are. Now, again, I am inclined to be more pragmatic. I'm not sure that you need a general statement—a "guideline" statement—about what ethics are in a paper of this kind. Rather, we need to know what is ethical in terms of sex therapy and sex research. The more general statement, while not completely irrelevant, diverts our attention from the specific question.

Finally, I was distressed at the frequency with which Tris used the term *life-style*—a rather recent term that has gained ascendency in the counter-cultures. I understand the meaning Tris is assigning to the term; he is trying to indicate that some choices about how you live are your own business. They are not matters of law and they do not involve ethical decisions, at least from the standpoint of an ideal concept of ethics. But I wonder why Tris used that particular term. It seems to me that he runs the risk of having people say, "Well, everything that we think is important, you call lifestyle."

To sum things up, I'm very appreciative, Tris: I thought it was a wonderful job. But thinking along somewhat more pragmatic lines, I wonder if all the baggage is necessary to bolster your excellent conclusions.

H. TRISTRAM ENGELHARDT, JR.: Thank you. Let me briefly rejoin.

I suspect that you would have more problems in defending pragmatism than I have in defending the role of freedom in a concept of ethics, and before you knew it, you would find yourself unpacking all sorts of conceptual baggage in order to make sense, for example, of why you were in favor of physicians wandering freely through prisoner-of-war camps. The reason I unpacked this bag was not so much to display the things that I have an investment in, but to suggest that if we are going to engage in the negotiation of moral intuitions, we will have to ask ourselves *why* we rank some values before others and what methods of ranking values we should generate. Therefore, I suggest that there may be various senses in which we are ethical or unethical, with the arguments in various areas being more or less strong. I think such elaboration is inevitable, unless one simply wants to assert one's own moral intuitions and hope that others agree.

ALBERT R. JONSEN: I have discussed this paper with Tris at some length and have a number of disagreements that I have never been able to satisfactorily articulate to myself, so I'm not going to try to do it now. As is the case with most of Tris's things, I like what he has to say, but I don't understand all of it. This paper seems to me to be peculiar in that by pointing out the strong arguments as opposed to the weaker ones, Tris has proposed a strong but thin argument in emphasizing the value of freedom, as opposed to what might be a thick but weak argument if he had stressed an ethics that depended on value preferences and their rankings.

But what particularly caught my attention was this: Tris's paper sets out a very interesting theoretical framework in which the most interesting problem gets short shrift in a footnote. (I have to admit that Jay and I did the same thing: We took the most interesting problem, sex therapy with adolescents, and put it into a footnote [see Chapter 4 under ETHICAL EVALUATION OF RESEARCH]. So I can hardly blame Tris.) The footnote about religious preferences and religious opinions [see Chapter 5 under MORAL-AESTHETIC CHOICES] is really a very important one for sex therapy. I'm sorry that Father Wilkerson didn't pick that topic up instead of being a philosopher for us. The freedom or free choice that Tris stresses is usually articulated and manifested and realized in personal value rankings. Persons who hold particular religious beliefs and value them highly are going to be met by therapists very frequently. Rather than merely proposing that the therapist not impose his or her own values on other individuals, I suggest that the real concern of the therapist should be that of learning to appreciate the various value rankings of these individuals and learning how to navigate in the archipelago of value preferences that clients bring to the therapy situation. Although I am not a therapist myself, I wonder whether the therapeutic effect isn't more likely to be realized if the therapist can somehow enter into and clothe himself or herself in the value preferences of the client? That seems to me to be a different problem from the problem of imposing values.

JEROME F. WILKERSON: Ah, I think that's a good point. I certainly could have dealt with that footnote of Tris's at greater length. He provides for the reality of religiously oriented values by showing how they can have validity outside of his philosophical system. The point I would make is this: I really don't think the connection between religious values and philosophy is so disjunctive and tenuous. A more realistic position would involve a rapprochement between reason and religious values, rather than the mere coexistence that Tris seems to propose.

H. TRISTRAM ENGELHARDT, JR.: My argument with respect to the role of freedom is simple. Communities can either be based on respect for the freedom of persons or they will be a vehicle to impose the views of some (perhaps the majority) upon an unconsenting minority. A community based on respect for freedom rather than force will not use unconsented-to force, will protect its members against unconsented-to force, and will not interfere with the consensual relations and beliefs of its members. Within such a community, some may come to discover which values are the most important. If they do, that is excellent; it is simply that they cannot as members of an ethical community (that is, in the sense of one not based on force) impose those views on unconsenting others. Freedom has a priority in the sense of setting the limits of an ethical community. However, that in no way speaks against the importance of values. It is like knowing you must keep your promises, before knowing which promises are important to make. But it is true that I hold little hope for establishing a particular religion on the basis of reason alone. It is for this reason that I wanted to recommend that the therapist attempt to avoid a secular inquisition while attending to the value preferences of particular groups, including religious groups.

As to Father Wilkerson's earlier remarks, let me simply make Kant's position clear. Kant never thought one had knowledge from morals. In fact, Kant held that one could never know whether there has ever been such a thing as a moral individual, much less a free individual, though we can think of ourselves as free (see, for example, the third section of Kant's *Foundations of the Metaphysics of Morals*). Nor do we, according to Kant, know the world as it really is, as God would know it. Kant in fact held that one could not know whether there is a God, as a review of Kant's *Critique of Pure Reason* shows.

On the other hand, Kant surely was a prisoner of his time—as we all are, to some extent. (For example, Alan Donagan's appraisal of Kant's view that sexual excesses are worse than suicide [12] may be seen as bordering on the hysterical.) In short, there are some things we can learn from Kant and other things that should be avoided.

Given the lack of any theoretical basis for the belief that there will be rational agreement concerning which sexual life-style is best, mine is a suggestion of one way to come to terms with disputes concerning sexual mores in light of the fact that medical practice and sexual ethics and attitudes change greatly over time. This fact does not provide us with a reason to refrain from making value choices. However, it should serve to remind us that we must recognize the source of the choices that we make. For instance, I may decide that Jackson Pollack's art is very good. There are probably a number of people who would disagree with me. The fact that I am not willing or able to coerce them into agreeing with me does not in any way diminish my fervor in pleading that Jackson Pollack created a number of very good paintings. So do not misunderstand me; my use of the word *life-style* is not intended to derogate the values that a given person embraces. I simply mean to say that there are sets of values that one can and does celebrate without believing one has justification for forcing others to share in that celebration, and that these should include values associated with particular sexual life-styles.

VIRGINIA E. JOHNSON: As I suggested before, it's easy to identify those people in this discussion who are actively involved in therapy, in contrast to those who are not. Seward Hiltner tried to bridge the gulf between them when he advocated the more pragmatic approach. The fact is that in spite of historical and philosophical influences, we as therapists have to deal at the level of what is operant within the individual or the individual couple at the time. To those of you who have been so complimentary as to say that Bill and I have made contributions or innovations in the field of psychotherapy, especially therapy with sex as a focus, let me say somewhat simplistically that it depends in large part on the extraction of the values operating within the individuals at the time of therapy—the reuse of the values that are effective for those persons and the identification of the few values that are not in any way helpful to them. In no way does our mode of therapy stem from a philosophical base. I am absolutely enthralled by these discussions, but the fact is that when you are working with people and you want something to happen that represents their own measure of effectiveness, you must draw from that which is operant within them. Al Jonsen made the point better than I can.

ALEX H. KAPLAN: I'd like to add this small point, which really is a continuation of Virginia's remarks: Successful therapy depends on the therapist's empathic ability to identify with the patient. Polanyi [13] called it "indwelling," defined as the perceptual process in which the analyst reconstructs the subject's orientation by dwelling within the patient's experiences and behavior while standing back from them sufficiently to enable him to detect configurations of intention, especially disavowed ones that the patient is living out in his experiences. It is the interposition of the therapist's own values—in contradistinction to what he or she has extracted or learned from the process of empathy or indwelling—that provides the opportunity for the patient to make those changes that are necessary for therapeutic change.

HAROLD I. LIEF: I think an important image was captured in Father Wilkerson's quotation from Kant, where he mentioned "the starry sky above and the moral law within." I always thought that Kant was referring to the eyes of God: that the stars were symbolic of God's eyes and that the "moral law within" was a reference to one's conscience. Another interpretation of the "starry sky" might be that it represents the laws of nature, establishing a distinction between science and religion. At any rate, the therapist has the task of trying to find out what mixture of these two basic value positions is present in the patients whom he or she sees and attempting to tread a path between the two—without trespassing on either. That's one way of looking at the difficulty we encounter in therapy.

SAMUEL GOROVITZ: Dr. Redlich asked a question earlier today that strikes at the very foundation of this congress. We are gathered here to consider ethics guidelines; he raised the question, What's so good about ethics—why should one be concerned with ethical matters at all? There was an echo of that inquiry in the remarks made about the footnote in which Dr. Engelhardt pointed out that morality is not always the only consideration. We have also heard some talk about reason and an alternative to reason (namely, revealed "truth," or a religious point of view). The cumulative effect of taking in all this conjecture is that I can no longer resist responding.

Sometimes when I am teaching an introductory philosophy course, which is an undertaking with a heavy emphasis on careful argumentation and reasoning, a student will ask, "Look, what's so good about reason? Here you are forcing us, possibly against our inclinations, to be rational and reasonable in everything we say and do in this classroom." I then have to point out to the students that there is no rational argument that will be effective in convincing someone of the value of rational argument, for in order to be susceptible to persuasion by that kind of argument, a person must already have accepted rational criteria as the appropriate basis for arriving at judgment and establishing belief.

Quite the same kind of issue arises when one asks—as students in my ethics classes invariably do at some point—"We've been studying morality and ethics, but why bother?" It is basically the same question that Dr. Redlich raised. Why be moral? What argument can be offered in support of the claim that one ought to be ethical?

Here we can learn from the epistemological parallel. There is no demonstration that will convince the irrational individual that he ought to give up irrationality (or nonrationality, which is a different thing) and become reasonable (insofar as he is capable of reason). However, the price that one pays for rejecting reason as a method of reaching judgment is the price of not being reasonable. Some people think the price is small and others think it a very great penalty to pay. The situation in regard to ethics is quite comparable. One does not have to be ethical, of course. I would point out only that the price one pays for not being concerned about morality and ethical considerations is precisely the price of not being ethical. If that does not provide sufficient motivation, no moral argument will serve to persuade the immoral or amoral person of the value of morality.

In short, the reason that we are all gathered here to formulate guidelines for the ethical conduct of sex therapy and sex research is simply that antecedently we are concerned about ethics and morality. That answers the question as to why we should be engaged in such an enterprise.

ROBERT C. KOLODNY: I wanted to link Professor Gorovitz's remarks with an earlier comment by Charles Fried .this morning, while talking about the rational bases for having such a congress or for formulating ethics guidelines or indeed for being concerned about ethics in general. In a very pragmatic sense, as Charles point-

edly and repeatedly told us, it is a matter of survival. As we are increasingly aware, as the public has been increasingly aware over the
past half-decade at least, there is less and less tolerance of transgres-
sions, whether real or imagined, of ethical propriety in the realm of
medical research and in the delivery of health-care services. The interest in bioethics within our own field is not isolated, but is mir-
rored by widespread concern about kidney transplantation, for example, and work in many other areas that I could cite. One reason
for doing our own housecleaning or tending our own shop comes
from self-preservation instincts. In my association with Masters and
Johnson, I've been very much impressed by their sense of responsibility for having, in effect, opened the doors through which many
people are now rushing; that is, having documented that there are
rather brief forms of therapy that can be reasonably effective in
treating people with sexual problems, we now find so-called sex
therapists springing up on every street corner and listed in the yellow pages of the telephone book—people who are sex therapists by
self-proclamation only, having so identified themselves in order to
open a bank account and to serve their own interests.

I don't think that taking steps to protect ourselves—and the public—from such persons can be labeled either good or bad in itself,
but as Charles was implying, at least it will allow for a greater lon-
gevity of the field. I think that has real relevance.

JEROME F. WILKERSON: I'd like to say, in response to Professor
Gorovitz, that I subscribe to his argument about the inability of
convincing someone who wants to be unethical or irrational of the
importance of ethics or reason, respectively. But I wanted to make
one thing clear: Insofar as religious convictions are concerned, I
think it's important not to leave them hanging out on such tenuous
branches as Tris did. I would endeavor to show the rational, reasonable underpinnings of many religious tenets. Some of them—at
least in origin—are purely of a revelational nature, but as Aquinas
pointed out, part of the motive for the credibility of revelation is
its frequent congruence with reason.

H. TRISTRAM ENGELHARDT, JR.: I was surely not suggesting that
religion or religious arguments are not important. My point was

rather that no matter how intense one's religious beliefs, one has no warrant to force those beliefs on others. That is, unless religion is lived within the bounds of toleration, one would reap a new inquisition. The only response, other than a rational response, would be some form of force—or just keeping silent. As long as one wants to participate in the larger community, one makes reason and rational arguments the governing criteria, unless one resorts to force.

My suggestion, given in a historical context of fluctuation with regard to moral intuitions, is that individual variability in this area, especially with respect to sexuality, is so great that it would be better not to impose specific moral strictures except in very narrow areas and with great hesitation. That was the intended thrust of my remarks.

JEROME F. WILKERSON: It's not a question of imposing the arguments of a particular religious cult, but rather of recognizing their rational defensibility.

H. TRISTRAM ENGELHARDT, JR.: The point is not whether one recognizes many of the values supported by religious arguments (which I surely do), but whether one believes that there are strong enough rational arguments on behalf of particular views of what are correct sexual life-styles to justify forcing them on others. My point, in short, is that if one uses force to impose values on others who are not using force, one's actions are incompatible with a community based on respect for persons rather than force; one is using force against the innocent. Here the innocent would include consenting adults engaged in what others hold to be "immoral" sex. Ethics requires toleration of those "immoralities" that do not involve the use of unconsented-to force against the innocent.

RICHARD GREEN: I share Gini Johnson's regret that Judd Marmor isn't here, because I think he would have supported what I am about to say. I don't want to let Dr. Kaplan get the American Psychiatric Association off the hook for committing whatever it is we are calling "value imperialism." He cited as an example the problem of classifying what has been termed *ego-dystonic homosexuality, dyshomophilia,* and so on. In this room there are a number of us who have been wrestling with that issue for about a year and a half, including Paul [Gebhard], John [Money], Judy [Kuriansky], and Harold [Lief], and there's still considerable lack of agreement. But I think my position was supported at least by John and by Paul and would be supported by Judd as well:

Homosexuality has the unique position in the forthcoming DSM-III [2] of being, if not the only psychological state, certainly one of the very few, that is not a mental disorder unless one is worried about it or wants to change it. It's hard to find many parallels. Pedophilia is considered a mental disorder, for example, whether the pedophile likes it or not; he's got a mental disorder if he's a pedophile. But I suppose one could claim that pedophilia is a crime rather than a mental disorder (unless the perpetrator happens to be disturbed about his preoccupation with child molestation). Paul, in some of his correspondence with Dr. Spitzer (the head of the nomenclature committee), had pointed out, for example, that there are people who are troubled by adultery—but we don't have any "dysadulteria" or "ego-dystonic adultery." Some people are troubled by masturbation, but no one is proposing "dysmasturbatia" or "ego-dystonic masturbation." Nevertheless, homosexuality is still there. I suggest, in the light of all the scientific evidence, that its unique classification confirms the existence of value imperialism within the American Psychiatric Association. I'm not really sure why that should be so; it may be that there are more adulterers or more masturbators than there are homosexuals in the APA. Certainly there are fewer pedophiliacs.

H. TRISTRAM ENGELHARDT, JR.: Thank you very much for the report.

ALEX H. KAPLAN: I'm not sure what Dick is trying to tell me. It seems to me that what he said is very similar to my feelings about the subject, so I don't quite understand the disagreement. I thought I indicated that psychiatrists have recently changed their minds about the meaning and diagnosis of homosexuality because of the modification of their previous value-laden attitudes.

H. TRISTRAM ENGELHARDT, JR.: I want to thank everyone for their very helpful comments on my paper.

REFERENCES

1. Saghir, M. T., and Robins, E. *Male and Female Homosexuality: A Comprehensive Investigation.* Baltimore: Williams & Wilkins, 1973.
2. Task Force on Nomenclature and Statistics of the American Psychiatric Association. *Diagnostic and Statistical Manual of Mental Disorders (DSM-III)* (3d ed.). Washington, D.C.: American Psychiatric Association, 1980.
3. Kant, I. *Sämmtliche Werke, Kritik de Praktischen Vernunft.* Edited by Hartenstein. Leipzig: Leopold Voss, 1867. Vol. V, p. 167.
4. Kant, I. *Sämmtliche Werke, Grundlegung zur Metaphysik der Sitten.* Edited by G. Hartenstein. Leipzig: Leopold Voss, 1867. Vol. IV, p. 269.
5. Walsh, W. H. *Reason and Experience.* Oxford: Clevedon Press, 1947.
6. O'Neill, N., and O'Neill, G. *Open Marriage.* New York: M. Evans, 1972.
7. Masters, W. H., and Johnson, V. E. *The Pleasure Bond.* Boston: Little, Brown, 1975.
8. O'Neill, N. *The Marriage Premise.* New York: M. Evans, 1977.
9. Redlich, F. The Ethics of Sex Therapy. In W. H. Masters, V. E. Johnson, and R. C. Kolodny (Eds.), *Ethical Issues in Sex Therapy and Research.* Boston: Little, Brown, 1977. Vol. 1, pp. 143–157.
10. Marmor, J. The Ethics of Sex Therapy (designated discussion). In W. H. Masters, V. E. Johnson, and R. C. Kolodny (Eds.), *Ethical Issues in Sex Therapy and Research.* Boston: Little, Brown, 1977. Vol. 1, p. 157.
11. Lowry, T. S., and Lowry, T. P. Ethical considerations in sex therapy. *Journal of Marriage and Family Counseling* 1(3):229–236, 1975.
12. Donagan, A. *The Theory of Morality.* Chicago: University of Chicago Press, 1977. Pp. 105–107.
13. Polanyi, M. *Personal Knowledge; Towards a Post-Critical Philosophy.* New York: Harper & Row, 1958.

CERTIFICATION AND TRAINING OF SEX THERAPISTS

HAROLD I. LIEF: Lorna Sarrel is going to highlight some of the issues that we dealt with in our paper on accreditation and training; then the members of the panel will make their presentations.

LORNA J. SARREL: I want to start out by mentioning a fact that Bill Masters and Virginia Johnson and Bob Kolodny shared with us at the first task force meeting, when we began talking about certification and training. They said that a number of state legislatures had contacted the Masters & Johnson Institute, seeking advice on the subject of certification and licensure of sex therapists. I asked Dr. Masters today just how many states had contacted him to date. He said that eleven state legislatures had asked for this kind of advice from the institute (and presumably from other places as well). In fact, Pat Schiller said that state legislatures have also contacted American Association of Sex Educators, Counselors, and Therapists (AASECT) for guidelines. This is a very real issue that the field faces. It marks a transition from relative anarchy and chaos: Now there is considerable consensus that we need some kind of regulation, some kind of order. There has been pressure from consumers as well as from people who want to be trained.

It's nice to reach a consensus, but when you come right down to the nitty-gritty, to the questions of who should be trained and what the certification process should be and who should implement it, you realize that there are a lot of thorny issues and they're not easy to settle. We didn't provide many definitive answers in our paper, but we tried to make some suggestions and formulate some guidelines.

One of the issues we highlighted was the issue of regulation versus no regulation. We presented arguments both for and against regulation: ten strong points in favor of regulation and five not-so-strong points against it. We didn't purposely weight the argument, but honestly marshaled all the material we could find for either side. I noticed in rereading our paper that one of our arguments against regulation [see Chapter 6 under DISADVANTAGES OF REGULATION (point 3)] could actually be used as an argument in favor of regulation. Setting official standards for training and practice in sex therapy could discourage or prevent physicians, marriage counselors, and other professionals from carrying out sex counseling or therapy in their respective practices, true; but from one point of view, you might want to prevent exactly that, if people are carrying it out without sufficient training. That was a point that Pat Schiller and I were discussing, and I think she will probably mention it later.

The whole issue of professional monopoly of practice versus pluralism raises additional questions: What actually constitutes sex therapy? Are there forms of practice that should be excluded from the definition of sex therapy, and if so, what are those forms of practice? What about new forms of practice and therapy that may evolve? Who is to say what should come under the rubric of sex therapy and what should not? If there is to be an authoritative body or organization that certifies, should the board of that group be charged with these decisions?

The definition of sex therapy is terribly complicated. Someone remarked earlier today that we don't yet know just who are the practitioners of sex therapy and we don't know exactly what is the practice of sex therapy. In our paper we had difficulty making clear distinctions between education, counseling, and therapy. We made an attempt—but I think there are other valid ways in which one could draw lines of demarcation, particularly between counseling and therapy. In fact, one could devote a lengthy paper to the definition of sex counseling alone. I think this actually is needed in the field, because there are and will continue to be many physicians, ministers, psychologists, social workers, and marriage counselors who are not trained sex therapists, but who ought to be trained to deal with sexual problems and issues to some extent, ought to be trained for something that we might call sex counseling.

Then we took up the issue of regulation. If we agree that there ought to be some type of regulation, what form should it take? Should it be certification or should it be licensure? There has been a steady nationwide trend toward licensing of psychologists; we don't know if there will be a similar push from legislatures or from particular pressure groups to license sex therapists. In general, we felt that certification was preferable to licensure. The reasons are spelled out in our paper. But even if there is a consensus that certification is the best procedure for the field at this time, there are still further questions: How should the certification be structured? Should there be certification by the individual states? Should a single organization such as AASECT be the certification body? Or should there be several organizations, so that different points of view are represented? Should there be something like a certification board, which would have only one function and would not carry out any other activities such as workshops or continuing education programs? For example, a board might be made up of appointees representing organizations such as the American Medical Association, the American Psychological Association, the American Psychiatric Association, and the National Association of Social Workers.

Then there's the whole issue of training—also quite a complex issue. Who should be accepted for training? We made some recommendations about that in our paper. We also raised the question of how many training institutions there ought to be and how these institutions should be approved or certified. What about the content of training? We proposed a tentative outline of recommended content for training. How broad should the training be, how narrow? This question has ethical implications in that the requirements could be defined in such a way that the training would be elitist and one would have to have a Ph.D. or an M.D. to qualify. Also, the necessary cost and duration of the recommended or required training could make it difficult for people to obtain it unless they were financially independent.

One subject that we didn't treat in as much depth as we might have was mentioned in the last paragraph of our paper. This was the fact that sex therapy practitioners include M.D.'s—although the majority of people calling themselves sex therapists probably are not M.D.'s. What is the role of the M.D., and what is the role of the therapist who is not an M.D.? In their earliest training, Masters and Johnson had an easy formula: They accepted couples for training only if one of the cotherapists was an M.D. This is a very good check-and-balance system to make sure that medical aspects of sexual dysfunction are not overlooked and that possible medical treatments are not overlooked, but the realities of the field now are such that many people who are not M.D.'s are and will be practicing sex therapy; in fact, many will be practicing alone without an M.D. cotherapist or a cotherapist of any sort. I think it's important not to lose sight of the medical component of sex therapy. How can this be built into the training? Perhaps we need to train people specifically for the role of liaison with an M.D., so they can learn how to work with an M.D. in the community. And perhaps there should be comparable courses for M.D.'s, courses designed not to create M.D. sex therapists, but to produce M.D.'s who would know how to work alongside a sex therapist.

Training is big business, at least potentially. There's a great deal of money involved in training for sex therapy; where there is a demand for training and where there are people willing to pay for it, there is also the potential for ethical abuse. There is a temptation to offer inadequate courses, courses thrown together quickly, either for easy personal gain or to enable one's university to receive credit simply for offering a course in the field. I think we have a real ethical responsibility to potential trainees—as well as to their future clients—to take a long, hard look at the kind of training we are offering and to set standards to ensure quality in this area.

HAROLD I. LIEF: Thank you very much, Lorna.

There is an overriding issue that has been captured in a quotation I'd like to mention. It comes from a recent book by Bledstein, *The Culture of Professionalism* [1]. The quotation is this: "The question for Americans should be, How does society make professional behavior accountable to the public without curtailing the independence upon which creative skills and the imaginative use of knowledge depend?" I think we will be returning to this question over and over again in our discussions.

The first panelist is Dr. Crenshaw.

THERESA L. CRENSHAW: In the time allotted, I would like to focus on some specific and limited aspects of this very broad paper and pursue some topics of particular interest to me.

I think that there is a significantly greater need for regulation and control in the field of sex and marital therapy than in many other disciplines. Our society is well educated in certain other areas: In medical emergencies, for example, most people know not to move an injured person; they've been taught to wait until competent help arrives, or perhaps they're sufficiently well educated to administer emergency medical measures. By contrast, if a person happens to mention that he or she is having sexual or marital difficulties, other people are more than willing to offer their advice and assistance—all very well intended, but often quite ineffective and very inappropriately directed.

The lack of education in this area and the corresponding need for quality training are not always recognized, even among our professional peers who do not work specifically within our specialty. I found to my surprise, when I returned to San Diego after a year of training here in St. Louis with Masters and Johnson, that physicians and other well-educated professionals often reacted with suspicion, as though I might have been a slow learner, having spent a year in training when a weekend ought to have been enough (or at most, a week or two), in their opinion. So I think there is a certain level of awareness that we need to aim for in educating other members of the health-care professions as well as the general public, before we start dealing with some of the concrete issues.

Among my colleagues I encounter attitudes ranging from "It's inappropriate to do anything right now because we know so little" to "We must do something immediately or it will be too late"; I can see some merit in both points of view. I've reached the somewhat uneasy resolution that it's important to confront realistically what we don't know when it comes to training, certification, standards, and these other issues, while simultaneously mobilizing our forces to synthesize what we do know in a way that is intelligible and teachable. This young field extends a significant challenge to all of us to achieve that twofold goal.

In looking at training standards and in formulating ethics guidelines, there must be a balance between idealism and pragmatism. I think it's impossible to separate entirely the two concerns. On the one hand, as recommended in the preamble to the draft of guidelines, we need to leave to specific groups and organizations the enforcement of ethics guidelines and training requirements; on the other hand, while neither lowering our sights nor exceeding the realistic applicability of some of the recommendations that will be made at this conference, we need to coordinate these guidelines and requirements in some practical way.

I'd like to make a few comments and observations on motivations for forming organizations for accreditation and licensure. In addition to those motives that are identified in the background paper, there are two others that I often hear people mention. One is that of the undertrained individual who is motivated out of fear and professional insecurity; the other is that of the extremely competent individual who has no need for further validation or professional stature but is motivated by a desire to establish limiting requirements in order to upgrade the overall quality of practitioners in the field. The interesting thing is that, as I look at both ends of the spectrum, comprising two very different groups whose motives are quite different and who judgmentally refer to each other as incompetents and elitists, respectively, I perceive that they share a single goal—and a very positive one: the establishment of higher standards in a field that needs the efforts of all concerned parties.

There is also the factor of legal protection. Here, too, I think we have a two-way winning situation: In forming organizations for accreditation and licensure, we will ensure better protection for the therapist—which I think is badly needed—and protection for the patient as well.

I'd like to underscore the need for a medical dimension as part of the education of a sex therapist. As I heard Lorna suggest that physicians might be trained to work together with nonphysicians in sex therapy, my immediate thought was that nonphysicians should be trained in medical aspects of sexual dysfunction so that they might better relate to the medical issues involved in sex therapy. Were we to institute an intensive educational and training program directed toward non-M.D.'s and designed to give them the raw material, the data, the kinds of questions to ask patients, and the types of differential diagnoses that are particularly relevant to sexual dysfunctions, we would produce a group of therapists who would know when to refer; they would no longer invite criticism for not being physicians themselves.

A few random thoughts: Sex therapy is following in the footsteps of many other disciplines in this 'ethical' meeting and fighting a battle that has been fought over and over again in many ways by practitioners of psychoanalysis, psychiatry, and marriage and family counseling, among others. With that advantage we should be able to facilitate much more rapidly the process that has taken place only slowly and painfully in other disciplines. One thing that I'm pleased to see is our accepting the responsibility of selecting trainees for our training programs. Our responsibility to patients could be equally pace-setting if we were to consider going one step beyond the follow-up concept that was pioneered by and introduced into psychotherapy a number of years ago—the attitude that once a patient walks out your door you're not finished with him, but are obliged to follow his progress to assess the effectiveness of your therapy. The further step that I entertain would involve utilizing our new resources in educational psychology and program evaluation to develop facilities whereby patients—with all efforts made to protect their security and their privacy—could enter into a pretest and post-test program. Through direct patient feedback, solicited by a disinterested third party, we might find a more objective way to evaluate our own results.

Another aspect of this is one that was mentioned by Dr. Kaplan earlier in regard to patients and the part they themselves can play in seeing that the quality of therapy they receive and their follow-up and evaluation is really sound. Educating the patient needs to be a prime responsibility of the therapists themselves, and they should not overlook the ethical dimension of this responsibility, particularly in such sensitive and controversial areas as the problem of therapists engaging in sexual interaction with their patients. One way to approach this problem is to educate and encourage patients to accept self-responsibility—not blame, but self-responsibility—in exercising judgment in this area. In our therapy-oriented society, a given patient is very likely to change therapists; putting more responsibility on the patient might tend to provide greater protection against ethical abuse in such cases.

Finally, one last point: It's very tempting, I think, to view ourselves as progressive or see ourselves as sophisticated when looking backward over the past. I would like to see built into the ethics guidelines a systematic and effective reevaluation process so that in future years, our work today doesn't become an anachronism—as it might have, had we convened during the Victorian era and tried then to arrive at definitive answers to all our questions and solutions to all the problems and issues that confront us now.

HAROLD I. LIEF: While Dr. Crenshaw represents a viewpoint of someone in the private practice of sex therapy, the other two panelists will be speaking, at least for the most part, in behalf of their respective organizations. Pat Schiller represents the viewpoint of the American Association of Sex Educators, Counselors, and Therapists (AASECT), of which she is the founder and executive director, and Fred Humphrey represents and presides over the American Association of Marriage and Family Counselors.

PATRICIA SCHILLER: Thank you very much, Harold.

I thought it would be a good idea to distribute some literature, because when I looked over your background paper, I saw that it was not limited to ethics, but was rather an attempt to establish alternative structures. I felt it was important for this group to have some factual information about AASECT, its constituents, and its activities as an organization.

For the record, we have a membership of 5,100 active members, over 600 of whom are physicians and over 800 of whom are behavioral scientists. They come from thirteen different professions and eighteen different professional settings, including medical schools, universities, secondary schools, and social service agencies—so there is a vast array of persons who are interested in identifying themselves as sex educators, sex counselors, and sex therapists. When AASECT was organized 11 years ago, a group of persons who were concerned not only with professional standards and ethics, but also with protection of the consumer, began to put their heads together. Even though AASECT was organized in 1967, it wasn't until 1972 that the professional training standards of sex educators were formulated and published.[1] This is a three-pronged approach: (a) a large body of knowledge; (b) skills; and (c) professional attitudes and values. A fourth factor would deal with experience. I'd just like to mention that when David Mace, the former head of our training and standards committee, was working with the group in developing and codifying this body of knowledge and skills, he told us he was going to Geneva to the World Health Organization's meeting on human sexuality and that this would be his basic working paper.

We called forty national organizations together to ask them what they thought of our proposed standards and our training recommendations. I want to refer you to these because they are very close to the recommendations in the paper of Lief and the Sarrels; the AASECT model could almost have been a blueprint for theirs, and if you look at it you will see that the content and the skills are very well defined.

The second question that arose was, How does one differentiate sex educators from sex counselors from sex therapists? We used a developmental model for the sex educator and a problem-oriented model for the sex therapist, and the respective skills were quite different. It was therefore necessary to develop separate committees to work on certification standards. (I could go on and discuss the details of our organizational structure—we now have ten national boards, for instance—but that is not really an issue here. What's at issue is the problem of how we can best set up standards for certification and maintain an ethics code, not only to ensure competency within our membership but also to protect the consumer.) Bob Kolodny is now serving as chairperson of AASECT's Ethics Committee; on Saturday, after our deliberations here and after your sorting out and working through the proposed guidelines, our committee will meet and possibly adopt some of this group's recommendations.[2]

---

[1] Schiller, P., and Mace, D. (Eds.). *The Professional Training and Preparation of Sex Educators*. Washington, D.C.: American Association of Sex Educators, Counselors, and Therapists, 1972; 2d ed., 1973.

[2] As a postscript, the final version of the Ethics Guidelines that evolved from this congress was adopted by the board of directors of AASECT in the spring of 1978. AASECT also devised an extensive set of implementation and enforcement procedures to supplement their code (*AASECT Code of Ethics*. Washington, D.C.: American Association of Sex Educators, Counselors, and Therapists, 1978).

As you can see in the printed material that has been distributed, AASECT's current Code of Ethics contains nine articles. This was the first ethics code that was formulated specifically for sex therapists and sex educators. It includes a general proviso at the end, sort of a catchall statement, concerning ethical behavior in the relationship between therapist and patient and some of the potential hazards; in a sense, we were both reacting to and trying to anticipate some of the issues and crises that were emerging in the literature and in the news media. The issue of the use of surrogates, for example, came up in the committee's deliberations. The recommendation was that once a person was certified, that person was considered competent to decide what therapy model he or she would use. It would then be at the discretion of the therapist to decide whether or not to use a surrogate.

My own feeling now is that perhaps we need to differentiate between sex therapy, sex education, and sex counseling in terms of ethical standards and their enforcement. The task of collating and and putting together an ethics code is not or need not be an insurmountable problem. The more difficult task is that of deciding who should be the investigative body; who should serve in a judicial capacity—should it be outsiders? Should it be members of the peer group? It is in this area that the very difficult and thought-provoking ethical questions are arising.

Within the organization we have also had to consider the matter of training. As a certifying organization, AASECT does not provide training in terms of giving or sponsoring programs that in and of themselves will produce sex therapists or sex educators. AASECT is concerned, however, with providing continuing education for those persons who already identify themselves as sex educators, sex counselors, or sex therapists. As of June of 1978, a written examination will be a part of the certification process. There will be separate examinations to cover requisite skills for educators and requisite skills for therapists. Boards will be set up to judge applicants' abilities through oral question-and-answer, and the element of experience will also be taken into account. At the present time, the requirement is 1,000 hours of paid experience, 200 or 250 of which must be under supervision. I do not want to burden you with additional details of the certification process, because I feel that the ethical issues involved in organizational life—and in the peaceful coexistence of various organizations—are more important.

The Lief-Sarrels paper discussed the fact that there is more than one organization that can handle these jobs. It has been AASECT's position that all interested organizations should do for their members whatever they can to enhance their competence and acceptability in sex therapy, whether they be social workers, clinical psychologists, physicians, nurses, or whatever; this provided the keynote for what we said when we brought those forty organizations together. We told them, "These are our standards. This is the machinery that we have set up to check out these standards. You go ahead and do whatever you wish in terms of setting up your own standards, but, please, let's be consistent. Let's be cooperative, so that we can work together to protect ourselves and the consumer."

I would say the same words to this group. I hope that during the next two days you will have a chance to examine our blueprints, our organizational structure, our standards. Finally, let me say that any organization that's only 11 years old is vulnerable and needs as much help as it can get. So far, we have received the support of the best people in the field. It is up to the members and to concerned persons like yourselves to further improve upon the machinery that will take us where we want to go.

HAROLD I. LIEF: Thank you, Pat. I got a mixed message from your address, but I'll leave it to the group to discuss it at length. You seemed to be suggesting that although some degree of pluralism would be beneficial, we should give our major support to AASECT, since AASECT is already established in the field, has its own standards, and has instituted a process of accreditation. That seemed to be the gist of what you said. Perhaps it can be clarified later on.

One minor point, Pat: You mentioned the World Health Organization and our reference to it. Just for the record, that reference was to the second conference of the WHO, not the first; David Mace was the organizer for the preparatory meeting, which was followed by a larger meeting a year or two later; it was from that later report that we quoted.

Fred Humphrey will now give us his point of view as president of the American Association of Marriage and Family Counselors.

FREDERICK G. HUMPHREY: Thank you, Harold.

I have been asked to share with you some background information about our organization and its experience in the training and accreditation field. I think it may be very relevant to what is happening now in the field of sex therapy.

The American Association of Marriage and Family Counselors was founded in 1942 and at its inception was very much a multidisciplinary organization. We had a heavy medical emphasis at the start, in terms of influences as well as numbers. We had people like Abraham Stone, Robert Dickinson, and Sophia Gottlieb. The group's work was closely linked to the sexual problems of couples in marriage, particularly in reference to the New York Community Church Service, which was sponsored by Hannah and Abraham Stone (who had worked with the Community Church and these problems back in the twenties). We also initially had many ties to education. Many of our early members had started out by teaching the newly emergent courses in marriage and the family at colleges and universities. Students and other people approached them for help because it was assumed that anybody who taught about marriage and family would know how to help them with their problems. (Incidentally, the same assumption is made in the field of sex therapy; if somebody lectures about sexuality, he or she is assumed to be an expert to whom people may turn for help.)

Some of the early pioneers in marriage and family relations set up clinics and treatment centers. The first facility of this sort was the Stones' in New York City; it had a medical orientation. Paul Popenoe, a zoologist by training, was probably next; he organized the American Institute of Family Relations in Los Angeles. Popenoe's groups, and later other groups, began to offer various short courses, weekend seminars, lectures, and so forth, with the objective being part-time preparation for professional work. As time went on, the phenomenon of what we called "three-day wonders" was a very real problem to our own American Association of Marriage Counselors. In the 1960s, when I served on our admissions committee, we encountered great difficulty in trying to determine what qualifications, if any, these persons had after having simply attended one or more of these short lectures or weekend workshops. There was no supervision and no accountability; they merely had a piece of paper saying that they had heard a lecture or participated in a seminar.

The third center to be started was that of our own Emily Mudd in Philadelphia. Emily's original work was done in her capacity as a helper to her husband Stuart, who was an eminent physician. He was one of the most influential figures in her approach, which employed both the medical model and the scientific method in dealing with human problems. Kenneth Appel, former dean of the Department of Psychiatry at the University of Pennsylvania, was also a major influence on Emily's career. Over the course of two decades she developed a multidisciplinary postgraduate training program—that which Harold Lief now directs at the University of Pennsylvania. It was patterned on the academic year of residency and based on access to the lectures and resources of a great university and medical school. It included a supervised practicum that took place right in the clinic where the organizers worked and taught. The program served and continues to serve postgraduate students in social work, medicine, theology, education, nursing, family relations, and psychology.

Alongside but apart from the development of clinics and centers of service and training there arose a professional organization, the American Association of Marriage Counselors. For the first 25 years of its existence it was composed of only a few hundred persons. It had stringent membership requirements; everyone except the clinical social workers had to have a doctoral degree. Members had to go to approved training centers such as the Marriage Council of Philadelphia; the program—now defunct—at Merrill Palmer Institute; and the Menninger Clinic in Topeka. They had to have additional experience under supervision, had to submit case material, and also had to submit their academic transcripts. Character references as well as professional references were obtained. Finally, if deemed appropriate or necessary, applicants for membership had to have a personal interview with a screening committee. Such restrictive measures resulted in a group of highly qualified practitioners and helped to promote a positive image of the marriage counselor in the public understanding. Accompanying this buildup of the Association was the adoption, very early in the history of the organization, of a code of professional ethics, a code that underwent further development over the years.

Gradually our association developed a system of "approved" training centers. We could not "accredit" these centers because official accrediting groups in those days did not deem marriage counseling to be a professional field, a step which would have been necessary for accreditation to have taken place. By the same token, colleges and universities sometimes rejected the services of our approval teams because we could not offer them official accreditation. We were caught on both sides of the fence. However, many organizations affiliated with colleges and community centers were willing to take advantage of our group of visiting experts, and utilized them to evaluate the various programs and to advise them on ways to improve or to gain public recognition. This system of approving programs was developed by the AAMFC throughout the United States and Canada, particularly during the 1950s and 1960s. Would-be marriage counselors were attracted to these centers largely because they had received approval, and this provided trainees with the assurance of a certain level of quality in training.

By the late 1960s, the term *marriage counselor* was being increasingly used by different types of professional persons—persons with various specialities—who were involved in helping couples to cope with distress in their marriages. For example, many social workers stopped describing their jobs as "marriage and family casework" and started using the term *marriage and family counseling*. Similar relabeling of professional activity occurred in pastoral counseling, in clinical psychology, and finally even in medicine. By this time, however, our AAMFC was being accused of elitism. Our stringent membership requirements also severely limited our monetary resources, the result being that we barely survived the financial distress of those years.

Three developments helped us round the corner: First, our membership standards were altered so that the minimum degree required was the master's degree. This increased our membership, broadened our financial base, and squelched the protests that we were an elitist organization. Second, we changed our name from the American Association of Marriage Counselors to the American Association of Marriage and Family Counselors, thus recognizing the fact that our members were increasingly involved with the family unit as a whole and not just with the marital unit. Third, we instituted a system of approved supervisors throughout the United States and Canada, thus providing a readily identifiable and accessible reservoir of competent clinical trainers for prospective practitioners to draw upon.

For many years we had a standing committee called Training and Standards. This committee concerned itself with approving the various training centers. As our program of approved supervisors grew, a group of supervisors constituted a subcommitte on training and standards. Later a separate committee on supervision was formed to carry out this work. The supervisory committee was charged with two activities: (1) recommending to the board of directors the standards necessary to become an approved supervisor in the field, and (2) screening the applicants for this particular task. Our approved training center system has now become more formalized. We have now established a nearly autonomous accreditation committee consisting of nine persons, three of whom are representatives of public consumer groups. We have an accreditation manual as well as a manual on guidelines for establishing training programs, both in and out of academic settings. We spend a great deal of time and money on planning sessions, on training sessions, on site visitation and evaluation teams, and on overall administrative support of this ongoing program.

In the mid-seventies our national association was reorganized into two separate bodies: the AAMFC, a trade association legally incorporated in Washington, D.C., with its administrative headquarters in Claremont, California; and the American Association of Marriage Counselors Foundation, legally incorporated as a tax-exempt foundation in New York State and concerned with furthering research and educational work in our field.

We are currently under consideration by the U.S. Department of Health, Education, and Welfare to accredit training in the field of marital and family therapy on a nationwide basis. Our application for this was opposed by the Council on Social Work Education and by the American Psychological Association on grounds that I interpret as "turf" issues. That is, these two groups felt threatened by our emergence as a new mental health discipline. They both went to DHEW with the claim that their own organizations were involved in training marriage and family therapists, claims that we effectively refuted.[3]

In related matters, we have actively supported the licensing of marital and family therapists. The first licensing in this field occurred in the early 1960s in California; New Jersey and Michigan soon followed suit. In more recent years Nevada, Utah, and Georgia have also licensed our therapists. During this same time period, however, we have failed in our efforts to secure licensing in this field in over twenty other states. Some of the failures have been the direct result of active opposition by groups representing related professionals—groups that claim preeminence in the field, even though their own accredited training programs generally do not prepare people for marital and family therapy. Other failures to obtain licensing can be attributed to the antiregulation philosophy that currently dominates state legislative bodies. (I might add that our group is not large enough to mount an extensive and high-powered lobbying effort in many places.) Finally, and perhaps most important, widespread acceptance of licensing has not yet come about because the public—voters as well as consumer groups— has not been convinced that the field of marital and family therapy needs licensing regulation. Legislators say very bluntly that not enough people have yet been hurt by unethical and incompetent marriage and family therapists to justify licensing.

At present, therefore, we are a group that performs two sets of functions. First, we are a professional interest group: We organize programs. We operate a continuing education program. We publish the largest professional journal in its field, the *Journal of Marriage and Family Counseling*.[4] We evaluate and accredit training programs. Second, in the forty-four states and in the six Canadian provinces where there is no licensing in the field, we serve as a

[3] On June 23, 1978, the DHEW Advisory Committee on Accreditation and Institutional Eligibility unanimously voted to recognize the AAMFC's Committee on Accreditation as the national accrediting organization for the field. This designation was made official by the U.S. Commissioner of Education in September, 1978.

[4] In January, 1979, the name of this journal was changed to *Journal of Marital and Family Therapy*.

"credentialing" agent for the profession and protect the public by ensuring the competence of marriage and family therapists who practice as members of our organization.

Training practices and accrediting procedures are critical issues for an emerging profession. In our judgment, professional associations should turn the training of future therapists over to colleges and universities as soon as this is feasible. The professional association should not be directly involved in the preparation role. The AAMFC is emphasizing this by adopting new membership standards, effective July 1, 1978, which will require that applicants' background preparation (marriage and family dynamics, marriage and family therapy, sexuality, personality dynamics, psychopathology, etc.) be obtained from accredited colleges and universities. Both private and governmental bodies involved with the accreditation process, it should be pointed out, insist on the formal separation of the accrediting group from the credentialing and training functions of a given profession. In addition, we feel that the professional accreditation process should be almost entirely separate from the administrative branch of the professional association. In our case, we fund our accreditation committee, but we do not nominate its members. The committee itself selects its nominees and submits them to our board for acceptance or rejection.

Sex therapy, like marriage and family therapy, is currently practiced by professionals of diverse and often multidisciplinary backgrounds. Sex therapy cannot truly come of age, however, until it rests on a sound body of knowledge, develops its own enforceable code of professional ethics, and has an internal set of regulatory controls. In short, it must exhibit the characteristics and fulfill the necessary functions of a profession before it can claim to be one. Judging from the AAMFC's three and one-half decades of experience in the marriage and family counseling field, I would also say that sex therapy will not be able to stand on its own merits until turf and political issues are resolved. If the traditional disciplines all insist on claiming their piece of the action and refuse to accept or even to acknowledge the existence of the new discipline as an emerging profession, there is little that this group or any other group can do to establish the uniqueness, the exclusivity, or even a permanent place for sex therapists.

The AAMFC, which will probably soon become the American Association for Marriage and Family Therapy,[5] grew out of a multidisciplinary approach to problems of marriage and the family. As the years went by, the Association came to realize that any professional activity that is treated as a subspecialty of several other professions is likely to vanish or, at best, to be permanently relegated to a minor role. This tends to inhibit the supply of well-trained practitioners as well as inhibiting the advancement of knowledge and, further, deprives the public of the benefits that can derive from a unified and more specialized profession. I might mention that in the AAMFC we did consider certifying our members as sex therapists if they had the requisite background. We rejected this proposal three or four years ago for a variety of reasons. Our members are required, however, to be knowledgeable about sexuality, particularly as a factor in relationships and attitudes, but not necessarily in its dysfunctional aspects (where counselors are expected to make appropriate referrals).

Sex therapy in 1978 appears to me to be in a position similar to that occupied by marriage and family therapy in the forties. Where it goes from here and what type and quality of care sex therapy will offer will depend to a large extent on what actions are taken by people in positions of leadership in the field. If potentially influential leaders in sex therapy remain quiet and inactive, I predict that commercial entrepreneurs will increasingly take over with a self-serving, irresponsible, public-be-damned attitude. The choice, I suggest, rests with many of you who are assembled here. My predecessors established marriage and family therapy as a respected new mental health profession. You may be able to do the same thing for the field of sex counseling and sex therapy.

HAROLD I. LIEF: Thank you very much, Fred. The floor is now open to discussion.

RALPH SLOVENKO: Fred Humphrey pointed out that attempts to obtain licensing laws have failed in over twenty states. What about the efforts to obtain certification? I think they, too, would be

---

[5] This change in name was officially voted by its members in September, 1978.

doomed to failure in the present atmosphere. For one thing, there is the current antiregulation philosophy; for another, many legislators are simply unaware of the difference between licensure and certification. That leaves the profession to certify itself, as AASECT is currently doing.

CHARLES FRIED: It is probably no accident that the same philosopher whose words I quoted to you as proclaiming that attitude of openness and freedom to which this field probably owes its existence, also said that it would be unthinkable for the state to get into the business of licensing. Certification, yes; the state can say, "We certify that a person has certain qualifications to practice a particular activity." But for the state to say that it's illegal or criminal behavior for a person to practice that activity without those qualifications is a manifestation of the same repressive mentality that is probably responsible for the fact that studies of human sexuality are only now beginning to gain widespread acceptance. Therefore, I was surprised and dismayed to hear our last speaker express his disappointment that his campaign had failed to foist licensure upon the entire country. I would like not only to see that campaign fail, but I would also like to see some well-established professions de-licensed—beginning with my own, the legal profession.

In my opinion, licensing of lawyers has done more to bilk the population of money than it has done to protect the public. I think that most nonlawyers would agree with me. Licensure is a conspiracy in restraint of trade. It may begin with noble intentions, but it ends up being turf protection, self-aggrandizement, and a repressive closing-off of the field of professional practice. In medicine this is quite obvious—and yet, medicine has a much firmer grounding than the newer disciplines we've been talking about.

Let's be serious for a moment. Family therapy may be a very useful and laudable thing, but it is not a science like physics or mathematics. Sex therapy is a marvelous thing, but it, too, is a very approximate matter, to say the least. In view of this, the notion that any group has a lock or a patent on what constitutes sound practice—to the extent that anyone attempting to practice without that exclusive patent should be guilty of criminal conduct—is simply grotesque and absurd and demonstrates an utter lack of sense of proportion. Granted that the public deserves and requires protection, certification, not licensure, is the proper mode.

In sum, I was delighted to learn that the movement for licensing of marital and family therapists is meeting so many failures, and I shall applaud each new failure as I hear of it.

HAROLD I. LIEF: Charles, we needed that provocation.

PATRICIA SCHILLER: I agree with you that licensing can be very restrictive, politically motivated, and even—in some instances—destructive. But of course the consumer needs some basis on which to decide where to go and whom to choose as his therapist. Certification is certainly the logical first step in establishing a baseline of competency in the profession. AASECT publishes a register, a list of names of those persons who have been certified. Yes, the consumer can go to other organizations; but if he comes to us, at least he knows that those persons have passed judgment by their peers. At least the consumer has the assurance of knowing that certified therapists have signed a pledge to abide by AASECT's Code of Ethics and that they are subject to disciplinary action if they do not.

I'd like to ask Professor Fried whether there is something he would disapprove of, in terms of certification or licensing, and if so, what are the alternatives? What sort of protection would he offer the public?

HAROLD I. LIEF: Pat, let me interrupt: There's a difference between organizational certification or licensure, on the one hand, and state certification or licensure, on the other hand. Professor Fried was referring to the difference between state licensure and state certification, not professional certification.

FREDERICK G. HUMPHREY: Professor Fried's eloquent attack on me would have been more effective if his own profession had in fact done precisely what he would like to see it do.

The big difference between certification and licensure is in regulation or enforcement. Certification is simply a method employed by an organization or by a governmental group to say that certain specified prerequisites for preparation have been met or fulfilled.

No guarantee of acceptable practice is made or necessarily implied, and there can be no enforcement. I mentioned cases of unethical behavior; let me cite an example. There was a marriage and family therapist practicing in the community where I lived in Connecticut for several years. He was a member of our professional association, and I received all kinds of complaints about his highly questionable "therapy" methods. We could do nothing about it, unfortunately, partly because people would not testify against him in an ethics case and partly because we are unlicensed and uncertified. The state government would do nothing until the situation got so far out of hand that the man was arrested for statutory rape, practicing medicine without a license, and other very serious charges. In short, an unethical and incompetent practitioner can generally continue to practice within the community unless there is some type of group effort or recognized machinery to put him out of action. That's the rationale in favor of licensure.

H. TRISTRAM ENGELHARDT, JR.: I protest. You distinguished between licensing and certification by using an argument that could actually lend support to either alternative. Charles Fried's point was that there could be government supervision to the extent of informing the public of an individual's credentials and also of whether the individual has failed to meet the stipulated requirements, and that this could be done through certification: Licensure is not necessary in order to accomplish these goals. The argument you gave is a mixed one that supports certification as well as licensure; why turn to licensure if you are able to achieve the desired result through certification alone?

FREDERICK G. HUMPHREY: Because licensure ordinarily contains the components of certification as well as provisions for regulation of the practice. Certification simply deals with the title and informs the public about the therapist's qualifications, while licensure actually regulates the practice. I feel that licensure provides a greater degree of consumer protection.

ROBERT L. STUBBLEFIELD: I could not agree more with Dr. Engelhardt. I'm a physician, a psychiatrist; I have lived and practiced in several states and currently live in Connecticut. The legislature is currently in session in the state of Connecticut, and no man's life or wife or business is safe. Let's face it: If you want to defeat the purpose you're trying to achieve, draw up a plan for licensure and leave it in the hands of the state legislature. In California, for example, approximately two thousand five hundred health bills are introduced each year. No society is large enough to deal effectively with that amount of legislation. I was on the American Board of Psychiatry and Neurology for eight years and was secretary-treasurer of it for three, and I became aware of an alarming nationwide confusion about the difference between technical training and professional training. At a meeting in Honolulu 10 days ago, I heard the chairman of a House subcommittee—a man who is very powerful in health legislation—refer to all members of the medical profession as "technicians." God help us if we are going to be demoted from a professional level, in spite of our accreditation procedures, to the level of technicians, and therefore subject to mandatory licensure! I beg all of you to consider that very carefully.

ARVIL C. REEB, JR.: Like the last speaker, I too had felt I would not speak, but I find myself with a great deal of emotion on matters related to labeling and territorial competition.

I would like to interject a new issue, or at least one I have not heard raised up to this point: namely, the possibility of a national health insurance plan being instituted within the next 5 to 10 years. As many of you know, there is a great deal of acrimony and rancor between psychiatrists, psychologists, and various other health-care groups, not so much now about who can do what, but about how it is to be described. I think back to when I was in graduate school in social work 12 years ago, when the issue was whether social workers did case work or psychotherapy; well, we have learned in the last 5 or 6 years that we do psychotherapy—because that's what we will be paid to do under third-party health insurance plans. I note with some interest that both the sex therapists and the marriage counselors are now emphasizing that they are therapists, the idea being that they treat illness or injury as opposed to problems of living—since the latter are probably not going to be paid for under national health insurance and under third-party schemes. The point I am making is that the proposed method of payment for these services can have some bearing on the basis for choosing between certification and licensure.

I might add that I'm glad that the licensure efforts of marriage and family counselors are meeting with defeat, and I certainly hope this group doesn't endorse the idea that we should license sex therapists.

ROBERT C. KOLODNY: I'd like to change the direction of discussion somewhat by pointing out that although the details of certification that have been discussed both in the background paper and by the panelists are necessary to ensure attention to some very important problems that may be resolved in our deliberations, the fact of certification in itself does not ensure competency for a given individual. The act of certification merely points to the fact that certain prerequisites have been met. It provides no assurance of what will be done—or insurance against what may be done—in the future and no guarantee of the emotional or physical stability (past, present, or future) of the practitioner. An organization or a state that offers certification is really attesting only that the certified practitioner possesses the necessary credentials—the minimum requirements for practicing. I am not trying to downplay the importance of credentials, but I think when we get into a discussion of some of the guidelines, we must maintain a separation between issues of certification per se and issues of competence—which cannot be subsumed under the heading of certification. Certification may be an important way of conveying to the public and indeed to fellow professionals basic information about whom one might turn to or refer to for treatment, but evaluation of overall competency involves other considerations as well. We'll be getting into those later.

HAROLD I. LIEF: Issues such as peer review and recertification, for example, should be taken up at least in our small group discussions.

I want to ask Fred Humphrey what practical differences there are between state certification and state licensure: There are six states that have either licensure or certification of marriage counselors; three of them provide certification and three of them provide licensure.

FREDERICK G. HUMPHREY: As I noted, Harold, certification restricts the use of the title: In the states that have certified marriage and family therapy, only those qualified under the certification laws can so list themselves and represent themselves to the public in that capacity. Licensing, however, is concerned with the way in which persons in a particular professional capacity actually perform that function, as well as how they were trained to practice.

HAROLD I. LIEF: Fred, that's not what I was asking. I want to know what happens in actual practice—what are the resultant differences, if any, between the three states that certify and the three that license?

FREDERICK G. HUMPHREY: There really aren't a lot of differences. One of the big problems—which I regretfully concede to my opponent, Professor Fried—is that a licensing law is no better than the will of the state to carry out the mandate of that law. In California, for instance, former Governor Reagan refused to allow any funds paid in licensing fees to be used by the state regulatory agency; hence, the regulatory agency was powerless to act, even though it was aware of widespread abuse of the licensing law.

MAE A. BIGGS: Fred, you mentioned earlier that the name of your group is going to be changed to emphasize the therapy aspect of marital and family counseling. What effect will this change have on your members who practice in states that have licensing laws?

FREDERICK G. HUMPHREY: Well, names are extremely important to all of us. The prospective name change to "family therapy" is, I believe, a constructive move in response to pressure from our members. Issues such as allowance of third-party insurance payments and clarification of the functions performed by these people—regardless of what they are called—have direct relevance. In our opinion, based on the experience of our representatives in various places, the word *counselor* has assumed so many diverse meanings that the term is almost useless for our purposes—particularly when we are attempting to communicate with legislators and with government regulatory agencies. The word *therapist* has a more precise meaning, and I am not aware of any law that restricts the use of the term to any particular specialty. The new name American Association for Marriage and Family Therapy was recommended by our board of directors because our organization's membership includes persons who call themselves therapists as well as persons who call themselves counselors. While we hope the new name is accepted, we want to continue to allow and even to encourage flexibility among our members, many of whom have an emotional heritage in the word *counselor* or an antipsychiatric bias against the word *therapy*.

PATRICIA SCHILLER: The term *sex therapist* has been associated primarily with persons who treat sexual dysfunctions, but as we in the profession know, there is quite a wide range of presenting problems, going far beyond the treatment of sexual dysfunction. AASECT, in terms of its organizational setup and certification, has grouped the various categories of treatment, excluding the treatment of sexual dysfunctions, together under the title *sex counselor*. A person who qualifies for the sex counselor classification and works in an institutional setting will have a certificate that reads "Sex Counselor of Planned Parenthood, Washington, D.C.," for example, or "Sex Counselor of Michigan University Counseling Service." So long as that person stays within an institution that is approved by the certifying committee, he or she can be called a sex counselor; but we are not permitting anyone in private practice and unaffiliated with an institution to be certified as a sex counselor. We don't know how effective this approach will prove to be in solving the problem of offering protection to the public without unduly restricting practice, but we had to come up with some kind of solution in response to pressure from organizations such as Planned Parenthood, where so many seemingly qualified people are doing sex counseling in areas other than sexual dysfunction.

HAROLD I. LIEF: Are you saying, Pat, that a person doing sex counseling in private practice would have to qualify as a sex therapist in order to be certified by AASECT?

PATRICIA SCHILLER: Yes, that's true at the present time.

RICHARD GREEN: I hate to go to bed more confused than I was when I woke up. Let me try to clarify something and ask my friend Charles Fried a question.

I'm a diplomate of the American Board of Psychiatry and Neurology: This serves the same purpose as certification in that essentially it's a quality-control device that has uniform standards throughout the country. In addition, I am licensed to practice medicine in four states. The licensure rules, as Charles has pointed out, can actually be used to *deny* me the right to practice (in spite of my being certified) in some states, if these states would not grant reciprocity with my licensure. This is absurd, since the human body in North Dakota is precisely the same as the human body in Maryland, where I received my medical training. There is no justification for that kind of restraint on my practice.

Now, we all agree that we are concerned with quality control and consumer protection; what is at issue is the method of implementation. I would like to ask this of Charles: Are you suggesting that rather than licensing physicians and surgeons—for example— we would do better to offer certification to those who are qualified and, at the same time, educate the public to select and patronize only those who have been certified as surgeons or physicians? In other words, this would be advocating a "consumer beware" policy, placing more responsibility on the public as informed consumers and less responsibility on the state as a licensing agent (with potential powers of prosecution).

CHARLES FRIED: That's a complicated question, but let me try to answer it.

First, I wasn't seriously making a proposal in respect to surgery, for a number of reasons: One of them is that it is awfully hard to turn the clock back (or forward, if you prefer to look at it that way). I realize that.

Second, there is a high degree of objectivity about what constitutes good and bad surgery, whereas in the area of marital and family counseling, sex therapy, and sex counseling we are much farther away from anything resembling the standard meter bar in Paris, to say the least. Rather, we are in a domain in which cultural values play an important role and in which there is—and must be—a great deal of diversity. The notion that the state can determine who has the "truth" about matters pertaining to sexuality, sex counseling, and sex therapy is so grotesque as to be preposterous.

What I am suggesting for this field is certification—but a type of certification that would not prevent an uncertified practitioner from practicing, as long as he or she states that he is uncertified. I would object to the quite unnecessary restriction that says you cannot call yourself a sex therapist unless you are certified. You may call yourself a sex therapist, but you must say, "I am not certified." Then people can take their choice. Would this mean that an uncertified sex therapist could rape his patients or otherwise harm them with impunity? Of course not. The uncertified person would be subject to the same criminal and civil liabilities that the certified person is subject to.

I don't know whether that answers your question.

FREDERICK G. HUMPHREY: I'd like to make just one quick comment in partial rebuttal. I respect very much the arguments that have been presented here against licensure. I respect your high ideals. But I would like the record, at least, to show that we are aware that we live in the real world. The reality is that if you fail to do something constructive about this situation, other people— perhaps unscrupulous people—are going to step in and take action.

Three years ago in my home state of Connecticut, I got a call one day from a legislator in regard to a proposed marriage and family counseling license. The bill—which did not pass—had been introduced to the state legislature by a radio announcer. He and his local representative were having a few beers together, and they arrived at the conclusion that some legislation—or at least some publicity—was needed in this area. Although nothing resulted from it, something might have—for better or for worse.

So, to sum up, your arguments scare me. If you are unwilling to involve yourselves in the dirty business of legislation, someone else will; and you may not be happy with the consequences.

VIRGINIA E. JOHNSON: I too had promised myself that I wouldn't take part in this particular session, because I truly have nothing significant to add to the discussion of certification and licensure. But there is an artifact of this field that helps, I think, to articulate the dilemma that we face in looking at this particular issue. That's the very name *sex therapy*.

Sex therapy is a self-delimiting term, considered in its semantic purity. In fact, in actual practice there's no such thing as "pure" sex therapy, as we who do it know: There is psychotherapy or counseling for sexual dysfunction or sexual problems. Anyone who becomes involved in the pursuit of this health-care goal will soon discover that it consists of much more than mere reassurance and dispensing of information: It is indeed part and parcel of what I personally identify as psychiatry. Psychotherapy is an art; I agree with Charles. It is not a science, as such, but it must embody scientific knowledge.

The cardinal arts and allied disciplines are side by side as we contemplate the issue of certification and licensure. We can certify and license to our hearts' content, but we have always to bear in mind what it is that we're representing. We have to be something, we have to know what we are, and we have to be able to describe ourselves and what we do. In other words, we cannot ignore the problem of terminology and the related problem of semantics.

Let me give you a little historical note, for what it's worth. Had I been—in the present-day terminology—a more assertive woman in 1966 when *Human Sexual Response* was published, or even in 1970 when *Human Sexual Inadequacy* was published, this issue might not be posing so many problems for us now. We had to decide whether to publish for general consumption and perusal that which we had developed in terms of psychotherapy—the natural evolution and outgrowth of our work, stemming from the basic scientific research. I have to admit that I deferred. I felt that we should postpone publication until we had on our staff a psychiatrist who could absorb and disseminate in the psychiatric format the work that we did. At that time, I felt that the only appropriate framework—protective framework—for the presentation and dispersal of this material was psychiatry, because it embodied what we were trying to establish: namely, the recognition of the total psychosexual person in all its medical, behavioral, and social aspects. Now, that was—and is—my own bias, and it does not mean that I feel another discipline cannot develop or represent the pursuit of reversal of sexual dysfunction. (As a footnote, in defense of other disciplines seeking to provide health care for sexual problems and dysfunction, I would not be surprised to see something equally effective evolve within their respective frameworks.)

At any rate, it was lack of assertiveness that caused us to withhold the mode of therapy we had developed until we could share it within a protective framework. I now feel that in so doing, we failed to confront the issue of the terminology of sex therapy as a professional discipline. If it was a timely issue then, it is a crucial issue now. Protection of the name in an appropriate framework is our only assurance that we can somehow come of age as an individual discipline or a separate health-care entity.

HAROLD I. LIEF: Gini, it's interesting to reflect on what might have happened if sex therapy had developed, as you suggest, wholly within the framework—and with the terminology—of the psychiatric profession. If it had, perhaps we would not still be struggling for legitimization eight years later.

SALLIE SCHUMACHER: I think we missed some of the points that Fred was making. We were getting hung up on the subject of accreditation, certification, and licensing—but he also outlined a 30-year development of a professional field. I don't think we paid enough attention to that.

Let me reinforce what Gini just said: We are in the process of trying to describe what sex therapy is and where it belongs as a discipline. We ought to talk next about training requirements and training programs. By whose sanction can an organization now certify sex therapists, when there are no professional training programs? Let's get back to the background paper's topic of major focus and expand upon some of the points it made and the topics that Dr. Crenshaw raised in her presentation.

HAROLD I. LIEF: Are you saying that you think we are being premature in talking about certification at this point?

SALLIE SCHUMACHER: Yes, I certainly think we are.

JOHN MONEY: I keep sensing a hidden agenda in the discussion. I have two or three comments to make. First of all, whether you call it certification or licensure, there is a high degree of trade unionism and monopoly involved in that issue. It appears to me, from my knowledge of affairs in this country, that there is a focus of interest in St. Louis, another one on the West Coast, and another one somewhere in the New York/Washington area. We didn't ask the West Coast people what they thought, although California is partially represented here. The one and only school that a state has chartered to grant a degree in human sexuality, the Institute for the Advanced Study of Human Sexuality (located in San Francisco), has no representative here. And they have a head start on us: They have an institute, a dean, a president, and a degree they can give to people whom they have trained in what they want to have them trained in.

That brings me to my second point, which is that while we haven't resolved the issue of who's going to be king of the castle and who is going to own the monopoly of sex therapy—if there is to be one—we are still dependent on someone else to train our sex therapists. Although we (in this gathering) haven't yet tangled with the problem of whether we are going to require our trainees to have an M.D., a Ph.D., an M.A., an Ed.D., or whatever, they're all going to have to go through and come from someone else's training program. If they come with the Ph.D. in psychology or the M.D., they will have their own professional memberships, their respective certification or licensure, and their respective professional codes of ethics. They won't really need ours. On the other hand, if they don't come with these credentials, then we are harping on a theme that is familiar throughout the mental health profession these days: Should we—and if so, how do we—produce "cheap" practitioners who hold lesser degrees than the top ones? And that has a great deal to do with what one or two speakers had to say regarding the ultimate arrival of national health insurance and the question of who will be paid for services.

So I believe that we must give serious attention to the proposed curriculum for sex therapy; to the contents of the first textbooks— which really haven't been written yet; and finally, to the selection or sanction of the particular degree-granting agencies or institutions. Only then will we be in a position to settle that other very important point, accreditation. And incidentally, I wonder if there hasn't been some misunderstanding this evening about accreditation, for it is institutions, not individuals, that are accredited. Furthermore, we'll have to determine the rules, the finances, the entire process whereby accreditation will take place.

Finally, if the federal and state governments do not get into the business of either certification or licensure, then we could do what most of the other medical disciplines do: We could set up our own board and administer our own examinations. But this is the last thing on the agenda—first we have to develop a very good curriculum on the basis of which candidates will be examined, and of course we have to have institutions where persons can receive training in that curriculum.

HAROLD I. LIEF: John, I'm happy to hear you say this. Although we dealt with each of those issues in our working paper, perhaps now we can all deal with them more thoroughly.

I thank you all for your participation.

REFERENCE

1. Bledstein, B. J. The Culture of Professionalism: The Middle Class and the Development of Higher Education in America. New York: Norton, 1976.

14

THE PROPOSED DRAFT
OF GUIDELINES

ROBERT C. KOLODNY: This morning, moving away from the background papers that were discussed in the panels and summaries yesterday, we shall begin to direct our attention specifically to the draft of ethics guidelines developed by the task force in preparation for this meeting. The guidelines resulted from a series of meetings of the task force and from the background papers prepared by members of the task force, who also profited from a detailed examination of existing codes of ethics or codes of conduct of a number of different organizations both in this country and abroad (for example, various psychiatric associations, the American Psychological Association, the American Association of Marriage and Family Counselors, and the American Bar Association).

We have asked several speakers to give us their reflections on specific sections of the guidelines. During the panel discussion there will be relatively little time for dialogue between the panelists and the other participants. But immediately after the coffee break following this discussion, the entire group will be divided into small discussion groups, which will meet concurrently for the remainder of the day. Each small discussion group has been assigned one section of the guidelines as a starting point and as a topic of primary focus. However, this is not meant to restrict their considerations to that section of the guidelines: The chairpersons of these small groups are free to expand the scope of the discussions as they see fit to encompass other sections of the guidelines as well.

Tomorrow morning we shall return to the plenary format, starting with a summary report from each discussion group of the major points that that group touched upon; the remainder of the meeting will be an open session with discussion involving the entire group.

The proposed guidelines are offered not as a final document, but as a working draft, subject to revision. I would like to emphasize this point. We have convened this group in order to solicit the creative input of all the participants. We welcome your comments and suggestions about points of content, points of omission, and stylistic points with regard to the language of the document.

With those few remarks, let me introduce the first of the panelists, Dr. Fritz Redlich, formerly of Yale University and now of the University of California, Los Angeles, who has been involved in our work with this subject for close to four years. He will begin by discussing the section dealing with the competency of sex therapists.

FRITZ REDLICH: I read the guidelines with great interest, and I am in general agreement with them—knowing, of course, as you all do, that such guidelines leave the reader with more questions than answers. In my comments I would like to raise a few of those questions.

The guidelines differentiate the broad and complicated concepts of competence and integrity. At times we are inclined to ask about therapists, What is more important, competence or integrity? Of course, this doesn't make much sense unless you specify levels of integrity or levels of competence. For instance, I once trained a clinical specialist who was not much of a human being but was very competent; I decided to retain him, because in this particular situation it was more important to have somebody who was very competent. In other situations, this may not be so. As a matter of fact, I would venture to say that in a field that Louis Thomas would consider a field of low technology—and I think all psychotherapists, including sex therapists, fall into this category—integrity is probably the most important quality for a therapist to have. Now, you might want to argue against this; in a field of low technology, characterized by low competence, the difference between low competence and no competence may be very small but is vitally important.

We are looking for competence in a particular situation. From the point of view of the patient or client, this means competence to treat the disease or disorder at hand. Take a patient with gall-bladder stones—cholelithiasis—for example: Such a patient would want to know the comparative prognostic statistics for an operative course and for a conservative course of medical management; the possible complications; the probable duration of illness in both situations; the approximate cost involved. He wants to know about his surgeon or internist: How many cases has he handled? In how many cases has he operated? How many cases has he treated con-servatively? What is his "score"? It is almost impossible even for a professional person—a referring person—to get this kind of infor-mation, let alone a member of the family or the patient himself. There are reasons for this difficulty. One is the complexity of the problem. One is the uncertainty of outcome. But most important is the secrecy that prevails in our field.

Of course, there are professional directories, directories contain-ing information about the training and educational background of practitioners, but these are not readily accessible to the lay person. We do not have anything like an efficient consumer report in the health-care professions. I think we are on the way toward that—I think the degree of secrecy is decreasing. But when you (in the guidelines) postulate that therapists should describe themselves, you are ahead of the times; such descriptions do not exist at pres-ent, and I think most therapists would be unwilling to supply them. One reason is that self-description is considered advertising, and the professions frown on advertising. But, as I said, this will gradually be considered legitimate and a certain amount of profes-sional description will become more frequent and—ultimately—even customary. Finally, the consumer, the patient, the client will exercise his or her right to ask for such descriptions.

The other argument against publicizing this information is that the patient would not understand it. Patients or clients, particu-larly when they are ill—even with relatively minor disorders—are often too upset to fully understand what a professional person tells them. Indeed, research has confirmed this fact—but this is not suf-ficient cause to argue that such information should not be given.

What *is* generally provided today in the major health profes-sions, particularly in the field of medicine, is information about degrees, about certification, about licensure, and about accreditation. These conditions do not apply to the field of sex therapy except in rudimentary form. Should we move toward them? That is the big question.

Before I give a tentative answer to this (and of course, only my own opinion), let me raise the question whether sex therapy should be a defined subspecialty or a specialty. I would argue against it at this point. For instance, I can imagine a team of researcher-therapists—a Masters and Johnson, if you will—who would be concerned with the field of sleep (after all, an enormously important activity). We spend one-third or at least one-fourth of our time sleeping. There are a great many people who have sleep disorders. Let's hypothesize that somebody might combine real scholarly knowledge about sleep with an effective therapy in this area. Would this justify the status of a subspecialty in science? I think not.

There are other examples in medicine of specialization stopping short of a full organization with boards, certification, and so on, as, for instance, diseases of the liver (hepatology) or diseases of the kidneys (nephrology). People interested in these fields form organizations, get together, and exchange knowledge, but they are not really specialists in the same sense as, say, specialists in pediatrics or specialists in surgery. The question is where they should stop.

I think the task for sex therapists at this point is to establish, to define what the field of knowledge is, both in theory and in practice, and to set standards. This must precede certification of practitioners, accreditation of organizations, and licensing by the state. Of course, as far as licensure is concerned, we are in a state of flux. It could well be that the issue of licensure will lose its importance in the light of evolving concepts of recertification. Whether those professions that have licensing today—in the health field, medicine, dentistry, and nursing—will relinquish these licenses and the right to license is another question. They might do so because in fact there are disadvantages to licensure; certification may offer fewer disadvantages. (To some extent, of course, we are talking about symbols of prestige within the profession, independent of consumer concern. This is the self-dealing aspect of a profession—and one can have very little use for that from an ethical point of view.)

Although I would argue against setting up rigid standards for sex therapy at the present time, I think that the profession ought to establish clearly who should administer training and what the training should consist of. It is my impression that training has been downgraded to some extent by quick courses, courses that were given insufficient planning. This has given the public the idea that sex therapy is a field in which one can become adept in a very short time, which obviously is not the case. The establishment of high training standards is therefore of the utmost importance.

I would also argue that there should be no certification at this time for sex therapists per se—that sex therapy should come from existing professions, namely, medicine, nursing, psychology, social work, and the counseling ministry (possibly others as well). If sex therapists come from these professions, professional standards will prevail; sex therapy will then constitute an additional area of knowledge and expertise for these professional persons. This would set up an automatic dichotomy between the therapist and the non-professional helper. Insofar as other dichotomies are concerned, I can see a clear differentiation between the sex therapist and the sex counselor. I am less certain about a real differentiation existing between sex counselor and sex educator; I believe that in general, the theoretical boundaries will be very easily transgressed. You will not find the clear separation that you may wish to see in this field. Nevertheless, the distinction between professional therapy and non-professional help should be recognized and preserved. There is no doubt that innumerable persons suffering from sexual disorders are helped by their partners, spouses, lovers, casual contacts, and prostitutes. But this is surely different from therapy.

This brings me to the question of surrogates. I personally think that the disadvantages outweigh the advantages of using sexual surrogates in a contractual relationship, but this is an issue that must be discussed. It cannot be ignored. In California I have heard of persons who serve as independent professional sex surrogates. This doesn't make sense to me; such persons would fall into the category of help, not therapy. Again, we should try to differentiate along these lines.

We will have to find answers to these questions.

ROBERT C. KOLODNY: The next speaker will be Joshua Golden, who will talk on issues of confidentiality in sex therapy.

JOSHUA S. GOLDEN: I'd like to expand on a few of the guidelines that were drafted. Because those in my section are brief, I will read or summarize the separate points and address my comments to each point specifically.

In the second recommendation on confidentiality it is suggested that "the very existence of a therapist-client relationship is a confidential matter, since there are circumstances under which the identification of such a relationship would imply the presence of sexual problems or difficulties on the part of the client." I thought this point might be expanded and that perhaps there should be some consideration given to the naming and physical structuring of facilities that treat sexual problems. Some facilities use disguises or employ euphemistic terms to describe themselves. Some clinics refer to themselves as sexuality programs rather than sexual dysfunction programs, and many facilities are set up in such a way that patients cannot be seen entering or leaving the premises. The reception areas are usually private; people can come and go without attracting attention. On the other hand, reflecting back to a point that Dick Wasserstrom raised in his paper—and the clinical experience underlying it—might it not be therapeutically advantageous to alter or mitigate a person's view that sexuality is something that needs to be hidden and that it is embarrassing or shameful to admit that one has a sexual problem? One useful therapeutic technique is to inform patients that a great many normal people have sexual problems as a consequence of the enforced sexual ignorance of our cultural conditioning. It may benefit the patient to be persuaded that certain aspects of his beliefs and attitudes about sex should not be kept private. At times in therapy it may be helpful to patients whose goal is overcoming a sexual problem to try to alter the concept that sex should be a completely private matter.

I recently treated with success a man who had had erectile failure subsequent to a coronary bypass operation. He used to come to our clinic. His son, a professional counselor who was visiting over the holidays, asked him why he was going into Beverly Hills once a week; he assumed his father was seeing either a doctor or a lawyer. The man was reluctant to acknowledge the fact that he was having a sexual problem. But after a few visits, he and his wife managed to reverse the dysfunction. About the same time, he told his son about it and felt very pleased that he had been able to do so. I will not go so far as to suggest that there was a causal relationship between telling his son about the problem and overcoming the problem, but it may be that there was a therapeutic effect in the sense that an attitude of openness can be beneficial—in this case, it was helpful to be able to accept the fact that not all sexual difficulties are pathological in origin.

Point 3 says that information received by the sex therapist from the client or prospective client or from diagnostic evaluation, treatment, or follow-up of a client may be divulged to the extent required only under the following circumstances: (a) "When the client provides written consent (except when this information has been obtained from another person whose privacy would be violated by unauthorized disclosure)" (I might add that this is almost always a possibility when sex therapy involves a partner). Examples that might be relevant would include employment inquiries, requests for security clearance, insurance applications, and the like, when reference to a patient being in sex therapy or being a subject in sex research might lead to the revelation of details of the patient's or subject's sexual practices that might place him or her in a disadvantageous position. I think we ought to give particular thought to such situations.

Point 3 (b) gives the following condition in which violations of confidentiality are permissible: "When there is clear and imminent danger to an individual or to society. In such an instance, disclosure should only be made to appropriate family members, public authorities, or professional workers (in assessing the necessity for such an action, it is permissible for the therapist to consult with other professionals, including a lawyer, as long as the consultation protects the identity of the client involved)." This obviously pertains to the principles raised by the *Tarasoff* case[1] in California. If one reveals a patient's identity with justification on ethical grounds, what responsibility might one have to ascertain that the person or institution to whom one gives this confidential material will protect it and use it with equal respect for the patient's welfare? It

---

[1] *Tarasoff* v. *Regents of University of California* (*Tarasoff I*), 529 P.2d 553, 118 Cal. Reptr. 129 (1974); *Tarasoff* v. *Regents of University of California* (*Tarasoff II*), 551 P.2d 334, 131 Cal. Reptr. 14 (1976).

seems to me that we are not discharging our ethical responsibilities properly if we divulge confidential material to someone who will then use it in a less than responsible manner. It might be advisable in such cases to consult a lawyer, the appropriate professional society, or someone who has already formulated a comprehensive plan of action. I leave it to the lawyers and philosophers among us to develop the general ethical principles of conduct that would apply.

Point 3 (c) provides another condition under which therapist-client privilege is altered: "When required to defend the sex therapist, employees or associates of the sex therapist, or the institute or employer of the sex therapist against formal accusation . . . by the client of wrongful conduct." Examples cited are court proceedings or hearings of an organizational ethics committee. I wonder if perhaps this is too limited a statement. There is also the possibility that a therapist or researcher might be accused by someone else—a colleague, a professional society, or an agency, for instance. This raises a fundamental question: When shall we sacrifice the patient's privacy for the well-being of the therapist by allowing disclosure of the therapist's records? When there is a conflict between the patient and the therapist, whose ethical needs shall take precedence? Would it be ethical to obtain consent after treatment has ceased, assuming that consent to disclosure was not obtained in advance from a patient entering therapy? I can foresee a situation in which a patient at the outset of therapy might perhaps be more willing to give his consent; the prospective patient might even feel that his acceptance as a client was contingent upon his giving such consent. In such a case, consent would not have been freely given. On the other hand, a given patient might be either more willing or less willing to consent to disclosure of information about him and revelation of his identity upon completion of therapy, depending on whether or not the treatment had been successful in his particular case. Again, consent obtained as a contingency of the outcome of therapy would not have been freely given. We should also remember that consent to disclosure, no matter how freely given, may be withdrawn at any later time.

Point 3 (d) is, I think, another controversial point providing an exception to the general confidentiality accorded to the client:

"When [it is] necessary to establish or collect a professional fee." Few persons are willing to represent themselves as openly mercenary, and yet we wonder whether the principle of confidentiality should be defended even when it costs us money. Should the question of fees be disregarded? If so, how is the sex therapist to survive, when his primary source of income is payment for professional services? Perhaps this issue could be resolved by securing an agreement from the patient in advance of therapy, whereby he consents to having his identity revealed if it becomes necessary in default of payment for services rendered. Of course, such an agreement would have to take into account the possibility of payment by a third party, for example, an insurance company, relatives, or Medicare.

The other points can be dealt with in the small discussion group. In conclusion, let me say that my general impression of this section of the guidelines as well as other aspects of our deliberations is that we seem to be in a position where our choices are not between ethical conduct and unethical conduct, but rather between two conflicting values. Keeping this in mind, it may be useful for us to attempt to spell out by example cases in which one value takes precedence over the other.

ROBERT C. KOLODNY: Thank you. The next speaker will be Joe LoPiccolo, who will speak about the section of the draft of guidelines having to do with the welfare of the client.

JOSEPH LoPICCOLO: I found almost nothing to quarrel with in this section. It was very well thought out. The points that I have to make are small ones—items that people could disagree about, and a few points on things that are not included in this section of the guidelines.

Items 1 and 2 are concerned with sex therapists' realizing the limits of their competency and not making exaggerated claims of efficacy. One problem I see here is that this whole section advocates a set of ethical principles for clinicians with regard to clients that are much less stringent than the corresponding principles for researchers in relation to research subjects. I find this somewhat puzzling in view of the fact that the researcher has, pro forma, institutional constraints on his behavior, whereas a clinician in private practice does not. On the other hand, we can hardly admonish sex therapists against making unsupported claims of efficacy or overstepping the boundaries of their professional competence unless the ethics guidelines include a requirement that clinicians gather outcome statistics on their patients, including delayed follow-ups after therapy. Without this, sex therapy will foster the sort of situation that has existed in psychotherapy for many years: Practitioners believe that certain modes of treatment are effective and they cite—as proof—the large number of patients they have treated, when in fact they may be describing spontaneous remission, placebo effects, and successful outcomes that actually result from other causes.

In reference to the section on fees [item 4], of course it's good that fees be discussed with patients in advance. Some of you may be aware that around the country there is a tendency for the fees for sex therapy to be considerably higher—even as much as ten times higher—than the fees for other types of outpatient therapy. I think there should be a statement in the guidelines to the effect that fees for sex therapy should be in line with established professional fees for other equivalent outpatient therapy. Furthermore, in settings where higher fees are charged in order to meet institutional costs or for other reasons, the therapist should perhaps be required to inform prospective clients that therapy is available in other settings at a lower fee.

I agree with the sentiment of the statement in item 5, "Sex therapists are encouraged to provide services to clients who are able to provide little or no financial compensation." But I think "are encouraged" is a little too weak. Since the typical legitimate sex therapist has received a good deal of his or her education and training at the taxpayers' expense, perhaps we ought to recognize a real obligation to treat a certain number of indigent clients.

Point 6—on conflict of interests—in an important one. It states the usual prohibition against treating one's employees, relatives, business associates, friends, or sexual partners. There are two other situations that might be mentioned here. One is that there is a potential conflict of interest when the therapist is being paid by a third party. Let's say, for example, that a police department therapist is seeing a policeman who has a sexual dysfunction. If the therapist or psychologist treating the case is a uniformed policeman himself, he is aware that he must operate within certain institutional restraints—or he'll be out on the streets in a patrol car, instead of doing therapy. On the other hand, he has a responsibility to the individual patient, and these interests may conflict. Another situation that should be considered is the possibility of conflict of interests after completion of therapy. For example, we recently had a case involving a husband and wife who had been referred to us. The woman had been in individual therapy with a psychiatrist for treatment of a sexual dysfunction. After about a dozen sessions, the therapy was terminated at the psychiatrist's suggestion. The therapist then entered into a sexual relationship with the woman. Now, I tend to see causality there: The therapist was well aware that it is unethical to have sex with a patient, and he stopped having therapy with her so he could have sex with her. Now, I think our guidelines ought to include a statement touching on this type of situation—perhaps a suggestion of some reasonable time interval that should elapse before professionals consider forming social, emotional, and perhaps sexual relationships with former patients.

The next point [item 7], that it is unethical for a therapist to engage in sexual activity with a client, could use some elaboration. Given the current debate over so-called sexological examinations and a recent trend to include some sort of "body work" in sex therapy, some therapists may have trouble interpreting this dictum, which does not specify whether or not such procedures are classified as sexual contact with the patient. If you ask the people who conduct a sexological examination, they say it does not constitute sexual contact. Yet, if the male therapist is stimulating the female patient's breast and pointing out that she gets a nipple erection, that sounds like sexual contact to me. At any rate, I think we need to be more specific in defining what constitutes sexual activity. Does it include sexological exams? Does it include massage? Does it include body work? I think we have to specify.

Item 8 admonishes therapists against observation of clients engaging in sexual activity. Perhaps my comments regarding this point will appear to be more philosophical than practical, but I see this as making an arbitrary distinction between vision and audition—and censuring only the former. That is, we talk with our patients continually about their personal sexual activity. At my clinic, the patients write it out for us. They keep diaries for us. I agree that there is a difference between actually watching them and merely listening to their report and talking about what they did. But the distinction is not always so clear-cut as this. What if you have the patients videotape themselves, and then you view the videotape? What if you send them home with a cardiac monitor, and they have sexual intercourse while you look at the EKG that's being transmitted to your laboratory? Are these examples classified as observation of sexual activity? I also think the justification given for the ban on observation is somewhat lacking in straightforwardness. It states that such activity would introduce undesirable elements of transference and countertransference into the therapy context. In my opinion, this type of language is simply a distancing device that we therapists use to make ourselves feel more comfortable with the fact that sometimes our patients are sexually attracted to us and sometimes we are sexually attracted to them. This attraction has nothing to do with transference and countertransference as those terms are classically defined.

Nudity is prohibited in this code of ethics [item 9]. Again, I think the ban should be stated in more specific terms. For instance, there are some possibly valuable body work workshops involving nudity or partial nudity; perhaps some allowance should be made for these. Certainly there are many persons who would disagree with the flat statement that nudity is always unethical.

Item 10 advocates that sex therapists give their patients objective assessment of their marital and relationship problems. This is a difficult area. We should not give the patient advice about *terminating* the relationship; I certainly agree with that statement in item 10. But I would go even farther, extending this admonition to include giving advice about *staying* in a relationship: I think it applies to giving direct advice about all sorts of important life decisions. With a narrower application—as it stands—this guideline implies that sex therapists are involved primarily in the business of saving marriages, which is hardly the case (and does not seem to be the intended force of the admonition).

Item 11 is concerned with a situation I think all of us have difficulties with: the potential dilemma that occurs when the therapist receives "secret" information from one of the two partners. For example, let's say you are doing an intake evaluation on a client, and the male tells you he doesn't really have an erectile problem: Although he never has erections with his wife, he experiences no sexual dysfunction with his mistress. However, he does not want this information to be revealed to his wife. Therefore, he says, "It's up to you, Doc; get me off the hook. I don't want to enter therapy with my wife, but don't tell my wife I'm having an affair." Now, this provision to keep such information from the wife seems to conflict with item 10, which states that we have a professional obligation to give our patients full and objective assessments of their marital situation or relationships. So we are to both provide objective assessment *and* not divulge confidential information provided by one member of a client couple. I don't know how to solve this dilemma. We struggle with it at least once a week in my clinic, because it is not uncommon for patients to relate secrets to their therapists, secrets that have definite implications for whether they should be in therapy or whether they should stay in the relationship. I think this section of the guidelines needs an acknowledgment of this dilemma.

Item 13 deals with the conflict of interests between research, training, and clinical care. As a researcher and clinician, I had a moderately negative reaction to some of this section—for example, the statement that you must modify your research in order to maximize the objective benefits to clients in therapy, if your research procedures are interfering with those objective benefits. But unless we do research on therapy, how will we ever learn what the "objective" benefits are? I honestly think the best clinical treatment occurs in research settings, where clinicians are examining critically what they are doing and trying to find out what works and what doesn't work. It took research by people such as Masters and Johnson to prove that many of the techniques used by psychiatrists and psychoanalysts for sexual problems were not actually in the client's best interests. I think the wording in this section of the guidelines implies that "real" clinical care does not involve research, and that clinical care in a research-oriented study is somehow inferior because of an automatic conflict of interests. But, in my view, research and therapy are interdependent, and good treatment must ultimately be based on research results.

The section on surrogates [item 14] is another item that I have some trouble with. It is stated in this section that the use of sex surrogates may be acceptable, but it is important to recognize that they are not sex therapists. Again, I suspect that this is essentially a use of semantics that has no clear relationship to the actual therapy situation. Certainly if you talk to patients who have been in sex therapy with a surrogate, you will find that they define the surrogate as the sex therapist. If you look at some of the literature, you will find that the surrogate is often described as the sex therapist. The therapist who *talks* to the patient is called the review therapist. So I think if we say that it is unethical for a therapist to have sex with a patient, but it is permissible for a surrogate to have sex with a patient, we are obscuring the issues involved in having sexual relations with a patient. I don't have the answer to this problem—but I don't think we can dismiss it so easily.

There are a few other things that I don't have time to go into extensively, but I will mention them briefly.

First, there is nothing in these guidelines about the issue of patients' access to the records of their treatment under the provisions of the Freedom of Information Act.

Second, in the section on research [section V] it is recommended that research subjects have an independent, objective advocate available to them for redress of grievances. It surprises me that this isn't advocated in the client welfare section as well. I think therapists should be obligated to inform their clients of the appropriate avenue for redress of grievances, if the clients are unhappy with therapy. And in general, in my opinion, client welfare is not best served by a sex therapist, but by a professional psychotherapist who happens to have been trained in sex therapy. Perhaps that should also be mentioned.

Third, I think we need to take a look at the problem of physically invasive surgical procedures such as clitoral circumcision, removal of clitoral adhesions, and pelvic surgery that involves drastic anatomical change that supposedly produces a desired sexual response. There ought to be an injunction in the client welfare section against performing this type of invasive surgery on a patient except under very special circumstances, with research required to demonstrate that the procedure is in the best interest of the client.

Finally, there is nothing in the guidelines either for or against advising patients to commit sex acts that are illegal within a given jurisdiction. We once asked the attorney general if by recommending that patients try oral sex, we were accessories to sodomy; the answer was yes. I think that issue deserves some consideration.

ROBERT C. KOLODNY: The fourth section of the guidelines deals with the welfare of students and trainees. I will be quite brief and will primarily summarize the section for you.

I believe it was Judy Long Laws who—at our 1976 conference—brought it to our attention that in federal codes of academicians there were at that time no provisions that prohibited sexual abuse of students by their faculty members. She urged us to consider our responsibilities toward students and trainees in the field. This section is included in the guidelines not as a theoretical issue alone, but because we have had direct knowledge of literally dozens of instances in which persons wishing to enter sex therapy training programs (or involved in sex therapy training or educational programs) were in some way enticed, compelled, or coerced into sexual activity on the pretext that it was a necessary experiential requirement for the program. While it may appear that students or trainees should have the ability to recognize the impropriety of such situations, it is remarkable that their good judgment is often distorted for reasons that range from the student's motivation to succeed to the general tendency students have to place automatic trust in their teachers. On the other hand, it is tremendously important to the vitality and integrity of our work to preserve academic freedom in its broadest dimensions. Just as our constitutional right to free speech does not condone slander or libel, so freedom of academic thought and action must be tempered by some checks and balances. This section of the guidelines aims at creating such an interplay.

The first point is concerned with preserving the confidentiality of the student or trainee while allowing for the teacher or trainer to be able to carry out objective evaluation of the students and trainees (including both evaluations for the benefit of the students themselves and evaluations in the form of job references or recommendations to other institutions or programs). It is stated [point 1 (c)] that disciplinary action would not be limited by the consideration for confidentiality.

The second point acknowledges the student's or trainee's right to periodic assessment of his or her performance, with advance knowledge of how and when this will be carried out.

The third point states that it is unethical for teachers or training supervisors to abuse their position of authority by compelling or enticing students or trainees into sexual activity.

The fourth point raises a sensitive issue: While we recognize the importance of the principles of privacy that, for example, Dick Wasserstrom expounded on so well, there is also a prevalent belief among workers engaged in clinical training in the field that it is important to know something about the personal sexual attitudes and sexual histories of persons who wish to become sex therapists and their motives for choosing to enter the field. If you were to discover, for example, that a prospective student has committed rape, perhaps it would be imprudent to admit that person to a training program. So point 4 discusses the propriety (while admitting the risk factor) of gaining access to limited amounts of such private information, pointing out that the student must receive assurance that this privileged information will not be misused.

The fifth point states that it is not ethical to compel students or trainees to serve as research subjects. Certainly the satisfactory completion of an educational or a training program should not depend on the student's participation in certain types (or a certain number) of research projects. We are not speaking of a requirement to conduct research—that's something else. We are talking about required participation as a subject in a research project.

In conclusion, I would like to ask Miriam Kelty to discuss the final section of the draft of guidelines, concerning the welfare of research subjects.

MIRIAM F. KELTY: First, I would like to endorse the notion of applying the same set of guidelines to research, training, and services. I think this is important, particularly in a young field, because it permits clinicians and researchers to switch roles and on occasion, to engage in professional activities other than their primary occupation. They are prepared to do so more easily and with greater competence if they have the appropriate training to work in these different areas. However, I think that in the proposed draft of guidelines the distinctions between research, training, and provision of services are somewhat arbitrary. There are areas of overlap. I recommend that the guidelines be examined comprehensively in an effort to determine which components really need to be separated out as distinct for persons whose primary work is in one area rather than the other two.

The addition of a rather specific preamble or introduction would benefit the guidelines. On first reading them, I wasn't sure about the extent to which they were intended to legitimize sex therapy, sex research, and sex education; whether the primary intention was to guide the activities of those persons working in the field; whether they were intended simply to raise the consciousness of those involved in the field; or whether the guidelines were formulated primarily as an educational device to stimulate students to look at broader issues involving the ethics of sex research, education, and professional practice—and later to apply these ethical principles to their respective specialties.

It's also unclear what the role of the guidelines is in the context of other ethics codes. I compared them with the code from my own professional organization, the American Psychological Association, and found them to be very consistent. I'm sure, however, that if one were to compare these guidelines with all the different professional codes of ethics, there would be some disagreement. Are these guidelines intended to amplify other ethics codes? Or should they take precedence over other codes for people whose primary work is in the area of human sexuality? This should be made explicit. Of course, there are some people involved in sex therapy and sex research who are not covered by codes of other professions, and the guidelines would appear to be particularly applicable to these persons.

I have some specific comments to make about the section on the welfare of research subjects. The introductory material states that sex researchers should conduct their investigations in such a way as to protect the dignity, rights, and welfare of their subjects. To me, the notion that patients, students, and research participants need protection has a negative connotation. I would prefer to see things stated in a more positive manner—for instance, advocating respect for participants and conduct of research in an ethical framework that reflects concern for the dignity, welfare, and rights of patients or research subjects.

The initial paragraph also maintains that an assessment of the risks and benefits of the proposed project should be conducted in making research decisions. It is not clear whether benefits include the advancement of knowledge, nor whether they have to accrue directly to the particular individual who was engaged in the research. It is also unclear how benefits are to be assessed. Suggested criteria for assessment of risks and benefits should be articulated, and it should be stated whether or not subjective criteria are to be acceptable. There is bound to be confusion about this issue, and I can envision some research review committees trying to delay approval of research until there are criteria that they consider objective, while others might be quite satisfied with a more subjective judgment.

The first guideline calls for identification of the responsible researcher to research participants. I suggest that this be made even more specific—recommending that information about the researcher be provided in writing. I have received telephone calls from former research participants who were looking for their researchers, whether to volunteer additional data for longitudinal studies, to get information contained in the records, or for some other reason. They frequently had some idea of where the research was carried out, but they seldom knew the name of the project or the researcher. Such inquiries could be greatly expedited if this information were routinely given to research subjects at the time of their acceptance for participation in a project.

The second guideline stipulates that research involving human subjects be designed to require the free and informed consent of subjects. I think the phrase *research involving human subjects* needs precise definition. The Commission for the Protection of Human Subjects of Biomedical and Behavioral Research has struggled with the definitions of *human subjects* and *research involving human subjects* for some time now; we recently came up with the following: A human subject is a person about whom an investigator—whether a professional or a student—in the process of conducting research obtained (1) data through intervention or interaction with the person, or (2) identifiable private information. Thus, the Commission suggests that neither secondary analysis of data nor public observation of persons in public places in which individuals are not identified constitutes research involving human subjects.

The concepts of free and informed consent are conflated in the guidelines. I would prefer to see them separated. Voluntary consent may be independent of being fully and accurately informed about the research and fully comprehending its purposes and procedures. The phrase *informed consent* is ambiguous, if not completely meaningless. I would prefer to see the components of information and consent dealt with separately, to make their import clear.

Point 2 (a) requires that the procedures and details of a given project be clearly explained to the research participants. Though it may be implicit, it should be added that the purposes of the study should also be explained to research participants. I would recommend further that written information about the research be provided to potential participants in order that they might review the purposes, procedures, and consent agreement at their leisure and discuss aspects of the research project with others, should they choose to do so.

Point 2 (b) addresses the problem of risks. It does not mention potential benefits, if any, for the individual participant and for the advancement of knowledge. I suggest that those be included.

Both points (a) and (b) of the second guideline state that participants should understand the material that is explained to them. This is much easier said than done. Perhaps this section could be expanded: I suggest that we consider the possibility of questioning potential research subjects about what they have been told—asking potential participants to summarize the information that the investigator has communicated, to make sure it was understood.

In my experience as a researcher, many participants have believed they would benefit from the research even though they were told clearly that they would not. When I was conducting sleep research it was virtually impossible to convince research subjects that recordings of their physiological and behavioral responses did not constitute treatment. It is the investigator's responsibility to explain such facts as clearly as possible. I also consider it the responsibility of the investigator to inform research participants that a certain degree of uncertainty is generally associated with research, and that if we knew what the outcome would be and knew all the risks and benefits, the research would either be unnecessary or it would be classified as treatment. I think that is a difficult concept to communicate, but it's a very important one to try to get across to prospective research subjects.

In addition, if a protocol has been approved by an institutional review board, potential subjects should be told of that; similarly, if the proposed research has *not* been reviewed or approved by an IRB, subjects should be so informed and should be told the reasons for the lack of review or lack of approval.

I applaud the recommendation that researchers who are not affiliated with institutions arrange for an IRB to review their projects—but I also realize that this would be a very difficult thing to control or monitor.

At the time of the initial agreement to participate in research, investigators should specify whether or not participants are to be paid for their time and effort.

The fourth guideline states that researchers should provide for protection of confidentiality. Point 4 (c) specifies that the identity of subjects be concealed in publications or public presentations. I would like to emphasize that concealing identities may involve more than merely changing names to code letters or numbers. On more than one occasion I have read papers or heard presentations containing descriptions from which I was able to identify particular research subjects about whom I learned things that were really none of my business. Researchers should guard against this.

Point 4 (d) relates to maintaining confidentiality of research-related records. It states that the participants should be informed of the limits that may apply to maintaining confidentiality, for example, in the event of subpoena of records. I think the guidelines should also remind researchers of the possibility of applying for grants of confidentiality from the Alcohol, Drug Abuse, and Mental Health Administration. In my paper at the 1976 conference, I mentioned that there had been a proposal to initiate standard procedures for securing such grants of confidentiality [1]. Currently there is no routine procedure, but requests are being considered on an individual basis—and one request, at least, has been granted. I saw a notice in the *Federal Register* for a project involving the use of sexual information to be conducted at a university where a grant of confidentiality was apparently made.

The fifth guideline affirms that sex researchers should strive for honesty and accuracy in their dealings with people. Since I don't know any professional persons who claim to be dishonest or inaccurate in their dealings with people, I question the necessity of including this guideline. Perhaps this type of exhortation should simply be included in a general statement about ethical principles or ethical behavior.

The sixth and seventh guidelines are important, and I'm glad to see them. Guideline 7 could be strengthened by stating that investigators have a responsibility to share the outcome of research with participants. Participants should have an opportunity to ask questions to help them interpret research data, and I would add that they should also be encouraged to request help in interpreting their own data if they are interested in doing this.

The ninth guideline addresses the treatment and welfare of research animals. Some reference might be made to the existing standards for animal care, treatment, and welfare established by the National Institutes of Health, the National Academy of Sciences, and the American Psychological Association. The same might be said for the eighth guideline, which refers to taking proper precautions when drugs are used in research: There are other existing guidelines in this area, which might be incorporated here by reference.

I'd like to conclude by making some general comments. This document states at the outset that it is intended as a guide both for professional workers and for the public. I think the document would be improved if it included definitions of sex therapy, sex research, and sex education. These terms are not clearly understood, particularly by the general public. In addition, the entire document would benefit from a summary review of the components that are applicable to sex therapists, sex educators, and sex researchers, respectively. The distinctions often seem arbitrary and without clear value. The section on competence, for example, contains many points that are applicable to all professional behavior and are not unique to sex therapy, sex research, or sex education. This was discussed earlier today; I would concur with Fritz Redlich and some of the others who viewed sex therapy in the more general context of psychotherapy, but I recognize that there are people involved in sex therapy who do not have a traditional background in general psychotherapy (and vice versa). I recommend that the more general principles of ethical behavior be separated from those that have specific applicability to persons involved in sex-related work.

Finally, the guidelines ought to acknowledge that both the state of knowledge and our societal values are changing. A provision might be made and a mechanism might be suggested to incorporate a periodic review of the guidelines, with revision as appropriate, and to ascertain what impact the guidelines are having—for instance, whether or not they are involved in legal proceedings. This was done with the code of the American Psychological Association covering research involving human subjects. It has been difficult to implement, and revisions are needed—though there is no consensus on what effect the present code has had.

On a more personal note, I am somewhat ambivalent about the potential usefulness of yet another set of professional standards and wonder what they will add to the existing professional codes for practitioners and the training codes for professions that have training qualification statements. And where research is concerned, I'm afraid we are all subject to federal government regulations. I acknowledge that the development of guidelines itself may be very beneficial to those engaged in the process, but the outcome may not justify the input—the hard work, time, and energy that goes into it. But the developmental process can be very educational in a direct way to all of us who are involved in it, and it will have a secondary effect on the persons who are trained by us. In anticipation of this, I suggest that before these guidelines are given a final revision, they be discussed as much as possible in open meetings or workshops in a broad array of professional and nonprofessional settings in order to engage as many people as possible in the developmental process and to sensitize them to the kinds of issues that the guidelines address.

REFERENCE

1. Kelty, M. F.   Ethical Issues and Requirements for Sex Research with Humans: Confidentiality. In W. H. Masters, V. E. Johnson, and R. C. Kolodny (Eds.), *Ethical Issues in Sex Therapy and Research.* Boston: Little, Brown, 1977. Vol. 1, pp. 84–106.

GROUP DISCUSSIONS:
SUMMARY REPORTS

ROBERT C. KOLODNY: At this time we will hear from the designated reporters, who will summarize the small discussion group meetings that took place yesterday.

PATRICIA SCHILLER[1]: Ours was the kind of meeting where there was no disagreement in terms of principles or in substance. It was, rather, an exercise in reworking, refining, and clarifying. It was truly a celebration of cooperative, interdisciplinary effort. All of us participated with great energy, but it was Fritz Redlich who really set the tone for our meeting by suggesting that we change the title of the section of the guidelines on the competence of sex therapists. Our new title is "Competence and Integrity of Sex Therapists." We also felt that there ought to be a reordering of the various subsections, progressing logically from a general statement of necessary requirements through a description of a specific body of content to an outline of particular skills and application of those skills.

Let me read directly from this beautifully edited paper, with thanks to Phil Sarrel—who gave up lunch to find a typewriter and gave up sleep in order to edit and type our revision. First, a definition:

Sex therapy is a form of psychobiological therapy which is directed to the treatment of sexual disorders. It is the ethical responsibility of every sex therapist to maintain high standards of professional competence and integrity. These guidelines are aimed at establishing clearly defined pro-

[1] Patricia Schiller was the reporter for discussion group I (topic: Competence of Sex Therapists). The other members of the group were Philip M. Sarrel (chairperson), Mae A. Biggs, Virginia E. Johnson, Alex H. Kaplan, Harold I. Lief, Fritz Redlich, Lorna J. Sarrel, and Robert L. Stubblefield.

fessional standards for the purpose of protecting the public as well as the proper development of the field.

We then list a number of categories under the heading *Competence:*

1. Prerequisites for practicing sex therapy include professional education and demonstrated competence in a psychological or biological clinical field *and* additional prescribed training in the treatment of sexual disorders.
   a. Sex therapists have earned an educational degree equivalent to a master's degree or a doctorate in human sexuality or in a related field such as psychology or medicine.
   b. Competence in another primary discipline such as psychology, psychiatry, or marriage counseling is not equivalent to competence in sex therapy. Those trained in such related disciplines bring professional experience and understanding, which provide a foundation on which sex therapy training can be added.
   c. Specific training in sex therapy must always include supervised experience in the conduct of sex therapy.
2. Sex therapists should possess adequate knowledge, skills, and therapeutic attitudes in the following areas:
   a. Basic information about
      (1) Sexual and reproductive anatomy and physiology
      (2) Developmental sexuality from a psychobiological perspective
      (3) Dynamics of interpersonal relationships
      (4) Sociocultural factors in sexual values
      (5) Marital and family dynamics
      (6) Ethics
      (7) Medical factors (drugs, pregnancy, etc.)
   b. Diagnostic information about
      (1) Sexual disorders
      (2) Psychopathology
      (3) Techniques of evaluation and referral
   c. Areas of knowledge and clinical skills, namely
      (1) Techniques and theory of sex therapy, including several different models

(2) Techniques and theory of psychotherapy

(3) Outcome evaluation, including basic research related to observation, experimentation, and outcome

This does not mean that a sex therapist must be able to provide a full range of treatment services for problems in each of these areas: Recognizing these limitations and the extent of one's professional competence and seeking consultation when necessary are integral parts of professional competence.

3. Sex therapists should recognize the necessity and benefits of professional growth by participating in continuing education, reading professional journals, and attending scientific meetings. Sex therapists should maintain knowledge of current developments in their field.

4. Credentials alone do not give evidence of full competence. The proof of competence is the ability to provide objective and responsible services to clients.

The remaining categories are listed under the heading *Integrity* and prefaced by the following statement:

Competence and integrity are interrelated qualities that are both requisite to the responsible provision of service to others: Competence without integrity or integrity without competence is an unsatisfactory compromise of professional standards.

Many aspects of integrity are taken up in other sections of the draft of guidelines and were presumably dealt with in the other discussion groups; here we present guidelines for maintaining professional integrity as it relates to professional competence.

1. Sex therapists should provide information to prospective patients and professional communities about their education, training, experience, professional affiliations, and competence, and about the nature of their services, in an honest and accurate manner.

   a. Educational degrees should be cited by sex therapists only when they have been received from an accredited institution that is recognized by a regional or national accrediting association.

   b. It is unethical to claim that clinical training in sex therapy took place by attending a lecture, demonstration, conference, panel discussion, or other similar teaching presentation, unless such activities are designated by an institution as a formal part of its training program, in which case actual supervised experience in sex therapy must also be a part of this program.

2. Sex therapists have a responsibility to maintain competence and integrity within the field of sex therapy.

   a. Sex therapists should not enter into association for the practice of sex therapy with unqualified or incompetent persons.

   b. Sex therapists should not recommend or accept for admission to a training or educational program or for employment any person known to be unqualified in matters of education, training, or personal characteristics.

   c. Sex therapists should not make referrals to unqualified or incompetent persons. It is the responsibility of the sex therapist to verify the competence and integrity of the person to whom clients are referred.

   d. If the therapist, because of emotional or physical impairment, cannot provide objective and responsible services, he or she should seek competent professional consultation or treatment and refrain from professional activities while necessary.

   e. Sex therapists who possess knowledge of violations of ethical principles of conduct or evidence of professional incompetence should notify the appropriate authority (certifying or licensing boards, organizations' ethics committees, etc.) unless constrained by legal and professional considerations of confidentiality.

Finally, with the concern that no matter how well thought out such matters are, there is a tendency to be too precise and to particularize, we felt that we needed to conclude the section with a catchall phrase. It would read as follows:

It is necessary to emphasize that integrity, competence, confidentiality, responsibility, and applicable standards are not always subject to finite descriptions which address every situation that may arise. Therefore, in the conduct of all aspects of their professional work, therapists are expected to act according to general principles of ethical practice that may not be directly dealt with in this code of ethics.

RUTH MACKLIN[2]: Amazingly, our group finished ahead of schedule yesterday afternoon—not because we exhausted the subject, but because the subject was exhausting.

We were supposed to be discussing confidentiality, but the discussion ranged far and wide. That is because problems involving confidentiality arise in virtually all the areas that these guidelines address. Most of our discussion fell into five major categories, which I shall identify before dealing with specific recommendations in each category (as well as a number of recommendations that do not fall into any particular category). In some cases the members of the group agreed, and in other cases they did not; I will indicate the points on which there was disagreement and perhaps a few of the reasons on one side or the other, but I'm going to assign authors to arguments or go through the entire line of reasoning that each one followed.

Let me simply list the five major themes or areas: First, there were comments about the nature of the guidelines as a whole—their wording, their structure, their ultimate purpose. Second, there was much discussion about the relationship between the proposed guidelines and the law. Third, the notion of contracts kept entering into the discussion—especially the possible use of contracts as a method of circumventing some of the difficulties that our group foresaw if the proposed guidelines were instituted. The fourth issue that arose was the question of the payment of fees. There was a great deal of discussion about that. And finally, the fifth general issue was the treatment of medical records: We talked about confidentiality with regard to medical records, the storage and retrieval of data, the presence or absence of identifying marks, the use of coding devices, and the ultimate disposition of such records in the case of the death or disappearance of their holder. Related to this issue was a separate question that the group considered, namely, whether the patient or client should have access to his or her own records. That led to discussion of what form those records should take. We also discussed whether or not the parents of patients or

[2] Ruth Macklin was the reporter for discussion group II (topic: Confidentiality in Sex Therapy). The other members of the group were Joshua S. Golden (chairperson), R. Christian Johnson, Nat Lehrman, William H. Masters, John Money, Ralph Slovenko, and Richard Wasserstrom.

research subjects ought to have access to their children's records, in the case of minors.

On one point there was unanimous agreement: There are social, legal, and ethical problems that we can't hope to settle in these guidelines or at this congress. There are two reasons for this. One reason is that a resolution of some of those problematic issues lies beyond the scope and purpose of these particular guidelines; the other reason is that reasonable, intelligent people disagree on some of the basic moral principles that underlie the opposing views. With that caveat, let me turn now to the substantive points that our group discussed under each of the foregoing headings and the recommendations that we made.

First of all, about the nature of the guidelines, their wording, their structure, and so on: The discussion began with the observation that the guidelines are made up of vague, high-minded, general statements interlaced with persnickety details. Members of the group offered criticism on both counts, namely, the vagueness of the general statements and the fact that no list of details, persnickety or otherwise, can be exhaustive or all-inclusive. Now, these were not mere stylistic recommendations; not only is the precision of the language open to question, but also the comprehensiveness or completeness of the guidelines, if they are intended to be complete (and if not, whether or not some omission might be significant). One succinct stylistic recommendation was that a number of hyperbolic adjectives and adverbs be deleted.

There was much discussion throughout the day about how to improve the nonstylistic shortcomings of the proposed guidelines. One suggestion was that the guidelines should include some general recommendations as a basis for any list of details (for example, about the legal and ethical dimensions of performance by therapists). A second suggestion was that wherever the exact meaning of a phrase or principle is unclear, either a precise definition or some specific examples should be included. For instance, look at section II, subsection 3 (b), namely, the phrase *when there is clear and imminent danger to an individual or to society*. Well, for at least the last three or four decades—perhaps much longer than that—the precise meaning of *clear and imminent danger* has been under debate. We are not going to be able to solve that problem by making the language more precise. Our group agreed, however, that the danger in question should be *serious* danger in order to warrant breaking confidentiality. We were nonetheless unable to come up with any clear criteria for determining serious danger. One recommendation was that we define the phrase *clear and imminent*, but two problems were foreseen here: First of all, there is a conceptual problem in framing such a definition—the problem of taking into account every possible situation that might come under consideration under this definition. Second, there is also a theoretical and factual issue that arises from the *clear and imminent danger* clause when the issue is one of breaking confidentiality. This theoretical-factual issue is the question of predictability in this field (whether it is the field of human sexuality, psychology, sociology, social psychology, or criminology). The problem is the lack of predictability of those likely to commit acts that pose a clear and imminent danger: Even if we were able to agree on a definition of what constitutes clear and imminent danger, there is an insufficient theoretical base—a lack of sufficient knowledge to form a data base, as the social sciences put it—on which to make such predictions accurately.

Much discussion surrounded this issue, which led to further questions. For example, what ought to be the moral presumption underlying these guidelines? Should the moral presumption be in favor of protecting the individual by adhering to the strict dictates of confidentiality? Or should the presumption be in favor of protecting society or other individuals from those persons who are deemed harmful or potentially harmful?

One member of the group proposed that some provision be made for non-police treatment of offenders, arguing in favor of retaining them in treatment settings for therapy and rehabilitation. (It wasn't clear to me whether this should go into the guidelines or not. I think this was in the nature of a general recommendation for improving the existing system. I suppose most of us wouldn't quarrel with that kind of recommendation; but of course we are not going to be able to reform society.)

After bringing up the much-publicized *Tarasoff* case[3] in California, the group agreed that there is no clear ethical solution to these

[3] The decision in *Tarasoff* v. *Regents of the University of California*, 13 Cal. 3d 177, 529 P.2d 553, 118 Cal. Reptr. 129 (1974), imposed on psychotherapists who

enduring problems in society. But it was suggested that we include this very point in the guidelines—namely, the fact that it is impossible to resolve certain issues once and for all (or at least that their resolution is beyond the scope of these guidelines).

Let me turn now to the second category: the relationship between the proposed guidelines and the law. There were two different ways in which this issue came up. On the one hand there was the observation of at least one member of the group that some of the points in the guidelines recommend disobeying the law or that they are actually in violation of existing laws. For example, section II, subsection 4 states, "A sex therapist who believes that an unjustified violation of the confidentiality and trust of the therapist-client relationship would occur if such material were divulged under legal edict in response to subpoena may properly refuse to comply and will not be viewed as acting in other than an ethical manner." This can be interpreted as an endorsement of refusal to obey the subpoena. The group acknowledged this feature of the guidelines, and some members were even prepared to argue for the separation of law and morality here on the grounds that it is sometimes more ethical to disobey laws—perhaps in the interest of getting them changed—than to obey them.

The other way in which the relationship between law and ethics came up in regard to these guidelines was the expressed fear that these guidelines, if they are adopted and promulgated, will open the door to even more litigation, malpractice suits, and so on. At least some reassurance was offered on this count; that is, we live in a litigious society already and it is unlikely that anything we might place in these guidelines or omit from them would have a direct manifestation in either more or less litigation. Lawyers will be lawyers, after all.

The third category was the notion of contracts. This came up in

---

have reason to believe a patient may harm someone a duty to warn the potential victim. In this case, a patient in treatment revealed his intention to commit murder. The therapist (a university clinical psychologist) informed the campus police under the supposition that he had a duty to alert authorities to the potential danger. The police initially detained the potentially dangerous individual, but later released him when he appeared rational and promised to stay away from his intended victim. Two months later, however, he murdered the victim with a butcher knife. She and her family had not been warned of the threat. Plaintiffs in the lawsuit that ensued, were the victim's parents, who brought a wrongful death action on the grounds of negligent failure to provide warning.

several ways and in several contexts in the discussion of confidentiality. The general question of what may be divulged to whom, and under what circumstances disclosure may be made, came up with respect to guidelines 3 (b) and (c). I have already discussed 3 (b) briefly; it contains the *clear and imminent danger* clause. Point 3 (c) is somewhat different: "When required to defend the sex therapist, employees or associates of the sex therapist, or the institute or employer," and so on. Here the group recommended that more emphasis be placed on the contract between the therapist, on the one hand, and the patient or client or research subject, on the other—that the contract should be emphasized as a protective device, particularly the initial contract and adherence to it.

The fourth category was the question of payment of fees. We spent virtually the whole morning session on this and related topics such as breaches of confidentiality brought about by third-party payments. Some people objected strongly to the inclusion of guideline 3 (d), which states that confidential information may be divulged "when necessary to establish or collect a professional fee." We debated that. One person in the group remarked that 3 (d) sounds like a blackmail clause. Another person observed that 3 (c) shows the same basic concern as 3 (d), namely, that of defending the sex therapist. We discussed that, and I think it was agreed that 3 (d) raises a rather different ethical problem from 3 (c). Later it was suggested that if a clause 3 (d) is to appear at all in these guidelines, it ought to appear elsewhere. We recommend moving it to guideline 9, which deals with providing information to outside agencies under necessary circumstances.

There was much discussion of third-party payments and how to deal with them, considering the need to provide information about diagnostic categories on insurance forms. The problem of breaches of confidentiality necessitated by third-party payments proved to be far too complex for us to solve. A specific suggestion was that the therapist ask prospective clients to think about this problem in advance of beginning therapy. But one member of the group pointed out that this may not be the ideal time, since people enter therapy, especially sex therapy, in a state of anxiety and distress; they may be irrational and may not even remember—at a later time—what they were told or what they agreed to.

Finally, the question arose—and it was debated—whether these guidelines should concern themselves with professional fees and their collection. That's a question that I shall leave with you: Should these guidelines discuss the payment of fees, for example, whether or not they should be prepaid? There was considerable debate within the group on the justice, equity, or appropriateness of having prepayment plans. While some members spoke in favor of prepayment, others objected on the grounds that a prepayment requirement can be used as an upper- and middle-class screening device—a method of screening out those who can't afford to pay, thereby denying them therapy.

On the issue of medical records—the fifth category—I'll say very little. Several specific proposals were made by one or more members of the group who had had considerable experience using computers in storage and retrieval of data, but these appear to be details of implementation that are not needed in the guidelines themselves.

The sixth and final category is simply miscellaneous concrete recommendations that came up. One suggestion was that perhaps we should include within the confidentiality section mention of a topic that does not now appear, namely, the patient's or client's right of access to his or her own records. Related to this was the question of parents' access to their children's records. That issue is not addressed in the confidentiality guidelines, and we thought it might be appropriate to do so. In connection with this, there was some discussion of how material included in patients' records might be worded in such a way that it is both truthful and accurate, but at the same time not harmful for the patient—or the parent— who reads it.

Another issue that involved some discussion had to do with possible conflicts between teaching and research efforts. The point was made that problems regarding confidentiality might arise if a researcher wanted to use, for teaching purposes, information about a research subject. The question was raised whether there was a need to mask that person's identity, if he or she had given informed consent to participate in the research. Our group had no specific recommendation. But I should add, for the record, that one member of the group felt that we should include a statement in the guidelines asserting the obligation of subjects of clinical research to allow unidentifiable information about themselves to be included in anonymous data in research descriptions and in the reporting of research results.

One final recommendation was put forward rather forcefully by two or three members of our group. It concerns the guidelines only indirectly in that it relates to one of the chief moral issues we faced in discussing the topic of confidentiality: namely, the conflict between the need to protect the individual and the need to protect society at large. (I'm going back now to the *clear and imminent danger* clause.) We all agreed that this was a major issue that could not be glossed over, but what to do about it remained problematic. The suggestion was made that a national ethics advisory committee be set up to handle difficult cases, and that cases be available for review. This would remove the burden of sole responsibility from the individual therapist or researcher. (If the recommendation of a national advisory body were incorporated in the guidelines, it would involve a change in guidelines 3 (b): The therapist would have to consult a committee, at least in some cases, rather than relying on the decision of an individual.)

I would like to close by enumerating briefly the potential problems I see with setting up and using a national ethics advisory committee. First of all, a national body might not reflect the regional differences that might be important in settling some of these issues. I'm not talking about differences in the law; I'm thinking of regional differences in the nature of cultural taboos and the acceptance of certain kinds of activities. Second, there is the question of what the composition of such a body ought to be—who are the experts? Should such a committee be modeled on the National Commission for the Protection of Human Subjects (certainly an exemplary body)? Should there be representatives of the public? Should there be direct public participation? Composition is always a difficult matter: Even if we were to stipulate that the composition should be representative, representative of what or of whom? Third, how would such a body be selected? Who would do the selecting? Who is qualified to select a body of experts in giving moral advice? *Are* there persons who can be called moral experts? I don't know the answer to that question; it's a deep question that philosophers have been talking about for at least 2,000 years. I don't think we will settle that question here.

MARTHA STUART[4]: Our group discussed the section of the draft of guidelines pertaining to the welfare of the client. I might begin by saying that throughout our deliberations, there was debate about the primary target of this portion of the guidelines: Participants never came to an agreement as to whether the purpose was to shape therapists' behavior or to inform clients of what they could and should expect from their therapists. We wound up with a general recognition that this duality of purpose is appropriate and should be retained. There was also discussion of the possibility of streamlining the guidelines by combining this section and section V (on the welfare of the research subject), particularly since an equalization in the stringency of requirements for informed consent between the two sections appears reasonable. However, no consensus was reached on this point.

I'll turn now to a point-by-point review of our discussion of section III. The opening paragraph didn't pose any particular problems. In subsection 1, we decided to eliminate the word *personal* because it could be interpreted as referring to the personal value system or life-style of the therapist and thus could become justification for "witch hunts." We noted that therapists may well have personal limitations, but it is only how such limitations affect professional competence that should be of concern to us. Our suggested revision of subsection 1 now reads, "Sex therapists should recognize their limitations to give competent therapy and should undertake and continue evaluation or treatment of clients only in areas where they are qualified."

In regard to subsection 2, our group did not reach any consensus. We all agreed that feedback from patients or clients was extremely important. A few persons wanted to require that all therapists maintain outcome statistics and follow-up data on their patients, which they would then cite to describe their efficacy, but others

---

[4] Martha Stuart was the reporter for discussion group III (topic: Welfare of the Client). The other members of the group were H. Tristram Engelhardt, Jr. (chairperson), David H. Barlow, Theresa L. Crenshaw, Frederick G. Humphrey, Stephen B. Levine, Walter L. Metcalfe, Jr., and Raymond W. Waggoner.

objected because this would place an undue burden on some private practitioners. In addition, it should be recognized that outcome statistics reflect the types of clients and problems being treated: A very competent therapist who treats difficult cases may have "poorer" results than one who only deals with easy cases, further complicating the picture. There did seem to be general agreement that all therapists should know the literature and be able to compare their efficacy with program statistics from other places.

It was agreed that subsection 3, detailing the requirement for obtaining informed consent from clients, was too lax. We felt that this should be spelled out in greater detail or that the same elements of informed consent that are discussed in the section on the welfare of research subjects should be applied to clients in therapy.

The first sentence of subsection 4 was amended to read, "Fees and costs should be discussed freely and openly with prospective clients, including discussion of the usual and customary fees in the field and mention of alternative service delivery systems (in a variety of price ranges)." Our group was unable to arrive at any formula for determining what constitutes a reasonable fee for inclusion in these guidelines.

Subsection 5—"Sex therapists are encouraged to provide services to clients who are able to provide little or no financial compensation"—was left unamended, although one or two members of the group voiced concern that it reflected a type of elitism (based on the assumption that therapists are wealthy enough to provide free services or will simply compensate by overcharging other patients to cover the cost of free care). One person felt the client should always pay something.

There was a fairly even split in our group regarding subsection 6. We all agreed on the following revision to begin this guideline: "The patient's benefit should be the first priority of all therapeutic interaction. A therapist will not use his or her therapeutic relationship to further personal, religious, political, or business interests." However, half the group wanted to retain the second sentence of the original guideline, while the other half wanted to revise it to read as follows: "Sex therapists should be mindful of the special problems attendant to treating their employees, relatives, business associates, close friends, or their own sexual partners (for example, loss of objectivity, loss of confidentiality, changing contexts of social relationships, and coercion)." This division was reflected in a long and involved discussion regarding the absence of empirical proof that treating persons such as employees or friends will have negative consequences.

Subsection 7 was retained in its original form, although there was discussion about the exact wording (specifically, about whether the word *activity* should be changed to *behavior*).

Subsection 8 was shortened. We felt that only the first sentence was necessary, with the addition of one word: "Sex therapists should not *ordinarily* observe clients engaging in sexual activity." It was recognized that there might be situations in which the therapist's observation of sexual activity might be beneficial to the client, but it was noted that nontherapeutic motivations might also occur. Although we wanted to discourage observation of clients stemming from prurient interests, we didn't want to contribute to an obligatory conservatism that would inhibit the development of new therapeutic techniques and knowledge. On the other hand, some members of the group expressed concern that our revised version would leave the door open to irresponsible behavior under the guise of helping the client. The second sentence of the original guideline was dropped as unnecessary psychoanalytic jargon.

Subsection 9 produced a substantial amount of discussion without final agreement. About half the group wished to retain it in its original version; one person wanted to delete it completely; one person wanted to incorporate it into the preceding guideline. Some members of the group suggested rewording this guideline to indicate that while client nudity (apart from physical examination) is generally inappropriate and improper, it should not be banned under all circumstances. There was also some discussion attempting to define who could properly be involved in a physical examination.

Subsection 10 was accepted as written in the draft, although most of us felt it was too wordy. One member of the group objected to the implication that sex therapists are involved in marriage counseling.

Subsection 11 was also accepted in principle, although prolonged discussion about the definition of *significant risk* indicates the problems that may occur in applying the final guidelines to real-life situations.

Subsection 12 was slightly condensed to the following statement: "The therapeutic relationship should be terminated when it is reasonably apparent to the therapist that the client is not benefiting from it. In such instances it is the responsibility of the sex therapist to suggest appropriate referral when it appears warranted."

Some of us wanted to omit subsection 13 because it is covered in section V [subsection 6]. If it is to be included, we suggest the following revision (which adopts a more positive tone):

Training of new members of a therapeutic team is an essential part of maintaining the professional community. In circumstances where it appears that the welfare of clients is being injured as a consequence of therapy conducted in such a training context, it is necessary to modify or terminate the training in order to maximize the objective benefits to clients, although the clients have consented to training-related therapy.

Subsection 14, perhaps the most controversial in these guidelines, was discussed at length. We altered point (a), and we decided to drop point (b) because it is covered in guideline 15. With regard to point (c), the suggestion was made that the use of partner surrogates should not be the first therapeutic intervention. We agreed with point (d) and retained it. The following revision of subsection 14 was generally agreed upon:

The use of partner surrogates in therapy for sexual problems may be an ethically permissible way of establishing a therapeutic environment, when conducted in a responsible manner. If partner surrogates are to be used at all, it should be understood that the partner surrogate is not a sex therapist or psychotherapist.
a. The sex therapist is held accountable for any breach of client confidentiality by the partner surrogate.
b. Sex therapists working with partner surrogates have a special responsibility to discuss in depth with partner surrogates, patients, and their respective spouses (if any) the possible social, psychological, physical, and legal risks pertaining to their roles.
c. In some jurisdictions, the use of partner surrogates may be counter to existing laws. In these circumstances, test cases may appropriately be sought or sex therapists may work toward changes in the law.

Subsection 15 was unanimously accepted as important and applicable to all sections of the guidelines.

To conclude, despite a great deal of attention to detail and difficult semantic choices that arose within a group including two psychiatrists, a lawyer, an ethicist, a psychologist, a marriage counselor, a sex therapist, and a visual media expert, we are proud of our work. Although we did not arrive at final answers, we were not trying to write a document for the legislature. We welcome your rejoinders.

STEPHEN B. LEVINE: Are you going to mention the discussion about federal guidelines?

MARTHA STUART: Yes. One thing that bothered some of us was that this group as a whole seemed to have a rather cavalier attitude about breaking state laws, but we are less casual when it comes to breaking federal laws. There was a suggestion that this was because the federal government is a major source of funding. That might be worth thinking about.

ROBERT J. BAUM[5]: Several members of our group observed at the end of the afternoon yesterday that although we had the briefest section to work with, we seemed to have found more to discuss than the other groups did. In contrast to the report you just heard on the preceding section of the guidelines, my report in general represents a consensus of the discussion group with regard to each of the points to be included.

One matter that we did leave up in the air is something that applies to the entire set of guidelines—that is, the language of the guidelines as a whole. Dr. Kolodny explained it as an intentional ambivalence in terminology whereby approximately half the statements are formulated in descriptive language (for instance, the first sentence of section IV in the draft) and the rest are in prescriptive language (using terms such as *should* and phrases such as *have the responsibility*). Although we discussed this for quite some time, we didn't arrive at a consensus. There are three possible strategies: to keep the bivalent wording essentially as it stands; or

[5] Robert J. Baum was the reporter for discussion group IV (topic: Welfare of Students and Trainees). The other members of the group were Robert C. Kolodny (chairperson), Samuel Gorovitz, Miriam F. Kelty, Judith B. Kuriansky, Joseph LoPiccolo, Arvil C. Reeb, Jr., and Jerome F. Wilkerson.

to go entirely one way or the other way. As our rewritten section IV is worded, it's still essentially in the bivalent form.

We rewrote the preamble to this section completely, but the thrust of it remains the same. Our changes were aimed at improving the style by reducing excess verbiage. It now reads, "Sex educators, counselors, researchers, and therapists have a responsibility to respect the rights and dignity of students and trainees, to maintain high standards of scholarship, and to preserve academic freedom." Then we added a statement that doesn't really fall under the rubric of the welfare of students and trainees, but which we felt should be made explicit somewhere in the document: "Status as a student or trainee does not exempt one from any responsibilities specified in other sections of these guidelines."

Going on to point 1, we added a qualification here to allay the group's expressed concern about unwarranted invasion of privacy. We expanded the second sentence so that it reads, "This provision of confidentiality does not preclude the use of such information when relevant in (a), (b), and (c)." We modified 1 (a) by deleting the word *objective*. We also modified 1 (c), in response to concern about possible narrow interpretation of *disciplinary action*; it now reads, "pursuit of disciplinary or other appropriate action. . . ."

Point 2: We recognized that there is a great deal of other information that should be available to the trainees and students in addition to knowledge of the timing and mechanism of evaluation procedures. Rather than providing an exhaustive list of specific types of information that should be available to students and trainees, we simply changed the guideline to read as follows: "Students and trainees are entitled to periodic evaluation of their performance and they should be informed fully and promptly of the results."

Point 3 we reworded as follows: "It is unethical for teachers or training supervisors to require, coerce, or defraud their students or trainees into sexual activity." Then we added a statement, which I have arbitrarily inserted as a new point 4; it could alternatively be added at the end as point 6: "Therapists should not accept into treatment students or trainees over whom they might have any supervisory control." And in conjunction with this, we recommend—reflecting point 6 of section III—that students and trainees be added to the list of individuals with whom there is a potential conflict of interests in taking them on as subjects.

Point 4 was reworded as follows: "Persons seeking or pursuing training in sex therapy, sex research, sex counseling, or sex education may be queried about their personal sexual histories and attitudes, since these may materially affect the competence and objectivity of professional performance." (The first "may" in that sentence is intentionally ambiguous; it can be interpreted either in the sense of granting permission to query trainees or as an admission that the possibility exists for querying them.) The remainder of the paragraph reads, "When such information is obtained it must be treated in a highly confidential manner. It is important that students be informed in advance that such information may be used in accordance with the provisions in section IV, number 1" (namely, the specification of conditions under which confidentiality may be breached). I might add that this was the single point on which we failed to reach a total consensus; I was the major dissenter, but I'll postpone my comments for the open discussion.

Point 5: We reworded the first sentence, which now reads, "It is unethical to coerce or require students or trainees to participate as subjects in research projects." We deleted the second sentence as being redundant, but we let the third sentence stand.

I'd lik to bring up one final point for your consideration. Although it does not relate to this section of the guidelines, it is something that our entire discussion group felt merited attention. Recognizing that there are some special problems encountered by sex therapists and researchers who are employed either by another therapist or counselor or by a large organization, we wondered if perhaps a new section might be added to the five sections of the guidelines as they now stand, a section that would address the professional rights of sex therapists, counselors, researchers, and educators as employees.

SEWARD HILTNER[6]: I plan simply to read to you the redrafted version of section V, forgoing detailed commentary on the revision

---

[6] Seward Hiltner was the reporter for discussion group V (topic: Welfare of the Research Subject). The other members of the group were Albert R. Jonsen (chairperson), Charles Fried, Paul H. Gebhard, Richard Green, Judith Long Laws, Jay Mann, Ira L. Reiss, and Sallie Schumacher.

process. But before I begin, I would like to share with the assembled group five matters of principle that the participants settled on during the course of our discussion.

First, we decided to edit the drafted section that we had before rather than starting afresh. This included the general retention of the hortatory form with its injunctions ("should," "must," and so on). Second, it was agreed that the document was indeed a statement of guidelines; that the detailed clauses that might eventually become a part of it for legislative or other purposes were not appropriate additions at this stage. Third, it was agreed that the document would not distinguish between research done in a clinical context and other ("pure") research, but would address itself insofar as possible to both types of research concurrently. In conjunction with that, we decided to include a brief definition of research. Fourth, there was a decision to avoid discussing the risk-benefit ratio. Both risk and benefit are mentioned, but we resisted the temptation to quote probabilities or statistics. Finally, the wide variety of topics, problems, and situations that may be encountered in sex-related research is not discussed as such, but tacit acknowledgement of this variety is made by the use of general, all-encompassing statements or by "compromise" language at points where one type of research is radically different from another.

Now, if you will simply follow along in your copies of the document, I will proceed to read our revision:

Sex researchers should conduct their investigations with respect for the dignity, rights, and welfare of their subjects. Research must be ethical at its inception and not justified solely by its outcome. These considerations apply whether the research is in conjunction with clinical treatment or not.

In both types of situation, research is any procedure for gathering data employed to develop generalizable knowledge, and which may affect individuals and groups in ways that are not designed to produce direct benefit to the research subject(s) on that occasion, and which may imply risks for those subjects.

1. Sex research should be carried out only by persons qualified to do such investigations or under the supervision of persons so qualified.

2. For each research project, a person or persons who assume the ethical and scientific responsibility for the conduct of the investigation should be designated and identified to potential subjects (wherever practicable, in writing).

3. All research that places human subjects at risk should be designed to require the free and informed consent of the subjects. This requirement consists of the following:

   a. The general purposes and procedures are explained to the potential subject.

   b. The physical, social, psychological, ethical, and legal risks of participation in the study are described to the potential subject, along with [a description of] any potential benefit(s) to the subject.

   c. The potential subject must be informed of his or her right to withdraw from the study at any time.

   d. If the study is in the context of clinical treatment, the subject must be assured that his or her decision not to participate or to withdraw without prejudice does not affect his or her continuing treatment.

   e. Researchers should attempt to ensure that the subject understands the points outlined above.

4. When subjects have diminished capacity (for example, children, the mentally retarded), diminished autonomy (for example, prisoners and students), or are particularly vulnerable to social reprisal, the investigator should attempt to obtain consent that is as informed and voluntary as the circumstances permit. The following conditions must be met:

   a. In the case of those legally incompetent or incapable by reason of diminished capacity (for example, children, the mentally retarded, the mentally ill), participation in research requires the informed consent of legal guardians and the assent of the subject to the degree possible. This permission can be validly granted if no more than minimal risk to the subject is involved or if [more than minimal risk is] justified by benefit(s) to the subject.

   b. In the case of adolescents, similar principles hold, except that with older adolescents consent of guardians may be dispensed with if risk is minimal.

   c. In the case of persons whose freedom of choice is limited by institutionalization or similar constraints, subjects may participate after giving informed consent only if there are adequate guarantees that no undue inducement or coercion exists. It may be desirable that an outside advocate be available to subjects.

d. In the case of persons particularly vulnerable to social reprisal as a result of participation in the study, the investigator must inform them of that risk.

5. Sex researchers must protect the confidentiality of research data, including the identity of participants.

a. All information obtained by the researcher (which information is not in the public realm and which could be linked to the specific subject) is confidential.

b. The investigator must take adequate measures to ensure that the subject's participation or identity is not revealed through exposure of records, publication, presentation, or other means.

c. Potential research subjects should be informed of the limits that may apply to confidentiality, as in the possible access to research records through a subpoena.

d. All considerations related to confidentiality in sex research remain in effect after the completion of the subject's participation in the study and [after] the conclusion of the study.

e. Information received from the research subject may be divulged only when

(1) The subject provides written consent

(2) There is clear and imminent danger to an individual or individuals

(3) There is need to defend the sex researcher, employees or associates of the researcher, or the institute or employer of the researcher against a formal accusation by the research subject of wrongful conduct

6. Concealment or deception may be used as a part of the research design only when alternate methodologies have been explored and found inadequate. Subjects must be informed that concealment or deception may be used and their consent [must be] obtained, unless the risk is minimal and the research

would be subverted by such disclosure. Explanation of the specific nature of the concealment or deception must be made as soon as possible after the subject's participation.

7. The researcher has a responsibility to provide or arrange prompt treatment or referral for adverse physical or psychological effects that occur during or after the study as a result of research participation. This responsibility encompasses all phases of research and specifically applies to situations in which the subject is assigned to a no-treatment group, placebo control group, or minimal-treatment group, where a determination is made that failure to receive other types of treatment is producing adverse consequences.

8. Debriefing of subjects is an important component of sex research. Debriefing should include (but is not limited to) explanation of the results and purposes of the study and an opportunity for subjects to react to the research, to ask questions, and to receive responses.

9. If the research poses the risk of medical complications, adequate medical resources should be available.

10. In general, all sex research should be carried out in accord with the federal regulations concerning protection of human subjects, which require review of research protocols by an institutional review board. Investigators not affiliated with an institution that has an accredited review board should arrange voluntarily to have their protocols reviewed and should voluntarily accept the judgments of the reviewing body.

OPEN DISCUSSION
OF THE DRAFT
OF GUIDELINES

ROBERT C. KOLODNY: We now turn to an open discussion of the draft of guidelines that has been under consideration for the last two days. In approaching this, although we have heard detailed reports and recommendations from the small group discussions of the separate sections, for purposes of organization and to facilitate locating references we will work from the draft that you have in your possession. This is not intended to negate the suggestions that have been made for revision and reorganization, but only to ensure that we are all working from the same document.

I am also going to arbitrarily impose time limits on discussion of each of the respective sections, since we have only two and one-half hours remaining for plenary discussion. I would like to reserve the first 15 minutes for the opinions of any persons who wish to speak against the issuance of a set of guidelines resulting from this particular meeting. If there are people here who would like to advocate abandoning any attempt to formulate guidelines, postponement of the release of guidelines, or other relevant matters, would you please indicate your preferences and reasons for those preferences at this time.

JOHN MONEY: I have given a great deal of consideration to the question that you have invited us to talk about, Bob, and my conclusion is that I am against issuing guidelines. I would like any dissemination of them to be postponed.

I would prefer to see, instead, something that might be described as an ethical casebook: a collection of particular cases that created great difficulty in decision-making, along with a delineation of the pros and cons in each case. With such a casebook we could develop a backlog of positive information, a sort of data bank out of which we could evolve general concepts—ethical concepts—that do not stem from too narrow a viewpoint.

Let me give you an example. Look at section 1, subsection 6: "If the therapist, because of emotional or physical impairment, cannot provide objective and responsible services, he or she should seek competent professional consultation or treatment and refrain from professional activities while necessary." Well, one would have difficulty in defining emotional impairment and even physical impairment, as loosely as these terms are used. What "objective" services are, I have not the slightest idea. I have less trouble with the concept of responsible services. I also feel it's somewhat insulting to say "competent professional consultation," as if there were a whole world of *in*competent consultation. The assumption is that even professionals in the field require guidance to determine who is competent.

We have here written a rule that can be used against ourselves in exactly the same way that Russians send dissidents to mental asylums: They can and do find reasons—albeit faulty ones—for doing so. There are plenty of abstruse terms in these guidelines that would allow and even encourage their misapplication. It's particularly likely to happen in this country in connection with sex: We live under an enormous taboo on sex. There is probably no other area of human activity that is subject to such a taboo—which makes us, in this profession, so peculiarly vulnerable to attack. If we promulgate a set of guidelines in which we ourselves, the national representation of the authorities in the field, say, "Thou shalt not . . . , thou shalt not . . ."—like a table of commandments—then we have simply provided ammunition for others to use against us. Believe me, such people are there; they are even in my own university and they are out to get me. Why? Because I show "dirty" movies to nice medical students. I think we should remind ourselves of the fact that we have a great horde of enemies who would like nothing better than to rid the country of everything and everyone dealing with sex—they are just looking for an excuse.

If these guidelines are widely adopted, it won't be long before we have spies among our ranks, trying to find out whether we are competent, whether we are providing objective services. Take, for example, the guideline that provided so much discussion in my group yesterday, concerning the right to inquire about the personal sexual histories of students and trainees [section IV, subsection 4]: Take a simple case of adultery, for instance. Many a sex therapist could have his career ruined if some hidden enemy decided to make a big issue of some adulterous relationship the therapist had had.

To sum up, I would urge that we use extreme caution in promulgating such detailed recommendations as are found in this document.

ROBERT C. KOLODNY: John, thank you. I know that your position is one that derives from extensive professional thought and experience. I must add, however, that I am surprised to hear you, of all people, question the inclusion of the phrase *competent professional consultation*, since your work in the area of gender dysphoria has pointed again and again to the lack of competency with which some individuals are being rushed through sex-change surgery without recourse to adequate diagnostic services.

ROBERT J. BAUM: I have difficulty accepting Dr. Money's strategic argument, which implies that one way of preventing outside criticism of the field of sex research and therapy is to admit that the field cannot define precisely what constitutes professional competence. It seems to me that statements of that type make the field all the more vulnerable to attack and criticism.

However, Dr. Money brought up a very important point, one that must be recognized and emphasized throughout the entire process of formulating and ultimately promulgating any guidelines: The point is that these guidelines are not to be seen as permanent, inalterable tenets that should be engraved in granite. Rather, they represent a working document, a document that will raise many difficult questions. Even in the course of the next two hours there will be numerous points brought up and questions raised that will require further study and consideration, perhaps for years to come.

I do second very strongly Dr. Money's suggestion that a project be established to collect and provide analysis of difficult cases. I myself found, in the discussion of the general principles underlying the guidelines, that various people were bringing different interpretations to bear on the respective principles because they were thinking of very different specific cases that would fall under a given general principle. I think that in order to understand the guidelines better and to make them more usable, there should be a group or body of selected persons engaged in in-depth analysis of specific cases as they relate to the guidelines.

SAMUEL B. GUZE: I'd like to carry Dr. Money's point a little farther. Several years ago the American Psychiatric Association assembled a task force on ethics in human research. I was appointed to chair that group. The members of the task force quickly and unanimously decided that they did not want to issue yet another set of guidelines governing research with human subjects. There were a number of reasons for this decision, but the most important one was the fact that so many sets of guidelines already exist, and they are quite similar in content, exhibiting considerable overlap.

As an alternative to issuing guidelines, we proposed that our group act as a voluntary review body that would be willing to evaluate any controversial research protocol for any institutional review body or for any independent investigator who was unhappy with a ruling. We felt it would be worthwhile to offer an opportunity for truly disinterested persons to evaluate judgments in cases that might warrant another review, while simultaneously building up a set of possible precedent cases for future referral.

Unfortunately, our proposal was not adopted—perhaps only because the recommendation was not couched in strong enough terms. But I think the suggestion that came at the end of Dr. Macklin's report, advocating some type of national review body, could be worked out and instituted, given further consideration to the details. What we need is a forum for the careful analysis of many difficult problems.

FREDERICK G. HUMPHREY: I was in the group yesterday that dealt with the welfare of clients. My guess is that one of the most pressing needs for a code of ethics in the United States is the demand of the consumer. Therefore, I would like to suggest that you consider drawing up a separate document for consumers, a document without unnecessary nit-picking and confusing details, which could be disseminated all over the country. Consumer groups could thus have early access to this instead of having to wait two or three years for a more formal and more detailed document for professionals in the field.

SAMUEL GOROVITZ: There is another problem that has to be taken into consideration. It is a problem that has to be faced by people who intend to be practitioners, particularly with respect to sex therapy. Sex therapy is being carried out in this country with increasing visibility by a very wide range of practitioners of every description. Some of them have impressive credentials and real competence, while others seemingly have neither credentials nor competence. There is a broad spectrum between the two extremes. This situation has been brought to the attention of the public by the news media, which would indicate that some sort of movement toward regulation will probably take place in the near future. One argument in favor of the promulgation of some carefully worded guidelines is their potential to influence the shape and substance of subsequent regulatory guidelines or legislation in this field. I predict that if reputable practitioners of sex therapy fail to make some statement about the differences between charlatanism and genuine competence, others who are not so well qualified will take the opportunity to usurp that privilege.

I am also troubled by the frequent and persistent juxtaposition of the terms *sex educator, sex counselor,* and *sex therapist,* as if somehow these were all of a piece. Sex education is one thing, but sex therapy is quite different and requires different training and controls and standards. Indeed, it seems to me that sex therapists and sex educators would make rather strange bedfellows, if I may say so. I suspect that because the distinctions are not entirely clear to the general public and because sex is big business, there will be continued growth in sex counseling services. (When I say "sex counseling," I am not using the term in any technically well-defined sense. I simply mean people hanging out shingles and offering their services, of whatever dubious value, often at substantial profit.) As a result, there will be increasing public concern for consumer protection and, ultimately, some type of regulation of sex-related advisory and therapeutic services. For my part, I would rather see this regulation formed by judgments of the sort that are arising here, than by judgments of the sort that emerge in legislative deliberations without benefit of specialized professional expertise.

MAE A. BIGGS: I agree with Sam [Gorovitz], and I'd like to call the group's attention to the fact that when the first section of the guidelines was summarized with recommendations for revision this morning, a definition of sex therapy was included. Parallel definitions of sex education and sex counseling were omitted, and perhaps we ought to consider adding these to the final draft that is adopted.

ROBERT C. KOLODNY: Thank you. I would now like to direct the discussion to the draft itself and to the various suggestions that have been made for revision and reorganization of the document. We'll begin with the preamble, before turning to section I.

I think we ought to try to concentrate on substantive issues at this time, since linguistic suggestions will be taken from the respective group discussion reports, from the tapes of those discussions, and from further consideration of the same material by the task force in their meeting at the conclusion of this congress.

HAROLD I. LIEF: This is a follow-up to what Mae Biggs said a few minutes ago. The first sentence of the preamble specifies "professionals working as sex therapists, sex counselors, sex educators, or sex researchers." But section I, dealing with competence and integrity, refers only to sex therapists. All the guidelines actually deal with sex therapists and sex researchers (and, of course, their patients or research subjects). I suggest that we either eliminate any reference to sex counselors and sex educators or specify in the preamble just which sections apply to those persons.

RICHARD GREEN: It seems to me that somewhere in the preamble we ought to make reference to the circumstances under which the guidelines came about, the deliberations that went into them, and the various background papers and the like that formed a predicate for them and for this conference. My suggestion relates to some of the objections raised earlier about the difficulty of the guidelines: If we specify the context in which the guidelines were developed, people will have a better frame of reference for understanding them.

ROBERT C. KOLODNY: Let us turn now to the first section, currently entitled "Competence of Sex Therapists" (but with a footnote stating that it applies equally to sex counselors, sex educators, and sex researchers in most points). In the group discussion a different treatment was devised.[1]

ARVIL C. REEB, JR.: I would like to comment on the omission of any reference to sociocultural factors in this section. Speaking as a social worker and noting that we are going to eliminate reference to social workers and nurses,[2] too, I question the lack of emphasis.

ROBERT C. KOLODNY: The text of item 2 (d) specifies "sociocultural factors in sexual values."[3]

LORNA J. SARREL: I might point out that our discussion group decided to include all three terms—bio-, psycho-, and social—in the revised opening paragraph of this section, containing definitions of sex therapy and sex counseling.

ROBERT C. KOLODNY: Thank you. Are there other comments on the section dealing with competence and integrity?

IRA L. REISS: I may be reading this wrong, but in section I, subsection 1 (b), am I correct in seeing implicit opposition to persons who practice sex therapy attending lectures or demonstrations or conferences, on the grounds that such activities might be harmful

---

[1] See Chapter 15 under PATRICIA SCHILLER.

[2] Mention of social work and nursing was retained in the final draft of the guidelines [section I, subsection 1 (a)].

[3] This wording was retained in the final version of the guidelines. "Sociocultural factors in sexual values and behavior" is one of the areas in which sex therapists and counselors should possess basic information [section I, subsection 2 (a) (4)].

Are there suggestions for possible additions to the list, either as it appears in your copy or in the revised version that was read this morning—important areas that were either omitted or subsumed under too broad a category?

JUDITH B. KURIANSKY: I'd like to suggest that principles of evaluation and referral—listed together as item 2 (j) in section I of the draft—be given separate categories and that the word *principles* be expanded to read "principles and techniques." Also, I suggest that another category be added, namely, "criteria for diagnosis" (especially in light of the emerging DSM-III[4] and its categories of sexual dysfunction).

HAROLD I. LIEF: With respect to Judy's comment, we did include those points in the revision.

ROBERT L. STUBBLEFIELD: I'd like to ask a general question. It appears to me that you are trying to include in a code of ethics a series of descriptions that belong to standards of training and education (and as such would find a more appropriate place in some other document). Suppose some of the people at this gathering or others involved in research in the field come up with some new ideas: Are you going to have to amend your code to include those new ideas in your training programs? In other words, is it necessary or advisable to have that much detail in this type of document?

ROBERT C. KOLODNY: In response to one subsection of your comment, I believe that the closing words of the preamble to the draft of guidelines make it clear that they do not pretend to be the final word on anything. These guidelines *must* remain flexible. As they are adopted by various institutions or associations or agencies, they will undoubtedly be modified in many ways. Of course, new developments, whether in research, in therapeutic techniques, or in cultural mores, will play a role in any decision to revise the document. It was never intended to be etched into marble, but rather

---

[4] Task Force on Nomenclature and Statistics of the American Psychiatric Association, *Diagnostic and Statistical Manual of Mental Disorders* (3d ed.). Washington, D.C.: American Psychiatric Association, 1980.

should be perceived as a starting point for ongoing revision and re-interpretation.

PATRICIA SCHILLER: I agree with Bob.

In response to Dr. Stubblefield's other point, when we included educational and training standards—specific skills and areas of knowledge—in the ethics guidelines, I think we did so on the basis of a general assumption that only ethical persons having high standards would seek training in this field. But perhaps this does not go without saying, and perhaps we need to include a general proviso concerning ethics, spelling out prior assumptions that should not be taken for granted.

ROBERT C. KOLODNY: There is a special problem inherent in this field. At the present time, most people who will ultimately function professionally in the field first obtain their education and training in other primary disciplines, entering the field only after receiving their graduate degrees and perhaps completing a practicum, internship, or residency. These persons, at least theoretically, have the benefit of having received training within a particular code of ethics and of having met the standards that pertain to their own discipline. But we are beginning to see a generation of students whose express interest at the outset of their graduate studies is in a professional career in sexology, sex therapy, sex research—a specific and delimited area, whatever terminology is used. Some of these individuals will have perceived themselves and identified themselves as sexologists; they will have obtained their primary advanced education from programs that may be affiliated with departments of psychology, for example, or psychiatry or medicine. It is possible that many of these persons will have had no training in general ethical precepts—at any rate, we cannot assume that they have. We have to be aware of the changing nature of the field.

ALBERT R. JONSEN: I'd like to add a quasi-historical note here. The problem of competence and integrity is a particularly difficult one for your field, but one that has historical antecedents in the development of the AMA code of ethics. When the AMA code was formulated in 1847, it was practically impossible to define competence in medicine. There was nothing like a standard curriculum of medical science in the United States. There were a number of competing schools of thought, some of which considered themselves to be more scientifically based than others. The code was initially formulated to promote one view of medicine among the several competing views, but at that time there was almost no evidence that that view was any better than the others. In fact, it may not have been.

At any rate, in the formulation of the code of behavior a lot of material was included that was extrinsic or secondary to actually curing people. Certain types of practice (such as advertising or not advertising) and particulars of referral came to be looked upon as touchstones for the practitioner's ethical behavior. Integrity per se was not explicitly defined, but the implication was that one's integrity as a medical practitioner was precisely his or her adherence to the code of behavior. For nearly 50 years, that was the only measure of competence. Thus, the code itself served as a substitute for stated criteria for measuring professional competence in medicine until a standardized scientific medical education evolved, with clearly outlined steps for earning an advanced degree in the field, in the late nineteenth and early twentieth centuries.

Now, people working in sex therapy are in roughly the same situation that medicine was in in 1847. You have no clear curriculum. You have no agreement amongst yourselves about the exact scientific nature of your discipline, although some of you have argued that it ought to be defined in terms of the already existing discipline of psychotherapy. In writing a code at this stage, you are attempting to create a culture of those who work in a certain field in the same way that the AMA code created—or at least codified—the culture of medicine. But you will only gradually be able to define competence, as more and more people and organizations and institutions set up curricula. At this point, the competence section is more desideratum than reality. Integrity is the most important component, and here it refers not to moral integrity but to adhering to certain general modes of behavior that are viewed as characteristic of people who practice sex therapy. That is how I see this section of the guidelines.

SEWARD HILTNER: I'm afraid my comments may open a new can of worms.

The section we are discussing begins by aligning integrity with competence in some undefined sense. I'm very pleased that it does. But following this opening statement, the only remarks that have to do with integrity are certain specifics about referral and things of that sort—you might say they deal with integrity at the professional level. What about *personal* integrity? Suppose, for example, that a person who is regarded by his peers as a very competent sex therapist is accused—either by his peers or by someone else—of lacking personal integrity, merely on the grounds that he happens to be a person of homosexual orientation. Can a person of homosexual orientation be a good sex therapist? I don't see any reason why not. My guess is that most people in this room would agree with me. But is there anything in this document that would enable such a person to defend himself or herself against charges that that orientation alone and of itself indicates lack of integrity, whether personal or professional?

ROBERT C. KOLODNY: The question that you are raising, as I understand it, implies that we ought to try to identify and enumerate thousands of characteristics about people's behavior or culture or physical appearance that would not preclude their being professionally competent or possessing integrity. We have chosen the more concise approach of listing only the more obvious preclusions, which can be rather easily identified. The assumption is that anything *not* specified as exclusionary not be considered at more than its face value, as long as other criteria in the guidelines are met.

I recognize the importance of the point you are making, but we felt we had chosen a strategy that made sufficient allowance for the variety of situations and related concerns that might arise.

FRITZ REDLICH: Returning for a moment to Dr. Stubblefield's question, I believe that the inclusion of criteria for competence in an ethics code is appropriate, and I would cite a historical precedent for it, namely, the Hippocratic oath. In the Hippocratic oath it is stated that physicians should not cut stones: That is left to stonecutters (later known as surgeons). I think it is this delineation of the boundaries of competence that concerns us. Inclusion of such material does not mean that an ethics code should contain detailed prescriptions for how to teach or what to teach; that's a different matter.

The other point on which I would like to comment is the link between integrity and competence as it was perceived in this particular section of the guidelines. Obviously, we are dealing with only one aspect of integrity, namely, refraining from practicing in the absence of competence. If a practitioner persists in carrying out some activity that he lacks competence to do, he displays a certain kind of lack of integrity.

LORNA J. SARREL: I'd like to comment on subsection 6 of section 1: "Credentials alone do not give evidence of full competence. The proof of competence is the ability to provide objective and responsible services to clients." It occurs to me that those adjectives are completely inadequate. I think we need different words or additional words here. I agree with Dr. Money that "objective" service is a very strange concept; *responsible* should surely be retained, but perhaps the term *skillful* ought to be added: Otherwise, the statement is really quite meaningless.

RICHARD GREEN: This same passage has some bearing on Seward Hiltner's question as to whether a homosexual can be a good therapist and whether these guidelines could be used to discourage or prevent such a person from practicing: In section I, subsection 6, we read, "If the therapist, because of emotional or physical impairment, cannot provide objective and responsible services, he or she should seek competent professional consultation or treatment and refrain from professional activities while necessary." With what appears to be happening in *DSM*-III, a homosexual who is unhappy about his or her sexual orientation will be diagnosed as having a mental disorder. I suggest that the stipulation I just quoted could be used to disqualify such a person from practicing sex therapy on grounds of incompetence.

ROBERT L. STUBBLEFIELD: Although I share the concern of John Money, Seward Hiltner, Lorna Sarrel, Richard Green, and others about the precise wording of subsection 6, I feel that our recommended revisions are adequate to meet any situation that might occur. In commenting on the specific example that was raised, I would say that a homosexual could certainly be objective and provide effective therapy, but that the same homosexual might be abandoned by a lover and be depressed and temporarily ineffective as a result.

If we leave this guideline as it is worded, with the minor modifications that we recommended, it places the initial responsibility on the individual and his or her ability to deal with the problem. If emotional or physical or mental impairment occurs and the afflicted person does nothing about it, then the person's colleagues have the responsibility to do something about it; this is not expressly stated in the guidelines, but perhaps it should be. I direct a hospital where we treat doctors and nurses and their spouses, as well as other people in the health-care field. It is a very painful task to say to a professional person, "If you're going to leave, I feel that you should know that I, as medical director, shall have to inform the authorities that you are not yet ready to resume practice in your specialty." It's tough, but I think it's something we have to face.

Finally, if the impaired person's colleagues are unwilling or unable to do anything to make the person refrain from professional activities and seek treatment, the law will step in. The state of Florida passed a law called the Sick Doctor Statute [1], an attempt to deter old people from going to Florida to practice (ostensibly to retire). The American Medical Association developed a model or draft act, which was then circulated and presented in San Francisco at a conference attended by many people in social work, psychology, and law. We pushed that model and our recommended modifications state by state, and it has now been adopted in about twenty-seven states.

ROBERT C. KOLODNY: I would like to make one remark before we break for lunch—thus preventing any physical or emotional impairment on our part.

It is easy to think about competence in terms of outcome statistics or—to use a word that you just used, Bob—"effectiveness" of therapy; and yet, we have to recognize that the two are not equivalent. Two highly competent and skilled practitioners may report very different outcome statistics reflecting factors such as patient motivation, the duration of the illness, disability, or dysfunction, and many other variables, depending on the nature of the cases seen. We also know that there are practitioners who are less than fully competent (or even incompetent), who may have successful outcomes in at least some of their cases. In other words, outcome statistics are not a reliable index of competence, even though they may appear at least superficially to reflect "effectiveness" of therapy.

[RECESS FOR LUNCH]

ROBERT C. KOLODNY: We shall now consider the second section of the guidelines, dealing with issues of confidentiality in sex therapy.

One of the more thought-provoking and discussion-provoking points in section II is subsection 3 (b), the provision that confidentiality may be breached when there is "clear and imminent danger to an individual or to society." Ruth Macklin identified some of the problems on both sides of the fence in reference to this [see Chapter 15]; the various codes of ethics of different organizations take up different positions in regard to this; there have been legal decisions and cases in the courts dealing with this.

Since Ruth mentioned the utility of providing some specific examples of situations that might arise, I'd like to cite one that was mentioned in our 1976 conference. That is the case in which a couple enters therapy, the husband is found to have active syphilis, and the wife has no knowledge either of the presence of the disease or of any sexual behavior on her husband's part that would have exposed him to it [2]. In my opinion, this type of situation poses a clear and immediate danger and would justify the revelation of a limited amount of information.

I would like to point out that the general lead-in to subsection 3 specifies that information may be divulged *to the extent required*, which is different from a blanket permission to divulge any and all information that must otherwise be regarded as confidential. I'll open discussion of this section of the guidelines by asking for opinions or thoughts on this particular dilemma.

RUTH MACKLIN: It's worth pointing out that in the examples that were mentioned, both from the previous conference and in our discussion group's deliberations, there was disagreement and debate about whether or not the cases described were instances of "clear and imminent danger." As I reported, one member of our group suggested changing the wording of that phrase to make it more precise, in addition to including some examples. But if we can't agree on what examples would be considered instances of clear and imminent danger, I don't know how we can deal with this issue in the guidelines.

CHARLES FRIED: It seems wise to me to include this provision. The concerns that people have about the breach of confidentiality can and should be met, given the fact that such provisions as these are present, by clearly informing the consumer—whether he or she is a student, a research subject, or a patient—that there is that possibility. The one thing that is open to question is the conditions or circumstances that should be specified.

R. CHRISTIAN JOHNSON: In our small group discussion of these possibilities, I think we were considerably less permissive about breaking confidentiality than some of the general remarks have indicated. I also think there are probably ethical alternatives to breaking confidentiality that might ideally be explored before confidentiality is broken. In the case of the couple in which one of the partners is a patient and is found to have syphilis, the physician could probably think of some reason to require a medical examination for the other partner, on which occasion syphilis could incidentally be diagnosed if it were in fact present.

ROBERT C. KOLODNY: Dick, I'm not sure I understand your point. Are you advocating deception in preference to breaking confidentiality?

R. CHRISTIAN JOHNSON: No, I'm advocating something other than full disclosure.

ROBERT C. KOLODNY: But when you mention (hypothetically) finding syphilis during a physical or medical examination, are you recommending that this diagnosis be made even when there is no such active disease?

R. CHRISTIAN JOHNSON: No. I mean that if it is likely that the infected patient's spouse has syphilis, the physician should find some pretext for discovering it where it exists, if at all possible to do so, rather than breaking confidentiality; that is, he or she should explore all other possible ways of dealing with the problem before resorting to breach of confidentiality.

RICHARD GREEN: I believe that deception may sometimes be appropriate as the lesser of two evils. I might try to solve the problem by finding another plausible reason for treating the spouse with penicillin. The therapist has to consider the entire contextual framework in which the couple lives, keeping in mind the fact that he or she is treating a relationship, possibly a marriage, as well as a disease. If there is any way to preserve certain aspects of the whole relationship without endangering the safety or well-being of the individual person, then some form of medical deception may be appropriate and more prudent in terms of the therapist's overall responsibility to the parties involved.

ROBERT C. KOLODNY: That might be a viable alternative in some cases, but I don't know if it would be applicable if only the affected individual—that is, the individual with the venereal disease—were in therapy, while the spouse was not. There would be no pretext then for medical treatment of the spouse. How would you handle that, Dick?

RICHARD GREEN: Well, most people have a family physician and undergo periodic checkups. So I suppose there might be a way of prudently communicating the necessary information to the spouse's family physician.

THERESA L. CRENSHAW: I'm very concerned for women in this issue, in view of the insidious nature of the disease processes to which they are vulnerable and the resultant difficulty of diagnosing venereal diseases in the female. Undetected gonorrhea in a woman can lead to sterilization or tubal pregnancy—literal risks to life. A physician who administers penicillin, ostensibly for a sore throat, to a woman who may have active but symptomless venereal disease might be called into question for violating both medical and ethical standards of conduct.

FREDERICK G. HUMPHREY: I would like to speak out against a loose interpretation of the circumstances under which confidentiality may be violated. In a case of syphilis, if one partner in a couple unit is having an affair and will not tell his or her spouse, it's a rather simple matter to inform the deceptive partner in a private, confidential session that the information in question is important, that it should be shared with the spouse, and that you—as the therapist—are unwilling to continue working with the couple unit unless the information is shared. I do not believe that the therapist should assume the responsibility of making the decision about what should be done in such a case, which would entail either compounding the element of deception that is already present or committing an impermissible breach of confidentiality.

RICHARD WASSERSTROM: I don't know much about syphilis, but as I'm imagining this hypothetical case, the spouse of the person with syphilis runs a serious risk of contracting the disease through sexual intercourse. I don't understand the ease with which people adopt the position that there's nothing to worry about in this situation. I would think that the potential health risk in itself would be sufficient reason for telling the spouse, completely apart from considerations about disclosure of extramarital relations. I imagine syphilis is an extremely unpleasant disease to have.

RICHARD GREEN: Preserving confidentiality is quite important, of course, but so are many other things in life, including protecting others from needless injury. Perhaps we have to learn to view confidentiality in a more reasonable moral perspective, particularly where issues involving sex and health are concerned.

RICHARD WASSERSTROM: I think it might be useful to cite another type of example, a situation not so far-fetched that it has never occurred, in which the risk of injury is even more obvious: Occasionally patients who are unhappy or dissatisfied while undergoing a course of psychotherapy threaten reprisal against the therapist or against the therapist's family. Now, if the therapist is told by his patient that a bomb has been planted in his wife's car and that the bomb is due to go off in 30 minutes, I fail to see any virtue in the ethical rigor of upholding the confidentiality of the client-therapist relationship by refraining from informing the person who is in imminent danger of being blown up. While this is admittedly an extreme example, nevertheless it illustrates the same principle as the example involving a case of syphilis. Granted that the degree of risk, the urgency of the situation, and the actual danger may be greater in the case of the bomb threat: They are still comparable situations that deserve similar consideration.

ARVIL C. REEB, JR.: I'd like to remind the group that the wording in this section is that information *"may* be divulged," not *"shall* be divulged." My understanding of this issue is that a therapist *may* breach confidentiality under certain circumstances, not that he *must* do so. The circumstances given do not make disclosure mandatory, but they provide legitimate or permissible grounds for breaching confidentiality should the therapist feel it necessary. The implication (which perhaps is not spelled out as clearly as it might be) is that the individual circumstances and particular details would all be taken into account, including the probability or actuality of a clear and imminent danger.

RICHARD GREEN: I understand what you are saying, but I would prefer to have it stated that breach of confidentiality is to be a last resort, something that is done only after all other possible alternatives for removing the danger have been explored and found lacking. That is to say, the mere existence of clear and imminent danger is not adequate justification for violating confidentiality as the first approach to dealing with the problem. For example, a bomb threat would call for a request for intervention by the bomb squad, rather than immediate revelation of who you think planted the bomb. I think that should be spelled out in the document, because if these provisions are to have any force, they must lead people toward consideration of the seriousness of maintaining confidentiality. Otherwise, I'm afraid that confidentiality will be seen as the first and inevitable casualty in any situation involving clear and imminent danger.

ROBERT C. KOLODNY: Although I agree that alternate paths of action should be considered, it seems to me that calling the bomb squad involves a violation of confidentiality in its own right.

JOSEPH LOPICCOLO: This discussion illustrates a problem that we are going to have to recognize. We appear to be trying to formulate guidelines that will clearly indicate how we should act in any situation that may possibly arise—as if we were attempting to avoid having to ponder each case individually. Unfortunately, there is no easy formula; it's a useless enterprise to try to find universally applicable rules of conduct. There is really no alternative to giving each individual situation the consideration it deserves, each time it occurs.

ROBERT C. KOLODNY: I would reinforce that by pointing out that we very deliberately chose the term *guidelines* to emphasize the idea of guidance as opposed to rigid rules of conduct. Perhaps that concept should be made more explicit than the terminology implies.

I would like to call on Father Wilkerson, who has, I presume, a unique perspective on this because of his particular professional background. Knowing that many problems of confidentiality are confronted by a practicing clergyman, do you have any thoughts on the subject as it pertains to the deliberations of this group, Jerry?

JEROME F. WILKERSON: It's true that there are some parallels. The confidentiality in a confessional matter is absolute, but there are other situations—in pastoral counseling, for example—that approximate the types of examples that have been given. I myself tend to be overscrupulous, if anything, in matters involving confidential information. I think Dick Green's point is well taken, that breaking confidentiality should only be a last resort and that the guidelines in question should be so worded as to emphasize that. But I agree that there are conceivable situations in which there is a higher value than confidentiality.

RUTH MACKLIN: It's clear to me from the remarks made on this topic that we are not going to be able to agree either on the examples or on the principles involved. Those who are in the helping professions may assign a greater value to confidentiality in their ideal hierarchy of values than do those of us who happen to have a moral perspective (as moral philosophers, for instance). Confidentiality has a particular place and meaning in the medical and helping professions, in Father Wilkerson's profession, in the law, and so on, and our lack of agreement in part reflects the diversity of this group and the dichotomies between the persons who are members of those several professions and those who are not. Some would advocate deception in preference to loss of confidentiality; others would place a higher value on absolute honesty. I myself assign a great value to health; I would place a risk to health (as in the case of venereal disease, for example) much higher than even the risk of dissolution of marriage. If that's my bias, so be it; I don't think everything is quite as subjective or personal as the range of responses to that particular example, but it is clear that we are not all going to agree on any specific hierarchy of values or on any set of illustrative examples here. So perhaps we ought to work a little harder at making the language more precise, specifying only the degree of danger and the corresponding likelihood of harm resulting from the danger.

ALBERT R. JONSEN: One final point on subsection 3 (b): I recommend that we strike the words "or to society," while retaining "danger to an individual." The reference to society is too vague and could invite misinterpretation.

ROBERT C. KOLODNY: Moving on to a new topic, I'd like to bring up a question that was raised earlier today, concerning whether there should be any treatment in the guidelines of the subject of clients' rights to access to their records related to sex therapy. These records may take different forms: They may be primarily written; they may be entirely or partially on audio tape; they may be partially on videotape. They may be simultaneously therapeutic session records and data composites in the context of research that includes clinical observations. There is no current law uniformly governing disclosure. Does anyone have strong opinions, pro or con, about patients having access to such records?

CHARLES FRIED: I'd like to know what the argument would be for the patient not having access to his or her records, if someone could articulate that.

ROBERT C. KOLODNY: One point would be that knowledge gained from evaluations and comments within the record might be detrimental to the well-being of the patient; also, under some circumstances, particularly involving couples in therapy, there would be problems involving confidentiality of information received from one partner in the couple.

RALPH SLOVENKO: Our discussion group also brought up the problem of protecting the confidentiality of information reported by third persons, including the spouse who was not in treatment; the recommendation was that a separate record be kept for each individual who contributed information related to the case, regardless of whether that person was a patient. This would offer a greater degree of protection from unnecessary disclosure.

RICHARD GREEN: I can provide Charles with an example in which access to records could be psychologically disastrous for the patient—though I think John Money has much more experience in this area than I have. In the medical syndrome known as the testicular feminization or androgen insensitivity syndrome, persons who are genetically male appear to be—and believe themselves to be—female. If a person with this syndrome gained access to records and suddenly became aware of the condition, it could produce a tremendous psychological trauma, especially in an older individual who has lived "her" entire life as a female. I would never under any circumstances release that record to an adult "female" who was unaware of the existence of this medical condition. To do so would demonstrate irresponsible professional conduct.

ALBERT R. JONSEN: There are several states that have statutory provisions allowing patients access to their own records. I think it's reasonable to allow patients access to the *completed* record (that is, an edited or summary version). In the process of therapy, a number of tentative strategies may be employed and recorded by the therapist(s); I think the therapist has an exclusive right to that portion of the record. The courts seem to be making an effort to determine just what information the physician has the right to retain and to withhold from the patient.

ROBERT C. KOLODNY: We shall have to move on to the next section of the draft of guidelines: section III, dealing with the welfare of the client.

CHARLES FRIED: My remarks will apply to revisions that have been made not only in this section, but also in the section on the welfare of students and trainees, having to do with sexual activity between therapist and client, between teacher and student, or between supervisor and trainee. It seems to me that these and related matters were correctly handled in the original draft of guidelines, with stipulations stating simply and explicitly that there should be *no* sex between therapist and client, *no* voyeurism—that's what I prefer to call it—and *no* nudity. I realize that there are undoubtedly therapists who think, in good faith and perhaps with good reason, that therapies involving one or more of these things are acceptable and even laudable. There is room for these people, and that's why I was so adamant yesterday in advocating certification as opposed to licensure. But this is a set of guidelines for conservative, rather old-fashioned sex therapists: That's what this group represents— the "right wing" of the profession. I think it's very important that you maintain that stance. The profession has many wings and it should be allowed to fly in many directions, but I think you're wise to hold the position you took in the original draft, as long as you don't say that that is the only possible way of doing things.

H. TRISTRAM ENGELHARDT, JR.: I support what Charles Fried just said, for the most part, and I think that was the general consensus within our discussion group, even though it may not have been made clear this morning. When those issues were discussed, the group was almost evenly divided between those who took a more stringent view and would have preferred to see all such behavior banned from the profession by licensure, and those who favored the use of language that would allow practitioners outside the orthodox fold to ethically implement more adventuresome therapies while still making it clear that these guidelines do not recommend or endorse such therapies. The discussion returned repeatedly to the issue of observation of sexual activity, as we tried to steer our course between a Scylla and a Charybdis. On the one hand, we did not want to endorse those therapists who are simply engaging in voyeurism per se, but on the other hand, we did not want to take a stand so conservative that it would exclude the possibility of ever finding out whether there are ways of observing clients engaging in sexual behavior that are therapeutically beneficial and do not exploit the clients.

RICHARD WASSERSTROM: On the point about nudity, I wondered what the potential risks were, given the other restrictions. I can't think of any great risk, provided all sexual behavior was precluded. And isn't it paradoxical that you go on to endorse client nudity when it occurs in the context of a physical examination?

H. TRISTRAM ENGELHARDT, JR.: I think the consensus was that if guideline 7 were taken seriously and maintained, there was no reason to preclude absolutely either nudity in therapy or observation of clients engaging in sexual activity.

ROBERT C. KOLODNY: Part of the problem is that whenever a therapist engages in sexual activity with a client or observes sexual activity between clients, almost without exception the rationale given is that this is in the client's best interest. The difficulty that many have voiced is that in fact, concern for the client's welfare is a sincere motivation in only a very small percentage of such cases. This is true even though one rarely hears a therapist admit, "I am engaging in this because it turns me on and I am fully aware that it is unlikely to help my patient." On balance, it appears to be those who are least competent and least qualified who make the most extensive use of strategies or modes of therapy that include this sort of thing. But I don't think even the most conservative among us would wish to endorse a statement that could be used to preclude the possibility of evolution or innovation in therapy techniques.

VIRGINIA E. JOHNSON: I wouldn't want to leave Charles Fried—or the profession that he represents—with the impression that we are so conservative that we don't have an unorthodox side. I think the whole field has emerged and developed with an attitude of willingness to try anything that works well for the individuals who are seeking our help; I think we are exceedingly open to suggestion, experimentation, and innovation. In spite of the fact that Charles was inspired to call us old-fashioned, the field is so new that our work is still largely a matter of selecting those methods and procedures that "work." I can speak only about the methodologies with which I am personally familiar, but essentially the framework for choosing what succeeds in therapy is defined by the values, the background, the life-style, the whole existence of the clients or patients at the time at which they present to us for therapy. But because it's a new field, in mapping out a set of guidelines we are making our way deliberately along a path that may give us the appearance of being overcautious or ultraconservative. I think we have to err on the side of conservatism in breaking new ground— paradoxically—both to remind ourselves that we are not omnipotent and to avoid taking on the entire burden of making decisions in which others should play a part. The whole idea is to develop the guidelines in such a way that they remain flexible and can be used as a point of departure.

It is against this background that I have to tease Charles for accusing us of conservatism. Many of us—certainly my own partner and I—can lay claim to nothing other than lack of orthodoxy in the field.

RICHARD GREEN: I think the guidelines have suggested an appropriate stance regarding sex between therapist and patient, and I was glad to hear that the wording of the corresponding passage in the section that dealt with students or trainees and their teachers or training supervisors [section IV, subsection 3] was changed. If you talk about "enticing" students into sexual activity, I'm afraid that a teacher who wears a new suit to work one day might be judged as overstepping the boundaries of the guidelines, since his sartorial splendor might be "enticing." Although this may be a silly example, it illustrates how carefully we must choose our words.

ALBERT R. JONSEN: An important point specifically discussed during the meetings of the task force is that there is no prohibition of either nudity or observation of sexual activity in the section on the welfare of research subjects. Thus, innovations can be made in therapy by first conducting clinical research (although this requires implementation of other measures to protect the client-subject).

ROBERT C. KOLODNY: The point here is that claims of efficacy for new therapeutic strategies should be supported by research evidence. Well-designed investigations serve a dual function in this regard, providing needed information and—potentially—directions for further work, as well as preserving the rights and dignity of clients.

Although some of you may regard the Masters & Johnson Institute as a haven for conservatives (possibly because of our interest in ethical concerns), not too long ago Masters and Johnson were considered mavericks who pursued unorthodox ideas. I believe that their meticulous attention to compiling research data has had a great deal to do with the scientific and public acceptance of their work.

FREDERICK G. HUMPHREY: I must change the subject in order to state my concern for one particular issue that hasn't yet been mentioned. Section III, subsection 10 addresses certain issues of marital or relationship problems, while earlier in the document there is an emphasis on the need for professionals to recognize the limits of their competencies and to make appropriate referral. I want to suggest that a statement be made that it is unethical for sex therapists to treat marital or family problems unless they are clearly qualified, competent, and have been trained to do so.

ROBERT C. KOLODNY: I recognize the territory you are trying to protect, Fred, but I fail to see how it is possible to separate sexuality from marriages or relationships. There is often major overlap in such areas—and I doubt that all marriage counselors would be willing to refer people with sexual problems to sex therapists, in the complementary situation.

MAE A. BIGGS: The guidelines already define the fact that sex therapists and counselors should only treat problems within the scope of their competence [section I, subsection 2]. We can't really suggest every example that might arise—such as referring patients with urological symptoms to a urologist or patients with dermatological problems to a dermatologist—or we will have an unwieldy document that no one will read. Since sex therapists should be knowledgeable about marital and relationship dynamics, as mentioned specifically in the draft of guidelines, they can decide on an individual basis when to treat and when to refer.

ROBERT C. KOLODNY: Because of time limitations, we must now turn to the next section of the guidelines [section IV], which has to do with the welfare of students and trainees; a suggestion was made by a speaker this morning that it might be a good idea to add a similar section on the protection of employees.

R. CHRISTIAN JOHNSON: Our discussion group spent considerable time on subsection 4 of section IV. The emphasis on the word *both* in the last sentence will draw your attention to the passage we were discussing. We tried to think of examples of personal matters affecting academic or professional performance that would not at the same time be part of the person's academic or professional record. For example, a person might have a marital problem or be committing adultery; this could certainly affect the person's academic or professional performance, in which case the record of performance would reflect it. A teacher's or supervisor's recommendation would naturally be expected to contain comments on the person's competence and performance, but to speculate on possible reasons for unsatisfactory performance would be unnecessary, unjustified, and unethical, in my opinion. If there *is* some personal characteristic in an individual that renders him or her unsuitable for employment, the ethical obligation of the teacher or supervisor is to apprise the student or trainee of that fact or discourage him or her from continuing in the field, at some time prior to writing letters of recommendation. To retain a student for the duration of a training program in anticipation of future employment, only to thwart the student's prospects by an unfavorable letter of recommendation, is highly unethical in itself.

ROBERT J. BAUM: I want to add my strong support to what Dick Johnson has said, which was a point that I was making yesterday in the small discussion group as a minority of one. I would argue that subsection 4 should be struck completely; I can see no justification for querying anyone about his or her personal sexual history and attitudes. This is not just a question of invasion of privacy; it has to do with relevance. I agree with Dick's point that the only thing at issue is the person's competence or performance. No empirical evidence has been provided to show that personal sexual histories and attitudes are relevant to the training or certification of sex therapists or researchers. But it is a fact that such considerations could be used to bar entire classes of individuals from entering the profession from the very beginning, if a particular admissions panel operated with the basic assumption that persons with certain sexual histories or attitudes should not be sex therapists. What is relevant is whether a given individual is capable of dealing effectively with various types of patients in various circumstances.

Now, if someone can provide empirical confirmation that a certain sexual attitude or a certain element in a sexual history will *definitely* prevent every person with that attitude or history from being a competent sex therapist, fine; but the only indication I heard in the discussion yesterday was the general expression of an intuition or feeling that certain types of sex histories or certain sexual attitudes could *possibly* affect a person's competence. It seems to me that when things are this vague and fuzzy, there is not adequate justification for invasion of privacy, nor is there adequate justification for depriving a person of an opportunity to prove his or her competence and ultimately to enter the profession. It is for these reasons that I recommend deletion of subsection 4.

ROBERT C. KOLODNY: Having agreed earlier in this program that there are other areas of human existence, such as personal finances, that are at least as important as sexual matters to some people in terms of privacy and confidentiality, we might consider for a moment the following hypothetical situation: The head of an investment firm that manages other people's money is interviewing applicants for the firm's investment training program. He asks one particular candidate about his personal financial history and learns that the person has been irresponsible, has shown poor judgment, and has experienced three personal bankruptcies. The interviewer weighs the evidence and decides against hiring and training that person to manage large sums of money for other people. I think this is a parallel situation to many situations in which the guideline in question might apply. We should not forget that sex happens to be the area wherein clinical services will be provided; any invasion of the private or confidential sexual domain is solely for the purpose of protecting prospective clients, not for prurient or spurious reasons. Would it be prudent to have a self-confessed rapist as a staff member conducting sex therapy at your university or clinic?

H. TRISTRAM ENGELHARDT, JR.: I am uncertain of the extent to which one can make reliable predictions from such past experience, even in the financial area. And I am not at all sure that this reasoning can be transferred to sex therapy. Would it mean that people who had had a number of divorces could not be good marital counselors? I do not know, but I would surely think not. Yet, after reading guideline 4 and hearing Bob Kolodny's remarks just now, I take it that many of you in the profession would consider anyone with a personal history of divorce a poor risk to train or hire as a family or marital counselor. And if you do not want that assumption to follow, you had better either make some distinctions in this guideline or delete it entirely (as Bob Baum suggested).

RICHARD WASSERSTROM: I think that perhaps part of the difficulty we're having with subsection 4 is that it deals with several different kinds of situations. On the one hand, how much personal—especially sexual—information can a person reasonably be asked to provide about himself or herself as a condition for entering a training program? Obviously, the more intimate the solicited disclosures, the more certain you ought to be that such information is relevant to the screening process for the training program. On the other hand, in writing a recommendation for someone, you may have information that is clearly personal but at the same time relevant, in your opinion, to the person's future professional behavior and performance—even though it may not have directly precipitated any problem during the training process. For example, let's suppose someone had been in your training program and had shown himself or herself to be quite competent in dealing with adult clients.

But through personal acquaintance, you discovered that this individual was extremely cruel toward his or her own children. I happen to think, as a potential user of a therapist's or counselor's services, that it would be useful to know—and for his or her prospective employer to know—that this individual treated his or her children very badly. That information seems to me to be potentially relevant to the way a therapist might behave, even though nothing in the therapy training program had elicited such behavior. In short, I would argue that some types of personal information are important and relevant and appropriate as part of a letter of recommendation for employment or academic or professional training.

R. CHRISTIAN JOHNSON: With reference to the particular example just cited, I think there is good reason for not continuing a person in a training program if you think he or she has serious problems of that nature, since one cannot counsel adults without continuously encountering people who have children. Most people who have children have dealings with them, and there might be a real danger of the therapist's attitude toward children adversely influencing his clients' relationships with their own children, in such a case. On the other hand, dissemination of the personally acquired knowledge that a person beats his or her children could make it difficult or impossible for that person to secure employment of any kind—such information reflects on the person's character and places him or her in a very unfavorable light. Rather, I would suggest that the person be persuaded to seek another type of training in another field, thus avoiding the problem of having to give him or her an unfavorable recommendation or one that is ambiguous or misrepresents the facts.

SAMUEL GOROVITZ: Subsection 4 was the most controversial topic that we discussed yesterday in the group considering this section. We distinguished sharply—as the text in front of you now does not—between the issue of selection into a training program, on the one hand, and what information might be relevant to that; and on the other hand, the issue of recommendations for persons who are already in training. One of the difficulties that one faces in selecting people for a program is the problem of limited resources. In an ideal situation—if there were no limitation to training opportunities—one could simply admit everyone who had a reasonable prospect of becoming a sex therapist into the training program of his or her choice, and let the record of performance speak for itself. Unfortunately, that is not the existing situation. Because of space limitations, there is competition for admission to many facilities for professional training. Admissions personnel often have to make selections on the basis of marginal differences—minor differences that they hope will enable them to admit into the program the people who seem most likely to become successful practitioners—knowing full well that the selection process will exclude other people who might have turned out to be equally successful practitioners. (In the case of medical school admissions, the selection process may even be counterproductive—probably the best applicants are systematically filtered out by the process!) Under circumstances involving the allocation of scarce resources, it becomes appropriate to consider evidence of a less demonstrably relevant sort than would be justifiable in circumstances under which every applicant could be given a chance to demonstrate competence.

ARVIL C. REEB, JR.: Following up on Sam's comments, I'd like to describe what actually happens in the training situation. Trainees, like other people, often have personal problems, and sometimes they are encouraged to enter therapy themselves. In the setting in which I work—a student health service—we see this frequently. Many of the persons referred to us are trainees in psychiatry, psychology, social work, and so on. We have made it a practice never to release information about the therapy—sex therapy, psychotherapy, or whatever—to faculty members who have administrative authority over those trainees. In other words, we take the position as the therapist(s) of a particular trainee that we will not provide information to anyone who has to make an administrative decision about the person, even in cases where access to that information might prove helpful, because this would introduce a possibility of secondary gain into the therapy context (whether prior to therapy or after the person is in therapy). Once this happens, therapy cannot take place, and a valuable personal resource is lost to such trainees.

I would like to suggest that as trainers, educators, and supervisors, we consider it unethical to ask the student or trainee to waive his or her right of confidentiality relative to any personal therapy experience.

ROBERT L. STUBBLEFIELD: I'd like to return for a moment to the issue of selection screening procedures. The exact wording in section IV, subsection 4 is "may be queried." I have been involved in selecting medical students—also psychologists, social workers, and psychiatric residents. In my fantasies, the lady who was looking for Mr. Goodbar applies for training and she may *not* be queried at all about anything—that prospect disturbs me. I can't answer precisely the philosophical question of how you decide who is a good risk and who is a bad risk, but I submit that a certain amount of knowledge about a person's past experience will provide some clues to that person's attitudes about becoming a professional person. Maybe I would be more comfortable if the guideline read, "may be queried about their personality development, including sexual history when indicated."

ROBERT C. KOLODNY: Let's turn now to section V, on the welfare of the research subject. Dr. Hiltner provided us with a reading of the revisions that the committee prepared yesterday. Again, because you don't have the revised draft before you, let's address our remarks to the subsections as they appear in the original text.

ALBERT R. JONSEN: I'd like to call attention to what we thought might be the most problematic of our recommendations. It doesn't appear in the draft of guidelines; if it did appear, it would be in subsection 3, which deals with problems of compromised consent.[5] We made a specific reference to adolescents, indicating that both parental permission and the assent of the young person is a requirement *except* in the case of older adolescents, for whom parental permission may be dispensed with if risk is low or if there is particular benefit to the research subject. In using the words *dispensed with*, we may be inviting a morass of problems, since much of the controversy these days about sex education in the schools revolves

[5] In Seward Hiltner's report on the redrafted version of section V [see Chapter 15], this topic is discussed in subsection 4.

around the issue of whether parents should control the flow of information to their children even when they are older adolescents.

RICHARD GREEN: Speaking as another member of the group recommending that revision, let me say that we took into consideration the fact that adolescents—minors—receive contraception and abortion services without the knowledge and consent of parents. It's inconsistent to be able to offer such services without being permitted to ask these adolescents what they did to get pregnant, or to take a more elaborate sex history. There is room here for judgment with respect to the kinds of information one is attempting to elicit and with reference to the anticipated amount of benefit to science. But I can foresee practically no risk to the research subject, given appropriate institutional reviews of protocols and given the ethical considerations that are evolving in education, research, and therapy. I feel that too much would be lost by requiring the additional filtration system of persons who merely by virtue of being older have a coercive control over individuals who happen to be minors in the legal sense. I would even go a step farther than the recommendation stated this morning and eliminate the word *older*: I would dispense with requiring permission of parents or guardians in sex research involving consenting adolescents, if risk is minimal.

LORNA J. SARREL: I see some problem with the phrase *if risk is minimal*. I think it should either be defined more clearly or eliminated. What if the investigator and the adolescent envision no risk, while the parents see the procedure as extremely risky?

ROBERT C. KOLODNY: The same phrase poses the same problem with reference to research involving deception in the revised version submitted [section V, subsection 6; see Chapter 15 under SEWARD HILTNER], where the criteria are that alternate methodologies have been explored and that the risk is minimal. This is a continuing dilemma, particularly since—if I understood the suggested changes—the sentence in the introductory paragraph about the importance of weighing benefits against risks has been deleted.

A number of substantial changes were recommended in this section of the draft of guidelines. Are there comments on any of the other proposed revisions?

ALBERT R. JONSEN: I would like to point out that the last recommendation, suggesting the voluntary use of an accredited institutional review board, remains substantially as it was in the original draft, and it is an essential element here. Although review boards or certifying boards are not mentioned elsewhere in this document, they are a key concept in assessing such factors as minimal risk.

JUDITH B. KURIANSKY: As one who has been an independent evaluator of a number of studies, I'm aware of the three-way relationship that exists among the person evaluating the research, the clinician, and the research subject. I haven't seen any reference to the rights or welfare of the clinician in such situations, and I think something of the sort might be appropriate for inclusion in this section.

CHARLES FRIED: I would like to point out that the fact that we recommend referral to an institutional review board has the effect of making the remainder of the section—the entirety of section V, up to that last subsection—technically otiose. We are simply restating in the section those provisions and principles which the IRB by its charter is obliged to impose. This doesn't mean that we should omit the rest of the section and include only the final provision; rather, it draws attention to something that was discussed this morning, namely, that the purpose of these guidelines is to apply generally understood ethical principles to the special situation of sex research. Thus, it demonstrates the educational function of the guidelines.

R. CHRISTIAN JOHNSON: I'd like to comment on the recommendation that was read this morning regarding the guideline on deception in research [section V, subsection 6; see Chapter 15 under SEWARD HILTNER]. I believe it was implied that the requirement for deception in a protocol is sufficient to make its use ethical. In a discussion earlier today we reflected on the possibility that a research subject could be informed that deception might be used, without actually informing the subject about what particular type of deception would be employed. The subject would then have the opportunity of declining participation on the basis of not wishing to be subjected to deception. This small modification seems appropriate.

SEWARD HILTNER: Just to explain what we meant—since you don't have the revised version before you—the real purport of our recommendation was that it's highly desirable and normally obligatory to get the review board's approval for the use of deception. During the discussion we found that people had different views about whether any deception should ever be used. Our final recommendation represented a compromise: First, deception should be used only if there is no alternative (that is, when other possibilities have been explored and found wanting); second, subjects must be told that deception is going to be used, and they must consent to that; third, the nature of the deception must be explained to subjects after their participation has ended. When can any of those stipulations be abrogated?

CHARLES FRIED: Just one point of clarification, Seward: We admitted—over my half-dead body, I might add—that there were some circumstances in which it would be permissible to dispense with the general warning that deception might be used. This allowance would apply in those cases where the risk involved was minimal and where foreknowledge of possible deception would skew the results of the experiment.

ROBERT C. KOLODNY: Are there any other comments?

In closing the discussion, I would like to express to the audience my sincere thanks for your enthusiastic participation.

Bill Masters will now offer some concluding remarks.

REFERENCES

1. *Laws of Florida* Sect. 2, 69–205 (Florida Medical Practice Act). Sick Doctor Statute (added in 1969) Florida Statute 458–1201 [1(N)].
2. Masters, W. H., Johnson, V. E., and Kolodny, R. C. (Eds.). *Ethical Issues in Sex Therapy and Research*. Boston: Little, Brown, 1977. Vol. 1, pp. 13, 16.

CONCLUDING REMARKS

WILLIAM H. MASTERS

It was almost four years ago, in March or April of 1974, that Gini and I began talking—admittedly in a very desultory manner—about the ethics, or rather the lack of ethics, in this field. We wondered what, if anything, could be done to develop a measure of expression for the discipline that wouldn't appear to be self-serving. We soon incorporated Bob Kolodny into our discussions, and the three of us have been concerned with this problem for at least three and one-half years.

As I have listened to the proceedings both at this gathering and at our earlier conference, I have been overwhelmed by the number of ethical principles I have violated over the years, some knowingly, some unknowingly. That does not mean that I don't feel these deliberations have been a tremendous step in the right direction.

Our primary concern four years ago was to achieve some measure of academic, professional, and political acknowledgment of the existence of our particular discipline. In order to establish a competitive position in the health-care field, we had to do something to set our house in order. I think these meetings have contributed much toward the accomplishment of that goal.

Some of you may remember that our first ethics conference[1] was funded in part by the National Institute of Mental Health. When we were planning the second conference—the present Ethics Congress—NIMH offered to help support it. That was something I was delighted to hear. So a representative of NIMH came to St. Louis

[1] January 22–23, 1976, in St. Louis, Missouri; proceedings of the first conference were published in *Ethical Issues in Sex Therapy and Research*, Volume 1 (Boston: Little, Brown, 1977).

to see us and to discuss particulars of the program. But after this representative returned to Washington, we received a very interesting telephone call. The substance of it was that NIMH would indeed be willing to underwrite as much as 50 percent of the cost of the congress; however, they would reserve the right of review of any material that was presented at the meeting. If, for instance, there was discussion of the use of surrogate partners, it might have to be eliminated from consideration for publication in order for NIMH to provide financial support. That demand for censorship privileges scared me. Needless to say, we had to decline the agency's offer to consider financial support.

I think Bob Kolodny, who had the conversation with the NIMH representative, will corroborate my story.

ROBERT C. KOLODNY: They used a very specific term: They wished to reserve "veto power" over any guideline with which they disagreed.

WILLIAM H. MASTERS: I stand corrected—now I'm even more upset. The concept of governmental privilege of censorship of the proceedings of a professional meeting gives you something to think about. Maybe there are other groups in this country that could benefit from codes of ethics.

At any rate, I'd like to express my sincere appreciation to this group for your cooperation, not only in attending this meeting, but for your help over the past two years. I am pleased, proud, and delighted with what has happened.

I wish to thank our staff, of course, but there is one individual above all who has fostered this project from beginning to end: As you all know, that has been Bob Kolodny.

I wish you a safe trip home.

IV
ETHICS
GUIDELINES

ETHICS GUIDELINES
FOR SEX THERAPISTS,
SEX COUNSELORS, AND
SEX RESEARCHERS

(As Revised: March 1978)

This set of guidelines represents a systematic attempt to delineate the ethical responsibilities of professionals working as sex therapists, sex counselors, or sex researchers and those engaged in the education and training of these persons, regardless of disciplinary background.[1] The intent is to provide, within the framework of these principles, guidance both for professionals and for the public regarding standards of ethical conduct.

These guidelines·were developed over a four-year period under the sponsorship of the Masters & Johnson Institute (then known as the Reproductive Biology Research Foundation). Beginning in 1974, plans were made for a multidisciplinary meeting to identify and discuss the primary ethical issues pertinent to the conduct of sex therapy and sex research. This conference took place on January 22–23, 1976, and involved 32 participants. The proceedings were published in 1977 in *Ethical Issues in Sex Therapy and Research*, Volume 1. Following the 1976 conference, a 14-member task force was organized to prepare appropriate background papers and draft a set of guidelines to be considered in a subsequent meeting. The present guidelines are the result of extensive discussion and alteration of that draft during an Ethics Congress held in St. Louis, Missouri, on January 25–27, 1978.

[1] Status as a student or trainee does not exempt an individual from any of the responsibilities delineated in these guidelines.

These guidelines are designed to be adopted by whatever institutions, organizations, governing bodies, and agencies find them applicable. There is no discussion of topics such as employer-employee relations and other aspects of professional etiquette, the process of investigation of grievances, enforcement of these standards, or types of disciplinary action that might be appropriate, since these are properly within the jurisdiction of any group that adopts these guidelines.

Because not every situation that may present an ethical issue can be foreseen or specifically addressed, it is important to realize that the omission of a subject in these guidelines does not imply either endorsement or condemnation of related conduct: Any situation not covered must be judged by the application of general standards of ethical conduct. Recognizing that the development of new knowledge and changes in mores may necessitate reappraisal of what is beneficial or detrimental in the context of sex therapy and sex research, it is expected that this document will undergo revision and interpretation. It is hoped that these guidelines will serve as a flexible instrument, since unanimity of opinion rarely exists in the interpretation of what is ethical or unethical.

SECTION I: COMPETENCE AND INTEGRITY OF SEX THERAPISTS

Sex therapy is a form of psychotherapy integrating biomedical and psychosocial components in the treatment of sexual problems. Sex counseling is the use of biomedical and psychosocial knowledge to provide education or advice about sexual problems by means that do not include the use of psychotherapy. It is the ethical responsibility of every sex therapist or counselor to maintain high standards of professional competence and integrity. Both the public and other professionals should be protected from persons who represent themselves as sex therapists or sex counselors but who lack competence.

1. Prerequisites for practicing sex therapy include professional education and demonstrated competence in a psychological or bio-

logical clinical field *and* additional prescribed training in the treatment of sexual problems.[2]

a. Sex therapists have earned an educational degree equivalent to a master's degree or doctorate in human sexuality or in a field related to the practice of sex therapy, such as psychology, social work, medicine, psychiatric nursing, and counseling.

b. Competence in another primary discipline such as psychology, psychiatry, and marriage counseling is not equivalent to competence in sex therapy. Those trained in such related disciplines bring professional experiences and insights that provide a foundation upon which sex therapy training can be added.

c. Training in sex therapy must always include supervised experience in the conduct of sex therapy.

2. Sex therapists and sex counselors should possess expertise in a number of specific areas.

a. Sex therapists and sex counselors should possess basic information in the following areas:

(1) Sexual and reproductive anatomy and physiology

(2) Developmental sexuality (from conception to old age) from a psychobiological perspective

(3) Dynamics of interpersonal relationships

(4) Sociocultural factors in sexual values and behavior

(5) Marital and family dynamics

(6) Ethical issues in sex therapy and sex counseling

(7) Medical factors that may influence sexuality, including illness, disability, drugs, pregnancy, contraception, and fertility

b. Sex therapists and counselors should be knowledgeable about and possess clinical skills relevant to the following areas of diagnosis:

(1) Sexual disorders

(2) Psychopathology

(3) Techniques of evaluation and referral

---

[2] Alternatively, some persons may achieve competence by receiving their professional education in the area of human sexuality with commensurate clinical training in sex therapy without demonstrating competence in another field.

    c. Sex therapists should possess knowledge and clinical skills relevant to the following:

        (1) Techniques and theory of sex therapy, including several different models

        (2) Techniques and theory of psychotherapy, including several different models

        (3) Principles of outcome evaluation

    Sex counselors should have background knowledge of these areas but are not expected to possess clinical skills related to the practice of sex therapy and psychotherapy.

This does not mean that a sex therapist or sex counselor must be able to provide a full range of treatment services for problems in each of these areas: Recognizing the limits and extent of one's professional competence and seeking consultation or making an appropriate referral when needed is an integral part of professional competence.

3. Sex therapists and sex counselors should recognize the necessity and benefit of professional growth by participating in continuing education, reading professional journals, and attending scientific meetings. Sex therapists and sex counselors should maintain knowledge of current developments in their field.

4. Credentials alone do not give evidence of full competence. The proof of competence is the ability to provide skilled, responsible service to clients.

5. Competence and integrity are interrelated qualities that are both requisite to the responsible provision of service to others: Competence without integrity or integrity without competence is an unsatisfactory compromise of professional standards. The following points deal with professional integrity as related to professional competence:

    a. Sex therapists and sex counselors should describe their education, training, experience, professional affiliations, and competence, and the nature of their services in an honest and accurate manner.

        (1) Educational degrees should be cited only when they have been received from an accredited institution that is recognized by a regional or national accrediting agency or association.

        (2) It is inaccurate and unethical to claim that one has re-

ceived clinical training in sex therapy by attending a lecture, demonstration, conference, panel discussion, workshop, seminar, or other similar teaching presentation, unless such activities are designated by an institution as a formal part of its training program, in which case actual supervised experience in sex therapy must also be a part of this program.

b. Sex therapists and sex counselors have a responsibility to maintain competence and integrity within their fields.

   (1) Sex therapists and sex counselors should not enter into association for professional practice with unqualified or incompetent persons.

   (2) Candidates should not be recommended or accepted for admission to a training or educational program or for professional employment if they are known to be unqualified in matters of education, training, or personal character.

   (3) Sex therapists should not make referrals to unqualified or incompetent persons. It is the responsibility of the sex therapist to verify the competence and integrity of the person to whom clients are referred.

c. If a sex therapist or sex counselor, because of emotional or physical impairment, cannot provide competent, responsible service, he or she should seek appropriate professional consultation or treatment and refrain from professional activities while necessary.

d. Sex therapists or counselors who possess knowledge of violations of ethical principles of conduct or evidence of professional incompetence should notify the appropriate authority (certifying or licensing boards, organization ethics committee, etc.), unless constrained by legal or professional considerations of confidentiality.

SECTION II: CONFIDENTIALITY IN SEX THERAPY

The intimate, personal nature most people attach to information about their sexuality requires the sex therapist to exercise extraordinary precautions in protecting the confidentiality of knowledge gained in the course of evaluation, treatment, and follow-up of clients. Sex therapists should endeavor to inform clients in advance of establishing a therapist-client relationship of the circumstances under which confidential material may be divulged. The following considerations apply to the area of confidentiality in the practice of sex therapy:

1. There is a general responsibility on the part of sex therapists to treat all information received in a therapist-client relationship as confidential, even if some portions of the information appear trivial, irrelevant, or not meriting confidentiality.

2. The very existence of a therapist-client relationship is a confidential matter, since there are circumstances under which the identification of such a relationship would imply the presence of sexual problems or difficulties on the part of the client.

3. Information received by the sex therapist from a client or prospective client or from diagnostic evaluation, treatment, or follow-up of a client may be divulged to the extent required only in the following circumstances:

   a. When the client provides written consent (except when the information has been obtained from another person whose privacy would be violated by unauthorized disclosure). Special precautions should be taken when the release of confidential information has a high risk of being harmful to the client.

   b. When there is clear and imminent serious danger to the life or safety of an individual and when no other reasonable alternative can be found. In such an instance, disclosure should be made only to appropriate family members, public authorities, or professional workers (in assessing the necessity for such an action, it is permissible for the therapist to consult with other professionals, including a lawyer, as long as the consultation protects the identity of the client involved).

   c. When such information is required to defend the sex therapist, employees or associates of the sex therapist, or the institute or employer of the sex therapist against formal accusation (for example, court proceedings or hearings of an organizational ethics committee) by the client of wrongful conduct.

4. In cases in which a subpoena is served to obtain confidential information about a client, sex therapists should protect their material by claiming a privileged relationship in jurisdictions where this privilege is recognized. When such privilege is not clearly recognized, the sex therapist may obtain legal counsel and attempt to resist the subpoena. A sex therapist who believes that an unjustified violation of the confidentiality and trust of the therapist-client relationship would occur if such material were divulged under legal edict in response to a subpoena may properly refuse to comply and will not be viewed as acting in other than an ethical manner within the context of these guidelines.

5. If a sex therapist wishes to use identifiable information about a client or materials related to the evaluation, treatment, or follow-up of a client for purposes of education, training, research, or publication, the express free and informed consent of the client must be obtained.

6. A sex therapist may discuss in a professional manner information about a client or matters related to the evaluation, treatment, or follow-up of a client for purposes of consultation with professional colleagues, when there is reasonable assurance that the identity of the client will not be disclosed.

7. Since the normal functions of an office, clinic, agency, or institution where sex therapy may be conducted include exposure of confidential information to persons who are neither sex therapists nor health-care professionals, particularly secretaries, students, trainees, and assistants, it is important that the degree of this exposure be minimized insofar as possible and that careful methods be used to select employees, students, and trainees. Sex therapists should specifically instruct such persons in areas related to confidentiality.

8. Sex therapists are responsible for planning and maintaining the confidentiality of all client-related records, including (but not limited to) correspondence, evaluation notes, results of diagnostic testing, notes about therapy sessions, tape recordings

(audio or audiovisual), and case summaries. This responsibility extends to the ultimate disposition of such confidential records.

9. It is permissible for sex therapists to provide such information about a client to an outside agency as is necessary for matters of accounting, bookkeeping, data processing, banking, collecting, duplicating, microfilming, printing, or other legitimate purposes. Care should be exercised in the selection of such an agency, and the agency should be notified of the strict need for confidentiality.

10. When sex therapy involves one or more therapists working with a client couple, whether married or not, unusual circumstances pertaining to confidentiality may arise. In such instances, the following considerations apply:

   a. Disclosure of information that one client has requested be kept confidential from his or her partner should not be made without the express consent of the person providing the confidential information.

   b. When only one client of a client couple provides consent to the release of confidential records or information, the sex therapist is responsible for releasing only information about the consenting client and must protect the confidentiality of all information deriving from the nonconsenting client.

11. When sex therapy is done in a group therapy format, special and complex circumstances pertaining to confidentiality may apply. It is important for sex therapists to recognize this risk and inform prospective clients of it. Group therapy leaders should remain alert to the potential loss of confidentiality when other clients, not bound by professional ethics, may learn information of a private, intimate, or secret nature.

12. All considerations related to confidentiality in the sex therapist-client relationship continue after the termination of this relationship.

SECTION III: WELFARE OF THE CLIENT

The client is in a unique position of vulnerability in respect to the sex therapist for a variety of reasons. Vulnerability may stem from uncertainty about the differences between propriety and impropriety, the criteria for efficacy or harmfulness, and what constitutes common, accepted practice as compared with irresponsible or unusual therapy. Clients' abilities to make judgments about their welfare are potentially lessened by the wish to succeed in therapy, the belief that the therapist(s) will always act in the clients' best interests, and the assumption of competence, knowledge, and high ethical standards on the part of the therapist. Therefore, the sex therapist must be constantly mindful of the responsibility for protection of the client's welfare and rights and for the rigorous maintenance of the trust implicit in the client-therapist relationship.

1. Sex therapists should recognize their limitations to provide competent services and should undertake evaluation or treatment of clients only in areas where they are qualified.
2. Sex therapists should not make false or exaggerated claims of efficacy in regard to their past or anticipated results.
3. Treatment should not be undertaken without the free and informed consent of the client or prospective client. Sex therapists should discuss the methods and techniques they employ with prospective clients, as well as the reasons for their use.
4. Fees and costs should be discussed freely and openly with prospective clients. Arrangements for payment should be completed at the beginning of establishing a client-therapist relationship.
5. Sex therapists are encouraged to provide services to clients who are able to provide little or no financial compensation.
6. The client's benefit should be the first priority of any therapy. A sex therapist will not use his or her therapeutic relationship to further personal, religious, political, or business interests. Sex therapists should be mindful of the special problems attendant upon treating their employees, relatives, business associates, students or trainees, close friends, or their own sexual partners (such as loss of objectivity, diminished confidentiality, and the changing context of social relationships).
7. It is unethical for the therapist to engage in sexual activity with a client.

8. Procedures involving nudity of either the client or the therapist or observation of client sexual activity go beyond the boundaries of established therapeutic practice and may be used only when there is good evidence that they serve the best interests of the client.

9. Client nudity during a physical examination by a licensed physician, nurse, or physician's assistant is not prohibited or unethical.

10. Sex therapists may be confronted by marital or relationship problems of varying degrees. The sex therapist has a professional obligation to make objective assessments of such situations and to inform clients of such assessments. However, sex therapists should indicate to clients that the ultimate decision to alter or terminate a relationship, such as by separation or divorce, is solely the responsibility of the client. Because clients extend considerable trust to the therapist, and because clients consider therapists to be both knowledgeable and acting in the clients' best interests, therapists should be cautious in giving advice regarding the termination of relationships.

11. In treatment of a couple, when neither client has requested that any matters be held confidential or kept secret from the other, but when the therapist(s) judges that there is a significant risk to discussing jointly information not known to one client, it is the responsibility of the therapist to point out this fact to the relevant person and to obtain his or her consent before disclosure of such information.

12. The therapeutic relationship should be terminated when it is reasonably apparent to the therapist that the client is not benefiting from it despite the use of alternative therapeutic strategies and techniques. In such instances it is the responsibility of the sex therapist to suggest appropriate referral when it appears warranted.

13. When research or training is being done in the context of providing therapeutic services, a potential for conflict of interests exists. In individual circumstances, when it becomes known that the benefit to the client(s) is being compromised due to such practices, it is necessary to modify or terminate the research or training in order to maximize the objective bene-

fit to the clients from therapy, even though the clients have consented to participation in research- or training-related therapy.

14. Although controversial, the use of partner surrogates in sex therapy may be an ethically permissible way of establishing a therapeutic environment, when conducted in a responsible manner. If partner surrogates are to be used at all, it should be understood that the partner surrogate is not a sex therapist; surrogates should understand that their role is not that of either sex therapist or psychotherapist; and sex therapists working with partner surrogates must exercise diligence and concern for protecting the dignity and welfare of both the surrogate and the client.

   a. Persons functioning as partner surrogates should receive special education in matters related to client confidentiality.

   b. If use of a partner surrogate is contemplated, the sex therapist should be highly sensitive to the client's values.

   c. Sex therapists working with partner surrogates have a strong responsibility to discuss in depth with these persons and their clients the possible social, psychological, physical, and legal risks pertaining to their roles.

   d. Before employing a partner surrogate who is married, consent should be obtained from the surrogate's spouse.

   e. Before providing a partner surrogate for a client who is married, consent should be obtained from the client's spouse.

   f. In some jurisdictions, the use of partner surrogates may be counter to existing laws. In these circumstances test cases may appropriately be sought or sex therapists may work toward changes in the law.

15. Sex therapists should be aware of the personal value system that they introduce into the therapy context and should disclose these values to the client when such information is relevant to treatment. Moreover, therapists should avoid gratuitously enunciating opinions or prescribing values that reflect their personal biases rather than being responsive to the needs and well-being of the client. In this regard therapists should not condemn certain types of sexual practices, except those that are coercive or involve deceit.

SECTION IV: WELFARE OF STUDENTS AND TRAINEES

Sex therapists, counselors, researchers, and educators have an obligation to respect the rights and dignity of students and trainees, to maintain high standards of scholarship, and to preserve academic freedom and responsibility.

1. Students and trainees are accorded confidentiality in regard to information of a personal or intimate nature obtained by a teacher or training supervisor. This provision of confidentiality does not preclude the use of such information when relevant in the following:
   a. Evaluation of students and trainees by their teachers, including evaluations by committee
   b. Recommendations concerning students and trainees for their personal or professional purposes
   c. Pursuit of disciplinary, administrative, or other appropriate action involving students or trainees in matters pertaining to scholarship, personal conduct, or violations of ethical standards
2. Students and trainees are entitled to periodic evaluation of their performance and should be informed fully and promptly of the results.
3. It is unethical for teachers or training supervisors to require, to coerce, or by fraud to induce their students or trainees to engage in sexual activity.
4. Persons seeking or pursuing training in the field of human sexuality may be queried about their private, personal sexual histories and attitudes, since these may materially affect the competence, integrity, judgment, and objectivity of professional performance. Such persons should be informed in advance of the relevant limits to confidentiality pertaining to this material, as described earlier in this section.
5. It is unethical to coerce or require students to participate as subjects in research projects. The increased risk of conflict of interest or subtle coercion should be recognized and guarded against by educators who engage in research with their own students or trainees.

6. Sex therapists should not treat their own students or trainees or those over whom they have administrative authority.

SECTION V: WELFARE OF THE RESEARCH SUBJECT

Sex researchers should conduct their investigations with respect for the dignity, rights, and welfare of their subjects. Research must be ethical at its inception and not justified solely by its outcome. These considerations apply whether the research is in conjunction with clinical treatment or not.

Research is any procedure for gathering data employed to develop generalizable knowledge, including studies that may affect individuals or groups in ways that are not designed to produce direct benefit to the research subject(s) on that occasion and studies that involve risks for those participating.

1. Sex research should be carried out only by persons qualified to do such investigations or under the direct supervision of persons so qualified.
2. For each research project, a person or persons who assume the ethical and scientific responsibility for the conduct of the investigation should be designated and identified to potential subjects (in writing whenever practicable).
3. All research that places human subjects at risk should be designed to require the free and informed consent of these subjects. Such a requirement consists of the following:
   a. The general purposes, procedures, and details of study participation are explained accurately to the potential subject.
   b. The physical, social, psychological, legal, and economic risks of study participation are fully and accurately described to the potential subject, along with a description of any potential benefits.
   c. The potential subject must be free to choose whether or not to participate, without any element of coercion, force, or deceit.
   d. The potential study subject must be aware of his or her

right to withdraw from the study at any time without prejudice.

e. If the study is in a context of clinical treatment, the subject must be assured that his or her decision not to participate or to withdraw will not affect his or her continuing treatment.

f. The research should attempt to ensure that the subject understands the points outlined above.

4. When subjects have diminished capacity (for example, children, the mentally retarded, and the mentally ill), diminished autonomy (for example, prisoners and students), or increased vulnerability to social consequences (for example, transsexuals and minority groups), the investigator should attempt to obtain from those subjects consent that is as informed and voluntary as the circumstances permit. In these instances the researcher has a compelling responsibility to observe safeguards that preserve the rights, dignity, and welfare of subjects.

a. In the case of those legally incompetent or incapable by reason of diminished capacity, participation in research requires the informed permission of legal guardians and the assent of subjects to the degree possible. That permission can be validly granted if no more than minimal risk to subjects is involved or if more than minimal risk is justified by potential direct benefit to the subject.

b. In sex research involving adolescents, similar principles apply, except that permission of parents or guardians need not be obtained if risk is minimal.

c. In the case of persons whose freedom of choice is limited by institutionalization or other constraints, subjects may participate after giving informed consent only when there are adequate guarantees that no undue inducement or coercion exists. In such circumstances it is desirable that an outside advocate be available to subjects.

d. In the case of persons particularly vulnerable to social consequences as a result of participation in research, the investigator must inform them of that risk.

5. Sex researchers must protect the confidentiality of research data, including the identity of participants.

a. All information obtained by the researcher is confidential except information in the public realm or information that cannot be linked to the specific subject.

b. The investigator must take adequate measures to ensure that subjects' participation or identities are not revealed through exposure of records, publication, presentation, or other means.

c. All research-related records must be maintained with diligent and continuing attention to safeguarding confidentiality. It is the responsibility of the sex researcher to ensure this protection in regard to data collection, data processing, data analysis, and, finally, the disposition of research records.

d. Potential research subjects should be informed of the limits that may apply to confidentiality, such as the possibility of access to research records by subpoena.

e. All considerations related to confidentiality in sex research remain in effect on conclusion of a subject's participation in a study and after the study has been completed.

f. Information received from a research subject may be divulged to the extent required only in the following circumstances:

   (1) When the subject provides written consent

   (2) When there is clear and imminent serious danger to the life or safety of an individual and when no other reasonable alternative can be found

   (3) When the information is required to defend the sex researcher, employees or associates of the sex researcher, or the institute or employer of the sex researcher against formal accusation by the research subject of wrongful conduct

6. Sex researchers should strive for honesty and accuracy in their dealings with research subjects. Concealment or deception may be used as a part of the research design only when alternate methodologies have been considered and found inadequate. In such cases, unless the risk is minimal *and* there is potential direct therapeutic benefit, subjects must be informed during the consent process that concealment or deception may be used. Explanation of the specific nature of the concealment or

deception must be made as soon as possible after the subject's participation has ended.

7. The researcher has a dual responsibility to protect the welfare of subjects and to provide or arrange treatment for adverse physical or psychological effects that may occur during or after the study as a result of research participation, if the subject desires such treatment. Although this responsibility encompasses all phases of research, it applies specifically to situations of research in a context of therapy in which a subject is assigned to a no-treatment group, placebo control group, or minimal-treatment group and a determination is made that failure to receive full treatment is producing adverse consequences.

8. Research subjects are entitled to an explanation of the results and purposes of their participation in the study, including an opportunity to react to the research, ask questions, and receive responses.

9. Research involving the risk of medical complications should be conducted only when adequate medical resources are readily available.

10. It is recommended that sex research protocols be submitted to an institutional review board for evaluation of ethical propriety. Investigators not affiliated with an institution that has an accredited review board are encouraged to arrange voluntarily to have their protocols reviewed and to accept the judgment of the reviewing body.

INDEX

INDEX